ANTHROPOLOGY IN HISTORIC PRESERVATION

Caring for Culture's Clutter

This is a volume in

Studies in Archeology

A complete list of titles in this series appears at the end of this volume.

ANTHROPOLOGY IN HISTORIC PRESERVATION

Caring for Culture's Clutter

THOMAS F. KING
National Park Service
Washington, D. C.

PATRICIA PARKER HICKMAN
Department of Anthropology
University of Pennsylvania
Philadelphia, Pennsylvania

GARY BERG
New York Archaeological Council
Albany, New York

ACADEMIC PRESS   New York   San Francisco   London
A Subsidiary of Harcourt Brace Jovanovich, Publishers

ACADEMIC PRESS, INC.
111 Fifth Avenue, New York, New York 10003

United Kingdom Edition published by
ACADEMIC PRESS, INC. (LONDON) LTD.
24/28 Oval Road, London NW1

Library of Congress Cataloging in Publication Data

King, Thomas F
    Anthropology in historic preservation.

    (Studies in archeology series)
    1.   Historic sites—United States—Conservation and
restoration.   2.   Historic buildings—United States—
Conservation and restoration.   3.   United States—
Antiquities—Collection and preservation.   4.   Anthropol-
ogy—United States.   I.   Hickman, Patricia P., joint
author.   II.   Berg, Gary, joint author.   III.   Title.
E159.K56   069'.53   77-75574
ISBN 0−12−408250−5

CONTENTS

8

PREDICTIVE SURVEYS FOR REGIONAL PLANNING

9

10

Appendix A

Appendix **B**

A COMPLETED NATIONAL REGISTER NOMINATION

Appendix **C**

A MEMORANDUM OF AGREEMENT

Appendix **D**

LETTERS TO AGENCIES TO NOTIFY OF COMPLIANCE
PROBLEMS AND TO SOLICIT INFORMATION;
PERTINENT ADDRESSES

PREFACE

During the last 10 years, historic preservation has become an important aspect of American life. Legislation favoring the protection of historic properties, the recovery of archeological data, and the maintenance of integrity in the built environment has transformed the historic preservation movement from a modestly successful citizens' lobby into an influential force in government planning. The involvement of anthropologists in historic preservation has until recently been marginal at best. Archeologists have worked under the historic preservation laws but have seldom regarded themselves as historic preservationists. Sociocultural anthropologists have worked in community improvement projects and social impact assessments, but have seldom grappled with the laws and policies that give historic preservation its influence in public policy. We believe that increasing the involvement of anthropologists in historic preservation would be beneficial to both fields, providing historic preservation with needed methodological organization and breadth, and giving anthropologists an opportunity to put their skills to work. This book is designed to encourage such involvement. In it, we argue for the centrality of basic anthropological thinking to historic preservation practice, outline how historic preservation works and can work as an influence on government decisionmaking, and suggest ways in which both archeologists and sociocultural anthropologists can work effectively within the historic preservation system.

This book has been in preparation for some time, and it is a little difficult to recall its origins. In 1973–1974, working as private consultants in California, we were all involved in using such anthropological skills as we possessed in studies under contract that related to historic preservation. Like a number of other archeologists, we found it possible to use our studies for "responsible experimentation in techniques, method, and theory," and could envision their use in "examin[ing] processual questions and reconstruct[ing] culture history on a scale and at a depth never before imagined [Schiffer & House 1975: 6]." The rapidly expanding federal programs for historic preservation and environmental protection made possible a great increase in the number, scope, and sophistication of archeological studies conducted in advance of construction and land-use projects. Beyond the fact that the new laws and policies made it possible to conduct useful archeological research, however, we began to see that the historic preservation field itself had a goal that was compatible with and challenging to our training as anthropologists—the maintenance of a diverse, stimulating cultural environment. Moreover, we found that participation in historic preservation helped us clarify our thinking about anthropology and its practice. King and Berg participated in the case of *Warm Springs Task Force et al.* v. *Gribble et al.*, where the interests of the Mahilkaune Pomo and archeologists converged in opposition to the plans of the U.S. Army Corps of Engineers; Hickman became involved in a controversy with National Park Service historians over the value of William Keys' Desert Queen Ranch, an historic site with potential as a source of ethnohistorical data. We all found it necessary to define clearly and defend our beliefs about the value of historic properties in the face of antagonists. We were impressed with the fact that our opponents, when they lost, did so largely because their approaches to historic preservation lacked scope and at the same time failed to attend to the particulars of preservation policy. Our own weakest moments came when we failed to articulate clearly our anthropological values in the language of historic preservation.

Coming east, King and Berg assumed administrative positions with the New York Archaeological Council and Hickman entered the PhD program at the University of Pennsylvania. We all found ourselves in new intellectual, institutional, and bureaucratic environments, where we had to explain what we were doing to agency officials, public groups, and anthropological colleagues whom we did not know well. We found it difficult to be sure of a common understanding of terms and principles, particularly with many archeologists. Our new proximity to Washington D.C., and King's employment there by the Office of

Archeology and Historic Preservation during 1976–1977, greatly enhanced our understanding of the historic preservation system. We came to see very clearly that a book like this was needed, not only to explain historic preservation to our colleagues in anthropology, but to show our associates in historic preservation how we as anthropologists view them and the system in which we all work.

With such a history, we cannot hope to acknowledge all the people who have contributed ideas and stimuli to the production of this book, so we will only say that while we take sole responsibility for the interpretations and ideas we put forth here, we know that they are not entirely our own. We are specifically grateful to Fred Plog for helping with initial arrangements for publication, to Stuart Struever for his sympathetic reading of our first struggling chapters, to William Murtagh for his invaluable insights into the philosophy and history of historic preservation, to Adrian Anderson, Keith Anderson, Lawrence Aten, Mark Barnes, John Byrne, Kate Cole, Steven Gluckman, Myra Harrison, Fred Rath, Pete Raynor, Robert Rettig, Jerry Rogers, Douglas Scovill, Carol Shull, Charles Spilker, Ken Tapman, Jan Thorman, and Rex Wilson for the discussions that have provided much of our education in how historic preservation works, and to Jerry Stuchell, Mary Obear, and Cathy McElroy for their help with manuscript preparation, indexing, and editing. By no means least, we are indebted to the staff of Academic Press for their patience and understanding.

1

ANTHROPOLOGY AND HISTORIC PRESERVATION

The diversity of America's peoples and activities is a key factor in ... historic preservation. For example, the mansion on the hill was an important part of American life, but so were the workers' houses, transportation system, factory, churches, and all else that made up the town. The plantation house is understandable only with the slave quarters, the dependencies and the fields. Cultures of ethnic groups have given ... a rich history to the country.

—National Trust: *Goals* and *Programs*, 1973.
Mulloy 1976: Appendix 23

Today the fragmented nature of the American preservation movement still concerns the people who are most involved in it.

—Hosmer 1965:302

Historic preservation in the United States has a long and complex history that has periodically been interwoven with and unraveled from at least that of the archeological element of anthropology. In the last few years, in response to the opportunities and needs created by new historic preservation and environmental statutes, people trained in anthropology and those specializing in historic preservation have been working together in increasing numbers. We who have come into historic preservation from anthropology are often surprised to find preservationists expressing themselves as the National Trust did in the quote that heads this chapter. If we had thought of preservationists as little old people who kept detailed genealogies of their families and promoted the preservation of major patriotic landmarks, such expressions quickly disabuse us of the notion,

1

and make us feel much more at ease. At the same time, the fragmentation of which Hosmer speaks is very apparent to us; historic preservationists are by no means united in even their basic understanding of what should be preserved or of what constitutes preservation. We are biased enough in favor of our own academic tradition to think that anthropology has something to offer to the development of such understandings. This is not to say that anthropology has a simple formula for effective historic preservation, but to suggest that an infusion of anthropological thinking into historic preservation could help clarify the nature of the cultural diversity that modern preservationists seek to maintain, and provide improved methods for maintaining it.

One major purpose of this book, then, is to encourage anthropologists to participate in historic preservation. On the whole, anthropologists understand historic preservation very poorly. Archeologists do contract work under the historic preservation laws, and cultural anthropologists participate in Social Impact Assessments touching on historic properties, with minimal knowledge of either the statutes or the administrative systems that govern historic preservation. A primer in historic preservation for anthropologists is needed, and in this book we will try to provide it.

At the same time, we think it may be helpful for nonanthropologists engaged in historic preservation to see how their field is viewed by at least three anthropologists. We think we have things to say to historic preservation that are consistent with its evolving philosophy, but that may serve to identify problems and suggest solutions that are different from those that would occur to one trained in another discipline. We have not been shy about criticizing aspects of the historic preservation system, about pursuing operational issues to improbable extremes, or about proposing what may seem to some rather visionary solutions to what we see as preservation problems. We hope that this book will be absorbed by historic preservationists who are not anthropologists as a perspective worth considering in the daily conduct of their business.

ANTHROPOLOGY, HISTORY, AND SOCIETY

We take a very broad view of our discipline, summed up concisely by Clifford Geertz (1973): "The essential vocation of interpretive anthropology is not to answer our deepest questions, but to make available to us answers that others, guarding other sheep in other valleys, have given, and thus to include them in the consultable record of what man has said [p. 30]." Each anthropologist has particular theoretical predilections, particular "deepest questions" to ask, and particular valleys, flocks and shepherds to study, but as a group we are all seeking to build up and maintain the most extensive and precise body of data possible on human responses to the exigencies of life, for our reference and our children's children's reference when pondering how to respond to such exigencies in the future.

Seeking the answers given by other societies—or by our own—to the deep questions of human existence, or for that matter even defining the questions, involves a great deal of exploration, sorting and comparison of data, experimentation with methods of data acquisition and interpretation, development and testing of hypotheses, and so forth. Some kinds of answers to some kinds of questions exist solely as mental constructs without lasting physical manifestation. When, for example, a society faces environmental stresses demanding the maintenance of an efficient hunting unit in each village, and females do the hunting, the society might respond to the stress by developing a form of kinship terminology that renders only males in groups not resident at the village imaginable as potential spouses, and a residence rule that specifies that at marriage, men leave the village of their birth and move into their wive's villages, thus keeping daughters in the natal village after marriage so they can work in hunting parties with their sisters over familiar terrain. This sort of answer to a general sort of human problem (environmental stress) cannot be added to Geertz's "consultable record," at least in much detail, without interviewing the people who use the terminology and the residence rule. Other answers, however, have distinct and recordable physical properties. Suppose a loose-knit group of American pioneer farmers view themselves as threatened by an influx of newcomers, and respond by developing a religious sect whose precepts emphasize the goodness of pioneer qualities and whose ritual reinforces intrapioneer solidarity by demanding frequent and continual interaction among pioneer families. Eventually this response should begin to influence residence patterns—pioneer residences may tend to cluster together and become similarly organized vis à vis those of newcomers. The exchange of objects between households may follow upon the exchange of ritual obligations, so that pioneer households may share certain contents not shared by newcomers. A tendency to cling to and replicate the things of pioneer life—to go to town in Conestoga wagons, for example—may characterize pioneer households in contrast with newcomers. The solidarity of the group may be manifested in the construction of a church. The anthropologist seeking to define this group's answer to the general human problem of coping with incursions from outside the group could make substantial progress without interviewing the people, by simply looking at their houses, farms, artifacts, and general community organization at various times during the group's history.

The archeologist, of course, is involved with the second sort of research, seeking, conceptualizing, describing, comparing, and interpreting the physical leavings of human thought and its attendant behavior. Most new techniques and methods in archeology are developed for the ultimate purpose of expanding the range of behavior classes we can infer from physical leavings. Not long ago, most of what archeologists did was to describe the ways in which artifact classes appeared, changed, and disappeared through the culture histories of particular sites or regions. These descriptions were accompanied by musings about what phenomena (wars, invasions, etc.) might account for the changes observed. Advances in the rigor with which the archeologist forms hypotheses and tests, in the range of models available to inform these hypotheses and tests, and in the variety and sophistication of tools and methods for use in the field and laboratory, have set archeologists to the systematic study of settlement organization, subsistence practices, interaction systems, social organization, and a wide range of other kinds of human activity through which a given society's answers to deep questions may be at least partially expressed. The successes and failures of a society's attempts to deal with its problems are expressed in its archeological record, with varying degrees of clarity, and archeological methods are capable of bringing forth a description of each such experiment in living and adding it to our consultable record.

The study of the past is an important function of anthropology, then, because it expands the number of Geertz's sheep-filled valleys into which we can look—from those in which the shepherds can talk with us to those where only the bones of shepherd and sheep remain—and because it gives us the potential for seeing what led to the development of a given shepherd's answer and what its results were. One more advantage should be noted: The shepherd can lie, and even if he literally tells the truth he is necessarily the prisoner of his own perceptions. The study of his physical leavings may provide an important corrective even if the shepherd's own words have been recorded. This is not to say that the archeological record is more accurate than that derived from informants or written history; what people leave around is a biased and incomplete record of their lives, just as is what they say or write. But it is a *different* record, an essentially independent record, and in doing the complex work of searching out and understanding a society's answers to its questions, we need all the help we can get.

The ethnographer has difficulty understanding his or her record of a society if its only survivor has become senile. The historian has difficulty reading texts if they are infested by bookworms. The archeological record, locked in historic properties, is similarly subject to erosion and consequent misunderstanding. One function of historic preservation from an anthropological perspective, then, is to minimize the erosion of the information content of historic properties.

The dead are not anthropology's only concern, however. If the shepherd is still tending his flocks, we would like to talk with him, and we would like to make sure that he can keep tending his flock, in his own way, for as long as he wishes, working out his own answers to his own questions, and thus helping provide us all with the broadest and most diverse possible record. The craft of social anthropology lies in eliciting meaningful information from the shepherd even if he speaks in circumlocutions and acts in ambiguous ways. The anthropologist is thus especially equipped to serve as a translator of social values between groups. This provides a second role for anthropologists in historic preservation.

Suppose that our pioneer subculture has as one of its supreme social values the conviction that its church must be so oriented that its door always opens toward St. Louis. Let us further suppose that taciturnity and faith in the central government are among its most valued personal attributes. When the Conastogaland Department of Transportation decides to put a highway through the church site, moving the church and rotating it 90°, the pioneers do not complain—they are taciturn and moreover assume that the government knows best. But the change will be seriously damaging to their cultural system, and could be avoided with no trouble to the highway planners. Were the pioneers the preservationists of Boston in the late 1870s, faced with the destruction of the Old South Meetinghouse, they would raise hell, but they are instead a small and nonassertive minority group, and they cannot or will not take the legal and political initiatives offered by the historic preservation statutes on their own behalf. So they will probably lose the cultural integrity of their church, unless during the highway planning process a serious effort is made to ascertain just what their cultural values are, and how they may be related to tangible properties. Such studies are precisely the kinds of things that social anthropologists are trained to do.

We see two basic roles for the anthropologist in historic preservation, then: the identification of the useful information contained in historic properties, and the development of methods to preserve it; and service as a translator between groups with a cultural investment in historic properties and those agencies whose actions may affect historic properties.

HISTORIC PROPERTIES: A DEFINITION

An historic property, to us, is any place where people have created something that can contribute—through its study or through its continued availability for individual or group experience—to our "consultable record" of human existence. Olduvai Gorge, the church down the street, the tract house in the suburbs, and the arrangement of silverware on the table may all be historic properties.

No one would deny that Olduvai Gorge is an historic property. It provides a stratigraphic sequence of archeological loci representative of many important steps in hominid evolution. But what if, instead of the entire gorge, we had only one of its living floors, with its patterns of bones, waste flakes, and tools? Certainly any archeologist would still regard this as an historic property under our definition. It can still inform us about hominid behavior and when it is compared with other such living floors, and other sites, it can help tell us about variation and change in that behavior. What, then, if we had recorded 2 million such sites all apparently exactly alike—would the Olduvai site then *not* be an historic property? Obviously, the answer is no—it would continue to be a property useful in comparative archeological research, although our pragmatic approach to it might be different. If Olduvai Gorge as we know it today were proposed as a new reservoir site by the Tanzanian Corps of Engineers we would be most upset; if a similar reservoir threatened 10 of our hypothetical 2 million living floors, we might find this loss tolerable—not because the 10 floors were not historic properties, but because we might feel we could afford a .000005% loss of this particular class of properties.

The church down the street was built in 1750, remodeled in 1825 and 1900. Its architecture thus reflects changes in style and fashion through 150 years of American history. It is associated with a cemetery whose organization reflects that of the congregation—there are family plots; wealth and status are reflected in the size and elaboration of tombstones, and so forth. The church has been a focus for community activities—town meetings, pot-lucks and, most recently, bingo games. These activities have resulted in the deposition of some debris on, and eventually in, the ground around the building. The activities that produced the debris can be reconstructed, with varying degrees of success, by studying the debris and its distribution. The church thus reflects human behavior in a number of ways, and if maintaining access to these reflections as part of our consultable record is important, then the church is an historic property. The differences between the church and Olduvai Gorge are differences of scale and kinds of perceived value. The church represents a shorter span of human history than does Olduvai, and we may regard the information it contains as less important to our understanding of history—less necessary as part of our consultable record. On the other hand, the church may be a great deal more important to our neighborhood's sense of its own historical integrity than Olduvai Gorge could possibly be; it may thus be vital to the maintenance of our neighborhood as a viable valley in which a particular kind of shepherd is working out answers to human questions.

The house just built in Shady Acres, a suburban development, represents one of five basic floorplans that, with cosmetic modifications, define the range of house-types available to purchasers. Compared with a typical house in Sunny Shores, the 5-year-old development next door, it shows several innovations. The fireplace, for example, is built of blocks containing bottom ash reclaimed from the local power generating plant as an antipollution measure. It is faced with old brick from an eighteenth century church lately razed during an urban renewal project. It contains a built-in garbage compactor, a special alarm system for calling the Shady Acres Security Patrol, and carefully designed insulation advertised as conserving energy. Thus before it is even occupied the house contains physical elements that reflect current social concerns—environmental protection, personal security, and energy conservation—and which by comparison with the adjacent older development will permit us to identify changes in these concerns. As such, it may be regarded as an historic property for study in the future if not in the present. It will have other characteristics once it has been occupied, as its occupants fill and reorder its spaces in accordance with their culturally influenced standards of order, propriety, and aesthetics. Not only will these orderings be amenable to study, to shed light on the behavior and beliefs of the house's occupants; they may also assume special significance to the occupants themselves, as reflections and reinforcers of their cultural system. The characteristics of the house may be trivial—the occupants may not care much about how this particular house is organized, and it might be more efficient to measure change in societal concerns by comparing records of materials purchased by the builders of Shady Acres and Sunny Shores than by using the developments themselves as objects of study. The fact remains, however, that the house *may* be an historic property; the question of triviality must be answered through evaluation based on an understanding of the house and its cultural context.

Modal patterns for the distribution of silverware on a dining table are defined by rules of etiquette. Variation from the rules reflects the differential formality of dining occasions, the involvement of particular dining groups and individuals in the standard protocol patterns of Western society, and the distinctive rules observed by different social and ethnic groups. These variant patterns are expressed differently through time; our generation, for instance, is supposed to be less formal than some of its predecessors, and this distinction is sometimes taken to reflect a significant change in social values. Insofar as the dinner table distribution of silverware thus reflects an individual's values and patterned behavior, that distribution may be taken to define an historic property. This is a marginal example only because the transcience of the distribution renders it practically intangible. The distribution, and the sociocultural factors that define it, clearly constitute information about our culture (a "cultural resource," as defined on page 8), but their intangibility makes our dinner table rather dubious as an historic property. If suddenly overwhelmed by a volcano and held immobile for a space of time, however, our table and its silverware would become an obvious historic property. Its value, like that of Olduvai Gorge, would depend on the extent to which the data it contained could be better obtained elsewhere.

We may appear to be on the verge of suggesting that everything is historic, based on an anthropology of the absurd. We agree that everything *does* have the potential for being of historic value; it does not follow, however, that everything thus should be preserved or otherwise afforded special treatment. Historic preservationists make decisions daily about whether something is sufficiently valuable to be given special attention. Most times, these decisions are made without lengthy thought—we throw away last night's beer cans rather than nominating them to the National Register of Historic Places. There is a point, however, at which decisions about historic significance, and about tactics for maintaining significance, should not be made offhandedly, and in this book we will be exploring how such decisions can be and are being made. We believe that if we start with the assumption that almost anything might be of historic value, we will make wiser decisions about what really *is* valuable.

HISTORIC PRESERVATION, CULTURAL RESOURCES, AND SOCIAL IMPACTS

What we will be talking about in this book sometimes passes under other names, or is at least related to things that pass under other names. We need to define, at the outset, how historic preservation relates to the fields of study called "cultural resource management" and "social impact assessment."

The federal government is obligated by such laws as the National Environmental Policy Act (NEPA) to take what may be called the "social environment" into account in planning projects and programs. Social impact assessments are done to ascertain what the effects of a given federal action may be on the social environment. In this context the social environment includes all organized behavior by groups of human beings, and the products of such behavior—economic systems, religions, governments, schools, housing. Social impact assessments are very general studies that tend to deal with broad patterns of social and economic behavior that occur in the area where a federal action is planned. They attempt to predict the results of the federal action in terms of possible changes in such patterns of behavior (cf. Vlachos *et al.* 1975).

Any society has aspects of its behavior, products of its behavior, and systems of thought that affect its behavior, that are ordinarily thought of as cultural. A society's history, traditions, arts, religious beliefs, sciences, and educational systems are expressions and products of behavior that have meaning to the society's perception of itself as a society. The cultural aspects of any social group or area that may be affected by a federal action must be taken into account by the government under the mandate of NEPA. Assessing the nature of cultural resources requires special techniques and methods, and these may be thought of as "cultural resource management." This term has been frequently used by archeologists to label the activities that they carry on under federal contract (cf. Lipe & Lindsay 1974; McMillan *et al.* 1977), or to describe what we think of as historic preservation (cf. King 1975), but we regard this as both confusing and a little pretentious. Culture, after all, is more than archeology, and it is also more than historic sites and structures. These are tangible expressions of culture, but there are also tangible cultural things that are not historic or archeological (libraries and opera houses, for example) and a great range of intangible cultural institutions, values, and beliefs that should be considered in federal planning. Cultural resource management should deal with all aspects of culture.

Culture does produce a clutter of material things, however, and this is the subject matter of historic preservation. Historic preservation, and the laws and policies directly supporting it (preeminently, the National Historic Preservation Act or NHPA) deal with the tangible remnants of past cultural systems and activities—historic properties. Much of the social and cultural environment must be studied in order to identify and understand such properties, so documentary

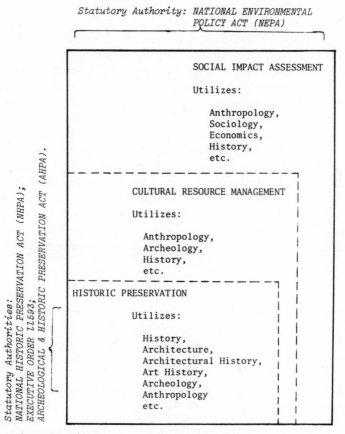

Figure 1. *Relationship of historic preservation to cultural resource management and social impact assessment.*

history, folklore, ethnohistory, and ethnography are involved in historic preservation, but the foci of attention are the historic properties themselves.

When a federal action is under study, social impact assessment, cultural resource management, and historic preservation can be thought of as nested within one another, making a total multidisciplinary package as shown in Figure 1. Each portion of the package requires special kinds of expertise and methods, however. We will be concerned with historic preservation in this book, rather than with the broader fields of cultural resource management or social impact assessment, because it is historic preservation that has the largest, most complex, best established set of laws, policies, and procedures with which to work, and because it is the field with which we have worked most closely and hence have the most to say. The appropriateness of integrating historic preservation with other approaches to the study and maintenance of the social environment should not be ignored, however.

Finally, we should note that we use the term "historic" to apply to properties that originated both before and after the European invasion of the New World. This is consistent with general federal government usage, and we believe that it is also less confusing than the division between "historic" and "prehistoric" would be. Lumping all expressions of the histories of all America's peoples, indigenous and immigrant, under a single term seems most efficient for the purposes of historic preservation; historic preservation is certainly not concerned only with the remnants of literate social groups or of Euro-Americans, and no one has ever found it necessary to propose enactment of a prehistoric preservation act. Using a single term for all the objects of historic preservation's interest also helps discourage the unwarranted but pervasive assumptions that archeologists are concerned only with prehistory, that structures are the sole province of the architect, and that once written records are available about a people only historians need study their leavings.

With this prelude, we can begin with a look at how historic preservation has developed in the United States, as a basis for understanding its condition today.

2

A HISTORY OF HISTORIC
PRESERVATION IN AMERICA

Few anthropologists are very familiar with historic preservation, either as a discipline or as a body of law and policy. Even North American archeologists, who work with the stuff of historic preservation and very often are funded because of its laws, have difficulty relating to the field and tend to have only a vague idea of its principles or its history. As we define it, however, historic preservation includes archeology—at least to the extent that archeology is practiced with preservation of data as one of its goals. This is, to us, a fact of modern life, and one with which we are not uncomfortable. The association of archeology with historic preservation also has a rather long history. Archeological research and the movement to preserve historic properties were closely intertwined at their roots in the United States. They were practiced by the same groups of people, based on rather similar premises, and they made common cause in legislative efforts. It was only with the Great Depression that the threads of historic preservation unraveled, and even then, both archeology and the preservation movement experienced similar social and economic pressures that resulted in similar conceptual changes. A major problem for modern historic preservationists is to bring archeology and preservation together again; we believe that looking at the entire field anthropologically can be an aid in solving this problem and in making all of historic preservation work more effectively.

This chapter will trace the histories of American archeology and the preservation movement, leading to what we think of as a modern unified historic preservation discipline. Through this history we hope to show something of what archeologists (and more broadly, anthropologists) share with preservationists, and how they have grown apart during the twentieth century. This should provide a basis for discussing the reunified discipline and how it can work.

BEGINNINGS: CONQUEST AND VENERATION

Early American efforts at both prehistoric archeology and preservation of historic sites were undertaken by private individuals working for or under the auspices of private scientific, antiquarian, or patriotic organizations, and were involved with political and social issues of national concern. Thomas Jefferson first developed his interest in local archeology through careful excavations of prehistoric sites in Virginia. Later, as president of the American Philosophical Society, he asked members to obtain data on American archeological sites wherever they might be found (Willey and Sabloff 1974:37). Both the American Philosophical Society and the American Antequarian Society focused their interests on the extensive and elaborate mound-groups of the Ohio and Mississippi Valleys. The basic research question addressed by these groups was of general public concern for a nation engaged in taking land from aboriginal owners. The "mound-builder controversy" boiled down to the question of whether the Indians could have built them. A conclusion that they could not, and did not, and that the mounds had in fact been built by Vikings, Irish, or Israelites would have supported the idea that the Indians were not very civilized and hence not worthy of much consideration, while simultaneously establishing a sort of aboriginal title to the land for Europeans. The earliest government-sponsored archeological research began in 1846 with the establishment of the Smithsonian Institution, and this research also focused upon the mound-builders (cf. Squire and Davis 1848; Squire 1849).

A similarly nationalistic concern, the "cult of Washington," characterized the early days of preservation in America. The deification of George Washington as the "father of our country" was in full swing during the middle of the nineteenth century; the Washington Monument was under construction, and statues of Washington were everywhere. It is not surprising that a site associated with Washington—his headquarters during the last 2 years of the Revolution—should have been the first successful acquisition for preservation purposes in the nation (Whitehill *in* Rains *et al.* 1965:37). This site, the Hasbrouck House in Newburg, New York, was acquired by the state of New York in 1850.

The fact that government acted to preserve the Hasbrouck House was unusual, as both archeology and preservation were largely interests of private groups prior to the 1870s. Community-level interest in preservation was beginning to show itself across the country. For example, in 1846 the residents of Deerfield, Massachusetts launched a drive to save the "Old Indian House," the last structural survivor of an Indian massacre that occurred in 1704 (Hosmer 1965:33). Though unsuccessful, the effort exemplified the type of community action on behalf of historic properties that characterized the development of preservation in New England for the next century. Individuals had preserved historic properties before, and a good deal of community feeling had been generated in Philadelphia when Independence Hall was threatened with destruction in 1813–1816 (Hosmer 1965:30), but these earlier efforts had been almost exclusively directed at the preservation of properties central to the history of the American Revolution and were often merely happy accidents.

The first national effort in preservation was, perhaps inevitably, organized around the acquisition of Mt. Vernon. Hosmer (1965:41–62) has told the story of Mt. Vernon and the Washington cult in detail. The movement to acquire Mt. Vernon from the Washington heirs and arrest its decay was organized by Ann Pamela Cunningham of South Carolina. Miss Cunningham organized state and local groups to collect money for the purchase, and later for the restoration and operation of Mt. Vernon. She enlisted the noted orator Edward Everett to travel about the country speaking on behalf of the cause. By 1858 the Mount Vernon Ladies' Association was able to purchase the property, and began its maintenance and restoration as a museum-house memorializing the founding father. Attempts to emulate the success of the Mt. Vernon movement by organizing national groups to protect Valley Forge and the Hermitage were not successful, however; preservation was embued with the Washington-cult, and only the great man's actual home could sufficiently excite the public imagination to justify a long-term commitment of work and money.

Fortunately, such long-term commitments were not always necessary, and local groups were successful in obtaining the assistance of state and city governments to acquire and protect a number of landmark buildings during the 1850s. John Hancock's home in Boston was lost to wreckers in 1863 after a lengthy preservation effort; of it, Hosmer (1965) says "In 'dying' the Hancock house contributed more to the preservation movement that it ever could have by remaining intact. Throughout the next five or six decades many preservationists used the Hancock Mansion as their rallying cry [p. 40]."

Thus, by the time the Civil War began, public interest had clearly developed both in archeology and preservation, and the government had begun to provide some support for each. The interests of archeologists centered on monumental sites whose origins were a political embarrassment, while preservationists sought to protect the shrines of a secular nation.

THE PRESERVATION ETHIC AND THE FEDERAL GOVERNMENT: 1870–1900

The years following the Civil War saw a considerable diversification in both archeology and preservation. The stage was set, in part, by the increasing pace of the movement westward that occurred during the 1840s and 1850s. As the federal government found itself in possession of vast new tracts of land requiring exploration, study, and subdivision into private ownership, the need to increase the complexity of the government itself became apparent. In 1849, after lengthy debate, the Department of the Interior was formed to manage the new federal lands, oversee dealings with the Indians, issue pensions, and engage in a host of other activities vaguely relating to the problems of settling the continental interior (Interior 1976:45–46). Surveys of western lands began in earnest after the Civil War, directed not only by the Department of the Interior but by the Army Engineers and the Smithsonian Institution. A study by the National Academy of Sciences in 1878 recommended that federal survey activities be coordinated within the Department of the Interior; the result was establishment of the U.S. Geological Survey in 1879. In the same year, the Smithsonian Institution established its Bureau of Ethnology, later to become the Bureau of American Ethnology (BAE). The Geological Survey and the Bureau of American Ethnology worked closely together under the directorship of Major John Wesley Powell.

In the year 1879, two organizations were founded that would play major roles in activities that eventually led to the passage of legislation concerning archeology and preservation. One was the Anthropological Society of Washington, which initiated the publication of the *American Anthropologist* and eventually merged with other groups into the American Anthropological Association. The other was the Archeological Institute of America, founded by a group of archeologists, historians and their associates around Boston.

Many members of the Archeological Institute of America became interested in preserving archeological sites in the American Southwest. This came about partly as a result of several other 1879 events: F. W. Putnam's archeological volume in the series of reports, *Surveys West of the One Hundredth Meridian* was published, thus bringing the ruins of the Southwest into the public eye, and anthropologist Lewis Henry Morgan was elected to the presidency of the American Association for the Advancement of Science. Members of the Archeological Institute sought out Morgan to obtain recommendations for a field project. Morgan offered an hypothesis concerning the evolution of architectural forms. He urged the Institute to launch an expedition to the Southwest to collect data pertinent to this hypothesis, and recommended A. P. Bandelier as its leader. Bandelier's reports exposed the damage being done to southwestern ruins by vandals and looters (Bandelier 1881). Two Institute members responded to Bandelier's report, and, in 1882, had a petition read on the floor of the Senate asking that:

> at least some of these extinct cities and pueblos . . . be withheld from public sale and their antiquities and ruins be preserved, as they furnish invaluable data for the ethnological studies now engaging the attention of our most learned scientific, antiquarian and historical students [Wilder & Slafter 1882, quoted in Lee 1970:10]."

Congress was not prepared for a petition of such general scope and the petition died in committee.

The next impetus toward congressional action came as a result of the 1886–1888 Hemmenway Southwestern Archeological Expedition. Mary Hemmenway, who endowed this expedition, was a prominant Boston figure who played a major role in the acquisition and preservation of the Old South Meetinghouse, one of the focal points of the New England preservation movement (Hosmer 1965:105). Now she dispatched Frank H. Cushing on a lengthy expedition that resulted in the description of the Casa Grande ruin and of the serious damage being done to it by vandals. This time the resulting petition to Congress, signed by such notable New England preservationists as Hemmenway, Francis Parkman of the Archeological Institute, Mrs. Henry Cabot Lodge, Oliver Wendall Holmes, and J. Greenleaf Whittier, was approved. The land around Casa Grande was reserved from sale and settlement, and an appropriation was made to permit the secretary of the interior to protect and repair the ruin. The federal government had thus taken its first step toward a formal program of historic preservation.

The BAE commissioned archeological studies, but its more important contribution to the history of American archeology and preservation may have been the philosophical direction it gave to American anthropology. By the time the BAE was organized, the Battle of the Little Big Horn had been fought and the destruction of American Indian societies as functioning entities appeared inevitable. Although BAE research addressed historical questions—for example, it was in large measure a BAE study that satisfied the scholarly community as to the indigenous origin of the great midwestern mounds (Thomas 1894)—a primary goal was the acquisition of data, objects, recollections, and pictures, in the hope of retaining some vestige of the fast-vanishing American Indian lifeway. This "salvage ethnography" approach came to be canonized by early American ethnographers in a research ideology now known as "historical particularism," the central idea of which is that understanding human culture and its history will come from the gradual synthesis of a great many small pieces of information gathered whenever and wherever opportunities arise. Historical particularism has provided the methodological context for much salvage research up to the present day (cf. King 1971).

The late nineteenth century also saw the growth of academic anthropology and archeology at such institutions as Harvard, Columbia, and Berkeley, and at major private museums. The research thrust of such institutions was usually consistent with that of the BAE—explore, describe, record information, and acquire specimens. One need only walk through the older halls of a museum like the Peabody at Harvard to see the fruits of these labors—case upon case of artifacts, often unlabeled though presumably described in a published or unpublished report somewhere. It must have been a frantic, frustrating, heartsick time, and it resulted in at least two generations of anthropologists and archeologists whose research was crisis-oriented and whose main goals were the gathering of data. One of the later BAE anthropologists encapsulated the philosophy of the period in rhyme:

Give not, give not, the yawning graves their plunder;
Save, save the lore for future ages joy;
The stories full of beauty and of wonder,
The songs more pristine than the songs of Troy,
The ancient speech forever to be vanished—
Lore that tomorrow to the grave goes down!
All other thought from our horizon banished,
Let any sacrifice our labor crown.

—J. Peabody Harrington
(Quoted in Laird 1975)

Not only were Indian societies vanishing; so were their material remains. As the profession of archeology developed within anthropology, the avocation of archeology did not obediently disappear. Some avocationals were honest and responsible researchers, but others had discovered that there were markets for antiquities, and they aggressively exploited this discovery. Archeological sites were also disappearing under the plow; the great mounds of the Mississippi Valley were particularly and dramatically susceptible to such destruction. Recognizing an immediate danger to the Great Serpent Mount in the Ohio Valley, Frederic Putnam of the Peabody Museum at Harvard took an unusual step; he raised money among preservation-oriented Bostonians, and bought the site through the museum, subsequently deeding it to the state of Ohio. This sort of activity was entirely in keeping with the approach to preservation then dominant in New England. New England, during this period, was the scene of widespread preservation action directed toward properties of regional concern and supported by private citizens. While efforts were still directed at the preservation of revolutionary shrines, interest was also growing in the protection of properties that reflected local history, represented particular kinds of architecture or periods of construction, or were associated with major intellectual events and trends (Hosmer 1965:104–122). House museums were appearing not only in the homes of revolutionary leaders, but in places that were esteemed as "faithful reproductions . . . of the primitive Colonial life of New England, [as] an atmosphere conducive to high aspirations, [and as the] historical treasures [of] every town in New England [Hosmer 1965:113–119]."

In the Middle Atlantic states, the sites and structures preserved continued to be scenes of important events associated with the Revolution. This was particularly evident in and around Philadelphia as government-sponsored preparations were made for the centennial celebrations of 1876 (Hosmer 1965:76–101). In the South, too, the major emphasis in preservation continued to be on homes of great men. Here virtually all preservation work was done by or with the assistance of the state or federal governments; only one substantial private group was successful in saving historic buildings. This group, the Association for the Preservation of Virginia Antiquities, was one of the first to direct its efforts to an entire district rather than to a single site. In the 1890s it arranged for a retaining wall to be constructed along the James River to keep the historic section of Jamestown Island from washing away (Hosmer 1965:67). In the West, an early focus of interest was on the Spanish–Mexican missions which had fallen into disrepair after secularization in 1834. Church interests contributed to these preservation efforts, but the bulk of financial support came from state governments.

The 1890s were a period of economic depression with few substantial government expenditures for archeology or preservation. Nevertheless, the Archeological Institute of American grew substantially during the 1890s, and established chapters in many parts of the country. Section H of the American Association for the Advancement of Science (that section concerned with anthropology) had been created, and a new "Anthropological Club" had been formed in New York in semicompetition with the Anthropological Society of Washington. By 1902, these last two organizations had merged to form the American Anthropological Association.

Increasing publication of archeological research results and popular accounts of prehistoric lifeways, expanding museum displays, and international exhibitions whetted the public's appetite for archeology. Support for archeology was thus developing, but this increased appeal to the public probably also impelled the growth of pothunting. During the 1890s new reports appeared describing the depredations of artifact collectors in the Southwestern pueblos. Nationalistic and chauvinistic sentiments were inflamed when in 1891–1892 the Swedish explorer Gustav Erik Adolf Nordenskjöld joined forces with the

Wetherill brothers—Colorado stockmen and archeology afficionados of, at best, checkered reputation—to excavate several ruins and remove their contents to Stockholm. The Wetherills and others were found to be filing homestead claims on lands containing ruins, for no other apparent purpose than the extraction of artifacts for sale, and when they cooperated with the "Hyde Exploring Expedition" in 1869–1879 to remove whole rooms from Pueblo Bonito for display at the American Museum of Natural History it sparked a petition to the secretary of the interior from the Santa Fe Archeological Society that led to a special investigation. The investigation strongly recommended the withdrawal of the whole Chaco Canyon area including Pueblo Bonito, pending its possible designation as a national park. Several other areas of ruins were protected by similar withdrawals during the 1890s. Since designation as a park requires an act of Congress, however, years passed before such areas were actually guarded in any way.

BEYOND CHACO CANYON: THE GOVERNMENT PRESERVES ARCHEOLOGICAL SITES

In 1900 a bill drafted by committees of the Archeological Institute and the American Association for the Advancement of Science was introduced in Congress giving the president the right to set aside reservations to protect archeological sites and areas of "scientific or scenic value." A counterproposal was offered in the House, forbidding the unauthorized disturbance of antiquities. A third bill was introduced directing the secretary of the interior to make a survey to identify southwestern sites worth saving. All three bills were finally referred to the General Land Office in the Department of the Interior, which introduced a modified version of the first bill in April of 1900. Interior was particularly interested in obtaining the authority to set aside lands for protective purposes, and was much less concerned with the essentially unmanageable prohibition of pothunting. The department was also anxious to obtain a broad mandate to set aside lands not only for the protection of archeological properties but of natural phenomena as well. As Lee (1970:44) points out, this concern was consistent with the general policy within the Roosevelt administration to take the management of western lands and water out of the hands of politicians and place it in professional hands within the executive branch. The Antiquities Act was one tool by which Roosevelt's scientific cadre could gain discretion over the public lands.

The fight for an Antiquities Act went on for 6 years, and is ably detailed by Lee (1970:47–77). The fight was not simply between Congress and the executive; at some times even the Smithsonian and the Archeological Institute were pitted against one another in support of slightly different bills. Eventually, under the leadership of Representative J. F. Lacey of Iowa, an Antiquities Act was passed in 1906. The Antiquities Act gave the president broad discretion to set aside lands—to be called national monuments—containing significant cultural or scientific resources, and forbade the disturbance of ruins or archeological sites on federal lands without the permission of the responsible land-managing agency. When President Roosevelt signed the act on June 8, 1906, the federal government had finally acknowledged a responsibility to archeology.

In 1907, the secretaries of war, agriculture, and interior agreed to uniform rules and regulations for administering the Antiquities Act. Although each department retained authority for issuance of permits, subject to recommendation by the Smithsonian, the secretary of the interior was given a lead role in the administration of national monuments. Centralization of responsibility for the management of federally owned historic properties in the Department of the Interior was furthered by the establishment of a unified National Park Service within the Department of the Interior in 1916, and by a reorganization in 1933 that assigned all federal parks, monuments, battlefields and historic sites to administration by the National Park Service. Thus the central role played by the Interior Department during the early days of the USGS and BAE exploration parties was strengthened but at the same time changed, the emphasis shifting from exploration and discovery to the management of designated areas.

Congress took another step toward development of a national archeological program in 1906 by granting a charter to the Archeological Institute of America. Chartering a national organization to acquire and protect historic properties had been regarded as desirable by preservationists for some time, but the single-purpose Mount Vernon Ladies' Association was by 1900 still the only successful example of a national preservation effort. The Daughters of the American Revolution and the National Society of the Colonial Dames of America both encouraged local preservation activities, but neither was capable of nor interested in national mobilization to acquire and protect historic properties (Hosmer 1965:131–152). In England, a national trust for historic preservation had been in existence for some time, and an attempt to emulate it was made in 1901 when the Trustees of Scenic and Historic Places and Objects in the state of New York was reorganized to become the putatively national American Scenic and Historic Preservation Society. The society performed useful services in disseminating preservation information and extending communications to preservationists in Europe, but it managed to acquire and protect only two buildings, both in New York State (Hosmer 1965:93–100). The Archeological Institute, upon receipt of its charter, turned away from preservation concerns toward the encouragement of overseas archeological expeditions. Forty-three years were to pass after the incorporation of the Archeological Institute before the federal government at last chartered a national group devoted to preservation—the National Trust.

We have dealt at such length with the beginnings of archeology and preservation because they illustrate some of the similarities and differences between the two aspects of modern historic preservation. The motives behind archeology and preservation were rather different; the one sought to preserve historic properties so that they could provide "data for ethnological studies";

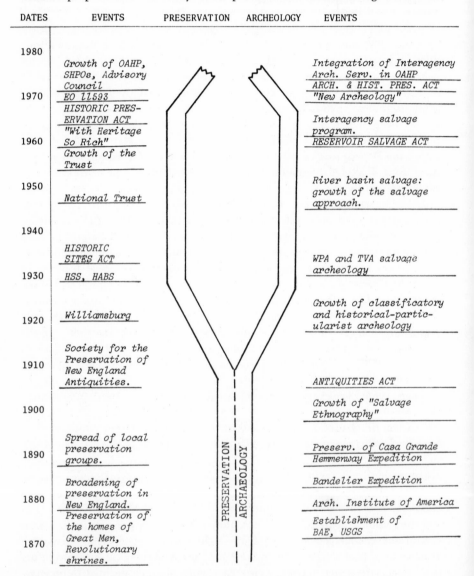

| DATES | EVENTS | PRESERVATION | ARCHEOLOGY | EVENTS |

Figure 2. *The development of modern historic preservation.*

the other sought to preserve historic properties in order to inspire patriotism, maintain examples of vanished lifeways, and retain examples of high architectural craftsmanship. Their strategies for preservation were similar, however, except that archeologists became primarily concerned about the public lands of the West, whereas most preservationists had to contend with the fragmented private landholdings of the East. Moreover, the people involved in archeology and preservation were often the same. The two fields of interest were intimately connected, but after World War I, an unraveling began that is only now being spliced (Figure 2).

INTO THE 1930s

World War I interrupted preservation and archeological activities to a considerable extent. Preservation groups continued on a local level, though often with only marginal success. A vigorous regional group founded in 1910, the Society for the Preservation of New England Antiquities, continued to grow and to acquire properties during the war. The society and its founder, William Sumner Appleton, pioneered the concept of "adaptive use" and the priority of architectural representativeness over patriotic considerations as a criterion for preservation (Hosmer 1965:237–259).

During the 1920s the single most ambitious preservation scheme in the United States was undertaken at Williamsburg, Virginia, under the direction of Rev. William A. R. Goodwin. With a generous endowment by John D. Rockefeller, Jr., Goodwin and his associates set out to restore the entire core of the old Virginia capital to its pre-revolutionary condition. Whitehill (in Rains *et al.* 1965:43) thinks that Williamsburg is a one-of-a-kind phenomenon because it requires vast amounts of capital simply to maintain and continue, but points out that the idea behind Williamsburg—that of regarding whole towns or large areas as preservation units—has caught on and is now a basic and important preservation concept. Another significant aspect of the Williamsburg enterprise has been its extensive use of carefully controlled archeological fieldwork as a basis for architectural and decorative reconstruction, for determining how rooms were used, and even for the replanting of gardens. Archeology had been used to document reconstruction before, for example at Ft. Ticonderoga in 1908–1909 (Hosmer 1965:92), but this application of archeological field methods was most extensively developed at Williamsburg.

Archeologists generally continued to concentrate their efforts in the Southwest, where the important research methods of stratigraphy and seriation were refined (Willey and Sabloff 1974:94–103). As the war ended and the 1920s began, private financing for archeological work reappeared and there seems to have been some increase in research volume. By this time much of the urgency of the "salvage ethnography" period had passed, as informants died off, and more attention was given archeology by the anthropological community as a whole. Archeologists began to seek ways of approaching the synthesis of their individual research projects that historical particularism promised. For example, attempts were made to devise classificatory schemes that could place the archeological phenomena of large geographic areas into a single frame of chronological reference (cf. Willey and Sabloff 1974:110).

A new era opened for archeology and preservation during the 1930s. The initial effects of financial collapse were presumably as traumatic for practitioners of the disciplines of historic preservation as for anyone else, but in the long run the Depression resulted in an unprecedented embedding of archeologists, historians, and architects in the federal system and the beginnings of a national program for historic preservation. It also set archeology and preservation on divergent paths.

When Franklin Roosevelt came into office, he initiated a variety of "make-work" programs for the unemployed. Among these was the Historic American Building Survey (HABS), designed initially to employ 1000 architects for 6 months making measured drawings, taking photographs, and accumulating other data documenting the nation's historic buildings. The project proved to fill a need, and was continued until the eve of World War II, by which time it had documented 6389 structures and placed this documentation in the Library of Congress (Bullock *in* Rains *et al.* 1965:139). The HABS program was formally initiated in 1934, shortly after the reorganization of federal land management responsibilities had centralized control of historic sites in the National Park Service; HABS was administered through the NPS, with the close cooperation of the American Institute of Architects.

With the initiation of HABS, the federal government moved beyond the public lands to assume interest in historic buildings regardless of ownership; thus HABS represents the first time that the general interests of preservation became embedded in the federal system. At the same time, the HABS approach to preservation represented only one very small (and often neglected) part of the traditional preservationists' repertoire. The HABS program recorded data about the nation's historic architecture, and it saw to it, through the Library of Congress, that these data were preserved. It did not acquire or otherwise preserve buildings themselves, though the interest that it generated, and the expression of federal concern for preservation that it represented, certainly stimulated local acquisition efforts. Moreover, HABS constituted a professional training ground for preservationists within the federal service, and provided a means for the infusion of preservation into various programs of the nascent National Park Service.

The propounders of the New Deal considered a number of possibilities for legislation to protect the nation's past. What eventually did emerge as part of

Roosevelt's legislative package for reorganization and reform was the Historic Sites Act of 1935, which for the first time asserted a broad federal concern for the nation's historic properties and authorized the National Park Service to conduct a tremendous variety of programs to locate, record, acquire, preserve, mark, and commemorate properties of "national significance." What the act did, in essence, was to specify further the Department of the Interior's central role in federal preservation, authorize the perpetuation of HABS-like programs beyond the time of national emergency, and make it easier for the federal government to acquire nonfederal properties of historic significance. Although the secretary of the interior now had the mandate to engage in a great range of historic preservation activities, the programs actually initiated under the act were modest. An historic sites survey was established to document nationally significant properties to be designated national historic landmarks.

Meanwhile, the make-work programs pushed archeology in a somewhat different direction. Archeology had obvious advantages as a work-maker: It could absorb a great many people, it could be integrated into federal and state-level programs, and it did not compete with anything that private enterprise might remotely be expected to undertake. The story of archeology during the depression has yet to be written, but in essence the Smithsonian Institution coordinated a program funded by the Works Progress Administration (WPA). Work under the program was focused in the Southeast, for two reasons: The greatest concentration of unemployed persons was there, and the inception of the Tennessee Valley Authority imperiled sites. As the TVA began damming the rivers of Appalachia, it was recognized that many archeological sites would be inundated, so many of the WPA teams directed their efforts to work within the reservoir pools.

Archeologists were employed to supervise field programs and they were supplied with (usually minimal) equipment for excavation together with military field supplies for camp maintenance. Workers were drawn from local unemployment pools, often in very large numbers. Unlike HABS, which had a definite provision for the preparation of final documentation and its maintenance at the Library of Congress, the WPA program included only sketchy provision for preparation of reports or permanent curation of collections; as a result, many massive WPA projects remain unanalyzed and unreported today, and substantial amounts of excavated data have certainly been lost.

Many archeologists now active as senior members of the profession got their start in WPA archeology. Often they found themselves, as fresh graduate students or undergraduates with very little fieldwork behind them, placed in charge of huge, often poorly equipped and always untrained crews responsible for the excavation of very complex sites. Archeology today is full of WPA anecdotes, and there is no question that this first mobilization of big crews to conduct research over large regions had long-range effects on the method and practice of archeology. Three aspects of the program deserve mention here because they affected the way archeology related to the developing federal preservation program.

1. The involvement of the Department of the Interior was minimal; the program was coordinated by the Smithsonian instead.
2. The emphasis of the program was on fieldwork, not on analysis or even documentation of fieldwork results.
3. The program was oriented in considerable measure toward reservoir salvage.

These characteristics, we believe, served to separate archeology from preservation, to the detriment of both. A whole generation of archeologists developed with the impression that federal archeology was a fast, dirty business of grabbing data behind dams. Within the then-dominant research strategy of historical particularism, this approach was justified by the assumption that archeologists would one day be able to integrate the fragments of recovered data into a grand synthesis; hence the federal responsibility was limited to assisting archeologists in removing such data as might be minimally necessary for that synthesis when a federal dam endangered them. The synthesis itself was the archeologists' responsibility, perhaps resting with the Smithsonian. Interaction between archeologists and preservationists was minimal, since they worked for and with distinctly different agencies. It was the Department of the Interior, however, that had both the legislative mandate and the responsibility to undertake an integrated national program directed at historic properties; the Smithsonian/WPA program was of limited duration and placed the needs of providing employment over the needs of archeology. Thus, from the perspective of federal preservationists, archeologists were out in left field someplace digging holes; as for the archeologists, they were much too busy digging to pay attention to the preservation movement.

GROWING APART: AFTER WORLD WAR II

World War II brought an end to the make-work programs, but when the war ended the separation of archeology and historic preservation generally continued. To maintain the economic recovery, the federal government undertook a massive public works program and reservoir construction was a major element. Archeologists naturally turned to their prewar coordinator, the Smithsonian, for help in dealing with the destruction that was to be expected and the Smithsonian organized the "River Basin Salvage Program." This program was infused with the same general philosophy as had been the WPA operations—it was aimed at the speedy salvage of data prior to dam construction, usually with only minimum reporting requirements, on the assumption that the data would somehow, someday, be useful. Lacking WPA funding to support the program, the Smithsonian was sometimes successful in getting money from the Corps of Engineers and other agencies actually engaged in dam construction, but it turned to the National Park Service for a more stable basic fund source. Under the authority of the Historic Sites Act of 1935, the NPS organized the Interagency Archeological Salvage Program in 1946; IAS thereafter worked as a partner with the Smithsonian in reservoir salvage activities, and gradually came to assume much of the financial and administrative burden for the program.

Meanwhile, preservationists were reorganizing both within and outside government. The postwar building boom was as shocking to preservationists as to archeologists, but their response was different. The HABS program and the other survey and inventory programs had been closed down by the war and there did not appear to be much prospect for their immediate revival. Preservationists were active within the National Park Service, but they were primarily employed in dealing with properties already in NPS ownership. Preservationists concluded that the private sector would have to bear major responsibility for getting the movement underway again. There was some reason to hope that the private sector would be equal to the task.

Such groups as the Society for the Preservation of New England Antiquities and the American Scenic and Historic Preservation Society were growing after the war both in size and sophistication. Several states had organized historic preservation units and enacted statutes encouraging preservation activities. Some pertinent national organizations now existed, such as the American Institute of Architects and the Society of Architectural Historians. The National Park Service had organized the Advisory Board on National Parks, Historic Sites, Buildings, and Monuments under the authority of the Historic Sites Act of 1935, and the advisory board provided an initial integrative medium.

In 1947, a group of delegates to a National Council for Historic Sites and Buildings met at the National Gallery of Art. The Society for American Archeology (which had formed in 1935), was represented by Frank H. H. Roberts and J. O. Brew. Historian R. F. Lee, who later was to write the definitive work on the development of the Antiquities Act, was a NPS representative. This participation by archeologists and the archeologically knowledgeable did not seem to bring archeology closer to preservation. The result of the council was the organization of the long-called-for national preservation organization, the National Trust for Historic Preservation. The trust was chartered in 1949, with the specific purpose of receiving and preserving historic sites, buildings, and objects in the public interest (Mulloy 1976:9–12).

The trust developed rather rapidly; it undertook education programs, developed criteria for evaluating sites and buildings, and, by 1951, began to acquire and manage historic properties (Mulloy 1976:13). The agitation of the trust, and its encouragement to local and state preservation groups, naturally fed back into the NPS to strengthen the role of preservation there. In 1957, HABS was revived, and a HABS inventory designed to record minimal data on as many historic buildings as possible was initiated. The Historic Sites Survey was also resurrected, and a program for the thematic designation and marking of national historic landmarks was begun. In 1956, the trust formed an Ad Hoc Committee on Planning to help assure a unified, nonredundant approach by these programs and by those of the trust and various private and state organizations (Mulloy 1976:23). Thus, as the 1950s came to a close, the preservation movement had become a large and complex enterprise involving the private sector and aspects of federal, state, and local governments, but lacking central organization beyond that provided by the trust.

Archeologists, meanwhile, were still digging. The 1950s were a period of extensive reservoir construction throughout the country, and the small amount of money available for reservoir survey and salvage was badly stretched. At the same time, the Smithsonian's interest in playing a focal role in the program gradually decreased and the National Park Service took on more and more responsibility. The NPS role was canonized in law by the Reservoir Salvage Act of 1960, which formalized the previously ad hoc program by ordering all reservoir-building agencies to notify the secretary of the interior when planning such a project, and to cooperate with the secretary insofar as feasible when he undertook survey and salvage operations. The secretary was then directed to undertake such operations. Unfortunately, the major dam-building agencies took the secretary's authorization to expand appropriated funds on reservoir salvage as an indication that they were *not* so authorized, and the support that had previously been provided from time to time by the Corps of Engineers disappeared. Nevertheless, by the early 1960s, the NPS had a national reservoir salvage program underway, with archeologists in various NPS regional offices and in special archeological centers administering a program of contracts that accounted for about $1.5 million annually. Salvage was growing to support a substantial percentage of the archeological research going on in the United States. With some exceptions, the WPA approach continued to infuse the Interagency Archeological Salvage (IAS) Program. As the IAS staff commented retrospectively:

> In the general absence of coordinated planning, adequately prepared research designs, and effective National Park Service contract monitoring, "salvage" tended to be piecemeal, executed on a "crisis" basis, and frequently only one step ahead of construction.

> Because of the difficulty of getting reports from many contractors, almost anything submitted as a contract report was accepted simply to close out the file on the agreement. Traditionally little more than descriptive reports of findings was explicitly required and reports were often accepted without

adequate professional critique or consideration of whether they met acceptable contemporary professional standards. Meeting National Park Service report standards had often come to mean an exceptionally low threshold of
adequacy [Interagency 1976a:14].

Like preservation, then, federal archeology by 1959 had come to be a
rather large but not very well coordinated activity. For both subdisciplines,
major changes were in the making, changes not only in organization but in world
view.

NEW PERSPECTIVES

In the 1960s, the catchword was "new." We embarked upon the "New
Frontier" with John Kennedy; children were taught "New Math"; geographers
grew increasingly concerned with models and quantification, and called it "New
Geography." There was also a new preservation abroad in the land, and 1962
ushered in the "New Archeology" with the publication of Lewis Binford's
Archaeology as Anthropology (Binford 1962). We do not propose to belabor the
issue, much discussed in some archeological circles, of whether New Archeology
constitutes a major paradigm shift or a simple outgrowth of older archeology.
What is important for our purpose is to see how New Archeology related to
salvage programs and to preservation.

New archeology was in part an expression of "neo-evolutionism," a body
of method and theory developed in reaction to the failures of historical particularism and strongly biased toward economic and materialist explanations for
culture change (cf. Harris 1968:684). The questions it asked of the archeological
record generally had to do with the linkages among environment, economy, and
social organization. "Environmental" archeology had a tradition going back well
before New Archeology came on the scene; it was traditional in historical
particularist archeology to describe the local environment of an excavated site,
and to seek information about what was hunted, gathered, grown, and eaten.
This interest in the environment, however, tended to be purely descriptive—
another attempt to describe the whole picture of the extinct group under
study—or to be organized around the answering of specific local historical
questions: Did the environment change and cause Culture B to replace Culture
A? New Archeology, by contrast, encouraged the answering of theory-based
questions about environmental and social relationships through the systematic
analysis of appropriate kinds of environmental, paleoenvironmental, archeological, and other data, starting from the premise that virtually any significant
anthropological question (by which was meant any question significant to a
cultural materialist), could be answered through the skillful use of the archeological record. Seeking *appropriate* kinds of data, rather than whatever data

happened to be apparent in a site, led new archeologists to look for kinds of data that had been little attended to in the past. As a result of their cultural materialist orientation, their research tended to have to do with settlement patterns, subsistence practices, and community organization.

The rise of New Archeology meant several things to salvage archeology. First, it diminished the credibility of salvage as archeology. Although Binford and other leaders of New Archeology had done important research using salvage funds (cf. Binford *et al.* 1970), they tended not to do it once they became well-known, and not to encourage it in their colleagues or students. Salvage, after all, demanded that you dig the site that was threatened, regardless of whether you had worked up research questions that could be addressed there, and salvage support agencies often were more concerned with how much dirt was moved, and how quickly, than with the scientific output of the work. Some would not even pay for the analysis and publication of data, on the assumption that their responsibility ended once the artifacts had been relocated in a safe place. Even the IAS program, with its professional archeological staff, tended to be dominated by historical particularists who would fret that the culture—history was not being properly addressed if one budgeted too much money for intensive survey, studies of soil or pollen, or other sorts of activities not directly related to the excavation of artifacts. Salvage was not a good field in which to do New Archeology, on the whole, and the New Archeologists turned instead to the National Science Foundation (NSF) and other funding sources for the conduct of "pure" research.

However, New Archeology could not help but influence the ideas of salvage workers. Many salvage operations were primarily directed, at least in the field, by graduate students who were experiencing the intellectual ferment of the 1960s in general and New Archeology in particular. Some began to attempt the use of salvage data to test hypotheses derived from theory in the new prescribed manner. These archeologists naturally began to look for new kinds of data. Where archeological surveying of reservoir areas in River Basin Salvage program days had been a matter of touring the reservoir pool to find the biggest, deepest sites to dig, surveying now began to be an end in itself, seeking to identify all the sites in a given river basin, and to describe them in detail, in order to answer questions about population size and distribution, use of the natural environment, and community organization. More attention than before was given to small sites and single-component sites, rather than the deep, stratified sites that had been the focus of culture—historical research. The small, shallow sites, often representing discrete identifiable activities, could sometimes provide more comprehensible information on the structure and activities of the social groups that created them than could the deep, stratified sites. Archeological analysis became more involved and began to employ more sophisticated and expensive tools.

Interdisciplinary studies, particularly those focused on environmental reconstruction, began to be common parts of salvage programs. Excavations, at the same time, often had to be more extensive and more careful than in the past to obtain a wider range of data. The growing popularity of probability sampling as a method of getting representative data from a site without completely excavating it helped to offset the rising cost of excavation, as did the increasing use of power equipment. But the fact remained that excavation became increasingly expensive.

One further influence of New Archeology on salvage was a broadening of horizons. Archeologists in general began to realize that there were archeological data inherent in a wider range of phenomena than was typically given research attention. A recently abandoned Apache wickiyup could be studied to help understand the organization of prehistoric communities (Longacre and Ayres 1968); colonial tombstones could be studied to elucidate the rules of stylistic change (Deetz and Dethlefsen 1967). Eventually archeologists would begin to study the organization of grocery stores and libraries (Schiffer 1973), the patterns of garbage disposal in modern Tucson (Rathje 1977), and the sociocultural implications of the National Temple of the Church of Jesus Christ of the Latter Day Saints before its construction was even completed (Leone 1977). One immediate impact of theory-based archeology's broadening perspective, then, was the infusion of anthropological thinking into the rather stodgy field of historical archeology, where research had been largely aimed at verifying historical documentation and contributing to restoration projects (cf. Noel-Hume 1969).

Meanwhile, preservation had also been going through a sort of identity crisis. Traditionally, the main basis for preserving something had been its association with some historic event or person. As preservation had developed, a new sort of value for historic properties began to be recognized. Historic buildings were seen to provide a character to a community or neighborhood, to add to its visual qualities and to the quality of life in it. The attraction of historical districts and communities that had retained their character was painfully obvious when these communities were compared with the sprawling subdivisions of the 1950s and 1960s. Architectural historians argued that buildings should be preserved for their architectural merits—not only classic architectural masterpieces, but buildings exemplifying styles, types, and trends in the architectural practices of the nation, its regions, and its social and ethnic groups. The architectural concerns blended well with the "quality of life" concerns; buildings began to be regarded as important not only for their historical associations but for their perceived importance to a community, for their significance to the architectural and aesthetic integrity of a neighborhood, and for their exemplification of changing cultural values and approaches to the living environment.

Thus, the directions in which archeology and preservation were moving in the 1960s were rather similar. In both fields, a particularistic tradition was giving way to a concern for the broader relevance of historic properties to society.

NEW ADAPTATIONS I: ENVIRONMENTALISM, PLANNING, AND PRESERVATION

The Eisenhower administration had initiated the development of a vast network of interstate highways in the late 1950s. Highway construction rapidly gained a reputation for running roughshod over other interests and concerns. While the concerns of archeology were handled, more or less, in various state-level highway salvage programs, preservation was not easily accommodated into highway construction programs. Many highways were designed to slice through the hearts of cities, taking out scores of historic buildings and segmenting historic districts. Preservationists were faced with a major challenge, as were citizens concerned with the aesthetic and economic value of their property. Neighborhoods subject to highway impacts began to fight back with petitions, public meetings, and lawsuits. Conservation groups complained about the impacts of highways on the natural environment. By the 1960s, the clamor began to be heard. But another threat to preservation had developed: urban renewal. By the early 1960s, the newly formed Department of Housing and Urban Development was assisting and encouraging local governments in a vast program of urban renewal in which whole downtowns were simply leveled for the construction of new facilities. The impact of urban renewal on historic buildings was even greater that that of the interstate highway system.

In combating these destructive forces, preservationists had certain powerful allies in government. The Rockefeller family has had interests in historic preservation and a willingness to contribute to it that goes back to John D. Rockefeller, Jr.'s support for the restoration of Williamsburg. Preservationists of the 1960s also had an important friend in Lady Bird Johnson. As first lady, Mrs. Johnson took as her personal project the beautification of America, and found common cause with a large number of local citizen's groups, the nascent environmental movement, and preservationists. In 1965, Mrs. Johnson convened a White House conference on national beauty. One spin-off of this conference was a Special Committee on Historic Preservation. The special committee was not conceived by the Johnson administration alone. Its basic precepts had been roughed out at a Seminar on Preservation and Restoration at Williamsburg in 1963, which had been convened to plan the future of American preservation on the occasion of UNESCO's declaration of 1964 as "International Monuments Year." The following 2 years had been a time of discussion and bridge-building between the National Trust's chairman, Gordon Gray, and Secretary of the

Interior Steward Udall, among others (Mulloy 1976:68–73). The groundwork for the special committee was well laid.

With sponsorship by the U.S. Conference of Mayors and staff drawn from the National Trust, the committee by early 1966 had produced a book-length report, *With Heritage So Rich* (Rains *et al.* 1966). The report synopsized American history and its leavings, gave a thumbnail sketch of the preservation movement to date, and discussed the crises then facing preservation. It strongly emphasized the idea that historic buildings are a part of the total modern environment, and emphasized the need to preserve them in order to maintain quality in that environment. Methods of preservation and preservation planning were discussed with reference to both the United States and Europe and a concluding section set forth recommendations. An Advisory Council on Historic Preservation was recommended to provide "leadership and guidance for the direction of interagency actions and to provide liaison" with groups outside the federal government. An expansion of the national landmarks list and the various other lists and inventories in the National Park Service was recommended, to form a National Register of historic "communities, areas, structures, sites, and objects." In contrast to the national landmarks program, the National Register was to include properties of not only "national importance" but state and local significance as well. A grants program was proposed, to assist states in the development of preservation programs, and modification of the Internal Revenue Code to encourage the maintenance of historic buildings was suggested. The recommendations also included proposals for loan programs, scholarship programs, state and local actions, and requirements to be placed on federal agencies to make surveys in advance of construction projects, to identify historic properties, and to consider them in their planning.

With notable exception of the suggested tax initiatives and the requirement for surveys in advance of federal projects, virtually all of the Committee's proposals were incorporated into the National Historic Preservation Act (NHPA) of 1966, which was signed as Public Law 89–665 on October 15. Preservationists now had a sophisticated statutory base upon which to build a national program. The components of the NHPA are discussed in the next chapter. Briefly, it established a National Register, to list districts, sites, structures, buildings and objects of importance in American history, architecture, archeology, and culture. It established an Advisory Council on Historic Preservation. It established a grants program to the states and the National Trust, but required that all states develop historic preservation plans to guide use of the money, and that the money be matched with state or local funds or services. It placed the National Register and the grants program in the Department of the Interior and added to the secretary's rule-making authority, but the advisory council was to function as an independent body. Finally, Section 106 of the act established the responsibility of all federal agencies to consult with the advisory council before participating in an undertaking that would affect a National Register property. It did not require the agencies to find out whether any properties that might qualify for the National Register lay in the path of their activities as the committee had recommended.

• Although Congress had passed the act, it did not immediately do very much to implement it. It was not until 1968 that any grant funds were available, and in that year the only grant ($300,000) went to the National Trust. Funding for the advisory council was squeezed out of the NPS appropriation. Nevertheless, the Park Service began to take some steps toward implementing the responsibilities of the secretary of the interior under the act. Park Service director George Hartzog, who had a considerable interest in archeology and preservation, established a three-man committee to study how to organize a historic preservation unit within the service. The committee consisted of representatives of the three disciplines now coming to be recognized as the constituent parts of historic preservation: Ronald Lee represented history, J. O. Brew represented archeology, and E. A. Connally of the University of Illinois represented architectural history. The deliberations of this committee resulted in the formation of the Office of Archeology and Historic Preservation (OAHP), which not only was to house the National Register and grants program, but also the Interagency Archeological Salvage Program, HABS, the Historic Sites Survey, and Historic Landmarks. Connally was named to head the program.

The initial concept of OAHP called for an independent, or at least semi-independent, highly professional institute linked to the National Park Service by funding only, if at all. It was clear that NPS had not, on the whole, made a very good showing in preservation; it had not undertaken anything approaching the vigorous, aggressive program that would have been possible under the 1935 act. The proponents of the 1966 act were determined not to see another opportunity frittered away by bureaucratic ineptitude; as a result, they put high priority on program building, development of a highly motivated, professional staff, and efforts to become as independent as possible from the National Park Service. However, independent status was not forthcoming. Instead, Connally was given additional responsibilities as NPS associate director for professional services, overseeing the in-park program of archeology and historic preservation as well as the OAHP (see Chapter 4), and every effort to move the office out of the service was met with new devices to fix it more tightly within the mother agency.

The staff of OAHP, and of the advisory council, was largely derived from the National Trust. Robert Garvey, executive director of the Trust, left in 1967 to take on a equivalent position with the advisory council. William Murtagh, director of the Trust's Department of Program, became keeper of the National Register. The extant staffs of HABS, Landmarks, the Historic Sites Survey, and the Interagency Archeological Salvage program were retained, but deliberate efforts were made to bring in new, and often more highly professional, staff members. Emphasizing the rebuilding of its own infrastructure, OAHP did not move with great vigor on the outside, and the burden of interagency coordination and consultation tended to fall on the advisory council. With little professional guidance from the OAHP, the council felt forced to move into standard setting and regulation itself.

Because of the slow start on the grants program, state programs did not become actualized with any great speed. In 1969, 25 states and territories received grants, but the largest grant received (by Missouri) was only $11,745.09; Maine received a munificent $788.51 (Mulloy 1976: App. 17).

No one could expect all the nation's historic properties to have been entered in the National Register overnight, of course, but even if this had been a technical possibility it would have been frustrated by the slowness of OAHP to get organized and take a leadership role and by the delay in initiating programs on the state level. As a result, by the time the 1960s came to an end, although the statutory basis now existed for a sophisticated national historic preservation program, the destruction of historic properties was proceeding apace. The failure of OAHP to provide clear leadership to other federal agencies left agencies to go pretty much their own ways and placed preservationists on something of a limb when they tried to press for better preservation planning. OAHP was primarily concerned with building its own program and those of the states; although this was certainly a rational concern, it meant that the provision of guidance to other agencies was underemphasized. In its desire to get state programs underway, too, OAHP tended to accept extremely shabby state plans. The NHPA included a clear requirement for the development of historic preservation plans in each state, to guide nominations and ongoing preservation programs. The Office of Archeology and Historic Preservation issued guidelines for the preparation of these plans that emphasized form rather than function; as long as the appropriate sections were present in the documentation of the plan, the plan and the program it allegedly described were acceptable. As a result, most state programs got underway with no real idea about where they were going or what they were doing other than nominating things to the Register and receiving federal funds for preservation projects that seemed nice to do. Naturally, the first properties with which most states concerned themselves were the most obvious historic sites and structures, and the first situations which contended with potential destruction were situations in which such properties were threatened. Thus, the NHPA was used less as a planning tool than as a club to wave at federal agencies when they threatened to damage obvious historic properties with great associative or aesthetic value. This vision of the act as a mandate to fight to the death for the preservation of National Register properties, and hence of the Register as a list of only those properties worthy of such a struggle, became fixed in the minds of many state historic preservation officers (SHPOs), of many segments of the public and to some extent even of the advisory council. When the council finally felt forced to issue its own procedures to guide its increasingly complex relationships with states and agencies, these procedures reflected the kinds of situations with which it had been dealing.

Despite J. O. Brew's involvement in the establishment of OAHP, archeologists did not respond with any great enthusiasm to the passage of the NHPA. The Society for American Archeology did form a committee to study archeological involvement in the programs established by the act, but on the whole the attitude of the archeological community ranged from apathy to outright hostility. Archeologists generally misunderstood the purpose of the National Register (and in many cases, continue to do so), confusing it with the National Landmarks program and thus believing that the NHPA merely extended protection to properties of landmark-type "national significance." Some archeologists feared (and continue to fear) that if they place their sites on the National Register, the information will become public knowledge and result in a swarm of pothunters. Quite accurately, most archeologists realize that the act did nothing to require federal agencies to do surveys and identify properties of National Register quality in advance of their projects. In essence, it placed this onus on the state historic preservation officers and the public by giving federal agencies responsibilities only when a previously designated National Register property was involved. Since one of the primary difficulties being faced by archeologists at the time lay in persuading agencies to do surveys so that sites could be located for salvage, most archeologists felt that the NHPA did rather little to address their problems. A few people with archeological propensities recognized that the Act provided a basis for comprehensive archeological planning, consistent with the regional perspective so important to most New Archeological research:

> Generous preservation, coupled with a climate of positive planning would seem to offer encouragement for problem-oriented archeological programs designed to incorporate regions corresponding to natural or cultural areas. Some support for these programs might be anticipated in the form of the familiar grants-in-aid. The usual condition for such grants is the existence of some sort of systematic planning by the recipient: meaning, in the case of archeology, research plans worked out by responsible scientific teams. Perhaps the provisions of the Historic Properties Preservation Act of 1966 (P.L. 89–665) will apply to such ventures in archeological planning. It certainly would be unfortunate to lack integrated plans at the time when shifts in public policy favorable to their implementation were to become effective. It is not at all too early, therefore, to begin to think seriously of ways in which archeology might relate creatively to the emerging planning climate. A policy-and-program gap can best be precluded by advance preparation [Barnes 1967:2–3].

By and large, however, the NHPA was passed and implemented with minimal archeological involvement or understanding. As late as 1975, in which year over $17 million was provided in OAHP grant funds to the states for survey, planning, acquisition, and preservation, the general archeological attitude toward the NHPA was articulated by McGimsey:

> Any number of states list their sites in the thousands. In the foreseeable future—the next five to ten years at least—neither the states nor the National Register are going to be able to handle such a work load. This suggests that for some time at least, the Register, of necessity is going to be less than a complete planning tool—an important, even vital tool, but not the only tool to be used in planning with respect to archeological resources.
>
> In the other direction, no state yet has any real control, in terms of hard knowledge, over the total extent, diversity, and distribution of its archeological resources. In many states, known sites are numbered in the hundreds while it must be presumed that sites actually present must be numbered in the tens of thousands. Thus even if, by some miracle, every site now known were to be placed on the National Register, it still would be years before the Register could function effectively as the sole planning document with respect to all archeological resources. In fact, I do not believe that with respect to archeological resources the Register will ever be able to so function. Our archeological knowledge and coverage will never be that complete [McGimsey 1975].

Archeologists could see little to the NHPA but the National Register and its misunderstood but odious implications. They tended to be suspicious of the new state historic preservation programs and tended to avoid working with them.

The attention of archeologists had turned, in large measure, to another outcome of the social and environmental ferment of the 1960s that had produced the NHPA. This was the National Environmental Policy Act of 1969, or NEPA.

The National Environmental Policy Act (see Chapter 3) requires the preparation of environmental impact statements (EIS) by federal agencies prior to making decisions about projects that may adversely affect the environment. Archeologists saw the requirement for EISs as a method of ensuring that archeological surveys were done. Moreover, they saw the requirement that EIS data be considered in project planning as a method of ensuring that salvage was done, since if sites identified in the EIS were not salvaged, their destruction would constitute unmitigated impacts of a project, and could be grounds for a suit to halt its implementation. On the whole, they were right, but NEPA turned out to be less of a panacea than it originally appeared to be. Lacking clear guidelines as to the need for archeological surveys in EIS preparation, agencies found many ways to avoid doing them. The Council on Environmental Quality, which set out standards for EIS preparation, merely suggested that the procedures of the Advisory Council on Historic Preservation be complied with, and all the advisory council could do at that point was insist that all National Register properties be identified and dealt with. Some agencies argued that, since the Reservoir Salvage Act authorized only the secretary of the interior to expend money for archeological surveys, they were therefore not authorized to do so, but would be pleased to incorporate any data that the National Park Service might like to provide. Gradually, such attempts at circumvention have decreased through time, but this has not been so much the result of improved agency attitudes toward NEPA itself as the result of further action in historic preservation, the growing effectiveness of OAHP, the advisory council, and the state programs, and to some extent, passage of the Archeological and Historic Preservation Act of 1974.

Still, EIS preparation did, in many cases, include the conduct of archeological surveys, and in most cases archeologists treated this work much as they had salvage contracts—as a method of funding research of interest to them. Seldom was there much attention to the agency's responsibilities to locate all the historic properties subject to impact, and to do something about them. Typically, archeologists simply surveyed the direct impact areas of projects and proposed salvage to "mitigate impacts." "Mitigation," in fact, became a sort of code word for salvage—the latter no longer being regarded as acceptable. Some archeologists, whose command of English apparently did not exceed their command of law, even made the transfer directly and referred to their activities as "mitigating sites." In some cases, however, EIS work did begin to produce useful research results (cf. Schiffer and House 1975), and occasionally these were used as the bases for sophisticated mitigation plans. One effort was made by a National Park Service Archeological Center to provide detailed guidelines for archeology in EIS work (Scovill, Gordon, and Anderson 1972), but criticism both from within the National Park Service and from outside agencies forced its withdrawal in favor of a much less detailed document (National Park Service 1973).

The failure of the NHPA to preserve historic properties endangered by federal activities was as obvious to preservationists as to archeologists, but the preservationists' tactics for dealing with this failure was different than that of the archeologists. What was clearly needed, for historic preservation as well as for archeology, was a requirement that federal agencies survey before beginning projects, and identify any properties that might quality for the National Register, and then go through the consultation procedures required by the NHPA, to find ways of minimizing damage. It had been impossible to have such a requirement written into the NHPA, and, although NEPA could be interpreted to place such a responsibility on federal agencies, it could at that time equally easily be argued that identification of already-listed National Register properties discharged an agency's identificatory responsibilities under NEPA. A better interpretation of NEPA's requirements for the identification of historic properties and a broader commitment of the federal government to the purposes of the NHPA, were needed and were obtainable from the executive branch without new legislation. The vehicle was Executive Order 11593, and the driving force behind its issuance was the advisory council. The council, still frustrated by inaction on the part of OAHP, consulted with the president's staff in the preparation of this order, which President Nixon issued on May 13, 1971. The order still stopped just short of explicitly requiring surveys in advance of federal projects, but it required three basic actions on the part of all federal agencies. First, they were to conduct "inventories" of historic properties that might qualify for the National Register. Second, they were to "exercise caution" until all such properties were placed on the Register to see to it that unnecessary loss or destruction did not occur. Third, they were to adopt policies that would contribute to the protection of historic properties on nonfederal lands. The advisory council was to be consulted in discharging these responsibilities and the secretary of the interior was given the authority to provide guidance.

The advisory council and OAHP now had a basis for promoting the systematic consideration of historic properties in the planning process preceding agency actions; identification, evaluation, and planning for the protection of such properties were clearly necessary parts of "exercising caution" and "contributing to preservation." Federal agencies were advised to conduct surveys in consultation with state historic preservation officers, obtain determinations from OAHP as to the eligibility of any discovered historic properties for the National Register, and consult with the advisory council concerning their proper disposition prior to implementing any undertaking that might damage them. This advice, however, continued to be only informal until 1973, when the advisory council, still seeing no sign that the Department of the Interior would ever issue implementing regulations, issued its own "Procedures for the Protection of Historic and Cultural Properties" (36 CFR 800: see Chapter 3 and Appendix A). Issuance of the procedures gave federal agencies a review process to which they could relate, if not always with great satisfaction. It also provided guidance to the courts in certain crucial cases where federal programs were restrained because of noncompliance with the NHPA or the executive order. Resolution of these cases helped clarify the intent of the authorities. For example, in *Save the Courthouse Committee* v. *Lynn,* 8 ERC 1209 (U.S. D.C.S.D.N.Y. 1975), the court held that NEPA and NHPA were in force so long as a federal agency retained discretion over execution of an undertaking. In *Stop H-3 Association* v. *Coleman,* 6 ELR 20424 (CA 9 1976), the court established that if, in a questionable case, the agency responsible for an undertaking failed to request a determination of eligibility for an endangered historic property, the secretary of the interior could unilaterally make such a determination.

The advisory council procedures provide little room for flexibility; they are designed to handle the case—typical in the early 1970s—in which a clearly preservable property of known historic value to the nation or some segment of the nation is threatened by an intractable federal agency. They are less relevant to the increasingly common case in which a dubiously preservable property possessing certain specific historical attributes is in possible danger from a relatively flexible agency program. This is not to criticize the procedures for doing what they do well; they have been tremendously important in causing federal agencies to take notice of their impacts on historic properties. It is a fact, however, that they work best and are most rational when applied only to a rather limited range of properties and circumstances. The fact that they do not work well or seem needlessly ponderous when applied to other sorts of properties and situations does not indicate an intent to preserve the wrong kinds of properties or to include too great a range of things on the National Register, as some have maintained (e.g., Grady and Lipe 1976); it merely means that as the states and agencies begin to develop better planning approaches to historic preservation, the procedures of the council must change to take account of the altered situation.

NEW ADAPTATIONS II: THE ARCHEOLOGICAL TRAJECTORY

In the early 1970s, archeologists began their first mobilization in support of legislation since passage of the Antiquities Act in 1906. The legislation that was to become the Archeological and Historic Preservation Act of 1974 grew out of the concerns of a group that called itself the Mississippi Alluvial Valley Archeological Program (MAVAP), whose primary leaders were Carl Chapman of the University of Missouri and C. R. McGimsey III of the University of Arkansas. The program was an attempt at multistate regional organization for purposes of research coordination and efficiency in data handling, goals that McGimsey and Chapman have continued to espouse in varying ways (McGimsey 1972:18–19; Chapman 1973:4–5). It was obvious, however, that little would be gained by coordinating research if in the meantime the resource base necessary for research was lost, and as MAVAP participants began to share notes, it became obvious that the loss rate among prehistoric sites in the region was extremely high. Most of the destruction was the result of federally assisted actions that did not come under the purvue of the Reservoir Salvage Act. A prime culprit was the Soil Conservation Service of the Department of Agriculture, which assists in programs of agricultural land leveling. McGimsey later described the situation:

> In Arkansas, for example, we discovered that only 20,000 acres had been leveled in all the years prior to 1953, the year in which the Federal cost-sharing program began. In the 14 years between then and 1967, the year

of our survey, the Soil Conservation Service, which handles this program, stated that 783,879 acres had been leveled.

In the Mississippi Alluvial Valley, the most popular location for Indian sites were the natural levees and other small eminences. These are precisely the places that are first leveled for purposes of irrigation, for rice farming, or often simply "to get rid of that high spot." Leveling of a natural levee serves effectively to obliterate the average Indian site located upon that levee. Even the larger sites are not immune; I stood by for a day and watched a team of three land planes almost completely destroy a Mississippian period village several acres in extent and dating from around A.D. 1400 and underlain by a Woodland site which was probably occupied around A.D. 1000. One pass of an earth mover was seen to completely cross section horizontally an extended burial; a few minutes later, the next pass oblitered the remainder. There were similar experiences with entire house patterns, and fire basins. With proper planning and funding the important information contained in this site could have been recovered without delaying or preventing the leveling [McGimsey in *Committee* 1973:92].

Technically, some control over such destruction should have been provided by NEPA, but such diffuse programs as those administered by the Soil Conservation Service are not as easy to bring under the NEPA spotlight as are the more obvious projects of the construction agencies. Technically, too, vigorous state programs to list archeological sites on the National Register would have brought at least some of the endangered properties under the protection of section 106 of the NHPA, but at the time of MAVAP's organization there were as yet no vigorous state programs, and the prospect for their development seemed relatively bleak. In addition, McGimsey and others in MAVAP had, at best, ambivalent feelings about the National Register. The conclusion by MAVAP was that new national legislation was called for, expanding the terms of the Reservoir Salvage Act to cover all kinds of federal activities and authorizing agencies to expend their own money on salvage rather than relying solely on the Secretary of the Interior to fund the work.

It was obvious to MAVAP that its problems were not unique, and it was also obvious that federal legislation could not be promulgated from the Mississippi Valley alone. Gradually, a national movement developed, with McGimsey serving as its principal moving part. Legislation was drafted and introduced simultaneously by Senator Frank E. Moss of Utah and Representative Charles E. Bennett of Florida; throughout its rather tortuous legislative history, beginning in 1970 and ending with its enactment in 1974, the bill was known as the "Moss—Bennett Act."

In drafting and promoting Moss—Bennett, archeologists lost one of their best chances for bringing the threads of archeology and historic preservation back together after their 40-year separation. Hindsight strongly suggests that the act would have been easier to pass and much easier to implement had it been tied more closely to NEPA and the NHPA and less closely to the Reservoir Salvage Act. Basing the new legislation on the Reservoir Salvage Act meant extension of provisions for salvage without any clear provision for advance planning or preservation. Moreover, by failing to tie salvage programs into the state historic preservation programs developing under the authority of the NHPA, Moss–Bennett gave federal agencies salvage responsibilities that overlapped but did not interlock with any of their historic preservation responsibilities; this naturally has served to confuse. Finally, Moss–Bennett extended the authorities of the secretary of the interior under the Reservoir Salvage Act, but failed to connect these authorities clearly with those given the secretary under NHPA, thus increasing the confusion among federal agencies which found themselves confronting duplicative reporting responsibilities and review authorities. The poor integration of the new act with the existing historic preservation program also has caused problems for OAHP in the preparation of implementing regulations. Perhaps the most serious failing of Moss–Bennett, in our view, was that it reinforced the salvage approach to the treatment of archeological resources in the minds of archeologists, encouraging many to regard Moss–Bennett as somehow superceding the preservation statutes and relieving them of any need to understand or work with them. These dangers were not apparent to many in the early 1970s, however, and with McGimsey's charismatic leadership the act soon enjoyed the near-unanimous and virtually unquestioning support of the nation's archeologists, both professional and amateur (including one of us: King in *Committee* 1973). It was also supported, albeit with some reservations, by OAHP and a number of State Historic Preservation Officers (cf. Connally in *Committee* 1973; Williams in *Committee* 1973).

We should make it clear that we do not think that something like Moss–Bennett was not needed, and we do not think that MAVAP was wrong to develop it. We do think it sad that it was not rethought during its long legislative career, and brought into closer alignment with the rest of the historic preservation authorities. We believe that a major opportunity for establishing a sophisticated national archeological program in conjunction with historic preservation was lost in the Moss–Bennett excitement.

Moss–Bennett, as the Archeological and Historic Preservation Act of 1974, became Public Law 93-291 on May 24, 1974. Its terms are discussed in Chapter 3. Although it was over 2 years before the legal ambiguities of the act could be resolved sufficiently to permit the issuance of implementing regulations by OAHP, many agencies began immediately to hire archeologists on staff and to fund salvage programs. The Interagency Archeology Services Division of OAHP, reconstituted from the old Interagency Archeological Salvage Program under the leadership of R. L. Wilson, established three field offices to coordinate work under the act.

SPLICING HISTORIC PRESERVATION

The reconstitution of a unified historic preservation program began before the passage of Moss–Bennett, largely through OAHP's efforts to implement the Department of the Interior's responsibilities under Executive Order 11593. Three executive order consultants were employed to meet with federal agencies and advise them about compliance matters. All three were archeologists; Roy Reeves was based in Denver, Jon Young in Tucson, and Lawrence Aten in Washington. If we were to pick a single individual who has been central to the restructuring of relationships between archeology and preservation, we would point to Aten. Quickly familiarizing himself with the workings of OAHP's various divisions (see Chapter 4), Aten made a deliberate, if not always successful, effort to represent the whole range of preservation concerns in his consultation with agencies. Like Scovill (1974) and others, Aten promoted the systematic integration of archeology into the preservation planning process prescribed by NEPA, the NHPA, and the executive order; uniquely, he was able to press this view on the rest of OAHP and on outside agencies. All three executive order consultants went a long way toward promoting agency preservation policies that dealt with all types of historic properties in a systematic way, and Aten, in particular, has pressed for better integration of anthropological archeology into agency and state preservation planning (cf. Aten 1975).

Outside the federal framework, Lipe (1974) called for a "conservation approach" to archeology, consistent with the basic philosophy of historic preservation. Surveys for EIS purposes began to deal with both prehistoric and historic sites and structures in a systematic, multidisciplinary fashion (cf. Levine and Mobley 1976; King and Hickman 1973). In 1975, the New York Archeological Council adopted survey procedures designed explicitly to insure compliance with the advisory council procedures (King 1975); these were widely distributed by Interagency Archeology Services. Archeologists also began going to court to demand proper treatment of archeological properties, and found that the historic preservation laws provided a much more solid basis for complaints than did NEPA and Moss–Bennett [cf. *Warm Springs Task Force et al.* v. *Gribble;* 378 F. Sup 240 (1974) *NYAC* v. *Train* (1975); King 1976].

In August, 1975, OAHP issued a "statement of program approach" articulating how it planned to implement its responsibilities under Moss–Bennett. Although basically consistent with premises advanced by Scovill some 2 years earlier (Scovill 1974) and accepted painlessly, the "statement" elicited complaints by some archeologists because it established eligibility for the National Register as the threshold below which historic properties would not be subject to treatment under the act (cf. Moratto *et al.* 1977). This recurring archeological failure to understand the National Register did not significantly deter OAHP in its administration of Moss–Bennett programs.

Issuance of formal regulations implementing either Moss—Bennett or the executive order continued to be a difficult process for OAHP, largely because of the many layers of review, sometimes by hostile bureaus, that must be gone through within the National Park Service. Other agencies, not surprisingly, have become frustrated and developed their own regulations. Many have also begun to develop substantial staff capabilities in the fields of historic preservation. Professionals are obviously needed on-staff to guide the inventory programs required by the executive order of such agencies as the Forest Service and the Bureau of Land Management. When the Moss—Bennett Act was signed into law, this opened the door for considerable staff development by the Corps of Engineers and, to some extent, other construction agencies. Thus far, agency staff development has emphasized archeologists, largely because the major land managing agencies administer properties in the rural West, where archeology is perceived as presenting more frequent problems than other aspects of historic preservation.

Although OAHP has been slow in developing regulations, its strategy of building state programs has begun to pay off. Grant funds available to states through OAHP have increased markedly from $6,000,000 in 1971 to $20,000,000 in 1975; this increase was largely the result of increasingly effective political action by preservationists nationally and particularly by the gradually developing cadre of state historic preservation officers who were knowledgeable about and dedicated to preservation. The existence of grants of respectable size made it possible for OAHP to become more demanding about the level of professionalism on state staffs, the quality of state plans, and the level of documentation supplied with nominations and requests for determinations of eligibility. Gradually, a true historic preservation infrastructure has begun to be built, in the Department of the Interior, in the advisory council, in the other federal agencies, and in the states.

Meanwhile, Congress has passed several other laws that have effects on historic preservation. The Housing and Community Development Act of 1974 and the Coastal Zone Management Act of 1972, among others, have ramifications for historic preservation that are not yet fully understood; these will be discussed in later chapters. In 1976, the NHPA itself was amended by P.L. 94—422 as a result of action by the advisory council. The amendments give new and clarified authority to the council as an independent agency. They incorporate the basic provisions of Executive Order 11593 into the statute itself, amending Section 106 to require attention by agencies not only to properties on the National Register, but to properties eligible for inclusion. This effectively requires that surveys be done in advance of all federal undertakings. The amendments also create a historic preservation fund, to supply the OAHP Grants Program with $150 million per year, and allow the secretary of the interior to change the federal—state match for survey and planning grants from 50/50 to 70/30.

Less than 2 weeks after P.L. 94—422 was signed into law, the Tax Reform

Act of 1976 (P.L. 94–455) was also enacted, including provisions for tax incentives for the preservation of historic buildings. Thus, over 10 years, the original recommendations of the Special Committee on Historic Preservation have been essentially implemented.

The year 1976 began a time of housekeeping and reorganization by OAHP. A task force was organized to completely rewrite the state plan requirements; procedures for requesting determinations of eligibility were drafted; procedures for locating and identifying historic properties under the authorities of the executive order and the amended NHPA were drafted clearly setting forth the need for surveys. Discussions began with the Office of Management and Budget about appropriate interpretation of the more confusing sections of Moss–Bennett, leading to the drafting of procedures for implementing this statute as well.

The schismatic tendencies of archeology had not been eliminated, however; as late as 1976, archeologists with strong involvement in work under terms of Moss–Bennett and NEPA were arguing vigorously that these statutes provided an adequate basis for the satisfaction of archeological concerns and that archeologists should eschew the complexities of the historic preservation procedures (Grady and Lipe 1976). One archeologist went so far as to say that "There simply seems to be no basis for an accommodation between the needs and requirements of archeological research and the conservation of the resource base and the currently accepted historic preservation philosophy and concepts . . . [Scovill 1976]."

Our intent in this historical overview has been in part to show that such positions lack merit. Public-sponsored archeology and preservation have common roots in North America, and diverged only in the 1930s when their respective incorporation into different kinds of make-work programs placed them in different environments subject to somewhat different influences. Yet changes in the two fields have been parallel; both experienced a broadening of horizons in the early 1960s and an increased politicization in the late 1960s and early 1970s. Both have gradually become more and more anthropological, turning from an exclusive concern with the homes of great men and stratified tumuli full of artifacts to a broad interest in properties that represent all aspects of human behavior and its history. Both now need, more than anything else, an organized and flexible methodology for dealing simultaneously with the great diversity of historic properties and the great diversity of federal programs that affect these properties. The legal basis for this methodology exists primarily in the preservation statues; the infrastructure that can implement it exists, in skeletal form, in the programs mandated by the NHPA.

What is still lacking is the comprehensive planning required to make the national program really work. Statewide surveys and plans continue to be generally haphazard and unsophisticated and agencies still tend to deal with preservation problems only when crises erupt. It is tempting to think about what things might have been like if some genius in OAHP had managed to establish clear procedures for statewide historic preservation planning in, say, 1970, neatly tying the provisions of the NHPA and the executive order to the requirements of NEPA and establishing a model identification, review, and preservation system that everyone could quickly understand and integrate into their own planning frameworks. It is hard to imagine a federal government program of any kind proceeding in such a way, however, and it may be too much to expect of human endeavor in general. The fact that now, 10 years after passage of the National Historic Preservation Act, there is hope for a stable, well-integrated planning approach to historic preservation—which justifies, in part, the existence of this book—is something to be thankful for.

3

REGULATING DESTRUCTION:
THE LAW

THE LEGAL BASE TODAY

Almost a hundred years of developing governmental concern for historic preservation has resulted in the existence today of a somewhat confusing, but nonetheless compelling, legal base. We have traced the historical development of this legal base; we now need only a brief synopsis of the statutes themselves and a consideration of their implications as a prelude to discussing how historic preservation works and how it could work better. Texts of the laws and procedures are given in Appendix A.

It is convenient to think about the authorities underlying historic preservation as divided into three parts. One set of statutes is central to the organization of the field; it sets forth basic responsibilities and powers. A second set of statutes is complementary to the first, at least in theory, providing methods for implementing the central authorities in particular ways or under particular circumstances. Finally, springing from both sets of statutory authorities, there is a body of regulation developed to organize the system provided for by both sets of statutes.

CENTRAL AUTHORITIES

The central authorities upon which historic preservation is based are the Antiquities Act of 1906, the Historic Sites Act of 1935, and the National Historic Preservation Act of 1966 as amended in 1976 and as implemented in part by Executive Order 11593.

The Antiquities Act has little day-to-day pertinence to the functions of historic preservation, but it established an initial federal concern for things of antiquity and of scientific importance. It continues to play a role in the activities of the Forest Service, the Bureau of Land Management, and other agencies that actually manage federal lands by providing a basis for prosecuting private collectors and vandals (in the unlikely event they are caught) and by providing a secondary check on contracted archeological activities undertaken by land users in order to comply with the National Environmental Policy Act and other planning statutes. An archeologist conducting a survey on some (but not all) federal lands for preparation of an environmental impact statement must not only satisfy the sometimes uncertain requirements of NEPA, but also the requirements of an Antiquities Act permit. These permits are granted by the responsible federal agency and (except on Forest Service lands) the National Park Service. Another function of the Antiquities Act is to provide the federal government with a means of guiding the development of basic archeological research in large parts of the country—for better or for worse. In much of the West, where most land is under federal ownership, conduct of noncontract research almost invariably requires a permit; and, the government can to some extent direct the future of research by selectively granting and withholding permits. As a "conservation" ethic has increasingly permeated the federal archeological establishment, for instance, it has become increasingly difficult to obtain permits for research that involves the destruction of archeological sites through excavation. Archeologists working under permit have thus been forced to reexamine their research needs, to adopt a more preservationist posture, and to undertake more surface survey and less excavation.

The 1935 Historic Sites Act is a basic authority giving the secretary of the interior both the power and the responsibility to collect information, conduct surveys, do research, acquire property, conduct preservation programs, own and operate historic properties, enter into agreements, perform educational activities, and make rules and regulations concerning historic properties. It also established the Advisory Board on National Parks, Historic Sites, Buildings and Monuments, and authorized the establishment of other technical advisory committees.

The National Historic Preservation Act (NHPA) of 1966 gave the secretary more explicit direction and established the Interior/Advisory Council/State triad that now forms the structural core of historic preservation. The secretary was authorized, first, to expand and maintain a national register "of significant historic properties." In fact, no national register had existed as such before; what had existed was the National Historic Landmarks program, linked to the Historic Sites Survey and the inventory of Historic American Buildings. It was the 1966 act that gave structure and purpose to this nebulous cluster of inventory activities and committed the federal government to the identification of all significant historic properties in the country. The secretary was further authorized to provide matching grants-in-aid to states and to the national trust for historic preservation purposes. The secretary was authorized to establish conditions for the receipt of grants by the states, and the states were required to prepare historic preservation plans to guide their use of grant moneys. The Advisory Council on Historic Preservation was established and federal agencies were directed to consult with the advisory council before adversely affecting a National Register property.

Executive Order 11593 helped implement the 1966 act by directing federal agencies to identify the nominate historic properties to the National Register and by requiring that care be exercised to avoid unnecessarily damaging properties that might be eligible for the National Register. This crucial aspect of the executive order was subsequently incorporated into the statute itself by a 1976 amendment to Section 106 of the act, which now calls for federal agencies to consult with the council whenever they may adversely affect a National Register property or a property that might be eligible for the National Register.

In sum, these statutes

1. express federal concern for the future of historic properties and give each federal agency a positive responsibility to identify them, protect them and consult with the advisory council in doing so;
2. establish the basis for a comprehensive program of historic preservation and interagency coordination within the Department of the Interior;
3. commit the federal government to developing a National Register of the nation's historic properties;
4. establish an infrastructure for historic preservation including the Department of the Interior, the advisory council and the state historic preservation programs with a complex set of structural interlocks and checks and balances;
5. require each state to conduct a survey and implement a plan for historic preservation and establish complementary responsibilities for federal agencies.

COMPLEMENTARY AUTHORITIES

Perhaps the most important complementary authority for historic preservation and for comprehensive cultural resource management is the

National Environmental Policy Act of 1969, which requires federal agencies to consider, during planning, the impacts of their activities on the environment. Since cultural resources are parts of the environment, the NEPA provides a clear responsibility for federal agencies to identify and plan for the protection of cultural resources, including historic properties, as a part of their overall project-planning and land-management programs.

A second useful complementary authority is the Archeological and Historic Preservation Act of 1974, amending the Reservoir Salvage Act of 1960. This act provides agencies with specific authority to engage in particular kinds of impact-mitigation when it has been established that their activities will damage or destroy particular kinds of historic properties. The act is aimed entirely at the preservation of data, not at the protection of historic properties as physical entities. Thus, the primary mitigation actions provided for are data recovery or salvage operations, and the properties to which the act applies are those that are "archeological" in the sense that their significance rests in whole or in part upon their capacity to yield useful information. The act also provides the secretary of the interior with additional authority, notably that of coordinating the entire national program of archeological and historical data recovery.

The Department of Housing and Urban Development (HUD) complements the national historic preservation program in a variety of ways, under a variety of authorities. Under the Housing and Community Development Act of 1974, for example, HUD provides communities with block grants that can be used for many purposes including surveys to identify historic properties, comprehensive historic preservation planning, renovation and restoration and archeological studies. Block grants can also be used for activities that destroy historic properties, of course, and the act places responsibility for compliance with NEPA and the historic preservation statutes in such instances with the community recipient, not with HUD. Comprehensive planning and management grants, provided to local jurisdictions by HUD under Section 701 of the Housing Act of 1954 may also be used for historic preservation planning.

Finally, certain statutes governing the operations of particular federal programs provide complementary authority or direction for historic preservation programs. For example, Section 4(f) of the Department of Transportation Act (23 U.S.C. 138) requires that all feasible and prudent alternatives be explored and all possibilities for minimizing harm be implemented whenever a transportation project requires the "use" of any significant historic site; 23 U.S.C. 305 authorizes the expenditure of federal-aid highway funds on archeological and paleontological salvage. The Coastal Zone Management Act of 1972 directs that cultural and historic values be considered in coastal zone management; the Federal Water Pollution Control Act as amended in 1972 directs that environmental impacts be considered in the development of areawide wastewater treatment plans, and so forth.

REGULATIONS

The mere fact that a law exists, with certain language that appears to require specific action, is no guarantee that such an action will occur. In some cases, agencies may deliberately or through negligence ignore their mandated responsibilities. We will discuss how this typically happens and what to do about it in Chapter 9. A more pervasive reason that the apparent requirements of law are not attended to is that laws, as they emerge from Congress, are both imperfect and incomplete. They authorize agencies of the executive, or others, to do things. They direct that certain things will be done and they authorize the appropriation of funds to do them, but they leave it to the executive branch to specify exactly how they will be done.

Sometimes, of course, Congress fails to appropriate the money that it has authorized for a particular activity and this tends to stall the activity. This happened with the Archeological and Historic Preservation Act of 1974, with the result that many of the things the secretary of the interior was authorized to do under the act have not yet been very successfully initiated. Sometimes, too, the exact intent of Congress is unclear from the statutory language. If ambiguities and contradictions cannot be settled during the process of rulemaking, they continue to clog up the implementing system until they are resolved either by amendment to the legislation or by the courts.

Rulemaking by an executive agency is a complex and frustrating activity. The idea of rulemaking is to establish a workable system through which the intent of the pertinent statute or statutes can be realized. Rulemaking also augments the statutes by providing technical standards that must be attained or methods that should be used in carrying out the statutory mandates. For example, when the secretary of the interior was charged by the Archeological and Historic Preservation Act with the responsibility to "coordinate all Federal survey and recovery activities [P.L. 93-291, Sec. 5 (c)]," he assumed rulemaking authority to issue guidelines for the conduct of such programs.

Rulemaking in historic preservation involves the careful balancing of congressional intent, as reflected in the legislative history of the statute, against professional judgments as to what is best for preservation, administrative judgments as to what will work, and legal judgments about how the rulemaking interlocks with other statutes and regulations. Proposed rules and regulations go through an elaborate review process before they are finally issued. When issued, they have the force of law, and are published in the Federal Register and incorporated into the Code of Federal Regulations. They are referred to by title and part in the code, separated by the letters "C.F.R." for "Code of Federal Regulations." Thus "36 CFR 800" means Code of Federal Regulations Title 36 Part 800. Sometimes a chapter number is also given: for example, 36 CFR VIII 800, but this is not necessary. Most pertinent regulations pertaining most directly to historic preservation have, of course, been issued by the Department of the Interior and the advisory council. Since the whole federal historic preservation system is continuing to evolve, change and development in the regulations is naturally constant. Most of the rulemaking discussed in what follows is in advanced draft form as this book goes to press; by the time it is actually published the structure of the regulations may have changed considerably. For example, it is very probable that 36 CFR 60, as redrafted in 1976, will be split into two parts in its final form, with one part (36 CFR 60) dealing with basic matters pertaining to National Register nominations, the other (36 CFR 68) dealing with historic preservation planning. It is also very probable that 36 CFR 63 and 36 CFR 64 will be combined into a single regulation dealing with the determination of eligibility process and the identification procedures required by that process. A more clearcut distinction will probably be made between actual regulation, which demands compliance by federal agencies, and simple technical guidelines and advice. None of these changes is substantive; the general direction of the rulemaking will remain the same, but readers should be aware that the precise construction presented here and in Appendix A is sure to change. The OAHP and the Advisory Council should be contacted for the most up-do-date regulations. As of early 1977, the principal pertinent regulations are the following:

36 CFR 60: *National Register of Historic Places: Criteria for Statewide Historic Surveys and Plans*

This regulation, massively revised in 1976, establishes the responsibilities of the state historic preservation officers (SHPO), sets standards for SHPO staffs and review boards and describes the statewide survey and planning process that each state must undertake. State historic preservation plans, as originally required under this regulation, were rather static documents and virtually no state exercised a great deal of sophistication in their preparation. The procedures now emphasize the implementation of a flexible process, assuring that all aspects of the state's history and prehistory will be addressed, that all historic properties will eventually be identified, and that the data acquired through survey will be used in a systematic and appropriate way in the review of land-use and project proposals. States are afforded a great deal of latitude in their development of surveys and plans; but they must develop them in accordance with the standards set forth in the regulation in order to obtain grants under the NHPA. This is a very important regulation for the development of regional and statewide preservation and research plans, not only under the authority of the 1966 act, but under other statutes that encourage such planning. We will return to it in Chapter 8.

36 CFR 63: *Procedures for Requesting Determinations of Eligibility*

When a federal agency comes to the secretary of the interior for a determination of the eligibility of a given property for the National Register, under terms of Executive Order 11593 and amended Section 106 of the Historic Preservation Act, it must provide the secretary with sufficient information to permit a judgment to be made. This regulation sets forth the information requirements and the steps involved in providing the information. This is an important regulation for those engaging in surveys for federal agencies because it indicates the kinds of descriptive and evaluatory information that must be supplied on each historic property discovered.

36 CFR 64: *Criteria and Procedures for the Indentification of Historic Properties*

Federal agencies are required by Executive Order 11593 to identify historic properties that might qualify for the National Register on lands under their jurisdiction or control. This regulation sets forth the methods to be used in making such identifications. In essence, it establishes general standards for the conduct of historic property surveys. Since the executive order was issued not only under the authority of the NHPA but also that of NEPA, these procedures are taken as applying to the conduct of historic property surveys during the preparation of environmental impact statements.

36 CFR 65: *Recovery of Scientific, Prehistoric, Historic, and Archeological Data: Procedures for Coordination and Notification.*

The Archeological and Historic Preservation Act requires that federal agencies inform the secretary of the interior when their activities are likely to destroy or damage historical or archeological data. It also gives the secretary the responsibility of compiling data and making an annual report to Congress. Furthermore, the act provides that the secretary may undertake certain kinds of data recovery activities on his own initiative and it authorizes the transfer of funds from other agencies to the secretary to undertake data recovery activities. This regulation spells out the procedures under which this information flow is to take place and specifies that data recovery programs under the act can be undertaken only after completing the planning processes required by NEPA, the NHPA, Executive Order 11593, and their implementing regulations. A very complex regulation, it is important to those actually involved in the management of agency actions or in questioning the appropriateness of those actions. It is also important to archeologists and others who may be asked to engage in data recovery activities by agencies that have not yet complied with their planning and preservation responsibilities. Such an archeologist may destroy a protectable site and may be placed in legal jeopardy by participating in such a project.

36 CFR 66: *Recovery of Scientific, Prehistoric, Historic, and Archeological Data: Methods, Standards and Reporting Requirements.*

These guidelines set forth basic professional standards for the conduct of data recovery activities under terms of the Archeological and Historic Preservation Act. It does not tell archeologists how to dig or architects how to measure; it does direct that all the classes of data that give a property its significance should be recovered when recovery is called for; it does stipulate that such data may include archeological, historical, architectural, and related ethnographic, geological, ecological, and other scientific data; it does stipulate that the data must be recovered in accordance with a reasonable research design; it does provide for the dissemination of data; and it does set standards for the professional qualifications of the persons doing the work. For archeologists, these standards are equivalent to those of the Society of Professional Archeologists (Jelks *et al.* 1976). These guidelines also establish standards for report preparation. These standards are binding on agencies when they notify the secretary of the interior of their data recovery projects as required by the act. Noting that one cannot recover data until one discovers the properties that contain such data, the regulation contains an appendix setting forth standards for surveys. These standards are identical to those in 36 CFR 64.

36 CFR 800: *Procedures for the Protection of Historic and Cultural Properties.*

Issued by the advisory council, these procedures tie the whole historic preservation program of the federal government together. They implement section 106 of the Historic Preservation Act and two sections of the executive order, Sections 1(3) and 2(b). Section 1(3) requires all agencies to establish procedures in consultation with the council to contribute to the preservation of nonfederally owned historic properties; the procedures at 36 CFR 800 constitute guidelines for the development of basic agency procedures, and have often been adopted verbatim by other agencies. Section 2(b) requires that caution be exercised on lands under the jurisdiction or control of federal agencies until the processes of identification and nomination are complete; the procedures at 36 CFR 800 are permanently binding on such federal lands (including federal project areas).

The basic procedures set forth in 36 CFR 800 are outlined in Figure 3. In essence, an agency (a) identifies historic properties in the environmental impact area of its planned undertaking (here complying with 36 CFR 63 and 64), and (b) consults with the state historic preservation officer to determine whether the

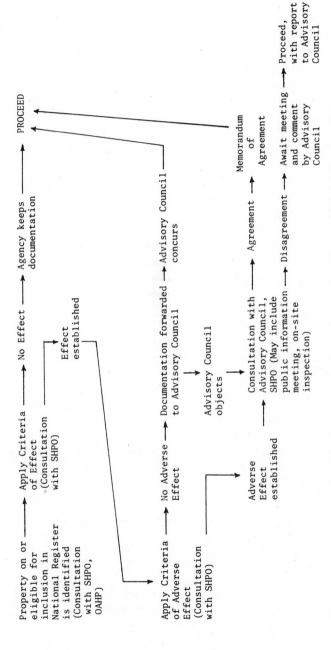

Figure 3. *Procedures of the Advisory Council on Historic Preservation (36 CFR Part 800).*

properties may qualify for the National Register and, if they are likely to, whether the undertaking will affect them and affect them adversely. The SHPO participates, as required by 36 CFR 60. If the properties appear to be eligible or if any responsible party raises a question about their eligibility, the agency asks the Department of the Interior for a final determination pursuant to 36 CFR 63. If the properties are eligible, the agency requests the council's formal comments. A process of consultation is thus triggered that should lead to agreement among the agency, the council, and the SHPO as to how to avoid or mitigate impact (here 36 CFR 65 and 66 may come into play). Once this agreement is signed, the project may go ahead in compliance with its terms; should an agreement not be reached, the project must be held up until the full advisory council can comment. Then it can proceed—over the council's objection if it wishes. Agencies seldom fly in the face of the council, however, considering that most significant executive branch department heads are represented on the council and considering the legal vulnerability to a charge of arbitrary and capricious behavior that an agency would acquire by so doing in the presence of a reasonable plan for avoidance or mitigation.

36 CFR 800 also sets forth various other powers of the council to comment, to object, and to advise.

THE INTENT OF THE LAWS

There is, then, a considerable body of law today that pertains to historic preservation. Before we begin to discuss how historic preservation works, how it is changing, and what part anthropology plays in its development and growth, we need to consider seriously whether the laws were intended to do what we, as anthropologists, would like them to do. After all, these laws have developed through 70 years of political cutting and filling and philosophical change; they are rife with semantic inconsistencies and vagueries. However, we think that it is possible to see a consistent thread of congressional intent in the key statutes, which can serve as a sensible legal basis for an anthropological approach to historic preservation.

In Chapter 1, we asserted that a major reason for studying and preserving the past is to have continued access to the experiences of our predecessors. Is there evidence that the maintenance of such access was an intent of those who wrote and enacted the laws under which historic preservation has developed?

The answer is superficially ambiguous. When the Historic Sites Act of 1935 justifies preservation for "the inspiration . . . of the people of the United States," did its authors mean to inspire us by allowing us to learn, systematically and thoroughly, about the events of the past or did they just mean for us to look at the walls of Mesa Verde and say, "Gee Whiz!"? Congressional testimony, by and large, is uninformative. Lawmakers typically express sincere generalized concern for historic values, while offering little clear definition of such values. Those testifying before congressional committees, not surprisingly, tend to bemoan the loss of impressive buildings, ancient sites, giant cemeteries, and the like. Such things have shock value, but they obscure the basic issue: Has Congress meant to preserve representatives of past human behavior useful to science and modern communities, or has it meant to preserve the big sites, the early sites, the beautiful buildings, the impressive structures—the places associated with specific exciting events in our history?

The events compelling congressional action, discussion of which often dominates the legislative history of bills, are not necessarily relevant. The general thrust of congressional interest is, we think, fairly clear. When Congress first expressed an interest in the preservation of archeological resources, in the Antiquities Act of 1906, it was impelled by an emergency—the despoliation of such sites as Mesa Verde for private profit. It responded by flatly forbidding such despoliation on lands of the federal government and by authorizing the president especially to manage properties of "historical or scientific interest." The Antiquities Act has been used to establish national monuments containing a great diversity of historic properties and to regulate the excavation of sites, great and small, impressive and nebulous, that are, in the words of the original petitioners for congressional action, the subjects of "ethnological studies [Lee 1970:10]." The original catalyst for action—the destruction of impressive sites—has not limited the act's implementation, because the law was written with broad language referring to a great range of properties. It was precisely the need for broad language (broadening the function of the statute even beyond the needs of archeology) that led to debate that delayed passage of the act for several years (see Chapter 2).

In 1966, in the NHPA, Congress found and declared that:

1. The spirit and direction of the nation are founded upon and reflected in its historic past.
2. The historical and cultural foundations of the nation should be preserved as a living part of our community life and development in order to give a sense of orientation to the American people.
3. In the face of ever-increasing extensions of urban centers, highways, and residential, commercial, and industrial developments, the present governmental and nongovernmental historic preservation programs and activities are inadequate to insure future generations a genuine opportunity to appreciate and enjoy the rich heritage of our nation; and,
4. Although the major burdens of historic preservation have been borne and major efforts initiated by private agencies and individuals and both should continue to play a vital role, it is nevertheless necessary and

appropriate for the federal government to accelerate its historic preservation programs and activities, to give maximum encouragement to agencies and individuals undertaking preservation by private means, and to assist State and local governments and the National Trust for Historic Preservation in the United States to expand and accelerate their historic preservation programs and activities.

This act was passed at a time when a new approach to preservation was gaining credence. This approach was .characterized by a concern with the preservation of an environment that truly represents the nation's social and historic diversity. In its broad language and concern with "significant properties" (as opposed to those of "exceptional value," dealt with in the Historic Sites Act of 1935), the NHPA was clearly responsive to modern preservation concerns. The use of the word "orientation" in the preamble is also enlightening. How does history "orient" people? Clearly, a number of totalitarian governments have skewed history to "orient" their people toward particular modes of thought, but this can hardly be an acceptable sort of orientation in a democracy. Orientation, for the citizens of a democracy, must mean developing and maintaining a feeling of direction based on an individual understanding of what has gone before. Such understanding can be reached only if a rational and unbiased sample of data about the past is preserved and made available to the American people, and if properties that embody and focus the beliefs and self-expression of each component part of American society are maintained as functioning elements of their environment.

Finally, the preservation of a past represented only by impressive sites and buildings is a subtle but pervasive form of discrimination. The builders of large, impressive, or beautiful structures have typically been the rich, the powerful, the elite, and—in post-contact America—the white. The selective preservation of such structures at the expense of the small and humble properties occupied by nonagricultural Indians, migrant farm workers, tenant farmers, or subsistence miners constitutes a skewing of the historical record in favor of the elite. We do not believe that such a warping of history was the congressional intent. Such an intent would be inconsistent with the whole recent thrust of civil rights legislation; surely access to and tangible representation in history is the right of every group that has participated in that history.

Thus, there is good reason to believe that the intent of Congress is to preserve a sufficient sample of historic properties and the data they often contain to permit the American people to tap thoroughly the experiences of those who have lived before, both in a scientific fashion and in experiential ways. We see no basis for believing that Congress intends that only impressive properties or those associated with particular exciting events should be preserved. The long-term problems of historic preservation lie in deciding how a proper sample is to be defined and preserved, while minimizing conflicts between the needs of historic preservation and those of economic development, environmental repair, and other useful activities.

HOW FEDERAL AGENCIES AFFECT HISTORIC PROPERTIES

All the historic preservation statutes refer most directly and completely to the operations of federal agencies, with the exception of the NHPA, which encourages the states to engage in systematic historic preservation planning. We will have more to say about state planning later, but now we should define how federal agencies affect historic properties.

Direct Effects

The easiest kind of effect to understand is the *direct* effect of a federal undertaking. If the Corps of Engineers bulldozes through a prehistoric site while building a dam, or if HUD finances the razing of a historic structure during urban renewal, these are obviously direct effects. Direct effects may take a great many forms, however, and some are less obvious than others. For example:

1. If the U.S. Army opens a new area for artillery practice or tank training, the explosive and erosive actions will be likely to damage any historic properties that may be present in the area. Since these actions are undertaken by agents of the government, as a direct result of governmental orders, they are *direct* effects.
2. If an interstate highway is funded in part by the federal government, any historic properties destroyed by construction-related activities are destroyed as a *direct* effect of the federal decision to fund the project.
3. If the American Tricentennial Commission finances the Town of Chickaluma's relocation of a historic structure, moving the structure away from its in-and-on-the-ground context, this loss of integrity is a *direct* effect of ATC action.

Permitted Effects

Permitted effects are often hard to distinguish from direct effects, but often there is at least an administrative distinction. For example, when the Corps of Engineers permits extraction of water from a navigable waterway under terms of the Rivers and Harbors Act of 1899, any damage to historic properties resulting directly from the construction of extraction facilities or facilities to convey the extracted water is a permitted effect because it could not occur in the absence of the permit, yet it is not done by the actual agents of the Corps.

Managerial Effects

Managerial effects occur as regular results of on-going management activities. If employees of the Bureau of Land Management loot ghost towns during the pursuit of their duties or if prehistoric sites are destroyed by erosion around a reservoir maintained by the Soil Conservation Service, these are managerial effects.

Contingent Effects

Contingent effects are those arising from the actions of nonfederal entities which *could not occur* without a direct action by a federal agency, although no formal permit is involved. Let us say, for example, that HUD guarantees flood insurance for housing construction downstream from a Corps of Engineers dam. The damage to historic properties resulting from the housing construction so insured is a contingent effect of the insurance authorization and the dam.

Infrastructural Effects

When a federal action alters the course of development on nonfederal lands, any resulting damage to historic properties is a special kind of contingent effect that we will refer to as an infrastructural effect. Infrastructural effects are more difficult to place boundaries upon than are other kinds of contingent effects; they are less predictable and yet may be more far-reaching. Some examples may clarify the type:

1. The Bureau of Reclamation brings supplemental water into an agricultural valley. This change in the valley's water supply allows increased irrigation agriculture, hence increased clearing and leveling of the land. These activities may damage historic properties (especially archeological sites); these damages are thus infrastructural effects of the federal action.
2. A new interstate highway is constructed through an area previously accessible only by barge. The area is hence opened for residential and industrial development. Any resulting damage to historic properties is an infrastructural effect of the highway construction.
3. The Environmental Protection Agency helps fund a sewer with a capacity to serve 150,000 persons, in a town with a population of 30,000 and an overtaxed sewerage system. EPA thus relieves a major

check to growth, and permits a fivefold increase in population and the concomitant construction of perhaps 24,000 new homes with all their appurtenant facilities. The resultant destruction of historic properties is an infrastructural effect.

The identification of infrastructural effects can be carried to impossible extremes. If the Federal Power Commission authorizes construction of a 500 kV powerline into a metropolitan area, it is permitting an input of energy that will very likely be expressed in new urban growth. However, in many cases, it is impossible to predict *where* this growth will occur and its occurrence will probably be controlled by variables other than power (circulation, job markets, etc.). Only the most nebulous assessment of infrastructural effects may be possible under such circumstances. Infrastructural effects are real, however, they are subtle, they are hard to figure out, but they are also often the most damaging of all effects of a federal undertaking.

APPLYING THE STATUTES TO THE EFFECTS

We do not take it to be the intent of the laws that protection of historic properties should be the paramount concern of all federal agencies, but we do understand it to be their mandate that each agency in advance of each action should make every reasonable effort to identify the potential effects of the action and to mitigate or avoid any effects that are adverse. We will try to show how the historic preservation statutes apply to each kind of effect just identified.

Direct Effects

No one really has serious argument with the responsibility of federal agencies to assess the direct effects of their actions on cultural resources, including historic properties. Section 101(b)(4) of the NEPA asserts the responsibility of the government to "preserve important historic . . . aspects of our national heritage," presumably through the preparation and review of environmental impact statements. Section 106 of the NHPA requires that National Register and Register-eligible properties be identified in advance of *any* project, with or without an EIS. Executive Order 11593, Section 2b also directs federal agencies to protect (federally owned) properties that may qualify for the *Register* and that might be "transferred, sold, demolished, or substantially altered." The Archeological and Historic Preservation Act specifies responsibilities with respect to properties valuable for their data content, and details a method (data recovery) for the mitigation of impacts upon such data. Cumulatively, these statutes require that all federal agencies conduct studies in advance of their land-disturbing projects, in order to identify historic properties, evaluate them, evaluate potential project effects on them, and devise avoidance or mitigation plans.

Permitted Effects

Effects permitted by explicit federal license, lease, or other entitlement, are also covered by most of the pertinent statutes. The Council on Environmental Quality, in its *Guidelines for Preparation of Environmental Impact Statements,* specifies the application of NEPA to projects "involving a Federal lease, permit, license, certificate, or other entitlement for use [40 CFR V 1500.5 (a)(2)]."

Similar language is found in the advisory council's *Procedures,* establishing the applicability of the NHPA and Executive Order 11593 (36 CFR VIII 800.3 (c)(2)). The AHPA specifically refers to "federally licensed" projects, activities, and programs in its primary direction to agencies concerning the recovery and protection of data (PL 93-291; Sec. 3(a)).

The responsibility for assessing and mitigating permitted project effects belongs to the permitting agency, but there is nothing in the statutes to keep the agency from making the beneficiary of the permit pay for the activities necessary for compliance. The permittee can and usually is required to identify historic properties and project effects upon them during preparation of its permit application, and mitigation of adverse effects can be written in as conditions upon the permit when issued. Assistance in impact mitigation may, in some cases, be obtained by the permittee from the Department of the Interior under Section 3(b) of Public Law 93-291.

Managerial Effects

The basic direction for the evaluation and mitigation of managerial effects comes from Section 2 of Executive Order 11593 and, less directly, from Section 106 of the NHPA. Section 2 of the executive order directs that agencies nominate all qualifying properties under their control to the National Register—thus bringing them clearly under the protection of NHPA Section 106—and in the interim, that they exercise caution in order to avoid inadvertently allowing properties that might be eligible for inclusion in the Register to be damaged or destroyed. The NHPA, as amended in 1976, requires attention to eligible properties as well as those listed, which has the same effect as the cautionary provisions of the executive order. The advisory council, in its *Procedures for the Protection of Historic and Cultural Properties* has issued "criteria of adverse effect," to assist agencies in determining whether their activities may affect properties included in or eligible for the National Register. Included is, "Neglect of a property resulting in its deterioration or destruction [36 CFR 800.9(e)]."

Thus, properties either on or qualifying for the National Register are not to be "neglected"; the managing agency has a responsibility under Section 2(a) of the executive order to identify such properties and a responsibility under Section 2(b) of the executive order and Section 106 of the NHPA to take care of them.

Contingent Effects

The Council on Environmental Quality's *Guidelines* contain language indicating the NEPA is to be construed as covering contingent effects. The definition of "types of actions covered by the Act [40 CFR V 1500.5]" is very broad, and covers such general actions upon which local activities could be contingent as, "contracts, grants, subsidies, loans, or other forms of funding assistance (except where such assistance is solely in the form of general revenue sharing funds) [40 CFR V 1500.5(2)]."

The council goes on to caution:

> In considering what constitutes major action significantly affecting the environment, agencies should bear in mind that the effect of many Federal decisions about a project or complex of projects can be individually limited but cumulatively considerable. This can occur when one or more agencies over a period of years puts into a project individually minor but collectively major resources, when one decision involving a limited amount of money is a precedent for action in much larger cases or represents a decision in principle about a future major course of action or when several Government agencies individually make decisions about partial aspects of a major action. In all such cases, an environmental statement should be prepared if it is reasonable to anticipate a cumulatively significant impact on the environment from Federal action (40 CFR V 1500.6(a)].

Executive Order 11593 provides further direction by requiring in Section 1(3) that all federal agencies:

> ... in consultation with the Advisory Council on Historic Preservation (16 U.S.C. 4701), institute procedures to assure that Federal plans and programs contribute to the preservation and enhancement of non-federally owned sites, structures and objects of historical, architectural or archaeological significance."

A federal action that serves as a necessary prelude to state or local activities damaging to historic properties can hardly be taken as contributory to preservation if the federal agency has not at least taken steps to help the local authority avoid or minimize destruction.

Infrastructural Effects

The authorization and direction of federal agencies to consider infrastructural effects in connection with their undertakings is essentially the same as those covering contingent effects. An explicit discussion of such broad effects is provided in the Council on Environmental Quality *Guidelines* as follows:

> Secondary or indirect, as well as primary or direct, consequences for the environment should be included in the analysis. Many major Federal actions, in particular those that involve the construction or licensing of infrastructure investments (e.g., highways, airports, sewer systems, water resource projects, etc.) stimulate or induce secondary effects in the form of associated investments and changed patterns of social and economic activities. Such secondary effects, through their impacts on existing community facilities and activities, through inducing new facilities and activities or through changes in natural conditions, may often be even more substantial than the primary effects of the original action itself [40 CFR V 1500.8(a) (3)(ii)].

Dealing with infrastructural effects in a reasonable and efficacious manner is one of the major challenges offered by comprehensive historic preservation planning. Discussion of possible approaches is given in Chapter 8.

CONCLUSION

We believe that federal law provides the basis for an understandable and efficient national historic preservation program. The laws do not demand that all historic properties be protected at the expense of other federal activities, but they do insist that an effort be made, every time a federal agency contemplates an action that may directly or indirectly modify the environment, to determine whether this action will contribute to the preservation of historic properties—including sites, buildings, structures, and districts, the cultural values they represent, and the useful data they contain. To the maximum extent compatible with other legitimate goals, such actions should be designed to so contribute. The *Procedures* of the Advisory Council on Historic Preservation prescribe a basic framework upon which the historic preservation programs of federal agencies can be constructed, but the purpose of the National Historic Preservation Act and its associated authorities is not to force agencies into rigid, unthinking compliance with bureaucratic requirements. The federal government is to "provide leadership [Executive Order 11593, Sec. 1]" and "encourage" and "assist" states, local governments and the public in preservation programs (NHPA preamble (d)). This implies an active, creative partnership involving federal agencies, other levels of government and the public with plenty of room for innovative policymaking and broad multiagency planning.

For more detailed information on federal agency policies, programs, and regulations, and the statutes on which they are based, the publications of the National Trust for Historic Preservation (1976a; 1976b) will be useful, as will a compendium now being prepared by OAHP and the advisory council (OAHP/ Advisory Council on Historic Preservation 1977). We will discuss the creative use of historic preservation law and policy in subsequent chapters. First, however, it is necessary to understand the bureaucracy within which historic preservation operates, which is the subject of the next chapter.

4

THE HISTORIC
PRESERVATION SYSTEM

Laws and regulations cannot be implemented without people and systems for their implementation. As the OAHP, the advisory council, the state historic preservation officers, and the various federal agencies have tried to figure out the new legal authorities, a complex cast of historic preservation characters has developed, a definite jargon has emerged, and a more-or-less well-understood set of methods has been hammered together.

THE CAST

First we will turn to the cast of characters: the secretary of the interior, the advisory council, the states, various types of federal agencies, and professional preservation contractors (see Figs. 4 and 5).

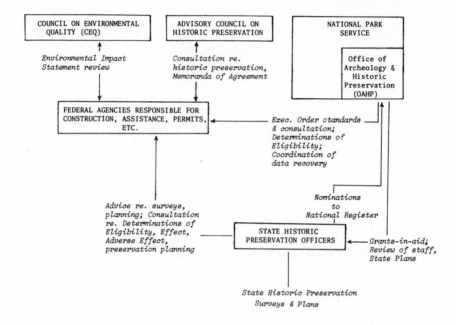

Figure 4.   *The historic preservation system: Major participants and relationships.*

The Secretary of the Interior and the National Park Service

The secretary of the interior heads a department with many branches—the Bureau of Land Management, the Fish and Wildlife Service, the Bureau of Reclamation, the National Park Service, and others. Although each has responsibilities for historic preservation, the secretary's coordinative responsibilities for historic preservation are delegated to the National Park Service, both by tradition and statute. This delegation is probably one that has outlived its usefulness, as we will discuss later, but it is understandable in historical context. The government's original preservation tool was designation to national monument status, and the administration of national monuments naturally fell to the National Park Service in the reorganization of 1933. As the years have gone by, the goals of the NPS and the preservation movement have progressively diverged, but the NPS has remained in essential control of the secretary's preservation responsibilities.

The National Park Service, too, is a thing of parts. And these parts get

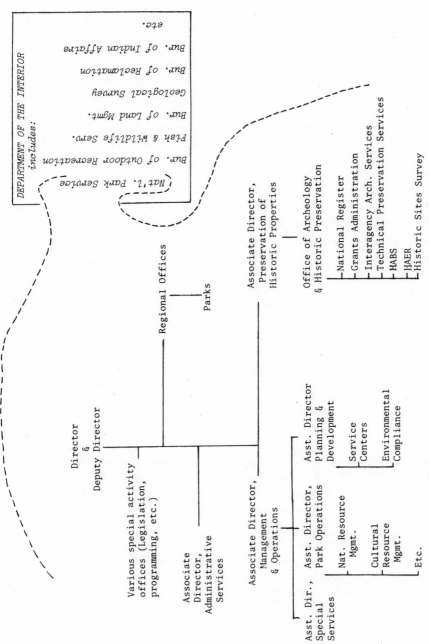

Figure 5. *National Park Service Organization (historic preservation functions are emphasized).*

moved about regularly, so the names and precise duties assigned to its elements in this chapter may not apply by the time it is read. The NPS, of course, is responsible for parks and monuments. Each park or monument has a superintendent, who has a staff. Often, this staff includes archeologists, historians, or architectural historians, depending on the unit's particular needs. The staff's central responsibility is to the park or monument, though staff members may be assigned outside responsibilities on behalf of the regional director. Superintendents answer to regional directors, of which there are eight across the country as of 1976 (In addition there is a special director for the National Capital Parks and two major department-wide service centers, one at Denver Colorado and one at Harper's Ferry West Virginia.) Each regional director is responsible for the parks and monuments of a region (Fig. 6). Each has a staff, which again may include archeologists, historians, and other preservation specialists. The regional director may also have specialized centers with historic preservation responsibilities; there are archeological centers at Tucson, Arizona; Lincoln, Nebraska; and Tallahassee, Florida, for example, which answer to the western, midwestern, and southeastern regional directors, respectively. Regional preservation staffs and archeological centers have regional responsibilities; they generally serve the needs of the region's parks and monuments. They may have extrapark roles to play; for example, they comment on environmental impact statements prepared by other agencies, and participate in the development of coordinated Depart-

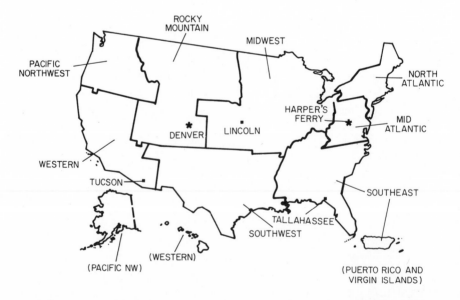

Figure 6. *National Park Service regions, service centers (*), and archeological centers (■).*

ment of the Interior responses to such documents either at the regional level or through the Park Planning and Environmental Compliance Division in Washington. Their first priorities, however, are the care of historic properties in the parks and monuments, the evaluation of potential additions to the park and monument system, and other duties centered on the lands held by the NPS.

The regional directors have a good deal of autonomy, but they do answer to the director of the National Park Service in Washington, who also has a staff that includes a Cultural Resource Management Division, consisting of archeologists and historians. These people are to the regional archeologists and historians as the regional specialists are to the park and monument staffs—high-level advisors and general policymakers.

The secretary's responsibility for the coordination of a national historic preservation program does not descend along this line of authority, although the regional directors do, from time to time, make efforts—sometimes successfully—to gain control of coordinative elements. Aside from their involvement in environmental review, the Cultural Resource Management Division, the regional preservation staffs, and park and monument preservation specialists are responsible solely for preservation matters within the parks and monuments.

The secretary's coordinative responsibilities descend through the director of the National Park Service to the associate director, preservation of historic properties. The associate director has two general theaters of operation. He represents the United States in international preservation circles, participating in various UNESCO programs and organizing exchanges and tours by preservation scholars. His main activity, however, is to oversee the operations of the Office of Archeology and Historic Preservation (OAHP).

Office of Archeology and Historic Preservation

The Office of Archeology and Historic Preservation (OAHP) was constructed during the late 1960s out of several smaller programs, with major new additions. The following are its components:

The Historic American Building Survey (HABS) was organized during the depression to document historic buildings with measured drawings, photographs, and other data. Summer teams of architecture students under professional supervision collect most of the data, which are edited by the HABS Washington staff and placed in the Library of Congress. HABS has become deeply involved in the applications of photogrammetry and in studies of the spatial organization of neighborhoods and small communities.

The Historic American Engineering Record (HAER) is modeled after HABS but concerns itself with recording engineering works. Like HABS, it places its results in the Library of Congress, but since HAER has been in existence only since 1969, its archive is of more limited volume. Besides preparing measured drawings and photographs, HAER conducts salvage documentation, films vanishing industrial activities, and prepares inventories of engineering works.

The Historic Sites Survey attempts to identify and document properties illustrative of broad "themes" thought to characterize American history. Once documented, such properties are reviewed by the Advisory Board on National Parks, Historic Sites, Buildings, and Monuments; this review results in the recognition of qualifying properties as national historic landmarks. Landmarks are automaticaly listed in the National Register and are given some special attention by the NPS, but are not necessarily acquired or protected.

Interagency Archeological Services includes the old Interagency Archeological Salvage program and the functional responsibility for Antiquities Act permit activities, together with other responsibilities. Interagency Archeological Services (IAS) issues and administers Antiquities Act permits on all Interior and military lands, subject to approval by the responsible bureau or agency and advice and review by the Smithsonian (The Department of Agriculture handles permits on its own lands, subject to Smithsonian oversight.) It also administers funds for salvage data recovery in advance of the construction projects of other agencies, utilizing funds appropriated for such purposes by Congress and those transferred to it by other agencies under the authority of the Archeological and Historic Preservation Act (AHPA). It advises other agencies on proper methods for the identification of archeological properties and for the recovery of archeological data, under the authorities of Executive Order 11593 and the AHPA, respectively. It reports to Congress on the overall national data recovery effort, receiving reports from other agencies on their preservation and data recovery programs and commenting on their adequacy. It comments to the Advisory Council on Historic Preservation on the adequacy of agency proposals for data recovery to mitigate or eliminate project impacts on archeological properties. It places reports on archeological fieldwork in a microfiche archive through the National Technical Information Service, for use in research. It contracts for special studies to develop methods useful in archeological planning, and publishes these as "cultural resource management studies." Contracts for data recovery programs under the AHPA are given through three field offices, in Atlanta, Denver, and San Francisco (Fig. 7). Control of these field offices and their contract allocations is the objective of continual internecine warfare between IAS and some of the regional directors, and authority over the offices shifts with changes in the NPS power structure. In addition to its specific duties, IAS provides archeological assistance to the other divisions of OAHP, and its chief acts as the secretary of the interior's departmental consulting archeologist, giving him broad advisory responsibility within the Department.

Technical Preservation Services reviews preservation projects funded by OAHP under the grants-in-aid program authorized by the National Historic

Figure 7. *Interagency Archeological Services (OAHP) field offices and areas of responsibility. Dotted lines indicate boundaries with reference to Corps of Engineers projects. Solid lines indicate boundaries with reference to all other projects.*

Preservation Act, to ensure their technical adequacy. It prepares, publishes, and distributes handbook material for use by other federal agencies and by state and local governments in the preservation of historic properties, under the authority of Executive Order 11593. It also comments on the preservation projects of other agencies, and on surplus federal property transfers that may involve historic properties. A major new area of responsibility for this division is the provision of guidance and review to projects undertaken by private property owners to maintain historic properties and thus gain tax advantages under the Tax Reform Act of 1976.

The National Register of Historic Places is the core division of OAHP. The Register is designed eventually to be a fully documented listing of all historic properties in the nation that are significant enough to require the attention of the federal government. Needless to say, it is not complete and will not be complete in the forseeable future. As of December 1976 the Register included 11,879 entries of districts, sites, structures, buildings, and objects of historic value. These entries are represented in the physical Register itself by files of descriptive and interpretive data, maps, photographs, and other documentation. Gradually, major portions of this mass of data are being computerized by a small Automatic Data Processing Section of the National Register Division. The basic work of the National Register staff is to receive nominations of properties from other agencies (including the parks and monuments) and from the states, verify insofar as possible that the information contained in the nomination is accurate, actually describes and documents a real property correctly located, and justifies the significance of the property in some defensible and useful way, file the documentation, and publish a regularly updated listing of registered properties. If the documentation submitted is not adequate, the nomination is returned for improvement, and a good deal of telephone discussion and correspondence usually ensues until the nomination can finally be accepted and the property listed. A recent court decision (*Stop H-3 Association* v. *Coleman*) verified the secretary of the interior's authority to place properties on the National Register directly, without having to rely on states or other agencies to nominate them. This raises the possibility that the National Register will begin preparing nominations itself, or receiving them from private individuals, but with the exception of a nomination now in progress on the Department of the Interior building in Washington D.C. such a program has not yet been instituted. The National Register is published by the Publications Branch of the Register Division, both in the *Federal Register* (on the first Tuesday of each February, with monthly updates) and in an expanded hardcover format.

As a result of the issuance of Executive Order 11593, the National Register Division took on another responsibility. Until they have completed studies of all lands under their jurisdiction or control to locate and nominate properties to the National Register, federal agencies are required by the executive order to exercise caution to ensure that no Register-eligible properties are improperly dealt with. Agencies that locate historic properties while so exercising caution must have a way to determine whether such properties are eligible. Thus the Register now receives requests for "determinations of eligibility." The review process for a determination of eligibility within the National Register staff is similar to that for a nomination, but it is expedited, and it is usually based on a different sort of documentation. Where nominations come in on standard forms (shown in Appendix B), requests for determinations may be accompanied instead by one or more archeological survey reports, architectural reports, bundles of photographs, site-survey forms, or environmental impact statements. Often these, too, have to be returned to the agency for improvement, but the National Register is attempting to set understandable and attainable standards for documentation that will facilitate the process (see 36 CFR 63 Appendix A; also King 1977).

The National Register shares with Interagency Archeological Services the responsibility to advise other agencies about methods to use in identifying historic properties in compliance with the executive order; as a result, it comments periodically on the adequacy of archeological surveys and other identification activities being conducted by such agencies.

The State Plans Branch of the National Register reviews the historic preservation plans received from each state and updated annually, to determine whether they are of sufficient quality to make the state eligible for grants and to submit nominations to the National Register, as provided for by Section 102 of the National Historic Preservation Act. Standards for state plans are set forth at 36 CFR 60 (see Chapter 8).

The Grants Administration Division issues matching grants to states and to the National Trust to engage in survey and planning activities and to undertake specific acquisition and preservation projects. These grants, which must be matched by the states and are dependent upon each state having an approved plan for historic preservation and an approved historic preservation staff, are issued annually upon receipt and approval of an apportionment warrant from each state historic preservation officer. Survey and planning grants are for use in developing and implementing the state plan, engaging in review of federal projects that may affect historic properties, conducting statewide surveys, and planning acquisition and preservation projects. They may, with secretarial approval, cover up to 70% of the state's survey and planning program costs. Project grants are made to cover up to 50% of the cost of acquisition, projection, restoration, and study of properties listed in the National Register. The Grants program in 1976 provided some $20 million to the states and the National Trust for these purposes, and the 1976 amendments to the National Historic Preservation Act (P.L. 94-422) authorize an increase to $150 million by 1980.

This description of OAHP, although it illustrates the diversity of activities brought together within the program, is static at best. As a physical thing, OAHP occupies most of the fifth floor of a leased building at the corner of 11th and L Streets, NW, in Washington. The National Register occupies a long, vaguely partitioned workspace with a number of attached small offices. Its staff numbers about 40, including both professionals and the clerks and typists who handle the immense paper flow with which the division must cope. The Control Unit verifies the technical details on nominations; are the Universal Transverse Mercator Grid coordinates correct? Do they match up with the map? Is the acreage accurate? The Review Unit of about 10 architectural historians, historians, and archeologists reviews the content of nominations and determinations, supplemented by a fluctuating staff of student interns. Their two supervisors are responsible for reviewing all staff opinions as well as taking care of regulation writing, correspondence with agencies, states, and the public, responses to congressional and other inquires, comments on agency procedures, and so on.

Immediately adjacent to the National Register, and in fairly constant contact, is Interagency Archeological Services. The IAS staff in Washington numbers about 10 including the departmental consulting archeologist, of whom 4 to 5 are clerical workers. One archeologist oversees Antiquities Act matters and personnel; the deputy chief of the division oversees the entire program of contract management, disbursement of funds, coordination with other agencies, comments on agency programs, preparation of regulations, publication, and so on; the deputy chief is assisted by 2 to 3 permanent, full-time archeologists and a floating population of temporary, part-time, and intern assistants. Lacking the record-keeping responsibilities of the National Register, the day-to-day activities of IAS tend to be highly varied, featuring a great deal of interaction with other agencies, development of guidance material, and communication with archeologists outside government. It is with these two divisions—Interagency Archeological Services and the National Register, that the anthropologist working in historic preservation is most likely to come in contact.

The Advisory Council on Historic Preservation

About five blocks from OAHP, the Advisory Council on Historic Preservation occupies offices at 1522 K Street NW. The advisory council also maintains an office in Denver to handle the western part of the country. With expanded funding provided by the 1976 amendments to the National Historic Preservation Act, the council is planning to open several other regional offices.

Officially, the advisory council consists of the secretaries of the interior, housing and urban development, commerce, treasury, agriculture, transportation, state, defense, and health, education and welfare, the attorney general, the administrator of the General Services Administration, the chairman of the Council on Environmental Quality, the chairman of the Council on the Arts and Humanities, the architect of the Capitol, the secretary of the Smithsonian Instititution, the chairman of the National Trust, the president of the National Conference of State Historic Preservation Officers, and 12 persons appointed from outside the federal government by the president. Practically, of course, the cabinet-officer members are represented by members of their staffs, and the actual work of the council is done by the council's own staff. Day-to-day operations are carried out by three major Divisions, overseen by the executive director. The council's *legal counsel* exercises considerable influence over general policy and the council's stance on particular preservation issues. The *Office of Intergovernmental Programs and Planning* interacts with other agencies, with Congress, and with other governments on broad policy issues, legislation, intergovernmental coordination, and long-range planning matters. The *Office of Review and Compliance* includes the Denver staff and most of the Washington staff under the supervision of a director of Review and Compliance. The compliance staff watchdogs agencies to encourage compliance with the council's procedures, commenting on environmental impact statements and other program documents, and alerting agencies when they appear to be in noncompliance. Staff members maintain constant contact with agency representatives and assist them in preparing case reports and in developing memoranda of agreement. With the exception of a staff archeologist and a staff historical architect, who have nationwide responsibilities, each compliance staff member is responsible for a block of states in which he or she maintains a working relationship with state historic preservation officers and agency representatives and is generally responsible for compliance activities.

The *Procedures for the Protection of Historic and Cultural Properties,* 36 CFR 800, circumscribe the council's functions, and are discussed at some length at the end of this chapter. The basic role of the council staff is one of negotiation with agencies –negotiation to get them to comply with the procedures in the first place, then negotiation through the procedures whenever a National Register or Register-eligible property is endangered, toward the development of a memorandum of agreement specifying what protective or mitigative actions will be taken to preserve the property's value.

As of early 1977, several proposals had been advanced in Congress and the executive branch for reorganization of the national historic preservation system. A bill introduced in the House of Representatives (H.R. 3602) would transfer the bulk of the National Park Service's preservation responsibilities (and all the functions of the OAHP) to the advisory council, while renaming the council and expanding its authorities somewhat. At the same time, one reorganization scheme under discussion by the Carter administration featured the combination of OAHP with the Bureau of Outdoor Recreation in the Department of the Interior. As this book goes to press, it is impossible to foretell whether any such reorganization will occur, what its nature might be if it does occur, or when it might occur. None of the reorganization schemes contemplate significant functional changes, however; the operations of each federal preservation entity would continue under new names and within different agencies.

State Historic Preservation Officers

Each state and territory has a state historic preservation officer (SHPO), except those few who in any given year fail to qualify for participation in OAHP's programs and hence are not certified. The SHPO is designated by the governor, but some states have passed legislation circumscribing the governor's choice in various ways. Regardless of who the SHPO is, he or she is required to maintain a professional staff in order to participate in the program. The minimum requirements for the staff are that it include a professional archeologist, historian, and architect or architectural historian. In addition, the SHPO must empanel a review board to review nominations to the National Register and provide other advice; this board must also include representatives of the professions that participate in historic preservation. Finally, the SHPO must undertake a statewide survey in accordance with an approved state historic preservation plan. Once these components are in place, the SHPO is prepared to receive grants from OAHP to undertake surveys and planning, to acquire historic properties, maintain them, study them, restore them, and so forth. These grants must be matched by state and local money, or by money equivalents, like volunteered time and donated property. The SHPO is responsible for a wide range of activities supplemental to his or her role as planner and grantsperson, including supervision of the state historic preservation staff and coordination with the review board, ensuring that nominations are prepared and transmitted to the National Register in an orderly fashion, supervision of an environmental review process undertaken by the staff to ensure that historic properties are considered in federal (and, where possible, state and local planning), participation in the compliance activities of federal agencies under the procedures of the advisory council and of OAHP, supervision of comments on environmental impact statements and similar documents, and provision of general information to federal, state, and local agencies and to the public. The SHPO is clearly a very important figure in the historic preservation system; he or she is consulted and involved at every step in the processes of compliance with the statutes and procedures, and is at the same time responsible for developing the general context of data and planning within which compliance takes place.

The National Trust for Historic Preservation

The National Trust was singled out for special perquisites by the National Historic Preservation Act. It receives substantial grants from OAHP annually, and of course collects funds and properties from private, local, and state sources as well as from other federal funding agencies. The Trust acquires and maintains properties, holds workshops and other education sessions on preservation topics, publishes educational material, solicits members, and otherwise actively promotes citizen involvement in preservation, publishes a newspaper called *Preservation News,* and places advertisements on radio and television and in newspapers and magazines promoting preservation.

The Council On Environmental Quality

Under the authority of the National Environmental Policy Act (NEPA), the Council on Environmental Quality (CEQ) performs a function similar to that performed by the advisory council under terms of the National Historic Preservation Act, but CEQ's ability actually to influence an agency's planning process is not as great as is that of the advisory council. The CEQ provides general advice to federal agencies concerning the maintenance of the environment, but its most visible structural role in federal planning is in its review of environmental impact statements. These statements must be prepared in accordance with guidelines set forth by CEQ, and they are reviewed in draft by CEQ to ensure that they are. Moreover, CEQ receives the comments of other agencies and the public on such drafts, and considers them in making its own comments. However, where the advisory council's procedures require that agencies refrain from initiating their undertakings until they (a) have shown that they will not adversely affect historic properties, (b) have reached an agreement with the council staff about how to mitigate such effects, or (c) have at least received the full council's comments on their activity, CEQ can only require that agencies prepare environmental impact statements according to particular standards, provide for their review, attend to comments and criticisms, and consider the results fully in the planning process. The agency is then free to proceed as it wishes, subject only to restraint through the courts.

Construction Agencies

Agencies that actually construct things have some of the clearest responsibilities under historic preservation law; they must identify properties subject to direct and indirect impact from their projects that may qualify for inclusion in the National Register, determine the eligibility of such properties in consultation with the SHPO and OAHP, and—if the properties are eligible—see to their protection or salvage in consultation with the SHPO and the advisory council. These consultations, and the studies that provide the basis for the consultations, should be fully documented in any environmental impact statement prepared on the project. As we will see, this is sometimes more easily said than done. The Corps of Engineers has faced up to its responsibilities by beginning the employment of archeologists, anthropologists, and historians in its various divisional and district offices; typically, these people do some minor fieldwork in connection with small or preliminary projects, and develop and administer contract programs to get the bulk of the work done. Other construction agencies are also beginning to staff up and develop contract programs, though none has yet reached the level of staffing attained by the Corps.

Land Management Agencies

Agencies like the U.S. Forest Service and the Bureau of Land Management also have clear, but particularly difficult, responsibilities for historic preservation. Section 2A of Executive Order 11593 requires that they conduct an inventory of all their lands to locate properties qualifying for the National Register. Considering the millions of acres managed by such agencies, fulfillment of this requirement will require many years of systematic survey work. Section 2B requires that they exercise caution to ensure that potentially qualifying properties are not unnecessarily damaged. This requires not only that the impacts of agency projects be scrutinized, but that the managerial impacts of general land use, public activities, and the processes of decay and deterioration be considered. Both the Forest Service and the Bureau of Land Management have begun to employ archeologists and other preservation specialists in considerable numbers, placing them both in field offices and in regional administrative positions. The Bureau of Land Management has also employed an archeologist at the Washington level to undertake general policy development and provide guidance to the field. In general, the responsibilities of preservation specialists in land-managing agencies are not unlike those of SHPO staff members; they seek to ensure project by project compliance with the advisory council *Procedures* while engaging in long-range planning for comprehensive survey and evaluation.

Assistance Agencies

Agencies that assist state and local bodies in projects that have direct, contingent, or other effects on historic properties have rather complicated responsibilities for historic preservation. Such agencies account for a large amount of damage to historic properties; the Department of Transportation assists in the construction of highways and airports, the Soil Conservation Service makes possible reservoir construction and land-leveling, the Environmental Protection Agency helps construct sewers, and so forth. These agencies are clearly required by NEPA to identify their impacts on historic properties. Their responsibilities under the NHPA with respect to properties listed in or eligible for the National Register are also clear. Their responsibilities under the executive order are less certain, depending on how one chooses to interpret the words "Federal jurisdiction or control" in Section 2A. If a highway right-of-way or a sewer easement purchased with a large percentage of federal money is thereby construed to be under federal jurisdiction or control, then the assistance agency is clearly responsible for taking care of any historic properties found there. If not, then the agency is only required by the executive order to attend to the mandate of Section 1(3), that it develop procedures to contribute to the preservation of non-federal historic properties. The responsibility of assistance agencies under the AHPA is even more ambiguous. Section 3A of this statute, which authorizes agencies to undertake data recovery programs either by themselves or by transferring funds to the secretary of the interior, does not mention assistance agencies but does refer to "Federal construction projects." Section 3B is specifically concerned with assistance programs, and authorizes the secretary to spend his own appropriated funds to untertake recovery when properties are endangered by assisted projects. Certainly many assistance projects fall within any rational definition of "Federal construction projects"; it would be hard to deny, for example, that interstate highway construction is not federal construction, even though the activity is carried out through state agencies and with state participation. In such cases, the assistance agency has a responsibility under the AHPA to provide for data recovery as needed. Other assistance projects are clearly *not* "Federal construction projects"; when the Department of Housing and Urban Development guarantees a loan that facilitates construction of a housing tract, it can hardly be said to be responsible for the construction. In such an instance, the AHPA confers responsibility upon the Department of the Interior to undertake data recovery, not upon the Department of Housing and Urban Development. Between these poles, however, there is a great diversity of project types over which argument can and does occur.

Until recently, most arguments over the responsibility held by assistance agencies for impact mitigation were somewhat academic, because those agencies that denied their mitigation responsibilities also denied their responsibility to identify historic properties subject to impact. The Soil Conservation Service, for example, assuming that its identification responsibilities sprang only from NEPA and Section 1(3) of the executive order, has issued very vague guidelines that leave each state conservationist to decide whether surveys will be done in advance of assisted projects (7 CFR VI 656). If there are no surveys, the probability of having to deal with mitigation problems is not great. Much uncertainty about the identification responsibilities of assistance agencies was cut away in 1976, however, by amendment of the NHPA. The amendment of NHPA Section 106, to cover properties eligible for the National Register as well as those already listed, in essence extended the advisory council Procedures to apply to the actions of all agencies on all sorts of land. This should help stabilize the current rather nebulous procedures being used by various assistance agencies to meet the requirements of NEPA and Section 1(3) of the executive order.

Besides those agencies that assist in the construction of projects, such agencies as the Department of Housing and Urban Development, the Environmental Protection Agency, and the Department of Commerce help local bodies in general land-use planning. Here there are important and often unrealized opportunities for historic preservation, which will be discussed in Chapter 8. The responsibility of a planning assistance agency is the same as that of any other assistance agency; it needs to identify the historic properties that its actions may affect and consider methods for avoiding or mitigating any adverse effects that may occur. Since its activities are general and programatic, its responsibilities for identification and preservation are of a programatic nature as well. It should ensure that preservation concerns are adequately considered in the planning programs it assists.

Permitting Agencies

Agencies that grant permits for land-use and development, such as the Federal Power Commission, the Environmental Protection Agency, the Corps of Engineers, and the various land-managing agencies, generally exercise their preservation responsibilities by requiring permittees to identify any historic properties subject to impact; permits can then be made conditional upon the avoidance or mitigation of such impacts. A flat requirement that all lands subject to permitted impact be surveyed can have results that border on the ridiculous, however, when the activities permitted may include nothing more dangerous than placing floating buoys in navigable waterways. By undertaking programs of general historic preservation planning in their areas of concern, as discussed in Chapter 8, permitting agencies can go a long way toward discharging their responsibilities without putting undue burdens on permittees. Having developed a broad general understanding of the distribution and nature of an area's historic properties, an agency can establish permit-application requirements that do not demand surveys when the probability of discovering anything is very slight. Most permitting agencies at the moment have only rather haphazard procedures for deciding whether surveys are necessary in advance of permitted projects, but many have expressed interest in making their procedures more rigorous.

State and Local Agencies

Unless they have their own statutes requiring it, state and local agencies are not required to be concerned about historic preservation when they plan projects unless those projects are done with federal money, assistance, or permission (see McGimsey 1972; Klinger 1975 for summaries of state statutes). Federal involvement in local programs is now sufficiently pervasive, however, that some local governments are employing historians, archeologists, or whole preservation teams, and the SHPO has become an important coordinative figure in state government. The growing importance of the SHPO creates great opportunities for state-level historic preservation; the SHPO is in a position to help influence state legislation, to advise state and local agencies in professional preservation matters, and to coordinate state agency and local preservation activities with the statewide survey and historic preservation plan authorized by the NHPA. On the other hand, the SHPO often comes under pressure from powerful state agencies whose programs are held up by federal requirements in which the SHPO plays a role. Instances of collusion between SHPOs and other state agencies to circumvent federal requirements are not entirely uncommon, and have thus far been the subject of at least one legal challenge (*NYAC* v. *Train et al.*).

An unusual case is presented by local governments that receive block grants from the Department of Housing and Urban Development under terms of the Housing and Community Development Act of 1974. The act conveyed to local governments receiving block grants the responsibility for compliance with NEPA, rather than reserving this responsibility to the Department of Housing and Urban Development. The department, in its regulations, extended this responsibility to cover compliance with the NHPA and Executive Order 11593. Thus block grant recipient governments must establish their own historic preservation policies in order to attend to their federal responsibilities. Another unique aspect of the Housing and Community Development Act is that it permits use of block grant funds as the local match for historic preservation grants from OAHP; this eases the burden of preservation planning on local governments by providing them, potentially, with 100% federal funding.

The Department of Housing and Urban Development is preparing guidelines to assist block grant recipients, as well as its own personnel, in dealing with archeological problems (HUD n.d.), and OAHP is preparing recommended procedures for historic preservation surveys using block grant funds (OAHP 1977a).

Contracting Entities

Most fieldwork in historic preservation today is done, and will continue to be done, under contract. The need for contractors to be responsible for what they do, to their sponsors, their professional ethics, and the historic properties on which they are working is becoming more and more urgent. Organizations that participate in historic preservation activities under contract include academic institutions, museums, private firms, private parties, and private organizations. All share the characteristic of working on a project by project basis, but there are many approaches that can be taken to this manner of working. Some contractors are, of course, flatly and exclusively interested in profit. Such an attitude is by no means exclusive to private firms and individuals, as some writers have implied (cf. McMillan *et al.* 1977); it is very common among academic institutions that look upon historic preservation activities as simply a good way to keep graduate students alive. Profiteers, especially academic profiteers, often do excellent technical work, but they are often poorly informed about historic preservation statutes and standards, and they are often unimaginative in their approaches and pliant to agency restrictions. A continuing serious problem with archeological contracting bodies of all kinds is their failure to become familiar with the historic preservation statutes and regulations. Such contractors take an agency's money to help it comply with the laws, and then provide reports that bear little relationship to that compliance. Some contractors, on the other hand, have learned that the federal government no longer simply funds an archeological survey and whatever salvage the survey report recommends. These contractors attempt to tailor their reports to agency needs. Some, of course, may tailor their reports to the point of assisting agencies in avoiding their preservation responsibilities altogether, but this appears to be rare. A good many—and this observation applies primarily to private firms and individuals—establish "cookbook" approaches to their work, conducting surveys, documenting properties, and writing reports in a very standardized fashion consistent with what they perceive to be the documentation needs of the agencies. Standardization has some obvious advantages, both for the processing of paperwork by federal review agencies and for comparative research, but cookbook approaches are often simply means of concealing an inability to do imaginative research. This, in turn, may indicate that the sponsor agency is receiving narrow, unimaginative advice that will be subject to question during review.

Some contracting entities make a concerted effort not only to understand the laws but to develop systematic plans for whole areas or activities, that give coherence to their individual contract projects. Most such plans are developed by university-based researchers or by multi-institutional organizations. Developed in isolation from, or ignorance of the statutory requirements of sponsor agencies, these plans can result in biased reports that do not fulfill the mandates of the law. For example, if a group of archeologists decided on a research design for a given area that systematically ignored prehistoric sites in favor of postcontact sites, implementation of this design through contract work would not fulfill the requirements of the law. Plans that do reflect understanding of the laws, or at least that do not conflict with them, are, of course, much to be desired; they will facilitate contract research and should be an integral part of statewide historic preservation planning. We will discuss such plans in greater detail in Chapter 8.

Professional Organizations

There are many kinds of professional organizations pertinent to historic preservation. There are established scholarly groups like the Society of Architectural Historians and the Society for American Archeology that publish papers, sponsor meetings, and otherwise promote information exchange. There are local, state, and regional groups that meet to discuss common problems both in research and in preservation. Increasingly, there are professional groups that come together for political action, and finally there are professional groups that attempt to regulate the professional activities of their members.

The need for regulation is clear. Contractors cannot balance their professional responsibilities against the demands of clients without some acknowledged set of professional standards. Professional employees of government need a clear code not only to follow but to use in their presentation of points of view within their agencies. Clients need help in identifying persons who will perform reliable professional services, and all need some forum in which to air grievances about professional behavior.

The dangers of regulation are equally clear. The primary long-term danger is simply that of closing research markets to innovative thought and cross-pollination from different areas and disciplines, resulting in intellectual atrophy. Some regional organizations have attempted this kind of closure in a fairly straightforward way, asserting that their understanding of their particular areas demanded that no one else be permitted to work there. Most regional groups, however, have recognized that such an attitude is both questionable legally and dangerous intellectually, and have adopted instead the quite defensible position that incoming scholars have a professional obligation to consult with local workers and to be sensitive to their research designs and priorities.

Certification for architects has been a reality for many years; nationwide regulation of archeologists has begun with the formation of the Society of Professional Archeologists and issuance of its first *Directory of Professional Archeologists* (Jelks et al. 1976).

Some regional and statewide organizations undertake contract work in addition to their data-sharing, standard-setting, and regulatory functions. This practice has obvious dangers if the organization acts in any way to exclude potential competitors, but it has advantages in that the total group naturally has greater flexibility and scope than does any one of its members, and can thus provide a broader range of services while maintaining high standards. One of the most promising undertakings for any state-level professional group is the establishment of a contractual relationship with the SHPO to participate in the statewide survey and preparation of the state historic preservation plan. The Illinois Archeological Survey pioneered this kind of relationship in 1970, and variations have since been adopted by the Washington Archeological Council, the New York Archeological Council, the Society for California Archeology, the Arkansas Archeological Survey, and the Ohio Archeological Council, among others. We will have more to say about the promise of this sort of relationship in Chapter 8.

THE LANGUAGE

Effective participants in historic preservation have command of a somewhat esoteric language, whose use and understanding are necessary to effective communication and practice. Some of the terms discussed in this section have been used in previous chapters in describing the evolution and current operation of the historic preservation system and its legal base. Here, we will try to present the meaning of the terms as they are understood by historic preservationists, and to discuss ways in which varying uses of each term may serve to confuse.

The National Register

The National Register of Historic Places is both a division of OAHP and a growing set of files precisely locating and describing the nation's significant historic properties. The Register is not meant to contain only preservable properties, or only properties that would serve as National Landmarks. Rather, it is meant to include all properties that should be somehow taken into account in planning modern land-use and development. Thus eligibility for the Register is the threshold that a property must reach in order to be considered extensively in agency planning. There are certain kinds of planning that can deal with properties whose eligibility for the Register has not yet been determined, and these will be discussed in Chapter 8. Such planning, however, still occurs with reference to the National Register because it simply puts off the time at which the properties will be evaluated and determined eligible or ineligible, avoiding impact on them in the interim.

Had all historic properties in the nation been located, identified, and fully evaluated, planning for their treatment would be relatively easy. Since this has not yet happened, surveys must be done.

Survey

Of all the words in preservation's lexicon, "survey" is perhaps the most misunderstood. It would perhaps be better to say that it is perfectly well understood, but understood differently by different kinds of people.

When the Historic American Building Survey was established, the word already served as a noun and a verb, with internally varying meanings. The noun meant, and means, both the process of surveying and the organization that undertakes the process. In the HABS context, the verb meant both to locate historic buildings and to subject them to detailed measurement and description. Rather little thought was given by HABS, or by the Historic Sites Survey which functioned within similar definitions, to the problems involved in locating historic sites and structures. The sites of historic events had usually not been lost to memory, and historic buildings were visible. The HABS and HSS teams came to emphasize the documentation aspects of survey; a HABS survey produces an enormous compilation of measured drawings, photographs, and other documentation on a selected group of buildings, while the proceses by which this group of buildings was selected out of all the things in the real world that must have been observed by the HABS team are not usually exhaustively considered.

Archeologists working for the River Basin Surveys defined the noun "survey" much as did HABS and HSS, but the verb was something else again. To River Basin Survey workers, the basic function of survey was to find sites appropriate for excavation. There was no particular need to record in detail all individual sites as they were found; real documentation, to an archeologist in the 1940s and 1950s working on problems of culture–history, usually required excavations. Archeologists thus came to define "to survey" as "to find," or at least, "to search for."

Over the years, architectural historians have increased the sophistication of their survey methods by using better measuring devices, better cameras, and photogrammetry, and they have developed detailed documentation procedures (cf. McKee 1970). The "searching for" aspects of survey have commanded little architectural interest; typically approved methods range from walking up and down the street to driving up and down the street, after conducting background research into local history.

Archeological survey methods have also improved greatly over the years, but the improvements have come largely in the methods employed in searching. A concern for controlling the observational biases of surveyors, who may notice only what they are interested in or only what they have been trained to regard as important, has led to the development of techniques to ensure that all ground surfaces in a study area are looked at in a reasonably consistent way. A similar concern has resulted in attempts to precisely define "site-ness"—to define standards by which one could decide whether one had found an archeological site when one had found something on or in the ground. New technology has been employed, ranging from remote sensing to the use of backhoes and power-augers, but the emphasis remains on searching rather than describing. In the recent past, a greater concern for documentation has emerged; archeological site record forms have tended to grow from the typical single page or edge-punch card of the 1950s to multipage forms that require information on the local environment, distributions of surface artifacts, topography, survey conditions, and so forth. These changes have arisen in part because of the requirement for increased documentation created by federal law, but they are primarily the result of a recognition by archeologists that a good deal of data could be obtained from survey alone that would be of assistance in dealing with research problems concerning settlement patterns, subsistence practices, and other acts that social groups perform on the ground. Although documentation of properties per se has thus improved, the modal definition of archeological survey continues to be: "the systematic search for archeological sites."

Historic preservation calls for both noun and verb surveys, and for both searching and documentation. Since the same word continues to be used for all meanings, it is important to understand the contexts in which it is used.

First, each state must conduct a "comprehensive statewide survey" of historic properties [NHPA Sec. 101(a)(1)]. This is a noun-survey; each state must institute a survey process. In many states, the process is implemented under the title of the State Historic Preservation Survey. The comprehensive survey is eventually supposed to identify all significant historic properties in the state; hence it is to provide for survey-as-search. Survey methods are to be fully documented, and the SHPO is to coordinate all other survey efforts done under federal sponsorship in the state to ensure consistency (Draft 36 CFR 60: Appendix A).

The comprehensive survey is not intended to be completed overnight; the survey data it produces are added to as the survey progresses, and are used in planning as they accumulate. The hoped-for product of the comprehensive survey should be a combination of the best sorts of surveys from both architectural and archeological points of view; we should be confident that the ground has been covered and all historic properties found, and we should have detailed documentation on each. Until all the state comprehensive surveys are complete, other kinds of surveys will continue to be necessary, particularly in advance of federal undertakings. Surveys of project impact areas are very much like state comprehensive surveys in microcosm, and they have the same ultimate ends: the complete identification of all historic properties, their documentation to a level sufficient to judge their eligibility for inclusion in the National Register, and their incorporation into the land-use planning process. A survey is not the "quick and dirty" run-through that it was in River Basin Survey days, to find the sites that looked best for excavation. Neither is it the detailed documentation of a few outstanding buildings to the exclusion of all other properties. Less-than-complete surveys have their place in the planning process, but the information needed for decision making about a project, or in the long run about the management of a state's repertoir of historic properties, can only be the fruit of both comprehensive search and careful recording.

It should be noted, however, that there is nothing in any of the historic preservation laws that says that federal agencies must conduct surveys in advance of their undertakings. The executive order says that inventories are to be made in order to identify properties; NEPA says that cultural and historical aspects of our heritage are to be preserved; NHPA directs that properties in or eligible for inclusion in the National Register be considered in planning, but nowhere are federal agencies directed by statute to conduct surveys. That states are expected to conduct surveys, in accordance with standards set by the Department of the Interior, is clear from the NHPA [Section 101(a)(1)]. In the long run, then, it is the comprehensive statewide surveys that are to identify properties eligible for the National Register, which should be preserved through wise federal project planning. The need for federal agencies themselves to sponsor surveys arises from the incompleteness of the state surveys, and the impossibility of otherwise identifying historic properties.

Plans

The statewide historic preservation plan is conceived of as a document that integrates a complete state preservation program. Such a program should be based on a clearly defined philosophy and executed by a qualified staff. It should include a systematic survey of the state, nominations to the National Register, interagency coordination to ensure that local, agency, and state programs are consistent with the statewide plan, review of proposed construction and other land-use projects, actions to acquire, protect, study, and restore appropriate properties, and public education. Documentation of the program on a periodic basis constitutes the plan, and is submitted to OAHP for review and approval (36 CFR 60; draft 36 CFR 60; Appendix A).

Just as local and project-level surveys should be consistent with and contributory to the comprehensive statewide survey, it is only plausible to think that local preservation plans and plans for the preservation of properties in connection with particular projects should be consistent with the state plan, and help fulfill its objectives. Most state plans at the present time are poorly developed and extremely unsophisticated, however. They do not provide sufficient guidance to constitute a basis for clear local and project planning. Since the amendments to the NHPA passed in 1976 provide increased funding for state historic preservation planning (see Appendix A), a rapid increase in the quality of such plans can be expected. We will have more to say about the potential development of state plans in Chapter 8.

Determination of Eligibility

Federal agencies that locate historic properties in compliance with NEPA, NHPA, or Executive Order 11593 determine their eligibility for inclusion in the National Register by first applying the National Register criteria set forth at 36 CFR 60.6 to them. They do this in consultation with the SHPO, usually by writing, with documentation, and saying "we think these things are eligible and these others are not; what do you think?" Ideally, the agencies are assisted in their determinations by professionals who located the properties during surveys, and whose reports include a careful application of the Register criteria. The criteria read as follows:

> *National Register criteria for evaluation.* The quality of significance in American history, architecture, archeology, and culture is present in districts, sites, buildings, structures, and objects of State and local importance that possess integrity of location, design, setting, materials, workmanship, feeling, and association, and
>
> (a) That are associated with events that have made a significant contribution to the broad patterns of our history; or
>
> (b) That are associated with the lives of persons significant in our past; or
>
> (c) That embody the distinctive characteristics of a type, period, or method of construction, or that represent the work of a master, or that possess high artistic values, or that represent a significant and distinguishable entity whose components may lack individual distinction; or
>
> (d) That have yielded, or may be likely to yield, information important in prehistory or history [36 CFR 60.6 & 800.10].

If the agency and the SHPO agree that the properties do not meet any of the criteria, the matter goes no farther and no further attention is paid to the properties; they may be destroyed with impugnity. The only exception to this rule comes when a responsible person (for example, the professional who recorded the properties) questions the appropriateness of the determination. In this case the agency should go to OAHP for a final determination; if it does not, it is possible for OAHP to take several steps, the most drastic being to determine unilaterally that the property is eligible over the heads of the agency and the SHPO (cf. *Stop H-3 Association v. Coleman*).

If the agency and the SHPO agree that the properties are eligible, or if they cannot agree, or if some other question exists about the eligibility of the properties, they should go to OAHP for a final determination. The documentation required by 36 CFR 63 should be supplied to OAHP (see Appendix A) if there is any question about the eligibility of a property. If no question exists, and the agency and SHPO have reached a consensus determination that the property is eligible, 36 CFR 63 allows submission of much less documentation.

Only when a property has been determined eligible does it qualify for preservation, either through physical protection or through salvage data recovery.

A careful distinction should be made between determination of eligibility and nomination to the National Register. Nominations are processed by the state historic preservation officer with recommendations from the state review board, which consists of professionals in architecture, history, architectural history, and archeology, plus citizen members, all approved by OAHP. There is a good deal of potential for political dealmaking and exercise of quixotic bias on state review boards. Ostensibly, the state plan should outline a basis for making decisions about nominations that would eliminate the possibility of bias dominating a review board's considerations, but few plans have yet reached such a level of sophistication. Determinations of eligibility do not go through the review board for consideration; there is seldom time in the project planning process, and in any event, the role of the SHPO, and hence of the review board, is only consultative, not determinant. Thus, the fact that OAHP may determine a property eligible for the National Register when the review board would not consider a similar property for nomination means nothing other than that the SHPO should reconsider the structure of the review board.

Memorandum of Agreement

A memorandum of agreement should be the outcome of consultation with the advisory council under its *Procedures* (36 CFR 800; Appendix A). Once an historic property has been determined eligible for the National Register, or nominated and accepted for inclusion in the Register, if an agency's action will have an adverse effect on it, the agency must consult with the council. This, of course, does not mean sitting down around a table with the secretary of agriculture, the secretary of defense, the chairman of the National Trust, and all their councilfellows. It means consulting with the advisory council staff to see what can be worked out. Technically, the agency must first prepare a "pre-liminary case report" setting forth the facts of the matter: What is the property? What is the undertaking? What will be the effects of the undertaking on the property? What does the agency propose to do about it? The council staff can then request further levels of consideration, if it feels they are necessary, during which the undertaking itself must be suspended in planning or implementation. An "on site inspection" may be called for, in which the council staff visits the property with whomever else seems relevant, in order to gain first-hand informa-tion. A "public information meeting" may be held at some location close to the property, to obtain public response and advice. These rather eleborate and time-consuming activities are not required by law or regulation, however. They are things that the staff *may* require if it feels they would be useful. The upshot of the whole consultation process should be a memorandum of agreement, signed by the agency, the advisory council, and the SHPO; an example of such a memorandum is given as Appendix C. The memorandum of agreement spells out what will be done to avoid or mitigate the adverse effects of the project on the property, and is binding upon the signatory parties.

In some cases it is possible for an agency to negotiate a "programatic memorandum of agreement" with the council when actual properties have not yet been completely identified. Such a memorandum stipulates what the agency will do to assure substantive compliance with the council's *Procedures* when literal compliance would be unreasonably difficult. For example, when an agency proposes to sell leases in a very large area for oil exploration, it may fund a predictive survey (see Chapter 8) and use its results to formulate a plan for specific identification and protection. Council approval can then be sought for the plan, in lieu of case-by-case compliance.

No Adverse Effect

If an agency can demonstrate to the advisory council's satisfaction that, even though its project may affect a National Register or Register-eligible property, the effects will not be adverse, it need not go through the consultation process. The agency makes a determination of "adverse effect" or "no adverse effect" in consultation with the state historic preservation officer, and sends documentation of the basis for this determination to the council. Unless the council objects within 45 days, the determination stands. In certain cases, as discussed in Chapter 7, it is possible to determine that the destruction of an archeological property, with appropriate data recovery, does not constitute an adverse effect. Such a determination is proper, however, only if all concerned are agreed that data recovery constitutes the best way to preserve the property's value. Appendix A includes the council's policy statement setting forth circumstances under which such a determination is appropriate (also see King 1977a for discussion).

Council Comment

In an adverse effect situation, if it is impossible to reach a memorandum of agreement, the council must be afforded an opportunity to comment formally on the undertaking. This comment is made by the council itself, not the staff, but it typically is based upon the staff position. The comment is made to a high level within the responsible agency. In the context of the review prescribed by NEPA, such a comment indicates that the undertaking will have irreversible and irretrievable impacts on the environment, and the project should be reconsidered in this light. If there are reasonable ways of avoiding or mitigating the impacts, the failure of the agency to adopt such methods is probably open to legal challenge. The council itself cannot halt projects permanently, however. It can delay them until it has commented, but if an agency wishes to take its chances and proceed despite the council's comments, it can do so.

The Advisory Council Procedures

Most of what has just been discussed is derived from the advisory council *Procedures,* the actual title of which is *Procedures for the Protection of Historic and Cultural Properties,* 36 CFR 800 (see Appendix A). The *Procedures* specify methods for compliance with two authorities, the NHPA and Executive Order 11593, and they interlock with the *Guidelines* issued by the Council on Environmental Quality for compliance with Section 101(b) (4) of NEPA (40 CFR V 1500; Appendix A). The *Procedures* have been discussed in Chapter 3, and diagrammed in Figure 3, but it may be useful to summarize the basic steps an agency must go through in compliance with them in advance of a project.

1. As early as possible in the planning process preceding the project, the agency must identify all properties in or eligible for inclusion in the National Register that are subject to possible effect as a result of the project. In the absence of complete comprehensive statewide surveys, this typically requires that a survey be done by the agency, covering all areas subject to impact in order to identify all kinds of historic properties (see Chapter 6). In consultation with the SHPO, the agency then applies the National Register criteria to each property discovered and, if any of them appear to meet the criteria, requests a

determination of eligibility from OAHP. If properties are already listed in the Register, of course, the determination step is eliminated.

2. If it turns out that eligible properties do exist within the area subject to impact from the project, the agency then applies the "criteria of effect" and "criteria of adverse effect" set forth in 36 CFR 800 to determine what its project will do the properties. This exercise is also done in consultation with the SHPO. If this consultation reveals that the project will have no effect of any kind on the properties, the agency merely retains documentation of this fact and proceeds. If an effect will occur, but the effect does not appear to be adverse, the agency makes a determination of "no adverse effect" and provides documentation of the basis for its determination to the council. This documentation can be quite simple—clear evidence that a highway alignment will miss an historic house and not intrude on its visual environment, for example—or extremely complex. When a determination of "no adverse effect" is made based on a program of data recovery, precise documentation standards must be met, the property itself must be shown to meet particular criteria, and a research design for the data recovery project must be submitted for review (see Appendix A). The council then has 45 days to consider the determination; if it does not object within that time, the project can proceed.

3. If it appears that an adverse effect will occur, or if the council objects to a determination "no adverse effect," the agency must undertake consultation with the council staff. This may or may not require an on-site inspection or a public information meeting. The agency prepares a "preliminary case report" discussing the nature of the historic properties involved, the nature of the project, and nature of the expected adverse effects, and proposals for avoidance or mitigation. The council staff, in consultation with the agency and the SHPO, then tries to develop a memorandum of agreement specifying effective methods of avoidance or mitigation.

4. If all goes well, the council, the agency, and the SHPO all sign the memorandum of agreement. The project proceeds subject to the terms of the memorandum. If the parties cannot agree, the matter must be taken up by the council itself at one of its regular meetings, and a formal comment offered to the agency. The agency can then proceed with its project, noting the adverse council comment (if, after consideration of the staff's recommendations, the council *does* comment adversely) in its environmental planning documents.

The Planning Process

When "the planning process" is referred to in most historic preservation contexts, what is meant is both the process of planning a project and, more specifically, the processes prescribed by NEPA, the *Guidelines* of the Council on Environmental Quality, and the advisory council *Procedures* for the considera-

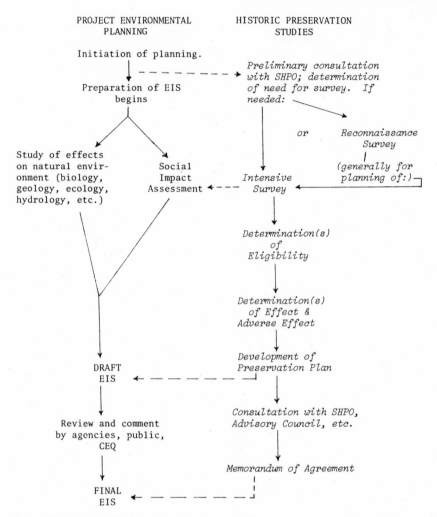

Figure 8. *General relationship of historic preservation to environmental planning on a federal project.*

tion of historic and other environmental resources during project planning. Figure 8 diagrams the integration of historic preservation planning into the overall planning process prescribed by the Council on Environmental Quality (40 CFR V 1500; Appendix A). How the planning process works, and how it sometimes breaks down, will be discussed in Chapter 7. (For more detailed information on agency programs and policies see National Trust 1976a and OAHP/Advisory Council 1977.)

The whole historic preservation system is clearly oriented toward the protection of significant historic properties, that is, those that qualify for inclusion in the National Register. Before we go further in discussing and illustrating how the system works, we need to confront the sticky problems surrounding the ways in which significance is defined.

5

SIGNIFICANCE

Sooner or later we shall have to face it: to modern man, all buildings are buildings of historic interest.

—Sir John Summerson, quoted by
R. W. Howland in *With Heritage so Rich*

The National Register is the pivot upon which historic preservation in the United States turns. Properties that qualify for the Register are the subject matter of historic preservation, and they are eligible for preservation, enhancement, and salvage. If they do not qualify, they are not worth worrying about. The bluntness of this pivot is one of the major sources of trouble for historic preservation.

Historic preservation has grown and evolved from an inchoate wish for the perpetuation of landmarks to a concern with the fabric of communities and the integrity of a scientific data-base. The boundaries of its expanding range of vision are broken and uncertain, however. They are represented by an uncomfortable but necessary modifier—"significant." The National Register is to list properties "significant in American history, architecture, archeology and culture [NHPA Sec. 101 (a) (1)]"; the Archeological and Historic Preservation Act mandates the recovery of "significant scientific, prehistoric, historic or archeological data [AHPA Sec. 3(a), 3(b)]." The very centrality of the significance concept has made regulation writers shy of defining it beyond the level of precision offered by the National Register criteria (30 CFR 60.6). In practice, evaluators tend to interpret the criteria as measures of utility. Does the property being evaluated have some sort of useful function in terms of our understanding or appreciation of the past, or in terms of maintaining the quality of our existing and future environments? To meet the criteria, the property must arguably have at least a potential role to play in maintaining the integrity of a community or neighborhood, in the maintenance of some group's sense of place and cultural value, or in the enhancement of human knowledge. A property lacks significance when it has no utility at all or when its role is already played by some other entity. If one can tell all one needs to know about the distinctions between Shady Acres and Sunny Shores (see p. 6-7) from examining available documents about their construction, are the building themselves useful for research? If it is useful to study the behavior of the two tracts' residents, and they are engaged in that behavior so that one can study them behaving, is it useful to preserve their houses as permanent repositories of data on their behavior? Though exceptions no doubt exist, we tend to think not. In both cases there are other more immediate and complete sources of data about the tracts than their buildings themselves—the buildings are redundant. If we find it important to learn about the people who lived in Shady Acres 20 years ago, however, and to do so we need to look at the chemical weathering evident in the bottom layer of wallpaper in the living room of each house, *then* the buildings are useful and the tracts have significance.

The same principle applies to non-data-related values. If the character of a neighborhood in Shady Acres is particularly expressed in the carved lintels over the front doors of the houses and this character is valued by the community, its visitors, or the International Siblinghood of Lintelcarvers, the lintels and their architectural context are good for something—their continued existence maintains the valued character of the neighborhood. But if every house in Shady Acres has a similar carved lintel, then it would be very hard to argue that the lintels of one particular neighborhood define its character—the lintels are redundant.

Decisions about this kind of thing are made every day by the National Register, the state historic preservation officers, federal agencies, and individual preservationists. Over time, the decisions have become progressively more difficult, as the properties being evaluated have come less and less frequently to resemble Mount Vernon and Olduvai Gorge, and more and more often to be like Shady Acres. A systematic, thoughtful approach to defining significance is needed.

We have said that there are two large contact points between historic preservation and anthropology—in dealing with the research values of historic properties, and in defining the cultural value of such properties to the communities and social groups that are somehow associated with them. We can consider each of these aspects in turn.

RESEARCH VALUE

In discussing research value, two pieces of statutory and procedural language need to be considered. First, the National Register is designed to include properties of "national, state, and local significance." Anthropologists are unaccustomed to thinking of their research as having significance to anything less than all mankind, but as we will see, these "levels of significance" may be useful to us. Second, the National Register criteria (36 CFR 66.6) set forth one general standard that must be met, and four more specific standards, any one of which must be met in order for a property to qualify for inclusion in the Register. The general criterion is "integrity." "The quality of significance . . . is present in districts, sites, buildings, structures and objects . . . that possess integrity of location, design, setting, materials, workmanship, feeling and association . . . [36 CFR 60.6]."

This criterion was clearly written with buildings in mind; with respect to many archeological research concerns it becomes virtually indecipherable. Clearly, the information content of an historic property's significance turns on the information contained in spatial associations among its constituent entities. A property's value may be impaired by loss of integrity of "setting" if the relationships of property to environment are crucial to its research utility. It thus seems to us that the "integrity" criterion has meaning only as it interacts with the more specific criteria upon which the significance of the property is judged. An example may clarify this circumloquacious statement.

• Suppose we are evaluating the significance of a scatter of Early Woodland chert tools and flakes in the plow-zone of a piece of former farmland, now surrounded by factories, in western Pennsylvania. The material has been thoroughly mixed by plowing. We observe that the research value of the site lies in the fact that it can give us information about local stoneworking techniques and about patterns of regional trade. The first kind of information is embodied in the manufacture-related attributes of the tools and flakes; the second kind is embodied in the chemical composition of the material, which permits us to identify its sources. Contextual information would be nice, but not necessary; all we really need to know is that these objects, with their physical and chemical attributes, exist at this spot. "Integrity of workmanship" is represented by the fact that the ways in which the tools were made, and the flakes struck, can be ascertained. The need for "integrity of location and setting" is satisfied by the fact that, for purposes of this site's research value, the only important environmental datum is the site's physical location, which has not been changed. Similarly, the need for "integrity of association" is satisfied because the only necessary associational datum in this case is the fact that all the items occur together at this particular location. It follows that the requirement for "integrity of feeling" is satisfied by the fact that, for purposes of this site's research value, the necessary data on its feeling are nil. Conversely, of course, if the artifacts and flakes had been tumbled by a stream until their technological attributes had been lost, or irradiated until their chemical composition changed, then the site's integrity vis-à-vis the research values attributed to it would be compromised. Similarly, if we wished to study how Early Woodland toolmakers related emotionally to the products of their craft, we might be hard put to show that this site had not lost its "integrity of feeling."

As already noted (p. 87), the specific criteria for eligibility are:

> (a) [association] with events that have made a significant contribution to the broad patterns of our history; or
> (b) [association] with the lives of persons significant in our past; or
> (c) [embodiment of] the distinctive characteristics of a type, period, or method of construction, or that represent the work of a master, or that possess high artistic values, or that represent a significant and distinguishable entity whose components may lack individual distinction; or
> (d) [history of yielding, or potential] to yield information important in prehistory or history [36 CFR 60.6].

In most cases, research significance turns on criteria (a) and/or (d). Properties valuable for their data are associated with important "patterns of ... history" or they would not be worth investigating; they can yield information or they are not investigable. It is possible to argue that archeological properties should always satisfy both criteria—that we must know to what "patterns" the information in a site may relate before we can decide whether the information is important. Although we believe this is true in a general way, if carried out rigorously it could have the effect of protecting only those research values we can clearly recognize today, to the exclusion of those we may discover in the future.

Glassow and Spanne have discussed this problem in detail:

> In the past few years there has been an explicit effort made to couch research designs for salvage projects, of the type that may be undertaken in the project area, in a "deductive framework" (T. King 1971). That is, many archaeologists are now attempting to collect data from salvage excavations

that relate to a set of hypotheses and covering theoretical problems that were developed for a comparatively broad region prior to the beginning of any one salvage project in that region. . . . This logic may be extended to argue that sites which should be preserved are those that are relatively more critical to regional research designs. But, as Lipe (1974:227) points out, this approach fails to consider the probability that research interests are bound to change in the future as new problems develop and new analytical techniques are discovered. Lipe feels that this problem may be solved, insofar as proposing archaeological preserves is concerned, by including in preserves "the main varieties of sites found" in a particular part of the country (1974:228). This answer does not really go far enough, however. In determining initially what the "main varieties" are, the establishment of a typology of sites would be involved and as every good typologist knows, each typology is based on a set of differentiating criteria—in this case, attributes of sites—that are selected by the typologist from a potentially very large number. What governs the selection of criteria for establishing a typology of sites? In essence, we are back where we started.

For purposes of determining the relative importance of some 80 archaeological sites on a portion of Vandenberg Air Force Base where facilities of the Space Transportation System will eventually be built, not only the importance of particular sites to regional research designs was considered, but also criteria that will have a high probability of relating sites to future, yet-to-be-defined research designs. These additional criteria may be divided into five categories: (1) habitat, (2) physical characteristics, (3) temporal distinctiveness, (4) activity diversity, and (5) quality of preservation [Glassow & Spanne 1976:101–102].

Glassow and Spanne's attempt to set forth attributes by which a representative sample of prehistoric sites might be preserved for future research is essentially the same approach taken by one of us in dealing with historic sites, although of course the attributes are different.

In one study, written records and oral testimony were used as the basis for a projection of the kinds of historic sites that could be expected in a California agricultural valley. This study emphasized preserving a sample of historic sites representative of all the ethnic and occupational groups who had contributed to the valley's history. The research significance of individual sites was to be considered in terms of each site's relationship to the sample. In the second example, the history of a single ranch site in the southern California desert was studied within the social context of the region . . . to identify social and economic interactions. This provided a basis for evaluating how the ranch could be used to test theory-based assumptions about relationships between regional and local sociocultural change [Hickman 1977].

Thus there are two basic questions to be asked in evaluating the research value of a property:

1. *What specific research topics can be addressed here?*

2. *Does this property exhibit attributes that suggest a need to preserve it against the time when new topics will be formulated?*

Answering either question requires a command of anthropological theory, a knowledge of ongoing general research in the area, and—particularly with reference to Question 2—a body of regional data such that the site can be compared with others. We will return to this need later in this chapter and in Chapters 6 and 8.

It is clear that any reasonably imaginative soul can come up with a research topic applicable to almost any historic property; the problem is deciding on a triviality line, below which a research question is not worth consideration. Every science faces this problem, and answers are never clear-cut. We may be able to approach the problem by considering the provision made by the NHPA for "national, state, and local levels of significance." The National Register makes no distinction among these levels in the treatment of properties; the levels are just blocks on the nomination form. They were apparently included as much to remind nominators that the Register is not just for national landmarks as to serve any recordkeeping function. They can be used to structure a determination of research significance, however.

The National Level of Significance

What does the United States need to know about its past? On the whole, the needs of the nation are presumably the same as the needs of humanity in general, so the broad research questions that archeologists and anthropologists characteristically think of themselves as addressing are pertinent at this level. The really big questions—"Why is there war?" "Why is their social inequality?" "What are the limits to growth?" "What is a balanced economy?" "What are the elemental structures of the human mind?"—give rise to a series of slightly more on-the-ground questions that are actually addressed by scholars: "What are the relationships among changes in population density, interaction, and political organization?" "What is the relationship between the distribution of energy sources and that of population aggregates?" "What are the effects of population—environment disequilibrium?" "How is space used by people under different sorts of social conditions?" These sorts of questions can be addressed through the systematic study and comparison of archeological data, often in concert with data derived from ethnography and history. Each property, or each region with its properties, is one of Geertz's sheepy valleys, where answers were attempted to the problems of human existence, and these attempts can potentially be observed in the archeological record. If the data represented by a property give promise of advancing the study of such a general research topic, the property may be said to have national significance.

National significance also has a more particularistic aspect—the filling in of the nation's narrative history and the answering of particular major historical questions. When did the first people enter the New World? What happened to the Roanoke Colony? What difficulties were faced in provisioning Valley Forge? The lack of general theoretical interest represented by some such questions does not detract from their value as attempts to fully describe major episodes in the past.

The State Level of Significance

States are uncomfortable entities with which to work as units of archeological study. Few correspond with natural areas, and since prehistoric settlement patterns usually do relate somehow to natural environments, they tend to cross state boundaries with some abandon. This very lack of synchronism with the order of the environment provides historic archeologists with some opportunities that might otherwise not exist: Where environment is held constant, what variations will we see in settlement patterns, use of resources, sedentism, or community organization between, say, "wet" and "dry" states, or states where prostitution is legal and those where it is banned? To address these kinds of questions nevertheless requires the perspective of a natural region; the existence of the state line simply provides a useful independent variable.

It is unfortunate that states are hard to deal with, since it is at the state level that most historic preservation planning is done. States naturally have particularistic historical concerns; New Yorkers are very interested in Dutch colonists and Californians are involved with Spanish missions. There is a real danger that these interests may dominate state historic preservation plans to the exclusion of broader concerns.

The state's role in the definition of research topics that convey significance to historic properties is best thought of as one of integration and translation. Most scholars engaged in research are not directly involved in answering big questions about culture change and stability; they are asking and answering little questions about particular cases. It is, or should be, a role of state planning to relate small, local problems to big, national/universal ones. A good state plan will do this; it will specify how the kinds of research that can be done in various parts of the state can be brought to bear on large scholarly issues. In so doing, it will presumably set priorities—asserting that one kind of research should be undertaken soon, another held in abeyance—based on such pragmatic factors as where land development is going on and where land remains undisturbed, or which problems can be successfully addressed using present research methods and which cannot. It is in this context that "state significance" for research is usually to be understood.

The Local Level of Significance When a property is judged to be significant or insignificant in terms of research that focuses on a particular region or locality alone, the judgment is made in terms of local significance. When we assert that stratified shell midden SX-20 can help us construct a cultural sequence for the Texas coast, we are dealing in local significance. The same is true when we say that a group of surface scatters of nails and glass can help us reconstruct processes of socioeconomic change among early twentieth-century cowboys in the Little Belt Mountains of Montana. These sites can, of course, immediately attain national significance if the questions that give them meaning are tied into some larger issues, but this high level of significance need not be demonstrated in order to bring the historic preservation procedures to bear.

The Role of the State Historic Preservation Plan

Research questions, then, can be framed to confer significance or insignificance upon a property at two basic levels—local and national—and these levels may be integrated at the state level. If this does not immediately help us to define a triviality line, it at least should indicate the arena in which disputes over its delineation should be fought out. This arena is that of the state historic preservation plan. One function of a state historic preservation plan should be to define the kinds of data necessary to address research problems of both national and local significance, and to derive from this classification a guide to types of properties whose data content should be preserved in various ways. The plan should not only consider those questions now being addressed by scholars; it should also give attention to the probability that other questions will be asked in the future, and attempt to define the kinds of properties and data that should be preserved to maintain the likelihood that such questions can be fruitfully addressed. Thus, it should, in a sense, preformulate the questions to be asked about any given historic property in defining its significance. Does the prehitoric flint-chipping station in the Tlakipaki Valley contain nonlocal Hotchikotchi flints? The plan indicates that such sites may be valuable to the study of Tlakipaki–Hotchikotchi economic interaction, which in turn bears on the problems of political evolution among incipient horticulturalists; thus the site has national significance. Is the occupation site 40 feet deep, with 50 possible living floors? Then it can inform us about the culture–history of the Wet River Basin and the plan will accord it local significance if no other research questions can be conceived of to which it pertains. Was the building occupied and modified by members of a Korean revivalist sect during the late nineteenth century? Since this sect played a key role in the region's economic and political development, we can assume that they will be worth study, though no precise research questions have yet been formulated. Well-preserved properties representing a valid sample of their leavings should thus be useful for future research, according to the plan; if this building fits into such a sample, it is significant.

This way of dealing with significance puts much weight on the state plan, of course. The plan becomes, in part, a sort of super research design. It is vital that such a plan be responsive to all the research needs of the state and its scholars, that it have elements of flexibility, and that it be updated regularly.

McMillan *et al.* (1977) have put forth a proposed arrangement for the formulation of a state plan responsive to research needs, which appears to be reasonable. One crucial element of flexibility that must be maintained, however, is the assurance that, if a scholar can advance a reasonable argument for or against the value of a given property, the fact that the state plan has predetermined such properties to be significant or insignificant will not automatically override the scholar's point of view. In essence, the definition of research significance always comes down to an individual scholar developing a case for or against a given property. The state plan should provide an orderly framework upon which such cases can be built.

CULTURAL VALUE

Properties that are of cultural value to a group of people must of course also meet the National Register criteria. The ways in which they meet them must be defined in terms of the group's own perceptions of value. Taking the integrity criterion as a case in point: Suppose an old church has been taken over and lived in for several generations by a communal society of radical Trotskyites. The church was designed by a master of late eighteenth-century ecclesiastic architecture but Trotskyite carpenters have removed the steeple, cut away the ornamented altar, turned the sacristy into a communal kitchen, and replaced the stained glass windows with aluminum-framed storm windows. Does the building have integrity? To most architects, probably not, but to its resident community it does. The changes that have been made in the original structure represent community tradition, and it is the modified building, not the original church, that constitutes the community's valued life-space.

The building may also meet the first and second specific criteria of eligibility. It is associated with the establishment and growth of the society—certainly "events that have made a significant contribution to the broad patterns" of the society's history—and with the society's founders who are certainly "persons significant" in the group's past. The methods used in reorganizing the building may represent the work of masters in the eyes of the community and thus allow the building to meet the third specific criterion.

This interpretation turns on the assumption that the words "our history" and "our past" in the National Register criteria refer to the group of people which perceives the property as important. Since everyone would agree that Mount Vernon is associated with someone important in our national history, it is of national significance, but the National Register works at the local level as well, and here "our history" must mean local history.

In the evaluation of our hypothetical church, the architect should clearly have a say; the offenses perpetrated against the integrity of the original crafts-man's work should be fully recorded. The perceptions of the Trotskyites in this case should be represented, however, and this representation may be a job for the anthropologist. The historic preservation system was established for the benefit of all the nation's people, not only those interested in landmarks, the mansions of the great, or the nation's architectural traditions. The founders of historic preservation, however, were primarily concerned with landmarks and the commemoration of great people, and such elitism is still far from unknown in the discipline. Anthropology's major function in historic preservation is to help ensure that properties important to all sorts of people, and to the understanding of all sorts of cultural phenomena, are intelligently and efficiently treated. A primary context in which anthropologists can make contributions is that pro-vided by the surveys required for the operation of the historic preservation system. The next chapter will explore some of the methods and approaches that can be employed in conducting such surveys.

6

PRESERVATION SURVEYS

Compliance with the historic preservation statutes requires that federal agencies acquire and act upon data and professional advice in the identification and evaluation of historic properties. We assume that among those who will read this book are people who furnish or would like to furnish these commodities to those who need them. Archeologists, architects, and to some extent, historians have engaged in contract work for years, on salvage, evaluation, and restoration projects. The modern historic preservation system, however, requires new and more comprehensive ways of locating and dealing with historic properties. Anthropology can provide preservation surveys with a structure and organization that we think are appropriately broad and inclusive.

BASICS

Certain basic features distinguish historic preservation surveys from those conducted under archeological salvage laws and other authorities. These features should be clear in the mind of anyone undertaking such a survey. First, the obligation to identify *all* historic properties subject to effect by the project under study should be recognized. Obviously, this obligation is somewhat hypothetical; no one can guarantee complete identification. Still, the laws treat all kinds of historic properties, so the agency that is complying with the laws is responsible for them all. When the agency then contracts with a scholar for a preservation survey, in a sense, it transfers some of its responsibilities to the scholar, who in turn is well advised to know just what has been transfered. In most cases, what the agency really wants (whether it knows it or not) is a complete package investigation that will identify and evaluate all sorts of historic properties—it is this sort of investigation that we will discuss in this chapter. Often, however, the agency may not know quite what to ask for; it may ask for an "archeological survey" or a "cultural resource reconnaissance" or an "historic inventory." One should not assume that the agency knows what any of these terms mean, and should seek an understanding with the agency before undertaking the study. If the agency limits the study to some particular class of properties (prehistoric sites only, for example), one should (*a*) question the basis for this limitation (Is someone else doing history? If so, should we not communicate? If not, why not?), and (*b*) make sure that the limitation is clearly indicated in writing, to protect oneself against liability for what may be the agency's error.

Assuming one is asked to conduct a complete historic preservation survey, one should guard carefully against one's own biases. Archeologists, for example, are accustomed to the salvage surveys of the 1950s and 1960s, in which one went and looked at a project area with whatever precision one chose, and noted the sites that one wanted to dig. Specialists in prehistoric archeology often stumbled all over historic sites, and rumbled in and out of old buildings, looking for flakes and projectile points. Not only were nonprehistoric properties ignored, but often only those sites that struck the research fancy of the archeologist involved were recorded, or at least recorded well. Similarly, architectural historians engaged in urban-area surveys tend to have difficulty with the facts that standing buildings can contain archeological data, and that such data can also lie beneath the urban surface. These biases are entirely understandable, but they cannot be given free rein in an historic preservation survey. If one is unequipped to identify and evaluate the full range of historic properties likely to occur in a study area, one should find help in doing so.

It is also important to reach an understanding about the land area to be surveyed. In some cases, the impact area of a project may be the same as the construction boundaries; but in other cases it may be much larger (see Chapter 3). The ways in which areas of permitted, infrastructural, and other indirect impacts may be treated in a survey may vary depending on the immediacy of the effect and the extent to which the agency feels compelled to cope with its responsibilities. Obviously, one should try to get the agency to identify all properties subject to all kinds of effect. If the agency insists on restricting the survey to the construction area in a case where indirect impacts appear probable, one is well advised to discuss the possibility of indirect impacts in one's report, and make it clear that the decision to limit investigation was made by the agency. This will help to keep the agency from passing off an incomplete survey as complete, and protect the surveyor from undue accusations.

One should also be aware of the minimum standards provided by OAHP for both describing and evaluating historic properties. These are contained in 36 CFR 63 (see Appendix A). The identification procedures prepared by OAHP (36 CFR 64; Appendix A) also sets forth standards for documenting historic preservation surveys.

Finally, in preparing one's report on a survey, one should remember that the purpose of the survey is to help the agency comply with the laws. Accordingly, the report must mesh with legal requirements. And the tighter the fit, the more easily and effectively the compliance process will work. In discussing the significance of a property, for example, the report should address the National Register criteria, and set forth the reasons for thinking that the property does or does not meet each criterion, rather than simply discussing significance in the abstract and leaving it up to the agency and its reviewers to decide what is meant in procedural terms.

There is obviously a good deal of potential here for the development of a rigid, procedure-bound approach to historic preservation. One could interpret the need to identify all historic properties rather than focusing on those in which one is interested as a mandate for the kind of undirected research that characterized the least productive salvage archeology of the 1950s and 1960s (cf. King 1971). One could also interpret our insistence that scholars take cognizance of federal standards and guidelines, and cast their discussions in terms relevant to the compliance process, as approval of bureaucratic restrictions on intellectual freedom. We recognize this potential, and we know that the dangers are real. We will return to some of these dangers in Chapter 10. We think the dangers can be avoided, however. We believe that the procedures now in effect—at least the general ones provided by OAHP and the advisory council—not only provide plenty of room for intellectual freedom and scholarly exploration, but can serve to enhance them. If used carefully, the procedures can improve communication both within disciplines and across disciplinary boundaries by providing a mutually intelligible language for the discussion of concepts and data. They should encourage scholars to make their assumptions explicit and to report their observations clearly, and they should necessitate exchanges of views and information that would otherwise not be exchanged. They should require the conduct of many kinds of useful research in order to identify and understand historic properties—not the mere collection of many kinds of data for their own sake. They certainly structure one's research, but the structure is not meant to

inhibit thought; it is meant to facilitate communication and assure account-
ability to the public.

CONDUCTING A SURVEY: GATHERING DATA

It is convenient to think of the data-gathering aspect of an historic
preservation survey as having several parts, each associated with a major discipline, which are integrated in the final product of the survey. The basic elements
are historical, ethnographic, architectural, and archeological.

The Historical Element

The historian's definitive attribute is a concern with textual material. The
historian is not the only person who deals with texts, but the historian is the
most dependent on them, and the most highly trained in their use. The historical
element of a survey involves the development of a body of data about the study
area through the analysis of texts. The historian should not be concerned simply
with writing a narrative history of the study area, though this is almost invariably a tool that will be used. The functions of the historical element are (*a*) to
develop a framework within which individual properties can be judged as to their
historical significance, and (*b*) to identify particular locations or general areas
where historic properties can be expected. The second purpose is the more easily
understood and widely recognized. One studies old maps, atlases, travelers'
accounts, local histories, and so forth, to identify the locations of houses,
industries, camps, battles, or other things that might have left remnants worthy
of consideration for the National Register. This can be an exacting task. In
California, for example, it is possible to work out the approximate locations of
historic Indian villages that contributed neophytes to the Franciscan missions
through analysis of mission baptismal and death records. Moreover, it is possible
to calculate the populations of the villages and the periods during which the
villages were missionized. Working out the locations, however, involves a pains-
taking process of triangulation among recipient missions combined with analysis
of explorers' accounts and other sources of data (cf. C. King 1973). One can
identify the locations of properties from historical sources at a number of levels
of specificity, restricting oneself to published atlases and easily available maps,
interpreting published county histories and other published sources, or ferreting
out obscure and unpublished documents like the California mission records. The
level of specificity used will depend on one's judgment about what is likely to
emerge from the endeavor. In California, mission-period villages are a relatively
rare phenomenon that promise high yields of research data concerning culture-
contact and acculturation, and that are often of cultural importance to surviving

California Indian and Mexican–American populations; thus their identification is worth considerable effort in the eyes of most scholars. In western New York State, no one has ever seriously considered the research value of nineteenth-century farmsteads, nor are there particular social or ethnic groups who have expressed concern about them; accordingly, most scholars satisfy themselves with checking published county atlases to locate such properties during surveys.

This brings us to the other purpose of historical research in survey—the development of an evaluatory framework. Historic properties discovered in the field mean very little unless one has a reasonable understanding of the region's history; development of such an understanding is crucial to evaluation. Our approach to the development of such an understanding has been to identify the range of social and economic activities that have taken place in the area, then to identify the social groups associated with each activity, and then to identify the types of properties that may be associated with each social group. Doing this almost invariably requires immersion in a dismaying quantity of diverse historical detail and, after much sorting out and tying together, writing one's own history of the area. This is necessary for several reasons. First, published local histories are often slanted toward particular segments of the population. The history of the southern Santa Clara Valley of California, for example, appears to be a history of cattle barons, railroad tzars, successful horticulturalists, and land developers, until one begins to seek out data on the occupational groups that supported the economy. Very little information concerning these groups—including Chinese, Japanese, Mexican, and Filipino migrant workers, refugees from the dust bowl, and others—appears in county histories or biographies, but data can be found in government statistics, in works on sociology and economic history, in diaries and personal recollections, in newspapers, and in novels (cf. King and Hickman 1973; Hickman 1977). These kinds of primary material also supplement the more easily available works on those groups that do dominate the published historical record. Second, a broadly based social and economic history of the area, distinguishing major changes, trends, and interactions, is essential to the development of research questions. These questions provide a basis for assigning values to particular properties once they are discovered. Finally, identification of the groups that have participated in the area's history makes it possible to determine where community interests may exist that ascribe cultural importance to particular kinds of properties. Here, of course, historical and ethnographic elements overlap to the greatest extent, and should inform and support one another.

The Ethnographic Element

Ethnography in historic preservation, like history, has as its purposes identification and evaluation. Informants are sought who know where things are or were, and who know what has happened in the study area. Informants are not mere passive suppliers of data, however. They contribute their own evaluations and perceptions, which should be taken into account (cf. Vansina 1961).

Archeologists traditionally do a kind of ethnography when they interview farmers to ascertain what has been found in their fields. This can become an elaborate process requiring considerable ethnographic skill—as any archeologist who has worked with dedicated relic collectors knows—and it is vital to many surveys. The farmers, the foresters, the artifact-hunters, the roadbuilders and ditch-diggers have seen the land in its varied seasonal configurations, over years, and they have often seen beneath its surface in their furrows, holes, cuts, and trenches. They can provide valuable information based on observations that the scholar simply cannot make. The informants' perceptions and training must be taken into account. "There're no Indian sites on my land," said a farmer to one of our colleagues; "My family never let 'em on the property!"

Another sort of ethnographic recording involves gathering data from historical societies, landmarks organizations, and other local interest groups concerned with historic preservation. These groups naturally often have access to detailed data on what used to be, or still is, where. Again, the perspectives of the informants must be allowed for: Ask about Victorian farm houses in the Santa Clara Valley and you will receive a wealth of facts; ask about the campsites of migrant strawberry pickers and you will receive blank looks.

To obtain data on less obvious historic properties, or those not associated with the economically dominant social groups, it will often be necessary to seek our informants associated with the particular groups that created or used the properties. These people can usually be identified, sometimes indirectly, from the historical data and through historical societies. In the Santa Clara Valley, one of us sought out representatives of Japanese, Filipino, Chinese, and Mexican-American groups to get information on historic sites associated with their ancestors who had worked in the area as farmers and farm laborers (Hickman 1977).

The ethnographer has a larger task than simply to identify properties; informants also have things to say about significance. Some informants, of course, are quite able and willing to defend their interests. When the Corps of Engineers proposed to dam up Tahquitz Canyon, near Palm Springs, California, the Agua Caliente Band of Cahuilla Indians not only supplied large amounts of ethnohistorical information to demonstrate the cultural importance of the Canyon, but helped collect and interpret archeological data and nominate the area to the National Register (cf. Wilke 1975). Others, however, may be more reticent. People and groups who are unaccustomed to participating in policy-making, or even to speaking in front of groups, may simply be unable to do so, whatever their deeply felt concerns may be. They may even be unable to put these concerns into words. It is a task for the ethnographer to ferret out these concerns and figure out how they relate—if they do—to the agency's historic preservation responsibilities.

Perhaps the most elaborate current instance of ethnographic research in the service of historic preservation has been the program undertaken in Alaska under terms of the Alaska Native Claims Settlement Act (P.L. 92-203). Here ethnographers have worked with native groups to define places of historical significance to be claimed by the groups, applying criteria equivalent to (but varying slightly from) those of the National Register, but translating these into terms appropriate to Alaska native cultural systems (Schneider and others, personal communication 1976). Apple and Rogers (1976) have discussed the need for a similar translation of the criteria for historic preservation studies in Micronesia.

More than other specialists, the ethnographer's concerns extend beyond historic preservation into the broader field of cultural resource management. Any tangible property that functions somehow in the lifeways, beliefs, or institutions of a local group is likely to merit consideration under the historic preservation laws, provided it is not of entirely recent origin. But the ethnographer will very likely discover cultural resources such as social institutions and group interactions that lack particular referents in space, but will nevertheless be affected by the project under study. Such resources must be considered under terms of NEPA, but are outside the purvue of historic preservation (see Chapter 1).

The ethnographic methods used in historic preservation surveys are relatively traditional: interviewing, application of questionnaires, and observation. Because of the time constraints imposed on most surveys, the first two methods are more commonly used than the third. Ideally, ethnographic research should be undertaken after historical research has reached a point at which local groups, economic patterns, and the general structure of local history can be sketched out, to serve as guides for the selection of informants.

The Architectural Element

Architecture is concerned with space and living environments. The architect in historic preservation is concerned with how space has been used, enclosed, and structured at different times, by different people, in response to different stimuli, and with how the space thus structured continues to be used today. Architecture thus overlaps significantly with both ethnography and archeology; the architect is concerned with large, complex, semistationary artifacts used by extinct and extant social groups. The architect has the advantage of working with very tangible things that protrude above the surface of the ground. Finding them is thus not ordinarily a serious problem: One walks or drives or flies around and looks. Urban settings may present special problems:

Facades may have been added, new buildings may have crowded in front of old ones, and so on. But by and large, the search for architectural properties does not require quite the detailed planning that, for example, archeological search does. One does, however, have to decide what one is looking for; describing and evaluating properties are the taxing architectural activities. Any building *could* be of interest. Some architects may wish to record every building in a neighborhood, whereas others restrict their attention to particular types of buildings or representatives of particular time ranges, at the expense of others. For example, one historical architect engaged in a recent evaluation for preservation purposes decided that the vernacular architecture of a California desert ranch was insignificant because the buildings there were of "patchwork construction" (Historic Preservation Team 1975). Another architect might have found the buildings interesting precisely because their patchwork construction illustrates how their builders designed structures to cope with extreme environmental conditions and a scarcity of building materials. These sorts of biases and differential interests must be clearly understood at the beginning of the survey; the definition of what constitutes an architecturally important property is fraught with subjectivity.

Like ethnography, the architectural element of a survey should be undertaken after the historical element has gotten underway. It may be useful to initiate a program of ethnographic recording before undertaking architectural studies, as well. History and ethnography may identify particular architects, artists, or craftspeople whose work is represented in the area. They should also identify building periods during which particular architectural styles may be represented. Social, cultural, and economic events that may be reflected in the building or rebuilding of structures may be discovered. Uses or perceptions of space peculiar to particular groups may reflect themselves in architecture and may be discovered during historical and ethnographic research. Most generally, history and ethnography should help the architect develop a feeling for the area's spaces, its particular structural characteristics, and the aesthetic and spatial orientations of its occupants. With this understanding, the architect can begin to record structures with an emphasis on their significant features, and to evaluate them in a locally meaningful context.

As complex artifacts, structures also have value as data, and are thus in a broad sense archeological. How space is used and structured is itself an important data category, but there are many others of a more specific nature. How did the old mill work, and what does this tell us about the textile industry in this area during the nineteenth century? Do the additions to this house reflect increasing prosperity, increasing family size, or the availability of indoor plumbing? If the trot in a dogtrot house is closed off, does this mean the weather is getting colder, or that new concepts of propriety in living quarters are creeping in? Here the architect, the historian, the ethnographer, and the historic or industrial archeologist should be able to interact fruitfully.

In an ordinary survey, architectural data are typically illustrated with sketch-elevations, photographs, detailed drawings of key elements, and maps. The documentation should be sufficient to convey to reviewers the overall feeling of the property, its crucial features, and the basis for the architect's judgments about significance (see 36 CFR 63; Appendix A).

The Archeological Element

By considering history and ethnography as separate elements, we are in essence reducing archeology to the search—in the field—for historic properties on and under the ground. This reduction is, of course, only an artifact of our chapter organization. Ethnography and history are vital parts of archeological survey, and should be tightly interwoven with it.

There are some kinds of documentary research that are uniquely necessary for archeological survey. Archeology is concerned with historic properties representing all time periods, but it is particularly well equipped to deal with prehistoric sites. As a result, archeology requires background data on premodern environments, known prehistoric site distributions, and comparative settlement patterns, as a prelude to fieldwork. If there were Pleistocene lakes in the study area, or if the modern farmland was a marsh when the Spanish Conquistadores rode through, one wants to know about it in order to plan one's survey; otherwise the old beach ridges might not be given sufficient attention while time was wasted crawling through fields that were under water until 10 years ago. If reliable local surveys have indicated that prehistoric sites always occur on low ridges, one wants to know this too—not necessarily to believe it, but to let it serve as a basis for making predictions about the settlement patterns of the study area that can be tested through fieldwork. If worldwide ethnographic data suggest that hunter-gatherers always live within walking distance of key food resources, and local ethnography indicates that the residents of the study area were nonagricultural gatherers of mongongo nuts, one wants to try to predict where prehistoric mongongo groves would have been and give these locations special attention.

Some of the data needed by prehistoric archeology can be derived from historic documents—travelers' accounts, old maps, ethnographic and ethnohistoric reports. Other data sources are more technical: Soil maps available from local soil conservation districts are usually valuable for environmental reconstruction, as are some kinds of aerial photoimagery (cf. Lyons 1977). Archeological publications and files of extant data on local sites obviously must be checked. The archeologist's training as an anthropologist should give him or her access to useful comparative data and models through the published professional literature and through the Human Relations Area Files and its associated publications (cf. Lagacé 1974).

Field strategy is devised on the basis of the background data. It must be attuned to the identification of both historic and prehistoric sites and structures, and it should assure systematic, comprehensive coverage of the area. This does not mean that every inch of ground must be physically inspected in a standardized way. If one has good reason to believe that nothing will be found in a given location, or under given environmental conditions, or that only particular kinds of things will be found, it is certainly reasonable to adjust field methods accordingly. One's report should document these adjustments and indicate where and why they were made, and one must be prepared to have one's strategy questioned by reviewers. An inept strategy may result in a requirement by the sponsoring agency that the survey be redone.

Field methods, of course, must be appropriate to local conditions, and should be described in a comprehensible way. If local archeologists have worked out an understood taxonomy of survey types, this should be referred to. In California, for example, many consulting archeologists use a taxonomy recommended by the Society for California Archeology (1974) that distinguishes among such field survey types as "uncontrolled intuitive," "controlled sample," "intensive general surface," "intensive subsurface," and "mixed strategy." When such taxonomies are used, however, one should remember that not all reviewers may be familiar with them, and the meaning of descriptive terms should be supplied in the report.

In the desert Southwest, where the most comprehensive archeological field surveys have thus far been done, surface observation is often sufficient to identify most kinds of archeological properties, although excavation of some kind may be needed to obtain evaluatory data. As one moves east of the Rockies and north along the Pacific Coast, the need for subsurface testing becomes steadily greater as vegetation and active soil formation processes obscure the present surface and bury old surfaces. Thus in forested or turf-covered areas, systematic "shovel testing" or other techniques for subsurface exploration must be employed, and in some locations substantial excavation may be necessary (King 1977b).

As noted, standing structures are not as hard to find as sites, but the archeologist may require some adjustment in order to recognize their potential for providing data. The same principles apply to the data content of a building as to that of a site. One seeks evidence of human relationships, activities, and perceptions in the organization of material things, and one looks for evidence of change in that organization (cf. OAHP 1977, Appendix A). Collier (1967:77–104) provodes a concise discussion of the data content of rooms currently occupied by living groups; the same sorts of observations can be made with reference to abandoned structures that still contain the accoutrements of living or working (cf. Hickman 1977). That the former nature of rooms and structures, and past activities within them, can be reconstructed is obvious from the extensive literature surrounding the archeology of historic buildings (cf. Noel-Hume 1969). The existence of a building also eventually results in the creation of a site around it, as things are built, buried, and lost in its vicinity during its use.

The basis for archeological field strategy is essentially the same in both rural and urban settings, but the strategies that result may be quite different. In rural areas, background ethnographic and historical research will indicate where surface search or subsurface testing should be concentrated, but typically the whole study area will be subjected to some kind of inspection. In urban areas, it is usually impractical to examine the entire study area in depth, because to do so would require the removal of modern buildings, pavement, and so forth. In such areas more extrapolation from background and comparative data is necessary. Historical data should indicate where old buildings, old natural watercourses, and other areas of differential archeological potential underly the present city-scape, and subsurface testing can be applied to these areas in particular (King 1977b).

Once an archeological property has been found, be it a site or a structure, of prehistoric or more recent age, its evaluation for purposes of archeological research involves the answering of a seemingly simple question—can it yield useful data? We have discussed this question at some length in Chapter 5; at this point we need only say that one's thinking about value should be based on good descriptive data and be fully documented in the report of the survey. Do you think this prehistoric site may contain a cemetery that would provide data on prehistoric social organization? Why do you think there might be a cemetery, how might it be used, and what good will it do anyone to know about local social organization? Is it your opinion that this scatter of potsherds will not yield useful data? What kinds of data, then, do you regard as useful, and in what way does the sherd scatter not provide them? Are there other possible inter-pretations of usefulness? If so, have you rejected them in reaching your conclu-sion? If so, why? Do you believe that this old farmhouse can yield information on economic interactions in an early twentieth-century farm community? What attributes of the place could represent such information, how might they be studied, and why do we need to know about such things?

Obtaining sufficient data for evaluations of significance clearly requires a good deal of study and description of the property. One cannot get by with just the knowledge that there is a prehistoric site or an old house at such and so location. One needs to know enough about the thing to make some reasonably educated guesses about what is in it, and one needs enough knowledge of the archeology and history of the region, and of relevant theory, to make support-able judgments about what those contents might be good for. This may require that test excavations be done, that further historical background data be com-piled and analyzed, and that specialists be consulted.

DESCRIPTION

Basic standards for the presentation of descriptive data were set forth by OAHP in drafts of 36 CFR 63 and 64 (see Appendix A). Part 63, "Procedures for Requesting Determinations of Eligibility," included as an appendix a discussion of how various types of historic properties should be described in a request for a determination. Part 64, "Criteria and Procedures for the Identification of Historic Properties," included an appendix on the data that should be supplied in describing a survey. Neither regulation demands the unthinking outpouring of descriptive data, but each sets forth categories of information that should be discussed in order to ensure that readers and reviewers can understand what the writer has found and what the basis is for the evaluations. If one decides not to present any of the categories of information solicited by 36 CFR 63 and 64, the reasons for regarding such presentation as unnecessary or undesirable should be discussed.

SEQUENCING AND SCALE

It is obvious that the elements of an historic preservation survey should follow a predictable sequence in relationship to one another. This sequence is shown in Figure 9. The historical background study and whatever background research is necessary to archeological fieldwork design are the first things undertaken. The ethnographic element is implemented after some understanding of local history has been gained. Architectural and field archeological work can then get underway, informed by both history and ethnography. History and ethnography may be called upon for new data to test and elaborate on architectural and archeological conclusions once the fieldwork is complete.

As we have outlined it, an historic preservation survey looks like a pretty imposing undertaking. Naturally, the extent to which each element will actually be developed will depend on the nature of the project and the area. If there are

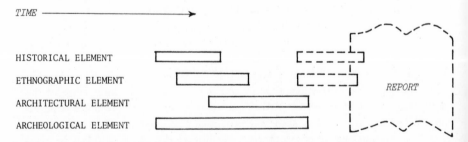

Figure 9. *Sequence of activities in an historic preservation survey.*

no buildings or structures in the area, an architectural element will be unnecessary. Historical research may very quickly show that some areas have had virtually no historic use, thus rapidly terminating both historical and ethnographic elements. Background environmental data or data on historic modifications of the land may show that prehistoric use of the area was impossible or that there is no chance that evidence of such use has survived, thus restricting if not eliminating the need for archeological fieldwork. If the project is one that will have only very limited, local effects—the replacement of an old sewer system with one of comparable size, for example, the need for extensive studies will be equally limited. Furthermore, as more studies are done, and their data internalized by scholars and incorporated into literature, future studies will become progressively easier.

EVALUATION

Once a survey has revealed the existence of historic properties in the area subject to effect by a project, if the sponsoring agency concludes that their existence will cause great difficulty to the development of the project, it is perfectly legitimate for the agency to decide not to proceed with the project, or to alter it to avoid any possible impacts. In such a case, evaluatory studies leading to a determination of eligibility are often not done, and the matter rests until some federal action does threaten the property or until it is evaluated in connection with the SHPO's comprehensive statewide survey or with a federal agency's surveys under terms of Section 2(a) of Executive Order 11593. Whenever evaluation does take place, there are things the surveying scholar can do to make it relatively easy and effective.

There are evaluatory implications in any collection of data. No one can help drawing boundaries beyond which things are just not regarded as significant enough to be observed. It is important to keep evaluation as separate from identificatory description as possible, and to specify how one progresses from the observation of what something is to the making of a judgment about what it may be good for. All too many statements of significance for archeological sites say things like: "this site represents the Midwestern Pluvial Tradition, which is over 7000 years old; therefore it is likely to yield important information." Similar nonsequiturs are found in historical and architectural statements.

All possible aspects of significance should be considered in evaluation, and each property recorded by the survey should be analyzed. If a property is considered to be significant, the reasons for thinking so should be set forth. If it is thought to be insignificant, the reasons for this should be indicated. Reference should be made to the National Register criteria (see Chapter 5) in such discussions; it should be shown that each property either does or does not meet

each of the criteria: 36 CFR 63 and the archeological recommendations provided by the National Register (see Appendix A) provide guidance in developing
discussions of significance.

IDENTIFYING EFFECTS

In most cases, one will have necessarily identified the types of effects that
a project will have when originally designing the survey (otherwise it would be
impossible to have defined an area in which survey was necessary). Once one has
actually identified significant historic properties, however, one needs to look
again at effects, as a basis for thinking about how good effects can be realized
and bad ones avoided or mitigated. Although it is relatively rare for a construction project to have positive effects on historic properties, the possibility of such
effects should be recognized. An urban renewal project that incorporates an
historic structure that was subject to deterioration and decay may provide for its
rehabilitation and reuse; an archeological site subject to vandalism and erosion
may be stabilized and preserved in the median strip of a highway. Sometimes, of
course, the effects of a project will be so heinous that no possibility exists for
balancing positive against negative. In most cases, however, it should be possible
to reach accommodations that protect historic values without stopping the
project. The first step toward doing so is to analyze carefully and completely all
the kinds of effects the project will have. Sometimes, the survey may uncover
data indicating effects that were not expected originally. Surveying a direct
effect area, for example, one may learn from local residents about expected
infrastructural effects. Even if one cannot then persuade the agency to study
these effects, they should be clearly noted in one's report, for reference by
reviewers.

One's discussion of effects should refer to, and utilize, the "criteria of
effect" and "criteria of adverse effect" provided by the advisory council *Procedures* at 36 CFR 800.8 and .9 (see Appendix A). These are very broad and
general criteria, but their use will help the sponsoring agency and its reviewers
relate one's comments to the agency's legal responsibilities.

RECOMMENDATIONS

The survey report should normally culminate in some recommendations
providing guidance to the agency in what to do next. Naturally, it behooves one
to know what the agency is legally obligated to do next, and at least avoid
recommending something illegal. Consulting with the SHPO and OAHP to obtain
a determination of eligibility is a normal next step after a complete survey, and

the SHPO is often consulted at the same time for assistance in applying the criteria of effect and adverse effect. The agency may need to be pointed toward the SHPO to engage in these consultations, and one's evaluations and comments on effects should provide the documentary base from which the consultation can proceed.

In most case, it is also appropriate to propose a preservation plan: a program for the avoidance and/or mitigation of adverse effects. If the plan is acceptable, it can simply be incorporated into the memorandum of agreement negotiated by the advisory council, the agency, and the SHPO at the end of the council's consultation process. An example of a memorandum of agreement is provided as Appendix C. If some (or all) of the properties dealt with in the preservation plan have not yet been determined eligible for inclusion in the National Register, the plan can be designed so that the elements referring to those properties can be dropped if the properties are determined not to be eligible.

Several general things should be kept in mind in drafting a preservation plan:

1. The advisory council and/or SHPO can request that other parties, beside themselves and the agency, be signatories to a memorandum of agreement. If the survey has identified local groups that have special interests in the properties subject to effect, one might recommend that they be involved in finalizing the memorandum. One might also discuss how to involve the group in order to ensure that the views of its members are really represented. The surveyor may know that the Bureau of Indian Affairs is not a recognized spokesman for a local Indian tribe, but the Corps of Engineers may not know unless it is told.

2. Normally, *in situ* preservation should be considered preferable to preservation through salvage data recovery, relocation of buildings, and so forth. Archeologists often have trouble with this priority, but the historic preservation laws are oriented toward the maintenance in place of as much of the historic environment as possible, and the need to preserve a reasonable sample of archeological data in the ground in now widely recognized (cf. Lipe 1974). On the other hand, one should not blindly assume that preservation in place is always preferable to relocation or recovery. If the house is infested with termites and dry rot, or the site is being eroded away, the best way to preserve anything at all may be to recover the valuable data and let the properties be destroyed. The reasons for each preservation recommendation should be spelled out.

3. Avoid trying to make the agency's policy decisions. It is important to stay within one's area of expertise, and not to try to tell the agency how to manage its overall affairs. It is up to the agency, taking a wide range of factors into consideration, to plan the location and nature of its project; one should not

try to insist that it would be a better project if located somewhere else or designed in some other way. This is not to say that relocation or redesign of the project should not be offered as preservation options, but one should not exceed one's expertise in arguing for or against a particular option. Similarly, one should avoid being influenced by considerations that go beyond historic preservation. The fact that a particular preservation option appears too expensive is not sufficient reason not to present it. It is in the agency's best interests to consider all options, rather than to have someone else suggest new ones during the review process. Conversely, the fact that one is biased against construction of a project because one regards it as an offense against a favorate natural ecosystem or a preferred trout stream cannot be allowed to influence one's recommendations unless the ecosystem or trout stream have something to do with historic preservation.

4. As many options as possible should be presented, in as much detail as possible, and the relative merits and demerits of each should be discussed. If particular options are favored, the reasons for favoring them should be specified.

THE PUBLIC NATURE OF SURVEY REPORTS

Some agencies are not above doctoring survey reports, or withholding them from review agencies. Reports that are prepared as base documents for preparation of environmental impact statements (EIS), are sometimes translated in peculiar ways when they are abstracted for inclusion in the EIS. One can seek several safeguards against this kind of misuse. If one's report is to be used for EIS purposes, and to be abstracted for inclusion in the published EIS, one can try to ensure that one's contract allows the author of the report to prepare the abstract. Every contract should include language guaranteeing that the author of the report will have continued access to the report and the right to distribute copies after acceptance by the agency. Each contract should clearly specify that a copy of the full report will be provided at least to the SHPO; in most cases it is wise to ensure that a copy is provided to OAHP or the advisory council, or both. If local groups or professional organizations are likely to have concerns about the properties discussed in the report, provision should be made for distribution to them as well. Not only is such distribution a basic professional responsibility; it will also protect the author from blame for the possible improprieties of the agency.

Thus far we have been discussing historic preservation in fairly abstract terms. We turn now to the problems faced by agencies and preservationists when these abstractions are applied to particular situations.

7

HISTORIC PRESERVATION
ON THE GROUND:
THE TANGLES OF LANGLES

However simple or complex historic preservation procedures may seem in the abstract, dealing with tangible cases is likely to bring them into focus. In this chapter we will construct seven cases illustrating the diversity of activities in which federal agencies engage, and we will discuss how historic preservation procedures are and can be integrated into these activities. In each case, we will try to identify problems and conflicts, and suggest needed changes in current policies and programs.

Figure 10 shows our study area, the coastal city of Langles and its hinterland. We will begin by discussing the kind of project with which archeologists and many other historic preservationists are most familiar: a reservoir.

DRY HOLE RESERVOIR

During the halcyon days of the 1892 Lead Rush, the town of Dry Hole was a boomtown with a roaring population of 15,000. It has declined today to a

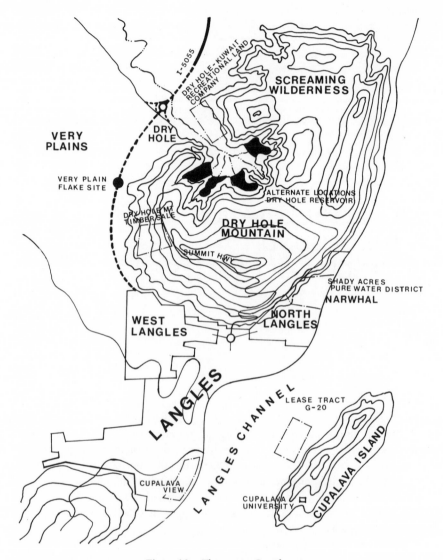

Figure 10. *The greater Langles area.*

population of 20 persons, mostly retirees who are decaying comfortably together with the town's old buildings and ruins. Increasing agricultural development on the Very Plains, west of Dry Hole, has created a need for additional
water, while the Dry Hole/Kuwait Recreational Land Company (DH/KRLC),
which has purchased a large tract north of town, has begun agitating for flood
control. Dry Hole itself is located on a bench overlooking the broad Dry Hole

Canyon, which experiences shallow flooding about once every 20 years. This flooding is sufficient to make it impossible for the DH/KRLC to obtain federally guaranteed flood insurance for potential homeowners.

At the request of a coalition of agriculturalists and land developers, the U.S. Army Corps of Engineers conducted a study, which concluded that a large earth-fill dam might be appropriate in upper Dry Hole Canyon. The dam will form Dry Hole Reservoir, a multipurpose lake to be used for flood control, irrigation, and recreation. Dry Hole Reservoir will hold between 120,000 and 250,000 acre-feet of water. The Corps now begins preliminary planning by considering several possible locations for the dam. Part of the planning involves preparation of an environmental impact statement (EIS) as required by NEPA. What must the Corps do about historic preservation?

Obviously, the reservoir will affect any historic properties located at the damsite or upstream. Since Dry Hole Canyon has never been subjected to a survey for historic properties, such a survey of the reservoir pool area is clearly necessary. Under 36 CFR 800, federal agencies must identify properties on lands under their jurisdiction or control that are eligible for inclusion in the National Register, and only a survey will make this possible in this case. The National Environmental Policy Act itself does not prescribe any particular treatment for historic properties; it merely requires their consideration, along with other aspects of the environment, in the agency's planning process. The Council on Environmental Quality's *Guidelines* for preparation of EISs, however, interlock with the advisory council's *Procedures,* so full compliance with the latter should be documented in the EIS. Thus, during preparation of the EIS all properties eligible for inclusion in the Register (or already included) should be identified, and consultation should be initiated with the advisory council and SHPO to establish methods of avoiding or mitigating adverse effects. An avoidance or mitigation plan should be presented in the EIS, ideally when the draft EIS is circulated for comment, and a memorandum of agreement should be comsummated prior to completion of the final EIS.

The Corps of Engineers, however, goes through many levels of planning in preparing for construction, and at its present very early planning stage, it is not willing to spend the money for the complete survey of all possible reservoir sites. Its preferred procedure is to conduct a "cultural resource reconnaissance" at this level of planning. The Corps defines this activity as follows:

> A literature search and records review plus an on-the-ground surface examination of selected portions of the area to be affected, adequate to assess the general nature of the resources probably present and the probable impact of the project [Corps of Engineers 1975].

This definition is compatible with that given by the Department of the Interior for a "reconnaissance survey," which is:

designed to provide a general impression of an area's historic properties and their values. . . . Although reconnaissance survey will seldom if ever provide sufficient data to insure identification of all historic properties in an area, it should make it possible to identify obvious or well-known properties, to check the existence and condition of properties tentatively identified or predicted from background research, to identify areas where certain kinds of properties are obviously lacking, and to indicate where certain kinds of properties are likely to occur, thus making possible a more informed and efficient intensive survey at a later stage in planning [36 CFR 64; See Appendix A].

Once a more advanced stage of planning is reached, and the options for location of the dam have been reduced, the Corps will ordinarily conduct a "cultural resource survey." This operation is defined by the Corps as follows:

An intensive, on-the-ground survey and testing of an area sufficient to permit determination of the number and extent of the resources present, their cultural and scientific importance, and the time factors and cost of preserving, recovering or otherwise mitigating adverse effects on them [Corps of Engineers 1975].

Once again, this is consistent with the Department of the Interior's description of an "intensive survey":

a systematic, detailed field inspection done by or under the supervision of professional architectural historians, historians, archeologists, and/or other specialists. This type of study is usually required to determine the significance of properties and their eligibility for listing in the National Register. It is preceded by adequate background research. . . . All districts, sites, buildings, structures, and objects of possible historical or architectural value are examined. . . . Persons knowledgeable in the history, prehistory, and folkways of the area are interviewed. . . . The surface of the land and all districts, sites, buildings, structures and objects of possible archeological value are inspected. . . . Systematic subsurface testing is conducted if necessary. . . . Documentary data necessary to the evaluation of specific properties are compiled and analyzed [36 CFR 64; See Appendix A].

The propriety of this multiphase approach to compliance depends largely upon the amount of discretion that the agency will have as it moves along in its planning process—that is, the extent to which opportunities will exist at a later date to halt or modify the project should it be found to endanger important historic properties. Most substantial Corps of Engineers projects proceed through many stages of planning, and often involve the preparation of EISs at several points along the way. Thus a phased approach to survey is generally regarded as appropriate to the Corps process. The reconnaissance survey serves to suggest where problems are likely to occur; the project can then be modified if possible to avoid them. Full compliance with the advisory council *Procedures* is put off until an intensive survey becomes a justifiable expenditure of public money, in advance of a fairly definite project.

The Dry Hole project will have other direct effects. A canal will carry irrigation water to the Very Plains; roads will be built, quarries opened, and fill obtained from borrow sources. During initial stages of planning, the locations of these activities may not be precisely defined, but their possible locations should be addressed by the reconnaissance. Once actual use areas are defined, a more thorough survey will normally be conducted.

The project may have managerial effects: For example, historic properties around the edges of the lake may be damaged by wave action, and boat-borne recreationalists may use them for new and destructive purposes. These effects should also be considered during the reconnaissance.

Contingent effects are also likely. Dry Hole will be used as a service center for dam construction crews. Once the dam is constructed, the town will be used by recreationalists for supplies and services. New buildings will go up and old ones will come down. Younger people with interests and world views different from Dry Hole's resident population will appear, and businesses will be established appropriate to the changing population. The lake and Dry Hole's services will facilitate other development. It will be possible to profitably subdivide the mouth of the canyon for recreation home development. Thus significant changes in the social and physical character of Dry Hole are contingent upon the reservoir project.

Similar to the contingent effects are the project's infrastructural effects. As more water for irrigation reaches the Very Plains, more land will be plowed and leveled. The region's characteristic temple and burial mounds, representing the little-known Hopeless Complex, will likely be lost, and subsoiling activities will destroy previously undisturbed village sites.

The responsibility of the Corps to assess the contingent and infrastructural effects of its project is a little less well defined than is its responsibility with respect to direct and managerial effects. While the latter are clearly covered by the tight provisions of the advisory council's *Procedures,* the former are the continuing subjects of argument, because they are so difficult to define precisely. Some consideration by the Corps is clearly necessary, however, in order to comply with the mandates of NEPA, NHPA, and Section 1(3) of the Executive Order. The following actions will probably provide the Corps with a sufficient data-base for its assessment of effects in the Dry Hole Reservoir EIS:

1. A reconnaissance survey of the lands subject to probable development by the DH/KRLC and to probable impact by changes in agricultural land-use.

2. A reconnaissance survey of Dry Hole to assess its significance as an historic archeological resource, to define those physical attributes of the community whose preservation is important to its historic integrity in the eyes of

local residents and visitors, and to determine whether it contains historic architecture of state or national significance. The last aspect of the study is clearly the province of the historian and architectural historian; the first should be an element of the archeological reconnaissance. The determination of Dry Hole's significance to the local community is a social anthropological activity, involving interviews, observation, and ethnohistorical research. It can easily be integrated into a program of social impact assessment, also a Corps responsibility under NEPA, but it should be closely coordinated with the other aspects of the reconnaissance survey to insure that all elements of the community's historic significance are being addressed in comparable fashion.

Ideally, then, the reconnaissance survey of the proposed Dry Hole project should involve a sample archeological study of the entire area where indirect and probable direct impacts can be expected, including full documentary research (see Chapter 8). It should also involve a reasonably detailed study of Dry Hole to ascertain its archeological, historical, and architectural significance in terms of research needs, national and state goals, and the needs of the local community. The results of these studies should be a management plan with several elements. It should be possible to predict where historic properties are most likely and least likely to occur among the various optional reservoir sites. It should also be possible to identify the types of properties whose loss would be most and least important in terms of the area's research potential. These two predictions should make it possible to rank the various reservoir locations in terms of their potential for damage. The same kinds of predictions should be possible on the lands subject to development and agricultural expansion. It should be possible to identify those elements of Dry Hole that should be preserved in order to retain its integrity as a research resource, as a representative of architectural styles and a reflection of historical events, and as a community with historical integrity. Based on these determinations and predictions, it should be possible to suggest means of mitigating some kinds of effects and means of more clearly identifying others. For direct and managerial impact areas, proper methods of survey can be prescribed, and potential problems noted for the guidance of the survey parties that may come later. For the contingent impact areas, it should be possible to prescribe land-use controls whose application by local government could protect the integrity of historic properties. For the area to be subjected to infrastructural effects, it should at least be possible to suggest that, if farmers want federally financed irrigation, and land developers want federal protection from floods, they should agree to keep their plows and bulldozers out of those areas identified as archeologically sensitive. As yet, no one has had much success in persuading the Corps of Engineers or a similar agency to withhold irrigation water pending an agreement by farmers or other users to protect historic values, but such a possibility is not unthinkable. It is even more thinkable that local government, given minor tax reforms together with a push from the water supplying agency, would provide incentives to landowners who agreed to preserve areas of historic value. In the absence of any real potential for protection, it should at least be possible to develop a survey-and-salvage plan based on the reconnaissance data, whose execution could then be funded by the SHPO using Historic Preservation Grant-in-Aid money or other grant sources during the years prior to delivery of the water. At least the preservation problems associated with the project would be identified, as they should be in an EIS, and the people and agencies of the area could begin thinking about ways to solve them.

At later stages of planning, it is doubtful that the Corps would be responsible for further study of its contingent or infrastructural impacts, unless a major problem had appeared whose resolution was crucial to the feasibility of the project. The Corps' responsibilities for dealing with direct and managerial impacts, however, are quite well defined. An intensive survey of the areas to be affected would have to be done, unless the reconnaissance had unequivocally shown that such areas were devoid of historic properties. Any historic properties discovered would have to be documented sufficiently to allow determination of their eligibility for inclusion in the National Register (see Chapter 5 and 36 CFR 63, Appendix A). The Corps would then consult with the SHPO to apply the National Register criteria and determine eligibility. Here several things can happen. If the SHPO and the Corps agree that nothing within the area of impact is eligible for the National Register, then the process is over; the Corps would keep documentation of this determination and go ahead with construction, without any further consideration of preservation needs. If all agreed that one or more of the properties did qualify for the Register, then it would be the Corps' responsibility to forward documentation to the OAHP for a final determination of eligibility. If the OAHP agreed that the property was eligible, then it would be the Corps' responsibility to take further steps as prescribed by the advisory council's *Procedures*. Before we follow the Corps through these steps, we should outline some other possible outcomes of the Corps–SHPO consultation.

If the Corps and the SHPO cannot agree about whether a property qualifies for the Register, then it is up to the Corps to request a determination from the OAHP, just as if they did agree that it was eligible. Such disputed cases naturally often take longer for OAHP to settle than do cases where agreement has been reached. If the professionals responsible for the survey, or any other responsible persons, assert that a property is eligible for the Register, and the agency and the SHPO both think it is not, the situation is more confused. It is OAHP's position that in such a situation the agency must request a determination from OAHP (36 CFR 63, 64; Appendix A). Some agencies, however, argue that the SHPO is the *only* person whose disagreement with an agency determination can force the matter up to OAHP for a decision. The advantage of this position to the agency is obvious; if it can get the SHPO in its pocket, *nothing* will ever have to be brought to the attention of the advisory council. Fortunately most agencies are coming to recognize the impropriety of such a position in a society that values checks and balances and open communication with the public.

Assuming, then, that something within the project impact area has been determined eligible, the agency must now decide whether the project will have an effect on it, and whether this effect will be adverse. The rather elaborate "criteria of effect" and "criteria of adverse effect" set forth in the advisory council's *Procedures* (36 CFR 800.8 & .9; Appendix A) are to be applied, but of course in most cases the nature of the impact is pretty obvious. If the project will have an adverse effect, then the Corps begins negotiation with the SHPO and the advisory council to work out a memorandum of agreement stipulating what will be done to avoid or mitigate this effect. This can be a lengthy and complex process, but it need not be. Let us assume that at Dry Hole Reservoir, everyone has done their work properly. There are 15 prehistoric sites of various kinds in the proposed reservoir area, plus an historic house. All have been determined to be eligible for the National Register—all because of their research value, and the house, additionally, because it is the last work of Dry Hole Daugherty, an eccentric but brilliant architect who practiced in the area before vanishing mysteriously into the Screaming Wilderness in 1937. One of the products of the survey sponsored by the Corps has been preparation of a mitigation plan. This plan calls for the full excavation of five prehistoric sites that lie between the high and low water marks of the reservoir and that will therefore be subjected to destruction by wave erosion. It also sets forth a public-interpretation and management program to preserve and use the three sites that lie in the management area around the lake shores. The other seven sites are to be sampled to extract information required for currently definable research purposes, or which might disappear through natural processes during the next few centuries, capped with riprap, and gently inundated; they will be inspected when the reservoir is drawn down every 10 years, and if their condition appears to be deteriorating salvage excavation or some other mitigation method will be applied. The house will be moved to a spot acceptable to the local community and the signers of the memorandum of agreement, and its original site will be carefully excavated. With this plan in hand, the Corps goes to the SHPO and obtains his concurrence. The Corps then goes to the advisory council, with a draft memorandum of agreement in hand. Within a matter of a few weeks the memorandum should be signed, and the project can proceed subject to the terms of the memorandum, which specify that the mitigation plan will be implemented.

I-5055 AND THE VERY PLAIN FLAKE SITE

The Langleland State Department of Transportation (LSDOT) proposes to continue construction of Interstate Highway 5055, which has reached the vicinity of Dry Hole, into West Langles. As this is in Interstate Highway, 90% of its funding comes from the Federal Highway Administration (FHWA). Thus the project comes under the purvue of federal environmental and historic preservation law.

The direct impacts of the project involve the construction area and occasional borrow sources. The only definable indirect impact is that the Interstate can be expected to permit increased use of Dry Hole, because an off-ramp will be constructed there. Since travel time between Dry Hole and West Langles (a major manufacturing center) will be cut from 3.5 hours to 45 minutes, rapid development of the Dry Hole area as a bedroom community for workers in West Langles can be expected.

The responsibilities of the LSDOT, acting for the FHWA, are similar in this case to those held by the Corps in the planning of Dry Hole Reservoir. The direct impact areas must be surveyed, and an attempt must be made to deal with the contingent effects of the new highway on Dry Hole. The LSDOT, however, faces a particular and unique problem, which is called "4(f)."

Section 4(f) of the Department of Transportation Act, as amended (49 U.S.C. Sec. 1653(f)(1970) requires that:

> The Secretary (of Transportation) shall not approve any program or project which requires the use of . . . any land from an historic site of national, State, or local significance as so determined by such (Federal, State or local) officials (having jurisdiction thereof) unless (1) there is no feasible and prudent alternative to the use of such land, and (2) such program includes all possible planning to minimize harm to such . . . historic site resulting from such use.

The FHWA is a bureau of the Department of Transportation, so the requirements of Section 4(f) apply to the programs and projects of state agencies that FHWA funds, including I-5055.

The courts have interpreted the requirement of Section 4(f) stringently, though most cases have involved impacts on parks and natural areas, also covered by the section. The Department of Transportation has found it necessary to require that very exhaustive analyses of all possible alternative locations for a transportation facility be conducted before use of a piece of land covered by Section 4(f) be seriously contemplated. In the case of *Stop H-3 Association et al.* v. *Coleman et al.*, the 9th Circuit Court ruled that any property determined eligible for inclusion in the National Register constituted a property to which Section 4(f) applied. Now, let us consider the quandry created by the existence of the Very Plain Flake Site.

The Very Plain Flake Site lies on the east edge of the Very Plains, at the foot of Dry Hole Mountain. It consists of a surface scatter of rhyolite flakes, presumably originating either in the rhyolite outcrop on the north face of the Screaming Wilderness Plateau or in the one on the north tip of Cupalava Island. It is the only historic property subject to direct impact by continued construction along the preferred I-5055 right-of-way. The site is determined eligible for the National Register because of its potential usefulness in providing information about prehistoric economic contact and technological change in the region. As a result, the LSDOT now has a Section 4(f) case on its hands.

The Very Plain Flake Site is in a rather precarious position, on a badly dissected outwash fan that is subject to severe ongoing erosion. It is also a popular spot for use by trail bike riders, who zoom up and down the eroded gullies and over the site, scattering flakes in all directions. It is conceded by all who know about the site and the area that the site will not last another 5 years, and the best thing that could possibly happen to it would be a systematic salvage project to recover its pertinent data. Scattered across the Very Plains are dozens of other archeological sites: Hopeless effigy, burial, and temple mounds, Lower Pineland village sites, and historic sites associated with the late nineteenth-century exploitation of bog-lead. It is very unlikely that the LSDOT could build a highway anywhere in the Very Plain without running into an archeological site that would qualify for the National Register in some way or other.

What is the LSDOT to do? Is it to explore every alternative right-of-way on the Very Plains? Is it to spend large amounts of money and wait several years while doing so, only to reach the obvious conclusion that the route through the Very Plain Flake Site is the best route—during which time the site will be destroyed by erosion and trail-bikers? This is clearly a distortion of the intent of Section 4(f).

Seeking a resolution of the 4(f) problem has led to attempts by some state highway agencies to avoid ever getting determinations of eligibility on archeological sites. In some cases, arrangements have been made to salvage sites without obtaining determinations of eligibility and consulting the advisory council. Sometimes these arrangements probably provide for the best possible treatment of the sites, but lacking the review provided by the advisory council's *Procedures* it is impossible to know. In other cases, political pressure has been exerted to force the SHPO to concur in plans simply to destroy archeological sites without any form of mitigation, or with only minimal "archeological monitoring" during destruction (Interagency 1976b). Sometimes such plans are put into effect even over the SHPO's objections. Clearly, this is the kind of independent exercise of irresponsibility that the historic preservation regulations are designed to control.

One possible solution to the problem may be available through the advisory council *Procedures,* coupled with what seems to be a reasonable interpretation of the intent of Congress in enacting Section 4(f). Under the advisory council's *Procedures,* once a property has been determined eligible for the National Register, the agency and the SHPO must determine whether the project will have an effect on it, and whether this effect will be adverse. Recognizing that situations like that on I-5055 occur with some frequency, the advisory council has notified federal agencies that it will concur in a determination of "no adverse effect" with respect to an impact on an archeological site if the following conditions exist:

1. The property is not a National Historic Landmark, a National Historic Site in non-federal ownership, or a property of national historical significance so designated within the National Park System.
2. The SHPO has determined that in-place preservation of the property is not necessary to fulfill purposes set forth in the State Historic Preservation Plan.
3. The SHPO and the Agency Official agree that:
   a. The property . . . has minimal value as an exhibit in place for public understanding and enjoyment;
   b. Above and beyond its scientific value, the property is not known to have historic or cultural significance to a community, ethnic, or social group that would be impaired by the retrieval of data;
   c. Currently available technology is such that the significant information contained in the property can be retrieved.
4. Funds and time have been committed to adequately retrieve the data [Advisory Council 1976; Appendix A].

Documentation that these conditions do exist, and that the data recovery will be consistent with the standards of OAHP (36 CFR 66; Appendix A) must be provided to the council along with the proposed determination. The council then reviews the documentation; if it does not object to the determination within 45 days, the agency can then proceed with the data recovery and the project.

Some archeologists object to the semantic difficulty of saying that destruction-after-salvage does not constitute an adverse effect. Some also fear that this procedure may not ensure proper mitigation of effects with the same certainty that is provided by full advisory council review. It is also clear that there will be real difficulties involved in deciding whether salvage is an appropriate treatment in particular cases; where are the thresholds beyond which it cannot be said that "currently available technology is sufficient . . ." or that a given proposed salvage project properly employs that technology? A very real problem is that of adequate review of proposed salvage projects. When the procedure was developed, in joint conferences by the advisory council staff and Interagency Archeological Services, it was anticipated that the latter organization would participate in the council's review and that notification would be provided to potentially concerned archeologists whenever a salvage project under the procedures was proposed, so that objections could be voiced if they existed. In the implementation of the procedure up to the time of this writing, neither expectation has been fully realized in the council's actual review of proposals.

These difficulties exist within the regular system for implementation of the advisory council *Procedures* as well, however. What the "no adverse effect" approach to approval of a salvage project does is simply to reduce the paperwork involved for the agency seeking approval of a project while potentially (assuming the review problems are worked out) shifting the locus where questions about the adequacy of a salvage program are asked from the advisory council staff to a broader arena where OAHP and outside archeologists can participate. The semantic problem is real, but also reflects a real-life condition. Salvage has always constituted a mixed curse for the archeological record. The argument that preservation is always preferable to salvage ignores some very real facts: The crucial data-content of an archeological site may be lost through deterioration while it is being "preserved"; it may be preserved from a federal project only to be lost to an uncontrolled, nonfederal activity; the recovery of particular data from one site may be crucial to the recognition or development of research topics that will help guide preservation efforts elsewhere. These facts can be used self-servingly, and some archeologists are naturally reluctant to accept the proposition that "we have to destroy the site to save it." At times, however, the proposition is entirely supportable, and in such instances it is arguable that the effect of the site's destruction is not adverse.

To return to the Very Plain Flake Site and Section 4(f), let us assume that the archeologist in charge of the right-of-way survey has developed a comprehensive plan for the recovery of all significant data from the site. A systematic surface collection will be made; sample excavations will be done; the site will be graded to seek subsurface features; full descriptive and comparative analysis will be done; the collections will be curated, and both descriptive and analytic reports will be prepared. The Langleland State Department of Transportation agrees to fund the project; the SHPO concurs in it, and concurs in a determination of "no adverse effect," which is then recommended to FHWA by LSDOT. The Federal Highway Administration forwards this determination as its own to the advisory council, together with the research plan, LSDOT's agreement to fund it, and the SHPO's concurrence. The council reviews the plan and concurs; FHWA approves the project and authorizes LSDOT to proceed.

What does this have to do with Section 4(f)? At this writing, this remains uncertain, but it seems to us that to say that under these circumstances the LSDOT is "using" the Very Plain Flake Site in the sense intended by Section 4(f) is to stretch the meaning of "use" beyond reason. Congress called upon the Department of Transportation, through Section 4(f), to be very careful about using land from parks, natural areas, and historic sites because the public has interests in such lands that would be injured by the use. With respect to most of the kinds of lands covered by Section 4(f) (parks, for example), it was, of course, inconceivable to Congress that placing a transportation facility on the land could be compatible with its continued utilization by the public or its continued viability as an environmental resource, so "use" was the word chosen to describe what the Department of Transportation should not permit without serious consideration. With respect to a site like the Very Plain Flake Site, however, the highway is entirely compatible with the archeological use of the site in the public interest. If all responsible parties are in agreement that the public interest in the historic value of the property is so well served by the project that they are willing to assert unanimously that the project will have "no adverse effect" on it, can the project really be said to "use" the property in the sense intended by Congress? We think not, and believe that in cases where a valid determination of "no adverse effect" can be reached, the requirements of Section 4(f) should not come into play. In cases where preservation would or might be preferable to salvage—where a determination of adverse effect is reached and the full advisory council *Procedures* must be gone through—Section 4(f) clearly should apply.

LEASE TRACT G-20 IN LANGLES CHANNEL

It has been discovered that substantial deposits of natural gas are locked within the continental shelf in the Langles Channel, between Langles and Cupalava Island. The Bureau of Land Management (BLM) is responsible for administration of the outer continental shelf. It issues permits for oil and gas exploration, and sells leases for the exploitation of oil and gas deposits. The U.S. Geological Survey (USGS) then oversees operations under the terms of the lease.

Cupalava Oil and Gas (COG) has responded to a BLM request for bids on Lease Tract G-20 in Langles Channel. What are the responsibilities of BLM, USGS, and COG toward historic properties?

Clearly, the outer continental shelf may contain a diversity of historic properties. As a rule, the oceans surrounding the North American continent have reached their present levels only within the last 7000–9000 years; hence there are undoubtedly early prehistoric habitation sites on the present continental shelves. Shipwrecks, disposal areas, and other cultural features that have been deposited on the shelves from the ocean surface are also to be found (Gagliano *et al.* 1976).

Just as on land, historic properties on the continental shelves cannot be assumed to occur everywhere with equal probability. Predicting where such properties will occur requires a detailed study of coastal geomorphology, marine geology, prehistoric settlement patterns both generally and locally, and the history of navigation in the vicinity (see Chapter 8).

The positions of BLM and USGS with respect to historic preservation on the continental shelves are somewhat unclear at present, but the policy supported by OAHP and much of the relevant professional staff within BLM would place great reliance on large-scale predictive studies. Where such a study had been done (as in the Gulf of Mexico: Gagliano *et al.* 1976), detailed surveys of actual lease areas would not be required in areas where historic properties were not predicted to occur. In areas where such properties are predicted to occur, remote-sensing surveys would be required prior to drilling, construction of platforms, or other substantial modification of the bottom. Side-scan sonar, magnetometry, and subbottom profiling are among the types of remote-sensing technology employed in such surveys, in a systematic search pattern. If a predictive study has not been done, then the methods that would be required in survey of a high-probability lease area should be employed in the survey of any lease area.

The Langles Channel has not been subjected to a predictive study, so the BLM and USGS conclude that a full survey must be done on Lease Tract G-20. This is provided for by including a stipulation in the lease requiring that the lessee conduct such a survey in advance of bottom-modification, and provide the results to BLM. Cupalava Oil and Gas, having won the lease in competitive bidding, now proceeds to contract with a Marine Survey Archeologist to conduct a study; this is often integrated with other surveys of the bottom required to locate dangerous obstacles to drilling and other features. Marine Survey Archeologists are certified by the Society of Professional Archeologists, based on demonstration of specialized training and/or experience in use of remote sensing instruments and knowledge of continental shelf geology and geomorphology, in addition to basic archeological expertise (Jelks *et al.* 1976). The survey reveals a shipwreck—an Italian submarine sunk during a World War II mission to bombard Langles. What now are the responsibilities of the participants?

If COG were intent on drilling through the submarine, or building a drilling platform on top of it, then compliance with the advisory council's *Procedures* would be necessary by BLM or USGS, before the action was permitted. Presumably, if the submarine were determined eligible for the National Register, a memorandum of agreement would be signed requiring COG to fund a salvage operation before being permitted to construct or drill. In fact, however, this has not happened and probably never will, because it is easier for COG to simply move its drill site far enough away to ensure that the submarine will not be affected. The BLM continues to be responsible for the wreck, however, since it lies on lands under the BLM's control. Under Section 2(a) of Executive Order 11593, it is BLM's responsibility to nominate the wreck to the National Register. Assuming it is accepted, the BLM must consult with the advisory council before permitting the wreck to be disturbed. Presumably the

BLM is also responsible for maintaining the wreck, but its tendency has been to leave well enough alone.

SHADY ACRES INTERCEPTOR SEWER

The community of Shady Acres, in North Langles, needs improved sewage facilities. Shady Acres, like most of North Langles, is a recently incorporated conglomerate of low-density housing developments that borders the older village of Narwhal, a small nineteenth-century whaling town. The area's rapid and rather poorly controlled development has seriously strained extant sewage facilities, and many homes use septic tanks that are coming to exceed the capacity of their leach fields. The population of Shady Acres is 5000; that of Narwhal 500. Realizing after several citations from the Board of Health that the septic tanks of Shady Acres are polluting the streams flowing into Langles Channel, the Greater Shady Acres Pure Waters District (GSAPWD) now proposes construction of an interceptor sewer system to carry its sewage and that of Narwhal to a treatment plant in Langles. The proposed interceptor will have the capacity to serve 15,000 people, in anticipation of future growth. The GSAPWD applies to the U.S. Environmental Protection Agency (EPA) for a 75% matching grant-in-aid to fund the project.

The responsibilities of EPA spring from NEPA, NHPA, and Executive Order 11593. Many of the actions required for EPA's compliance, however, can be transferred to the potential recipient of its largesse. Thus EPA requires that the GSAPWD conduct an environmental review of the proposed project, including a review of possible impacts on historic properties, and submit the results along with its application for assistance. Seventy-five percent of the cost of this review can be reimbursed by EPA.

In this project, as at Dry Hole, there are potential direct and indirect impacts. Direct impacts will occur along the right-of-way of the sewers. For the most part these pass along streets under pavement, and thus present a particular challenge for the archeologist attempting to identify historic properties. The Environmental Protection Agency prefers that inspections of rights-of-way be done in two phases. The first phase involves a relatively cursory inspection to identify what areas, if any, may require more intensive surveys. An appropriate first phase operation here is similar to the reconnaissance required by the Corps of Engineers at Dry Hole. Background research on the area's history, prehistory, and environment is done in order to predict areas where historic properties are likely to occur, and sample field inspection is made to augment and test these predictions, while providing information on the extent of recent disturbance, difficulties that may be encountered in intensive survey, and so forth. Since

EPA's project involves much more limited possible direct impacts than does the Corps', however, the reconnaissance often involves complete surface inspection of the right-of-way, with minor subsurface testing as needed. Intensive survey, if needed, then is directed toward the evaluation of actual discovered historic properties or the detailed exploration of high-probability areas.

At Shady Acres, it rapidly becomes apparent that 10 miles of the project will require no further inspection, since the right-of-way runs under the Langles Channel Highway, built in 1952 over what had been the Miasmic Swamp until it was diked off in 1937. Old records of the area indicate that prior to 1937 the entire area was under brackish water and alligators, while from 1937 to 1952 when the highway was built, every acre was used for growing potatoes by absentee agribusinesspeople. It also becomes clear that only certain spots within the greater Shady Acres area are likely to contain prehistoric sites. The moorlike coastal terrace has always been boggy, and both the sample survey data and the records of the Cupalava University Archeological Survey indicate that prehistoric sites here are always found on low knolls near springs. The right-of-way crosses 27 such knolls. The research also reveals that Narwhal burned in 1897 and was rebuilt on a different street pattern from that employed previously. Overlaying the modern town plan on the old, it becomes clear that in two locations the street down which the sewer will pass crosses sites where buildings previously stood. The research suggests that both buildings—a house of prostitution and a whale oil rendering plant—could contain data that would be useful to the reconstruction of Narwhal's social and economic history. A Phase II, intensive survey can now be planned in detail, emphasizing the areas where historic properties can actually be expected, providing for testing in areas where the data are insufficient to form a basis for reliable predictions, and ignoring areas where there is little or no chance that historic properties will occur. If testing of the knolls or the building sites, or other Phase II activities, result in the identification of historic properties, these must be documented and submitted to the SHPO and OAHP for determinations of eligibility. If they are eligible for the National Register, the EPA can (a) attempt a determination of "no adverse effect" just as the LSDOT did in the case of the Very Plain Flake Site, (b) go through full consultation with the advisory council, hopefully leading to a satisfactory memorandum of agreement to avoid or mitigate the project's impacts, or (c) get the GSAPWD to reroute the project so as to avoid any possibility of impact and hence any need for compliance actions.

There is, however, another and stickier issue involved in this case: indirect contingent and infrastructural impacts. The new system is designed to handle almost three times the output of the present local population. It is thus removing a check to growth that would otherwise exist, and can be said to have serious infrastructural effects. The effects will include the destruction of properties valuable for their information content through new housing and street construction and other improvements, and changes in the historic character of Narwhal. Contingent effects will result from the installation of a collector system, using local and state funds, once the EPA-funded system is complete. It seems clear that the EPA's responsibility here is identical to that of the Corps of Engineers in the Dry Hole case. It should make a similar effort to identify its indirect effects and work with the local community to mitigate them, or agree to fund only a scaled-down system sufficient to handle the present population's output. However, EPA does not accept these responsibilities with much grace; it tends to argue that the sewer system does not *cause* growth but merely services an expanded population that has already been projected by local planning bodies and whose eventual existence is inevitable. Leaving aside the question of the inevitability of growth, we do not believe that local or state planning agencies have always taken historic properties very fully into account in their plans for community development. As a result, the fact that a federal action merely helps permit fulfillment of a local general plan does not mean that the action does not facilitate activities that are contrary to the public interest in historic preservation. It follows that, unless the general plan that will guide local development does contain elements that will ensure adequate protection of historic properties (see Chapter 8), EPA has a responsibility to ascertain what the effects of growth will be and to help the community develop mechanisms to counteract those effects that are adverse.

CUPALAVA VIEW: LANGLES

On the scenic headlands overlooking the Langles Channel, Cupalava Constructors, Inc. has developed plans for a moderate-income condominium development called Cupalava View. Cupalava Constructors, Inc. applies to the Department of Housing and Urban Development (HUD) for a federal guarantee on its construction loan from the Bank of East Langles. No federal money changes hands; HUD is merely being asked to guarantee to the bank that, should CCI not make good on its loan, the federal government will settle up. The only federal action here, then, is HUD's agreement to back the loan. This action, however, has obvious contingent effects; it permits the construction of Cupalava View to begin.

The HUD loan guarantee programs are administered on the field level by small teams whose primary training is in real estate appraisal. In the case of Cupalava View, a HUD appraiser will visit the project site, inspect the plans, evaluate the terms of the loan, and decide whether the project is a good risk. If it is, he will recommend that the loan be guaranteed, provided the project appears to be in conformance with federal law. If Cupalava View were to be a racially segregated community, for example, the appriaser would not recommend that its loan be guaranteed. It is easy to say, formulistically, that if Cupalava View is going to destroy historic properties its loan should not be guaranteed either, and in fact HUD is not unwilling to take this position. The problem lies in finding out whether the project will have an adverse effect on such properties. Of course, HUD could say flatly that whenever a developer came to it with a request for a guarantee, the request had better be accompanied by the results of a survey showing to the SHPO's satisfaction that no impacts would occur, or by a mitigation plan that the developer was ready to implement. To make such a requirement, however, might not achieve the desired effect. If the Corps of Engineers were to refuse to construct Dry Hole Dam, it is possible that the Dry Hole/Kuwait Recreational Land Development Company could have built it with private funds, but it would have been a monstrous undertaking with relatively little immediate reward. HUD, by contrast, works with projects that come much closer to being feasible as purely private undertakings. If HUD places too many restrictions and conditions upon its applicants for guarantees, the applicants may simply forego the guarantees. In the case of Cupalava View, the developers may be quite able to obtain their loan from the Bank of East Langles without HUD's guarantee, if they are willing to put up with a higher interest rate. If HUD's restrictions are too onorous, they may do just that, whereupon all federal control over the project will be lost. As a result, HUD is very reluctant to become too hard-nosed; it needs ways to decide in advance whether a survey should be done and what it may reveal, and it needs ways for these decisions to be made by its appraisers. At this writing, HUD is preparing a handbook to assist its appraisers in making such decisions with respect to archeological properties (HUD n.d.). In general, this handbook will direct the appraisers to sources of data that may indicate whether an archeological survey is needed. The SHPO is one such source, of course, but HUD will try to direct its appraisers to a broader range of sources, and give them a basis for asking relatively sophisticated questions.

At Cupalava View, after consultation in accordance with the handbook, HUD requires a survey. It reveals two shell middens that are determined to be eligible for the National Register. One site is protected without difficulty. It lies on the bank of a stream that should be kept in open-space in accordance with local codes, so the developer simply agrees to include the site in open-space, cover it with a foot of topsoil, and plant the surface to discourage vandalism. The second site is on a prime building lot, and the developer balks at preserving it.

Here Interagency Archeological Services enters the picture, under the authority of Section 3(b) of the Archeological and Historic Preservation Act. This section authorizes the Department of the Interior to fund salvage on federal assistance projects. Interagency Archeological Services will first need to satisfy itself that (*a*) the advisory council's *Procedures* have been complied with (*b*) no viable means exists to preserve the site in place, and (c) salvage would be an undue burden on the developer. In this case, the advisory council is satisfied with a memorandum of agreement that stipulates protection of the first site and consultation with Interagency Archeological Services leading to salvage of the second. Preservation in place is not wholly feasible, but the developer is willing to minimize damage by covering the site with a thin layer of soil, building the house on piles without a basement, and writing a restrictive covenant into its deed requiring that salvage be performed in advance of any postpurchase subsurface alterations. The developer is working on a tight profit margin, so funding salvage would be a burden, but he can provide the assistance of a surveyor to map the site and locate where the foundations will go. Interagency Archeological Services now contracts for a salvage project addressing only those portions of the site actually subject to effect; HUD can guarantee the developer's loan, and Cupalava View can go into construction.

THE DRY HOLE MOUNTAIN TIMBER SALE

Up on Dry Hole Mountain, Dry Hole National Forest has decided to sell a block of timber. The Greater Langles Pulp Cooperative has already made an arrangement to harvest the trees growing on a private in-holding owned by one of its members within the forest, but it cannot accomplish the harvest until it gains access to the private block through the National Forest. It proposes to the National Forest Service that it be granted access across Forest land, and it also bids on the federal timber standing between the private block and the Dry Hole Summit Highway. As the Forest Service considers the possibility of making this sale, several things must be taken into account with respect to historic preservation. First, what impacts must be evaluated? Second, who must evaluate them? Third, what is the federal responsibility for the private lands? Fourth, who should pay?

Several kinds of activities connected with timber cutting will have obvious impacts, and the Forest Service is responsible for evaluating them. Haul roads, skid roads, landings, and work camps all require bulldozing or other disturbances of the landscape. Historic buildings can be pretty easily avoided even if they are not known about in advance, but the possibility of archeological sites makes a survey necessary. Some National Forests are much less willing to consider the simple cutting of trees to constitute a danger to historic properties, so it is often difficult to persuade them to conduct surveys of entire sale blocks. The impacts of tree cutting are easy to identify, however: The trees are not magically removed from their growth sites and transported through the air to the landing to be loaded on trucks, except where helicopters are employed. Instead they are dragged over the ground, usually by bulldozers, tearing up the surface and anything in it. Even in the case of helicopter logging, the falling trees gouge the ground surface and the removal of trees may alter the erosion-deposition regime in such a way as to result in damage to historic properties both within and outside the sale area. It is thus good practice to survey the entire sale area, and consider the possibility of impacts on adjoining areas as well. When historic properties are identified during the survey, the Forest Service is responsible for full compliance with the advisory council's *Procedures*.

The Forest Service has been among the nation's leading agencies in the recent employment of archeologists on staff, both in the forests and in regional offices. Although much survey and, where necessary, salvage work is done under contract, in-service archeologists handle an increasing load of fieldwork projects. Any in-service preservation specialist suffers under a conflict-of-interest burden not shared by outside contractors, but the Forest Service, with its tremendous range of activities that need archeological input, clearly does require full-time expertise in the field. Some Forest Service regions are training paraprofessional archeological surveyors, who assist regional and forest professional archeologists as fieldworkers and represent preservation concerns in the daily work of the forests and ranger districts. Although some archeologists are concerned about the quality of these paraprofessionals' performance, there is nothing in the historic preservation statutes to discourage their use, and our own experience suggests that they tend to do high-quality work. It is also difficult to imagine how the Forest Service could handle its diverse preservation needs without such paraprofessionals. Typically, the paraprofessional is a professional in another field—a forester, a geologist, a schoolteacher who works summers for the Forest Service evaluating timber or helping plan roads. Typically, they are trained to recognize the types of historic properties that are likely to occur on their forests and are responsible solely for the identification and description of such properties—not for evaluation or the development or implementation of mitigation plans. Once a property is found, the Forest Service archeologist or another professional is responsible for its evaluation. The Forest Service or regional archeologist also takes responsibility for the quality of the paraprofessional's survey (cf. Forest Service 1976). Quite often, outside archeologists are employed under contract to conduct surveys in cooperation with Forest Service paraprofessionals; this healthy arrangement gives the outside archeologist access to the paraprofessional's local information and knowledge of the area, while exposing the paraprofessional to professional views and training.

Dry Hole National Forest's responsibilities on its own lands are thus quite clear, and its methods of meeting them are generally effective. Its responsibilities for the private inholding controlled by the Cooperative are somewhat less certain. Under NEPA, NHPA, and Section 1(3) of Executive Order 11593, the Forest Service should seek to contribute to the preservation of historic properties on private land and assess the impacts of its actions on such properties, but it lacks specific direction in how to do so. Like HUD in the Cupalava View case, the Forest Service must be careful about pushing its private applicant too far. The Cooperative owns many bulldozers, and if it finds that historic properties on its lands are seriously entangling its business relations with the federal government there is nothing in federal law to prevent it from eliminating the problem by applying the bulldozers to the properties.

Typically in our experience, the Forest Service budgets its own funds for surveys and for mitigation activities, even when these are conducted in advance of timber sales that obviously benefit a private party. In cases where the Forest Service merely permits an activity—for example, when it allows an electric transmission line to be constructed through a forest—it requires that the applicant pay. The distinction lies in the fact that when a firm applies for a permit, the permitee is then known and can be required to do things, while when a sale is being prepared, in most cases the eventual buyer is not known and hence cannot be required to do things in advance of being awarded the timber. The survey, however, obviously must go on before the sale is made, so that preservation clauses can be written into the sale agreement. It is not clear to us why the cost of the survey is not then made a part of the price of the timber, or why the buyer is not required to pay for any salvage costs that become necessary. It also seems plausible that if the forest had accumulated a good body of predictive data about the distribution of historic properties through its general planning processes (see Chapter 8 and Smith 1977), it should be possible to foretell the costs of and need for surveys in particular areas with a fair degree of accuracy, so that buyers would not be subjected to unexpected increases in the price of purchase. As things now stand, the public is often paying for activities that are the proper responsibility of the lumber companies.

On Dry Hole Mountain, what will most likely happen is that the roads, landings, and other areas of obvious direct impact will be intensively surveyed, and an effort will be made to survey at least a sample of all the public lands where timber cutting will take place. The Cooperative will be encouraged to allow the survey party to look at its lands, too, but the inspection is likely to be rather cursory. Historic properties located on public lands will be avoided if possible, both by construction and by cutting. If avoidance is impossible, and the properties are eligible for the National Register, salvage will be done under the guidance of a memorandum of agreement with the advisory council and the SHPO. The extent to which the Forest Service will treat contingent effects on the private land depends on the aggressiveness of the staff and on the amount of encouragement it receives from the outside. Minimally, the Cooperative will be encouraged to protect any historic properties known on its land. Preservation or salvage may be made a condition of the Cooperative's timber lease and special use permit, if the Forest Service believes that this will not drive the Cooperative to destroy the properties in advance.

THE SCREAMING WILDERNESS

The high desert plateau north of Dry Hole Canyon is administered by the Bureau of Land Management (BLM). Recognizing its inaccessibility and the fact that it is the habitat of the Great Horned Condor and other endangered species, the BLM purposes to declare it a Wilderness under terms of the Wilderness Act of 1964 (P.L. 88–577). Vehicular access will be essentially eliminated, land and resource use will be restricted, and the land will be permitted, even encouraged, to regain and remain in a natural condition. In undertaking this action, what are the BLM's historic preservation responsibilities?

Interpreted literally, the advisory council's *Procedures* at section 800.4 appear to require that the BLM identify all historic properties in the Screaming Wilderness and consider impacts on them, just as if it were going to use the area as a testing ground for nuclear missiles. However, the Department of the Interior believes that the level of investigation conducted by an agency prior to an undertaking should be commensurate with the level of impact to be expected as a result of the undertaking (36 CFR 64; Appendix A). Thus, to the extent that the establishment of the Screaming Wilderness can be taken to protect its historic properties rather than impacting them, little or no survey is necessary. This does not mean that historic preservation can be ignored, however. The BLM will continue to manage the Wilderness, and it must consider what managerial impacts the change from unreserved to Wilderness status may have. Is it possible, for instance, that decreased accessibility will somehow increase the possibility of vandalism? Generally, this is a rather implausible possibility, but in the present case the BLM must contend with P.O. Thunter, an unregenerate vandal who lives on a pension in Dry Hole and spends his considerable free time digging in the dry caves of the Screaming Plateau. He has been apprehended on previous occasions only because the trail-bikers who ride the plateau have reported him. He is now on probation after an Antiquities Act conviction. Once he is off probation he will no doubt head for the Wilderness again, and if the trail-bikers are banned, what will be the result? In all probability, Thunter's activities will constitute an uncontrollable adverse effect, until his hopefully prompt demise, but they should be the object of consultation with the SHPO and advisory council.

A less far-fetched impact arises from the Wilderness designation itself. The Wilderness Act requires that designated lands be maintained in their natural, unmodified condition. The Screaming Plateau was the site of the Great Lead Strike of 1891, and the camps, cabins and mine shafts of the lead miners are still scattered over the landscape. Under the terms of the Wilderness Act, the BLM should undertake a program to remove these intrusions on the area's wild qualities. However, the historic significance of these properties has never been determined. Clearly, before the BLM undertakes their destruction, it must determine their significance and seek to protect their valuable attributes. These somewhat contradictory responsibilities may, of course, lead to irresoluble conflicts, but this cannot be determined until a beginning is made at identifying and evaluating the properties.

Two other BLM responsibilities are also relevant here. The BLM retains the responsibility to inventory the historic properties of the Screaming Wilderness under terms of Section 2(a) of Executive Order 11593. In addition, as specified by the advisory council's *Procedures* at Section 800.9(e), "neglect . . . leading to deterioration or destruction" constitutes an adverse effect that triggers an agency's responsibility to consult with the SHPO and the council. Thus the BLM, despite the Wilderness designation, must seek to identify the Screaming area's historic properties and strive to avoid the deterioration of those that qualify for inclusion in the National Register. These responsibilities converge with those of assessing the importance of the mining sites and structures before they are destroyed; the BLM should undertake a systematic survey of the plateau and develop a management program for its historic properties—which may involve the gradual elimination of some of them in conformance with the Wilderness Act. This survey need not be done before the Wilderness designation is made; it is part of an ongoing management responsibility that may be realized over a long period of time. Surveyors will, of course, have to avoid disturbing the condors.

SUMMARY

In this discussion we have tried to show how the basic responsibilities established for federal agencies by the historic preservation authorities are translated into specific actions by particular agencies engaged in projects. We have tried to point out problem areas, and to suggest means of resolution. We have emphasized the broad responsibilities of federal agencies to identify all historic properties that their activities may affect, and to avoid or mitigate all sorts of adverse effects. We have also tried to show how these responsibilities are sometimes circumvented, ignored, or lost in the shuffle, and are sometimes sources of conflict with other responsibilities held by the agencies. Finally, we have set a stage for Chapter 8 on regional planning. The reader, having struggled to this point, has probably wondered by now: "Why don't all these guys get together?" Why have not the Corps of Engineers, the Forest Service, the Department of Transportation, and the Bureau of Land Management jointly exercised their responsibilities toward historic preservation in the Dry Hole/ Screaming/Very Plains area? Why have HUD and EPA not cooperated in an integrated approach to the historic properties of the Langles urban zone? Why have the SHPO and the archeologists of Cupalava University not tried to build a comprehensive data base and evaluatory framework to be used by the agencies of the area in their compliance work, to ensure that the area's research needs were consistently treated? Mechanisms exist for getting everybody together—and the expectable result would be decreased confusion and conflict, decreased cost to the public both in dollars and in unnecessarily lost historic properties, increased research productivity, and a preservation effort that would be consistently sensitive to all the cultural interests of the region. These mechanisms, and basic approaches to regional historic preservation planning, will be discussed in Chapter 8.

8

PREDICTIVE SURVEYS FOR REGIONAL PLANNING

When our last-ditch defenses we man
Against projects we're trying to ban,
And bulldozers roar,
Smashing sites by the score,
We'll wish we had written a plan!

—Airlie Airs, 1974

We discussed how agencies typically should comply with historic preservation law, and how anthropologists can contribute to this compliance, in Chapters 4 and 6. We presented some specific complications and resolutions in Chapter 7. A broader sort of resolution is provided by general or regional planning.

It is apparent that the agencies whose activities affect the Langles area could, in most cases, benefit from a general understanding of where historic properties might most likely occur and what kinds of properties might be expected in which places. In some cases, were such data available, the need for surveys in advance of specific projects might be obviated. In other cases, surveys could be more finely tuned to expectable types of property, and hence be more efficient. It would be easier to evaluate discovered properties, since a comparative framework would exist. In some cases it might be possible to say that particular properties could be sacrificed with no mitigation of effect, and when mitigation was necessary the comparative data would make it possible to select appropriate mitigation plans with precision.

There are also arguments for regional planning as anthropological research. Almost invariably, the research value of an individual property is somehow related to its regional context, so it is clearly useful to understand something about the region before attempting to study a particular entity. Moreover, study of the region may itself answer questions of anthropological importance, or at least permit the posing of questions in a fruitful fashion. A regional perspective also can help anthropologists—and others—better understand the special problems and interests of particular local social groups, and address these problems.

Federal law provides considerable encouragement to regional historic preservation planning. The most obvious is that provided by the NHPA of 1966, which has as one of its goals "to grant funds to States for the purpose of preparing comprehensive statewide historic surveys and plans [NHPA Sec. 101(a)(1)]."

The NHPA, moreover, makes receipt of federal grants for historic preservation contingent upon the applicant's request being "in accordance with the comprehensive statewide historic preservation plan [NHPA Sec. 102(a)(2)]."

Other authorities are less explicit, but are consistent with the NHPA. The Coastal Zone Management Act of 1972, for example, declares as national policy the provision of encouragement and assistance to states in the development of coastal zone management programs "giving full consideration to . . . historic . . . values . . . [CZMA Sec. 303(b)]." Most other statutes establishing planning programs contain similar language. Funds for use specifically in historic preservation planning are authorized by both the Housing Act of 1954 (Section 701) and the Housing and Community Development Act of 1974; block grants provided under the authority of the latter statute can be used as the "local" match for federal money provided by OAHP under Section 102 of the NHPA.

Regional historic preservation planning has the same two aspects possessed by any other program of treatment for historic properties. First the properties must be identified, and then something must be done with them. In regional planning, however, the level of abstraction at which identification and protection take place is considerably higher than is the case when an individual property or small set of properties is being considered.

IDENTIFICATION

Whereas in the study of a particular project area, the preservationist's immediate problem is to identify particular properties, in regional planning the problem is to identify general classes of historic properties and plot their distributions. Ideally, of course, such generalizations should be based on complete survey data—the result of a full regional study including the professional examination of every structure and piece of land that might be of historic value.

Perhaps someday this ideal will be reached, but in most cases today it is necessary to settle for something less costly—a predictive survey.

The literature of prehistoric archeology has begun to reflect a growing interest among archeologists in attempts to predict the distribution of prehistoric sites. Such attempts are usually made as parts of an effort to account for the ways in which human populations distribute themselves over the landscape (cf. Hill and Plog in Gumerman 1971). Mueller (1975) has provided a valuable set of readings on the general topic of archeological sampling which includes important discussions of predictive sample survey. King (1977) has presented a less sophisticated discussion of sample surveys in a volume on preservation-oriented archeological surveys in general. As a result, our discussion here can be relatively brief and general.

A predictive survey sets out to identify the types of historic properties present in a study area, and to determine the relationships between property types and easily identifiable features of the natural or cultural environment, such as altitude ranges, drainage characteristics, and transportation routes. From these observations it is possible to extrapolate to the entire study area, with some degree of accuracy, thus predicting where different types and numbers of properties will occur throughout the area. For planning purposes, these predictions can be used much as can absolute data on specific properties, as a basis for identifying preservation opportunities and as a way of recognizing potential conflicts between preservation needs and modern land-use requirements before they become actual.

Archeologists have made predictive statements about the distribution of sites for many years, but these statements have tended to be vague, self-evident, or of limited value to planning. The statement, "rock art tends to be associated with rocks," for example, does not provide much guidance to planners if there is a great deal of rock in the region. The statement, "people tend to settle near potable water sources," although generally true in most places, can be used successfully only if one recognizes that under some circumstances (e.g., where defense requires that settlements be placed on high ground) potable water is not a primary settlement determinant, that old water sources can be obliterated and thus be invisible today, and that not all historic properties are settlements. Many predictive statements made in the past were mere intuitive reflections or, at best, conclusions drawn from simple experience. The problem with such predictions is that the experience of the person formulating them may not have encompassed a sufficiently broad sample of situations, and there is little or no way of knowing what the nature of that experience may have been. Formulating accurate predictive statements requires carefully developed research designs, systematic sampling techniques, and mechanisms for testing and adjusting initial predictions.

If predictive attempts by archeologists have tended to be vague and biased, predictive efforts by architects and historians have been almost nonexistent. Geographers have addressed the distribution of modern population aggregates, activities, and the structures that house them (cf. Berry and Marble 1968; Haggett 1965), but their perspectives have not commonly been employed in studies relating to historic preservation, except by archeologists. There is considerable unease in architectural preservation circles about the utility or applicability of predictive survey, but we believe that such an approach can be useful in regional studies of the whole range of historic properties.

Background Research in Predictive Survey

Background research in predictive survey is aimed at projecting where general types of properties will occur, rather than at the identification of specific properties. By studying the types of social groups that have lived in the area, and the kinds of things they did there, one should be able to hypothesize where their leavings should be, and what they might look like. One result of such a study might be the development of predictive tables like the example shown in Figure 11. In the study from which this table was derived, economic use of the land appeared to be the major determinant of activity type and location, and particular ethnic groups and occupation types tended to be associated with specific kinds of land use. The background research made it possible to project what site types would be found representing particular time periods and particular groups, and where they would occur. The same sort of approach could be applied to prehistory, as shown hypothetically in Figure 12. With respect to prehistory, however, relatively little may be known about the associations between particular social or occupational groups and particular land uses, except in a very general way (e.g., Archaic peoples were hunter–gatherers). However, given a good understanding of the natural environment, even low-level generalizations can be useful. For example, agricultural settlements can be expected to have some association with arable land; thus if one knows that a local prehistoric population practiced agriculture, a study of local soils may provide a basis for predicting the distribution of villages. Similarly, if one has knowledge of some archeological site locations, and finds a regular association between these locations and prominent environmental features, one can then plot the distribution of those features and predict the locations of sites. Figure 13, for example, shows a map projection of prehistoric site distributions in the greater Langles area, the product of a study undertaken by the Greater Langles Economic Betterment Commission using a Housing and Community Development block grant. Extant ethnohistoric and archeological records indicate that Indians lived mostly on the coast, along streams, and at the base of the mountains. Such areas have been designated "high density habitats" and then a distribution of sites similar to that found in known high density habitats has been predicted for all

Subarea	Period/Phase	Economic activity	Site types	Social groups
Baylands	Sp-Mex/Mission	First missions	Mission composite: bldgs, roads, cemeteries, etc.	Spanish missionaries Neophyte Indians
		Trade	Embarcaderos, probably not preserved	None resident
	Sp-Mex/Rancho	Hide and tallow shipping Refuge and subsistence agricult.	Embarcadero composites Camp/village	Californianos Post-secularization Indians
	Early American	Dairying Salt processing Strawberry production.	Ranch composites Evaporators Farm/packing	Swiss Anglos, nonresident Chinese
	Later American	Dairying	Ranch composites	Swiss, Italian
		Salt processing	Evaporators	
		Truck farming	Farm composites	Anglo, Japanese, Chinese.
		Oystering	Storage and processing composites	
		Shipping	Alviso composite	Anglos, Mexican
North Valley	Sp-Mex/Mission	Mission operation	Mission composites	Spanish, neophyte Indians.

Figure 11. *A predictive table of historic archeological properties. [From Hickman, in King and Berg, 1975.]*

habitats having similar natural characteristics (see Dincauze and Meyer 1976 for an actual example). Figure 14 is an example of a base data map developed under contract with the Cupalava Oil and Gas Company to predict the distribution of prehistoric sites underwater in the Langles Channel. It shows submarine topography and a graph of sea level changes over the last 60,000 years. Assuming that prehistoric people did not live underwater, or carry out activities likely to result in archeological sites there, the level of the sea—and hence the location of the coast—together with the distribution of rivers and inlets during any given time period, should limit the distribution of archeological sites developed during that

Subarea	Period	Economic activity	Site types	Social groups
Riverine lowlands	Archaic	Hunting/gathering/ fishing	Fishing stations, campsites	Migratory bands
	Early Woodland	Hunting/gathering/ fishing	Semipermanent	Semi-sedentary bands
	Middle Woodland	Hunting/gathering/ fishing/incipient agriculture	Permanent villages, burial mounds	Sedentary village communities.
	Late Woodland	Agriculture/Hunting/ gathering/fishing	Permanent villages, temple mounds, burial mounds	High-status lineages, bureaucrats, villagers

Figure 12. *Hypothetical predictive table of prehistoric archeological properties.*

time period. This map was useful in planning surveys of underwater drilling sites off the coast of Langles (see Gagliano *et al.* 1976 for an actual example).

Obviously, predictions derived from background research can be only as reliable as the data upon which they are based. The projections of regional distributions from the distributions of known historic properties is hazardous, since this practice may result only in the projection of old errors and biases. Archeological records on file with academic institutions and avocational organizations, for example, commonly contain data on two kinds of sites: those that have been recorded for specific research purposes and those that have been discovered accidentally. The distribution of the former represents archeological interests as well as actual site locations—if one is interested in Late Woodland cemeteries one is not going to spend time looking for Archaic rockshelters. Accidental finds, of course, normally occur in places where people spend a lot of time; projecting from the distribution of such sites would show clearly that prehistoric settlement patterns were largely determined by the placement of modern roads, picnic grounds, and housing tracts. Predictions from background data should be made cautiously, using all available data in a critical fashion. Such predictions should generally be regarded only as very preliminary hypotheses, and should be tested through fieldwork. Still, the generation of systematic predictions from background research is an important element of an overall predictive survey. Such predictions make it possible to design the fieldwork component of the survey with greater precision, and provide an initial comparative framework for the evaluation of historic properties.

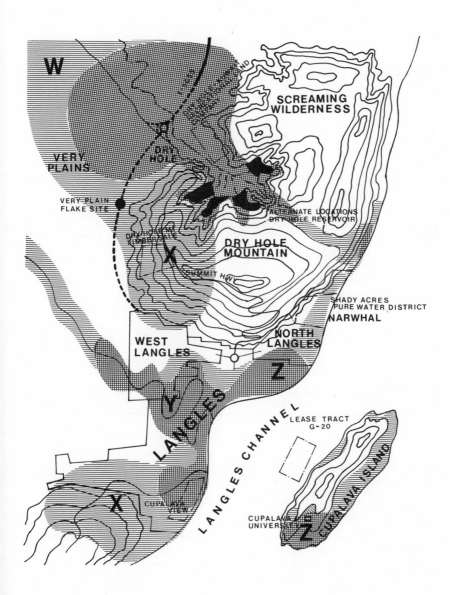

Figure 13. *Langles: high density habitats. Known areas are indicated by crosshatching; projected areas are indicated by horizontal lines. W = Plains; X = Foothills; Y = Riverine; Z = Coastal.*

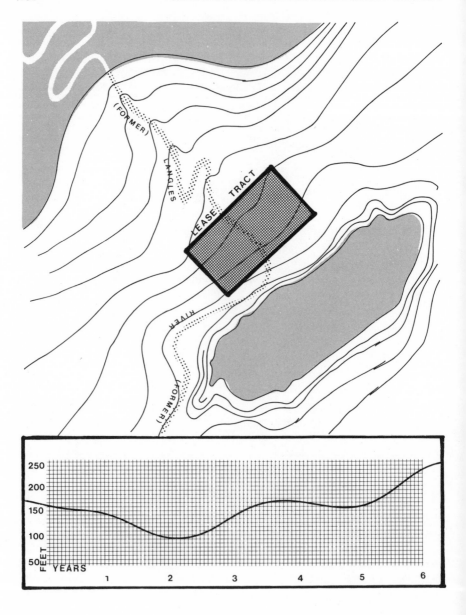

Figure 14. *Base data for projecting distribution of submarine prehistoric sites: Cupalava Island.*

Fieldwork in Predictive Survey

Background research as a basis for prediction provides one kind of incomplete "sample"—of data structured by the observational framework of the natural scientists who have compiled environmental data, by the biases of the historical record, and by the interests and logistic problems that characterized previous archeological studies in the area. Fieldwork provides the other basis for prediction, and there is an increasingly sophisticated and rapidly growing body of expertise in archeology which serves to assure that less-than-complete sample field operations are adequate for predictive purposes (cf. Mueller 1975). Mueller (1974) has described several simple types of sample field surveys, and we will use his terminology in the following discussion, returning to the tangles of Langles to illustrate the uses of various fieldwork methods.

Since fieldwork in a predictive survey is done on only a fraction of the total area under consideration, a system must be used for selecting the portions, or units, that will be inspected. This system is called the "sampling scheme." A variety of schemes have been employed by archeologists. Naturally, some are more successful than others, as the Corps of Engineers learned when it decided to do an archeological survey of the proposed Dry Hole Reservoir project.

When Congress first authorized planning the reservoir, the Corps requested that a local archeologist perform a reconnaissance of the various possible locations. Constrained by inadequate funding, the archeologist was unable to examine the entire area in even a cursory way. Instead, he concentrated his efforts in places where he expected to find sites—elevated benches above the flood plain along streams in the major drainages. He spot-checked places where he thought an occasional site might be located, and ignored places that were "unlikely." This, of course, he did on the basis of his previous experience in the area and with its ethnographic settlement patterns. In other words, since he always looked for sites in certain types of places—and occasionally found them there—he assumed that sites "always" occur in those types of places, and seldom or never in others. Since his experience was substantial, and his knowledge of local ethnography accurate, he did find several sites, and produced Figure 15 as part of his survey report.

Unfortunately (for the Corps) construction plans did not move along as expeditiously as hoped, and by the time planning was to begin in earnest NEPA had been signed into law. The Corps prepared its environmental impact statement, using the old survey data as a basis for its archeological element, but the adequacy of the EIS was challenged by the Langles Environmental Preservation and Ecological Rights Society (LEPERS). Seeking to bolster its case against the Corps, LEPERS turned to P. O. Thunter for information on the archeological impacts of the project. Thunter, of course, is primarily interested in the artifacts he can scavenge from dry caves along the canyon rims; he was unwilling to reveal

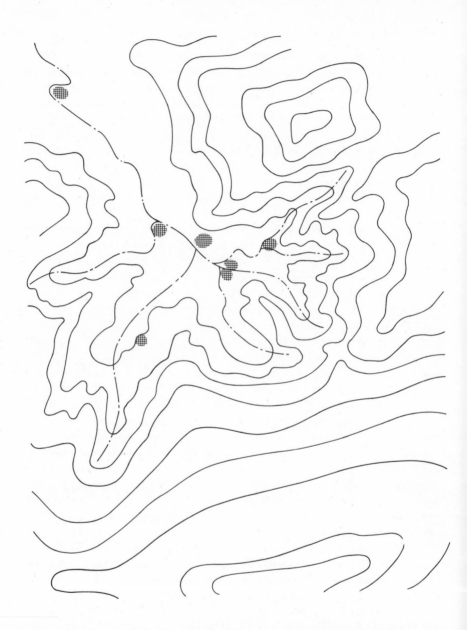

Figure 15. *Prehistoric sites recorded: initial survey of Dry Hole Reservoir area.*

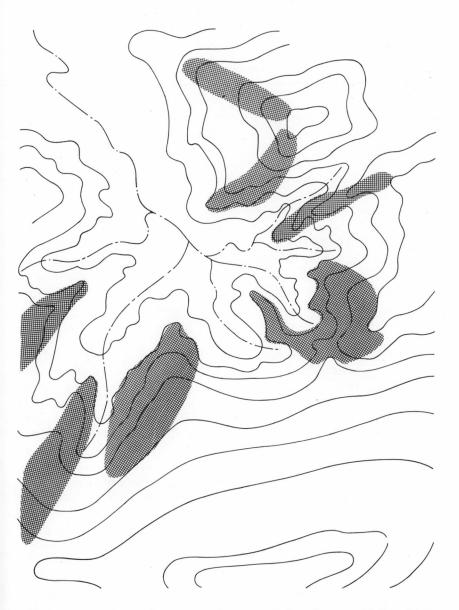

Figure 16. *Areas where, following P. O. Thunter, archeological sites are likely in the Dry Hole Reservoir area.*

exact locations for fear of competition, but he helped a LEPERS member develop Figure 16, showing general areas where important archeological discoveries might be expected.

Faced with this confusing information, the Corps concluded that more study was needed. At this point, however, several reservoir sites were still being considered and a preferred location had not been decided upon; the Corps was unwilling to fund a complete survey of the entire study area. It decided instead to contract with an archeologist to collect and restudy the data available on the area, including the original survey and Thunter's information, in order to develop predictions about the differential archeological sensitivity of the various reservoir sites. Had this restudy been done, the sampling approach employed would have been what Mueller calls "grab sampling," the most primitive of sampling schemes (if it can be called "sampling" at all). Grab sampling means simply "grabbing" whatever data one can from the area in question, without explicit design. As a field strategy, this approach is sometimes referred to as "intuitive" survey, because the choices of places to inspect are made on the basis of one's intuition about where things are likely to occur. The first archeological survey at Dry Hole was such a survey. Grab sampling may reveal sites, but it cannot be demonstrated to provide a representative sample of those that actually exist in the area.

By the time the Corps had reached this planning stage, however, Executive Order 11593 had been issued, as had the advisory council's *Procedures,* and the Corps began to think a little more seriously about its historic preservation responsibilities. It contracted with Cupalava University for a new study of the area, including new fieldwork, to produce reliable predictions. There was some divergence of opinion at C.U. as to what sort of sampling scheme ought to be employed. One archeologist felt that a simple random sample would prove satisfactory, because it would eliminate the biases that characterized the previous work. The study area would be divided into equal-size units, and each unit would be numbered. Using a table of random numbers, a percentage of the total units would be selected for intensive survey. From the results of this partial survey, predictions would be made about the whole area.

Although this approach certainly eliminated bias, it has been criticized as being too mechanical and for failing to utilize the expertise that archeologists may possess. Using this scheme, even if the archeologist knows perfectly well that a given portion of the area is very likely to contain sites, he cannot sample that portion unless it is chosen from the table of random numbers. Simple random sampling units also have a discouraging tendency to culster, failing to be well dispersed over the study area.

A way of avoiding the second of these problems has been sought using "systematic" sampling, and this approach was preferred by another C.U. archeologist. In a systematic sample scheme, the area is again divided into units on a grid, but rather than choosing sample units at random, the units are chosen at regular intervals (for example, every tenth unit on the grid might be chosen), resulting in a sort of checkerboard pattern. However, although systematic sampling disperses the sample units well over the study area, it does not make it possible for the archeologist to use data already available, the primary failure of simple random sampling as well.

The C.U. team eventually decided on a "stratified" sample, which has become the customary means of avoiding both of the major difficulties arising from random and systematic sampling. In a stratified sampling scheme, the archeologist uses background data or hypotheses about settlement distributions to subdivide, or "stratify" the study area, then samples within each stratum. For example, if background data suggest that some types of prehistoric sites tend to occur around the shore of a lake, while others occur in the nearby hills, one might subdivide the study area into a lakeshore stratum and a hill stratum. Each stratum would then be subdivided into potential units on a grid, and a sample would be selected using either random or systematic methods. At Dry Hole Canyon, of course, the first survey had indicated that some occupation sites lay along watercourses, while Thunter's data pointed to dry caves on the ridges. Each of these environments was usable as a sampling stratum, as were the several environments (dry lowland hills, for example) that had been ignored by both previous investigators.

Once the background research was complete, and sampling strata had been selected, the research design underwent some modification. A "cluster" sampling design was adopted to enhance efficiency. Clusters of potential sample units were defined, each cluster designed to represent the range of sampling strata defined for the entire study area within the smallest possible area. Sample units were then selected within each cluster.

Sampling units are the pieces of ground actually selected for field inspection. The size and shape of the units are important because they affect the number of units that can be chosen and the efficiency with which they can be inspected. Since sample survey became popular in the 1960s, the typical sampling unit has been the "quadrat," a square of variable size imposed on the study area by overlaying the area map or airphoto with a gridded plastic sheet or by drawing a grid system on the map. Figure 17 illustrates the Dry Hole sample survey using quadrats. Simulation studies and some on-the-ground experiments have indicated that "transects" may be both more effective and less costly than quadrats. A transect is, in essence, a long rectangle imposed on the area to be inspected. Since transects are long and skinny, they tend to crosscut environmental zones better than do quadrats, and since they can be walked out by simply following a compass heading and then swinging 180° and returning, they take less time to inspect than do quadrats. Figure 18 illustrates the Dry Hole sample survey using transects.

Figure 17. *Dry Hole Reservoir sample survey: quadrats selected for field inspection.*

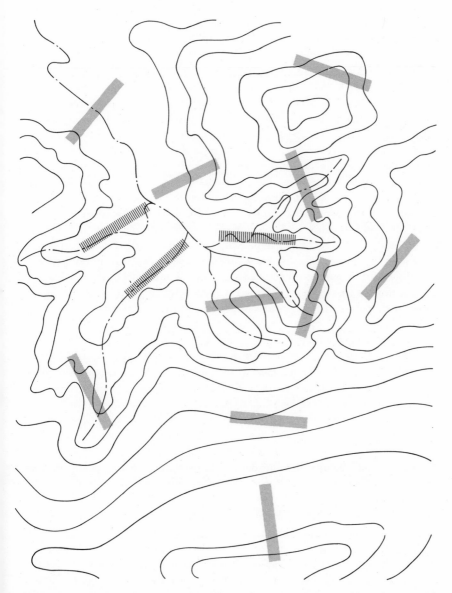

Figure 18. *Dry Hole Reservoir sample survey: transects selected for survey. The three odd transects are nonrandom.*

The next question to be confronted is, "How much area needs to be inspected in order to generate viable predictions?" The "sampling fraction" is that fraction of the total number of sampling units within the study area actually selected for inspection. In other words, the sampling fraction is the number of sampling units that must be inspected in order to make reasonable predictions. Sample sizes that have been used for predictive purposes have ranged from under 1% of the total study area to over 50%. General opinion about the size of sampling fraction necessary to project site densities ranges from about 15% to about 40%; these estimates, however, certainly reflect the different research interests of the estimaters and are probably biased toward reflecting conditions in the southwestern United States. A few recent studies outside the Southwest, however (cf. Lovis 1976) have tended to result in similar conclusions about the size of sampling fraction necessary.

Shifting to a somewhat larger and more complex frame of reference, Figure 19 shows the most basic output that can be expected from a predictive archeological survey. In this example, the basic relative density of prehistoric sites within the greater Langles area is projected, without comment on the types of sites present. Figure 20 illustrates a somewhat more sophisticated kind of study. It shows zones in which different densities and different kinds of sites can be expected. Both sorts of output can provide significant guidance to planners, identifying general areas where preservation opportunities exist and giving early warning of possible conflicts.

Thus far, we have emphasized surveys to predict prehistoric site distributions. We have done this because it is prehistoric archeologists who have developed predictive studies to their highest level of sophistication. The same principles and methods can be used to predict the distribution of post-Contact historic properties, but the variables used to stratify field samples and account for property distributions are likely to be different. Where a prehistoric hunter–gatherer can be assumed to have made decisions about settlement location based in part on the distributions of plants and animals, a nineteenth-century industrialist would be concerned about very different environmental features.

During the mid-nineteenth century, Langles was a small service center for local dairy ranchers. Milk was shipped by schooner from the mouth of the Langles River, and this is where the town of Langlesport initially sprang up. Dairy ranches sprawled along the riverbanks where water was available for the cattle. The only other local population center was Narwhal, to the northeast, where whaling and fishing were the main economic pursuits. Unsuccessful Narwhal whalers are known to have gone ashore and formed rustler bands which preyed on the herds of the Langlesport dairypeople. Rustled stock were driven into remote mountain canyons, then brought down in small, discrete groups or as butchered carcasses for sale to the citizens and shippers of Narwhal.

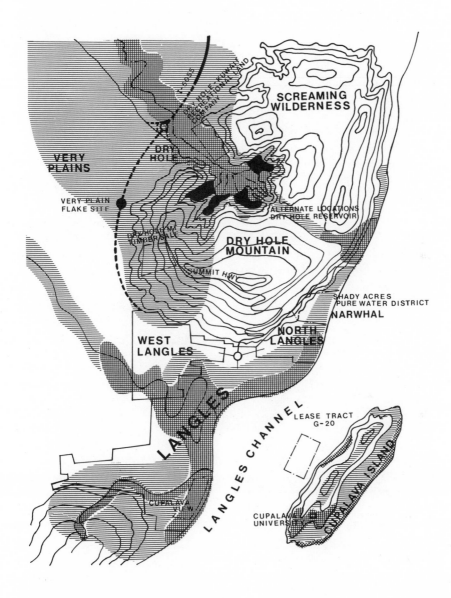

Figure 19. *Langles: projected prehistoric site densities. High density areas are cross hatched; moderate site density areas are indicated by horizontal lines; low density areas are clear.*

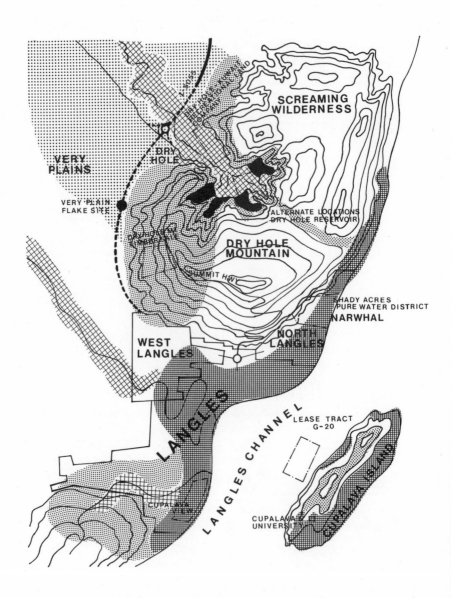

Figure 20. *Langles: projected prehistoric site type densities. Coastal shell mounds are indicated by close cross hatching, large interior villages by wide cross hatching, small foot-hill villages and special activity camps by close-dot stippling, open camps by wide-dot stippling.*

For this time period, then, four distinct populations can be defined: citizens of Narwhal, citizens of Langlesport, dairypeople, and rustlers. Each occupied a distinctive environment: Langlesport, Narwhal, the Langles River floodplain, and the canyons of Dry Hole Mountain. Each environment is definable, with greater or less accuracy, as shown by Figure 21. Each environment, then, can serve as a sampling stratum in which sampling units can be inspected in order to develop predictions about the distribution of properties associated with each population. The precision with which predictive maps of historic-period properties can be constructed will vary with the qualify of the data available and the complexity of the social and historical makeup of the community. Normally it can be expected that the distribution of post-Contact properties will be considerably more complex than that of prehistoric sites. Nevertheless, we see no reason to think that such distributions cannot be predicted, and we believe that such predictions would be as useful in planning as are predictions about prehistoric sites.

We do not mean to suggest, by all this, that predictive surveys involving the physical inspection of only a portion of a study area are real and permanent substitutes for complete surveys. It is a fact, however, that one can begin working with predictive survey data as soon as a small percentage of the total study area has been looked at. If one were faced with a large study area and attempted a straightforward complete survey—marching in at one end and hoping to come out someday at the other—it would be a very long time before one would be able to say anything reliable about the whole area.

There is, of course, nothing to cause one to stop with an initial sample survey. More useful data and more reliable predictions can be obtained as more studies are carried out and the sample actually inspected increases in size. In the long run, for regional and statewide planning purposes, a multistage hierarchical approach to predictive survey is most desirable. A hierarchical predictive survey is a phased approach to developing management data on a large region. Each phase represents a higher level of predictive precision, producing more and more useful information as the study progresses through its phases. In the long run, such a survey will result in complete inspection of the study area, but it is probable that virtually all the data necessary to implement a regional preservation plan will be in hand before physical inspection of the land surface has approached 50%. The nature of the phases in any given instance will vary, but hypothetically, we can suggest the following sequence:

Phase 1. A period of background research would lead to the development of predictive tables and, in some instances, crude predictive maps. General research designs would be formulated. Field survey strata would be established and a sampling scheme developed.

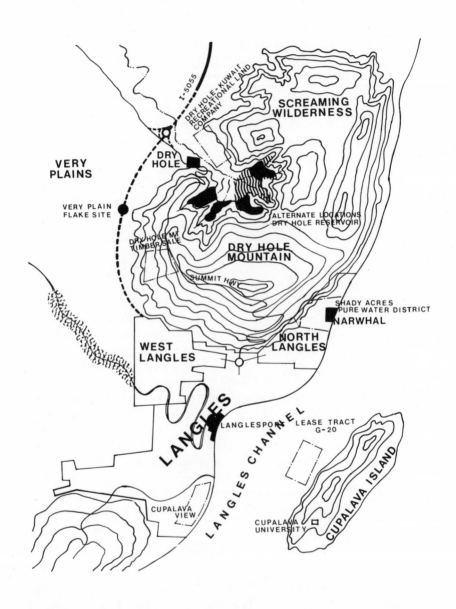

Figure 21. *Langles: premodern environments and projected distribution of historic sub-populations. Wavy areas show cattle rustling activities, sponge stippling areas show dairy farming.*

Phase 2. Initial sample fieldwork would be undertaken, perhaps together with further background research using sources identified during Phase 1. Depending on the size of the study area, the sample fraction might range from less than 1% to perhaps 10%; it would be designed to provide a crude and general projection of historic property densities and a rough check on the accuracy of the predictions generated from background research.

Phase 3. Once the results of Phase 2 have been digested, the sampling scheme can be refined, the sample fraction increased, and/or both field and background research redirected as necessary. This phase should result in refined predictive maps and supporting data.

Phase 4. This and subsequent phases would be aimed at further refining the study output, considering and reconsidering the output of preceding phases. Eventually, and probably well before field survey has advanced to 50% coverage of the study area, the output should begin to become repetitive, and at this point surveys for general planning could be terminated in favor of highly directed studies for specific preservation purposes.

PROTECTION: THE USES OF PREDICTIVE DATA

The data produced by predictive surveys can be used both for regional planning and for planning specific land-use projects. Maps of projected historic property densities can be used in planning for the preservation of open space and the acquisition of parkland. Zones of high projected density, or high projected density of properties meeting particular significance standards, can be identified as high priority areas for public acquisition or other forms of protection. Projected historic sensitivity can be one factor taken into account in zoning and in implementing other methods for regulating land use. Maps of projected historic property densities can be superimposed on general plans, maps of projected population densities, and other indicators of future land use, in order to identify danger areas where land use and the needs of preservation may come into conflict. This in turn will indicate where further survey and identification activities may be appropriate on a high priority basis. Figures 22–24 illustrate an example of this use of predictive maps. On a day-to-day basis, predictive maps and associated documents can be used as a basis for advising land-managing and land-modifying agencies about the need for surveys and preservation planning in advance of particular projects. Predictive data must, of course, be used with caution; it will seldom be appropriate to eliminate totally the need for survey of a project simply because it fals in a "low-sensitivity" zone on a predictive map, unless the map is based on extremely good data. It will probably often be

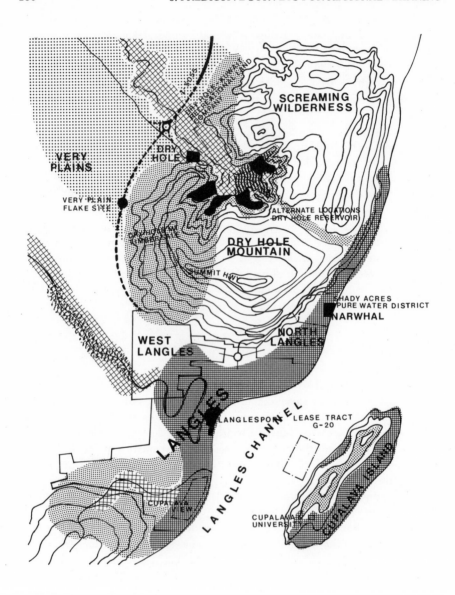

Figure 22. *Langles: projected historic property distributions. Area keys are as in Figures 20 and 21.*

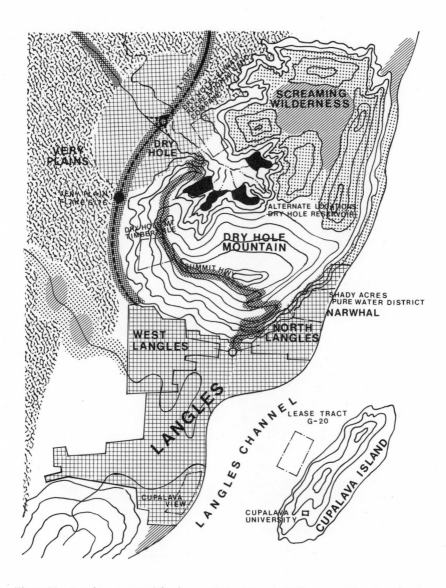

Figure 23. *Langles: projected land use, 1990. Sponge stippling: agricultural; wide cross-hatching: industrial, residential, and commercial; close cross-hatching: highway corridors; angled lines: parks; wide-dot stippling: planned open space.*

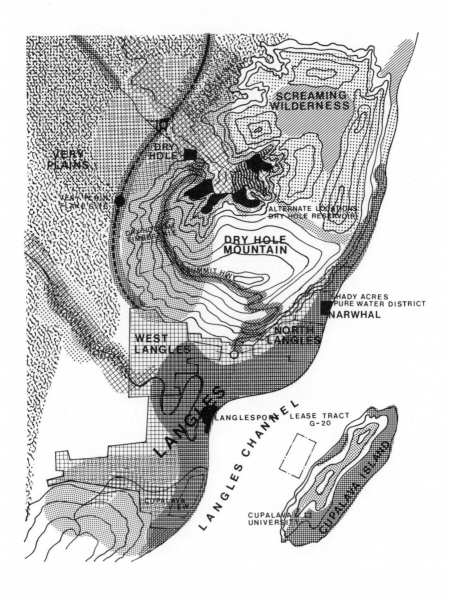

Figure 24. *Projected conflicts between land use (1990) and historic preservation.*

possible to conduct only relatively limited surveys in low-sensitivity zones, however, while doing more detailed studies in areas of higher sensitivity. If types of property, as well as densities, have been predicted, it should be possible to plan such surveys as are necessary with considerable precision and efficiency. Figure 25 illustrates a predictive map designed for project guidance use in connection with offshore drilling in the Langles Channel. In Zone 1, there is a

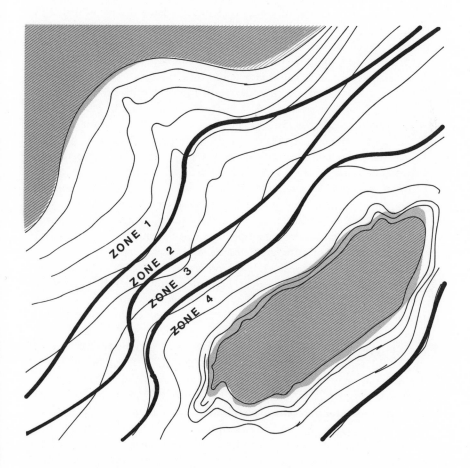

Figure 25. *Langles Channel: projected distribution of submarine historic properties.* Zone 1: *high density prehistoric sites high density shipwrecks;* Zone 2: *moderate density prehistoric sites moderate density shipwrecks;* Zone 3: *moderate density prehistoric sites low density shipwrecks;* Zone 4: *high density prehistoric sites low density shipwrecks.*

high probability of both historic shipwrecks and prehistoric occupation sites; project-area surveys here will require both magnetometer sweeps and the use of subbottom profilers to define old landforms. Zone 2 is likely to have fewer shipwrecks but some prehistoric sites; the subbottom profiler might be emphasized here rather than the magnetometer. Zones 3 and 4 are zones of low shipwreck probability but some prehistoric sensitivity, with Zone 4 having greater sensitivity because the shoals surrounding Cupalava Island represent areas exposed during the last glacial period, and because it contains very ancient shoreline features, the origin of which probably predates the entry of people into North America; here magnetometer sweeps might be eliminated altogether, but great care would be needed in searching for prehistoric sites.

It is important to understand the relationship between predictive studies and the processes for compliance with the historic preservation laws. The laws and their associated procedures were devised with the identification and protection of individual properties in mind. Predictive surveys will not, on the whole, deal with specific properties or generate data adequate to determine the eligibility of specific properties for the National Register. They will, however, greatly facilitate the compliance process for those agencies having regional planning responsibilities. As a result, many agencies are undertaking such studies (cf. Ritter *et al.* 1976, Weide, 1974, Smith 1977). Predictive surveys generate a large body of relatively low-resolution data in a short period of time; these data can be utilized in management immediately to minimize conflicts, leaving the complete recording and nomination of particular properties until a later time when immediate protection problems are not pressing.

One of the most promising uses of predictive surveys is as the basis for programmatic memoranda of agreement with the advisory council, that replace the exact steps outlined by the advisory council *Procedures* with region-specific, activity-specific, and property-type-specific methods of dealing with historic properties. The logic behind such a programmatic arrangement is simple: The NHPA requires that the advisory council be afforded an opportunity to comment whenever an agency finds that its undertaking may affect properties on or eligible for inclusion in the National Register—it does not say that this commenting must take place on a case-by-case or property-by-property basis. It is perfectly reasonable for an agency to recognize that a given *class* of action may have impacts on a given *class* of properties, then consult with the state historic preservation officer and OAHP to determine whether the class of properties is likely to represent eligible properties, and then consult with the advisory council and SHPO about general methods for preserving representatives of the class, arriving at a memorandum of agreement stipulating what methods will be used under particular circumstances.

Imagine—an admittedly great oversimplification—that the regional predictive study of the Langles Basin, funded jointly by the Environmental Protection

Agency, the SHPO (as part of the state historic preservation plan), the Langleland Coastal Zone Management Bureau, and the City of Langles using Community Development Block Grant funds, has led to the recognition of areas displaying three levels of historic sensitivity—high, medium, and low. It has also led to the recognition of three types of historic property—dairy barns, flake scatters, and temple mounds. The SHPO opines, and OAHP agrees, that all three classes represent eligible properties. The SHPO then proposes a treatment plan for each type of sensitivity area and each type of property:

1. Intensive surveys should be done in all unsurveyed areas of high sensitivity prior to any land disturbance.

2. Cursory generalized inspections, and specialized surveys to locate dairy barns, should be done in unsurveyed areas of medium sensitivity prior to land disturbance, since dairy barns are the only historic properties likely to occur there.

3. Surveys need be done in low-sensitivity areas in advance of land disturbance only if aerial photos or other data suggest the presence of temple mounds, since these are the only historic properties that can possibly occur there.

4. Dairy barns should not be disturbed without full consultation with the Langleland Order of the Sacred Cow, to whom the properties are often very important. Consultation must occur after a full architectural study, must involve professional ethnographic consultation, and must be conducted in accordance with the order's ancient standards of practice.

5. Flake scatters should be preserved insofar as is possible. Detailed consultation with the SHPO, Interagency Archeological Services, and a committee of 12 professional archeologists should be undertaken whenever such a site is endangered, to devise a preservation plan. All such sites that are preservable should be nominated to the National Register.

6. Temple mounds should be excavated whenever possible, in accordance with the research design given as Appendix IV:B:12 of the Langleland State Historic Preservation Plan, most current edition.

Now, the Environmental Protection Agency, or the Department of Housing and Urban Development, or the Department of Commerce for the Coastal Zone Management Bureau, should be able to approach the advisory council with a draft memorandum of agreement that simply commits the agency to comply with the treatment plan in all its undertakings in the Langles Basin. Assuming the council finds the treatment plan reasonable, it can sign the memorandum and thereafter serve simply in a monitor capacity, vastly simplifying the whole compliance system.

At the present, no such plan, and no such memorandum of agreement, have been developed, but the only thing to keep them from being developed is the lack of good regional studies. In the long run, of course, state historic preservation plans should be comprehensive enough to form the basis for all compliance; an agency should simply agree to comply with the plan and be free of further property-specific consultation with the council except as provided for by the plan itself. It will, however, be a long time before state historic preservation plans are able to bear this kind of weight.

Even now, however, SHPOs may have the greatest need of all for predictive surveys. The SHPOs receive notices of federal projects for review, and must advise the responsible agencies about the need for surveys or other kinds of preservation action. Agencies are unlikely to respond well to requests not based on some sort of real data. Routine requests for surveys on all projects tend to simply be filed and forgotten. Predictive surveys can provide a perfect documentary base upon which to build arguments for and against the expenditure of public funds on project-level studies. The SHPOs are authorized to undertake such surveys by Section 102 of the NHPA, and the procedures implementing this section (Draft 36 CFR 60) encourage the collection of predictive data. Funds, of course, are very scarce, but an aggressive SHPO has many sources open to him. Funds authorized by the Coastal Zone Management Act, the Water Polution Control Act amendments of 1972, and the Housing and Community Development Act could all be used to fund predictive surveys. Land managing agencies like the Bureau of Land Management and the Forest Service have inherant needs and authority to do such surveys. Data from individual project-specific surveys can also be incorporated into the development of predictions. Sewer projects, which often require the survey of long corridors through large and varied environments, can provide a substantial if not rigorous basis for the generation of predictions (cf. Johnson and Berg 1976), as can the survey of many discontinuous small plots planned for development in a large area (cf. King and Berg 1974). If well coordinated by the SHPO, these sources could be brought together with survey and planning grant funds from OAHP to develop a predictive survey of an average state in fairly short order.

EVALUATION AND PLANNING

We have talked thus far about the usefulness of predictive surveys for making relatively mechanical decisions about where specific projects need specific identification studies. Predictive surveys have another utility, however, as aids in evaluation.

Clearly, if a predictive survey has indicated that the Tlakipaki Valley contains 4,000,000 prehistoric potato processing sites, we are likely to be less concerned about the loss of one such site than we would be if we lacked this prediction. Similarly, if a predictive survey has identified a neighborhood that has been occupied since the 1850s by Latvian Taoists, we know that we may have particular kinds of cultural values to deal with should we be called upon to evaluate the neighborhood. It is quite possible that most of the problems experienced by federal agencies, SHPOs, and scholars with the evaluation of historic properties spring directly from the lack of a regional context for evaluation and/or the lack of early warning about potential conflicts with special values. Predictive survey is designed to provide both kinds of assistance.

Here, of course, is a place where historic preservation overlaps significantly with traditional anthropological research. Anthropologists tend to be oriented toward interpreting relationships and getting big pictures. Predictive survey results, integrated into regional plans, should portray such relationships and bring such pictures into focus.

Naturally, there are dangers in predictions and planning. The predictive surveys may be done poorly, and their inadequate results then canonized in plans. The plans themselves, while fine this year, may not reflect the cutting edge of scholarly thought a decade later. The responsibility for avoiding these dangers lies in large part with the professional disciplines involved in historic preservations. Each state must update its historic preservation plan regularly, and undergo review by OAHP (36 CFR 60). During the update period there should be ample opportunity for professional involvement and criticism; if not, comments can be lodged with OAHP during its review. We believe that the dangers of predictive surveys and regional planning are far outweighed not only by their advantages but by the dangers of not undertaking such activities. The existing compliance system is unwieldy and oriented toward coping with crises. It can be and is being effectively and creatively used in many instances, but it is too rigid to be easily applicable to all agencies, all properties, and all circumstances. Through the development and use of good regional plans based on solid predictive data, a needed flexibility could be introduced into historic preservation that would encourage compliance with the statutes and better fulfill what we take to be their purposes.

9

FORCING THE SYSTEM

We must now learn all the tricks
To be found in 106
When we find a fed whose EIS is lacking.
We must look 'em in the eye;
Holler "FAILURE TO COMPLY!"
And the legions of the Council start attacking

—Anonymous, 1974

Up to this point, we have emphasized how preservation professionals and, implicitly, concerned laypeople can work with planners and bureaucrats to realize the goals of historic preservation, assuming that we are all partners in the planning process. However, there are times when this partnership breaks down. When an agency fails to comply with preservation law in carrying out its activities, it is often necessary for someone outside of government to blow the whistle. Forcing compliance is a necessary part of historic preservation.

It is obviously not the purpose of historic preservation to stop construction projects. Its purpose is to maximize preservation in the modern world, not to keep the modern world from existing. However awful a project may be from an economic standpoint, or in terms of its effects on the natural environment, it should not be stopped or delayed as a result of historic preservation concerns as long as the properties in question, and their historic values, have been properly attended to. Such detachment requires some discipline, but the ability to separate one's emotional opposition to a "bad" project from specific points of fact and law distinguishes the effective preservationist from the hothead "obstructionist." In the privacy of our thoughts, we may harbor all sorts of hostility toward land development, but as an historic preservationist, one's job is to be sure that agencies comply with the law and protect historic properties while getting on with the jobs they are organized to do—not with stopping those jobs because we personally disapprove of them.

It is clear, however, that one of the best ways of getting agencies to take proper notice of their preservation responsibilities is to stop them in their tracks when they fail to do so. The laws and policies mandating the protection of historic properties, which we prefer to use as planning tools, can become weapons when one is forced to oppose agency decisions. Having discussed the use of the laws as plowshares at some length, we will briefly consider their employment as swords.

The basic preservation responsibilities of federal agencies are of course spelled out in the advisory council's *Procedures* (36 CFR 800), which interlock with the CEQ's guidelines for the preparation of environmental impact statements (40 CFR V 1500) and with OAHP's various procedures for implementing the NHPA, Executive Order 11593, and the Archeological and Historic Preservation Act. The Time involved in awaiting council comments pursuant to the council's *Procedures* can be considerable, and ignoring council comments without good cause can set an agency up for legal action as well as unpleasant questions from Congress and the executive. Consequently, in most cases, agencies do work with the council to reach memoranda of agreement, if they carry out the procedures at all. Some agencies, however, try to circumvent the procedures altogether, or seek some way of getting out from under them before they reach the memorandum stage. When this happens, the advisory council and OAHP can make a good deal of noise, but the "outside" preservationist is of key importance. It is the public that typically catches the agency, that brings its sins to the attention of the authorities so that they can act, that pursues the matter to make sure they do act, and that takes the matter to court if necessary. The public preservationist needs to know what he or she is talking about, however, and how best to present preservation issues. One can raise a lot of smoke, delay projects, draw a great deal of attention, and do absolutely nothing to protect historic properties by launching a protest without understanding what the laws and policies actually require. The reader should by now understand the basic requirements of the laws and the sometimes complicated ways they are interpreted. It will be useful now to consider how agencies typically try to slip away from their responsibilities under the advisory council's *Procedures,* and how they can be caught.

The "identification" requirement of the procedures, of course, implies that the agency has found out where all the historic properties subject to impact are and what they are like. It requires no thundering intellect to observe that one cannot apply National Register criteria to something one has not yet located or described. Yet it is here that some agencies circumvent their responsibilities, either by accident or design, by settling for a mere inspection of the published National Register or a chat with the local historical society as proof that nothing of value exists in the area. If the agency has had a survey done (see Chapter 6) or otherwise identified—within reason—all historic properties subject to possible impact, it must consult with the SHPO to decide on the significance of the properties, on whether the project will have an effect on them, and whether the effect will be adverse. This is another place where circumvention can occur. Through stupidity or cupidity, the agency's consultants or even the SHPO may advise the agency that significant properties are not significant enough for inclusion in the Register or that destroying such properties, somehow, does not adversely effect them. Sometimes political motivations may be involved: The SHPO may be under pressure from the governor to let the highway get built. Sometimes "professional" jealousies come into play: The old guard archeologist is not going to let these upstart "New Archeologists" tell him that flake scatters are important. Sometimes a simple misconception may be at the bottom of the problem: Someone in a position to impose his or her views may think of the National Register as an "honor role" of landmarks rather than as a roster of all useful historic properties, or may assume that salvage, or relocation of buildings, or some other action will always totally negate the adverse impact of a project on a significant property.

Finally, the agency and the SHPO, or a state archeologist, or some other seemingly official party may make an arrangement that truncates the compliance process short of review by OAHP and the advisory council. For example, for years one state never determined prehistoric sites eligible for inclusion in the National Register when they were endangered by highway construction; in return the state highway department funded minimal salvage excavations at all such sites.

If one wishes effectively to challenge crooked consultants, maleable SHPOs and wayward agencies, one needs to monitor what the agency, in each instance, is doing to make sure that (a) a proper survey has been done; (b) properties are properly evaluated; (c) effects and adverse effects are properly determined; and (d) the consultation process is carried through to a Memorandum of Agreement or a Council comment. Figure 26 shows the points at which one can force a recalcitrant agency to be responsible, and the sorts of general questions to ask at each point along the way.

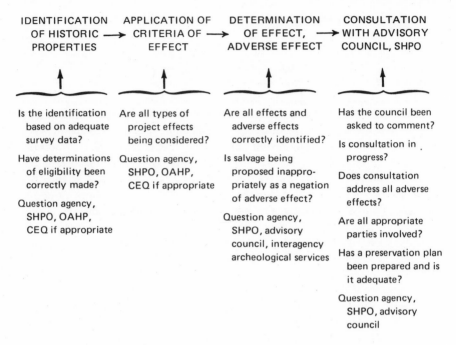

Figure 26. *Pressure points in the advisory council's* Procedures.

SURVEYS

When an agency issues a draft environmental impact statement or some similar sort of planning document on a project, the first question to be asked with respect to historic preservation is: Has there been a survey? There are obviously some projects that do not need surveys—those affecting only water quality, for example. Some projects may be so general, and at such an early stage of planning, that survey can be properly deferred until a later point in the planning process. As a rule, however, any project involving disturbance of the land, or of standing structures, or that will change patterns of land use, access to land, or the distribution of population should be subjected to a survey. The agency may be able to demonstrate that a survey has already been done, as part of the statewide comprehensive survey, for example, or on behalf of another agency engaged in another project, or it may be able to demonstrate that the project's impact area has already been totally disturbed in such a way that no historic properties could have survived. If such conditions cannot be demonstrated, then the agency itself is responsible for conducting a survey, and the survey should be described in the EIS or in other documents available from the agency to qualified persons.

If a survey has not been done in a case where it is needed, or if it has not been done well, one should protest to the agency, the advisory council, the SHPO, OAHP, and—if compliance with NEPA is involved, the CEQ as well. This may seem like a scattershot approach, or overkill, but it assures that everyone who might become officially involved in the case is informed. In many if not most cases such an action, or the letters of inquiry the agency begins to receive from the advisory council, OAHP and the SHPO, will stimulate the agency to have a survey done. If such does not prove to be the case, and if the agency does not demonstrate that a survey is unnecessary, one's action will at least have triggered reactions within the government that will build a record of official concern. This record will be useful in the event litigation becomes necessary. One should also never underestimate the power of one's senator or representative. All agencies respond with unseemly haste to inquiries from the Hill (though the responses are not always enlightening). One should always try to resolve things without dragging Congress into them, but if a response is not forthcoming in a reasonable period of time from the agency, OAHP, or the advisory council, a "congressional" can provide the needed motivation. Public information requests under the Freedom of Information Act can also be highly effective, especially when an agency has been unwilling to provide access to major documentation on its planning activities. For maximum effect, public information requests should be prepared in such a way as to anticipate attempts at obfuscation by the agency and head them off. An example is given in Appendix D.

If a survey has been made, it may not have been adequate. Agencies sometimes try to foist off one or more of the following as an adequate survey:

"There are no National Register properties in the project area. . . ."

One can respond to this by questioning how the agency knows there are no National Register properties in the area, but in most cases the agency will have checked the National Register and perhaps talked with the SHPO. The main thing to point out to the agency at this point is that Section 106 of the NHPA and Executive Order 11593 require not only that National Register properties but properties *eligible for inclusion* in the National Register be identified.

"There are no National Register or National Register-eligible properties in the project area. . . ."

The obvious next question here is, "how do you know?"

"The SHPO informs us that there are no National Register or Register-eligible properties in the project area. . . ."

One should ask how the SHPO reached this conclusion. Did the SHPO have a survey done? Did he or she have documentation that the area had already been adequately surveyed? Or were the files simply checked, revealing that no one had happened to record anything in the area?

"Dr. Gobbledigook of Cupalava University has informed us that. . . ."

What is the basis for Dr. G's opinion? Sometimes an agency will telephone an archeologist, historian, or architect (or almost anyone else) and ask: "Say, Dr. G., do you know of any important archeological (or other) sites out there in Dry Hole Canyon?" When Dr. G. says "No, I've never been there; my specialty is Minoan Crete," the agency representative thanks him and prepares a report saying that in Dr. G's authoritative opinion Dry Hole Canyon is devoid of historic properties. Even if Dr. G. was not thus being conned, did he know what he was being asked about? If he is a specialist in local prehistoric archeology, for example, he may not think about things like buildings constructed in the 1920s, or about the traditions of the Langles Indians who believe that their ancestors issued out of Dry Hole Canyon at the beginning of time. When he says "there's nothing there" is he considering all sorts of historic, prehistoric, cultural, and architectural properties? Has he made a survey, or is he just guessing? If he has made a survey, what kind of survey was it? What methods were used to ensure the identification of all potentially eligible properties? The agency should be prepared to answer these questions.

> "The National Park Service has been notified and will be allowed to conduct a survey in accordance with the Archeological and Historic Preservation Act. . .

One should point out that whatever the National Park Service may do under its AHPA authorities, the agency planning or permitting the project has primary responsibility under NEPA, NHPA, and Executive Order 11593 for identifying and avoiding or mitigating its impacts on historic properties. The AHPA simply provides one possible method for mitigating some kinds of impacts on properties valuable for their data content once they have been identified.

> "If the project is approved a survey will be done. . . ."

The advisory council's procedures clearly require integration of historic preservation planning into *early* project planning. By the time the project is approved it will be fully designed, and there will be little possibility of modifying it to protect historic properties. At that point only salvage archeology, salvage architectural recording, and other limited preservation options will be open, short of scrapping the entire project. The agency is setting itself up for a last-minute conflict, and is not in conformance with the procedures.

> "Before (or during) construction, archeologists will be given a chance to salvage important artifacts. . . ."

Clearly this approach bears no resemblance to what agencies are required to do by the historic preservation statutes. This should be pointed out. The agency should also be asked about nonarcheological historic properties, and asked how it expects the salvage archeologists to conduct their work. Archeologists, it should be noted, do not eat air, dirt, or time; it is the agency's responsibility to set forth some workable method for funding the activities necessary to avoid or mitigate project impacts, and present these to the SHPO and advisory council for incorporation into a memorandum of agreement.

"A survey was done in 1956 and revealed. . . ."

Surveys done prior to passage of NEPA and issuance of Executive Order 11593 are often, if not usually, inadequate to assure compliance with the procedures. The idea of locating all possible historic properties and developing means of protecting their value was little developed when most surveys were being conducted under terms of the Reservoir Salvage Act (see Chapter 2), as were the techniques of systematic archeological (and other) survey, description, and evaluation. At a minimum, the old survey report should be reviewed by the SHPO and OAHP for adequacy.

"A survey has been conducted by Drs. R.K. Ologist and R.Q. Tekt, who have submitted a report finding that. . . ."

Clearly, one should ask to review the report, and ask whether the SHPO has reviewed it and what his or her comments are. One should review the report with an eye to the technical guidelines provided by OAHP (36 CFR 64; Appendix A), and advise the agency, the SHPO, and OAHP of one's opinion of its adequacy.

REASONABLE EVALUATIONS

The agency may assert that in whatever sort of survey was done, no "significant" historic properties were discovered. One should be immediately suspicious of this, and ask whether the Department of the Interior (represented by OAHP) has reviewed any discovered properties for their eligibility. The agency may merely have a "professional" opinion that there are no important properties in the area, and may not have even received the SHPO's comments. It is also possible that the SHPO has erroneously concurred in an agency determination that no historic properties in the area are eligible. If this is a possibility one should ask to review the survey report and, if one disagrees with the SHPO's opinion about eligibility, raise one's questions with OAHP. In raising questions about eligibility with the agency, the SHPO, and/or OAHP, one should refer to the National Register criteria and to the documentation requirements set forth by OAHP for determinations of eligibility (36 CFR 63; Appendix A), and develop one's arguments accordingly. If the agency has not submitted its data to OAHP, and will not provide it to one for review, the agency probably has something to hide; one should immediately notify the SHPO, OAHP, and the advisory council of the situation. If one has independent information on historic properties that may be affected by the agency's project, one should provide this information to the agency, the SHPO, and OAHP, together with one's own opinions about the eligibility of the properties. An example letter is given in Appendix D.

If one has any question about the quality of review being provided by the agency, the SHPO, and OAHP toward determining the eligibility of properties subject to possible effect, one should ask to participate in the review process through either of the reviewing bodies or through the agency. The review process should not be conducted in secret, and unless there is a good and defensible reason for excluding one from participation, one's request can hardly be refused.

DETERMINING EFFECTS AND MITIGATING IMPACTS

If historic properties have been identified, and the agency fears that attendance to them will stop or delay its project—or if it simply does not understand the procedures—it may maneuver to escape its responsibilities to avoid or mitigate adverse effects. Several techniques are common.

Failure to Notify the Advisory Council

The agency simply does not let the advisory council know what it is doing. This is not too difficult to do, especially on projects that do not require environmental impact statements. The obvious response here is to notify the council oneself.

Determination of No Effect When Effects Will Occur

The agency may unilaterally determine that the project will have no effect on the properties; the SHPO may miss the fact that effects will occur, or be pressured into concurring in an improper determination. Since only the agency keeps documentation of a no effect determination (see Figure 3), the advisory council is not informed and the project proceeds without consultation. A similar maneuver can be used with a determination of no adverse effect, but this is riskier since the advisory council must be notified of such determinations (see Figure 3). If one has reason to suspect that an agency is up to something like this, one should immediately notify the council and state one's reason for objecting.

Misuse of the Archeological "No Adverse Effect" Guidelines

There are special ways by which an agency can escape its responsibilities with respect to archeological values. One method involves use of the guidelines for making adverse effect and no adverse effect determinations for archeological resources (see Appendix A). It is possible for an agency, confronted with an archeological property that really could be and should be preserved, to develop a salvage plan that it can sell to at least some archeologists and the SHPO. It then presents the plan to the council, together with the SHPO's concurrence, in such a way that the council sees nothing wrong with it. Particularly in view of the council's very limited staff in archeology, and the fact that, at present, OAHP participates only sporadically in the review of no adverse effect determinations based on salvage, it is not necessarily very difficult to delude the council into believing that an improper and destructive salvage project is really the best possible treatment for an archeological property. If one becomes aware of the possibility that an agency is attempting this kind of determination, one should immediately request the opportunity to comment on the determination before it is forwarded to the council. Copies of this request should be sent to both the council and Interagency Archeological Services in OAHP, which has authority to comment on data recovery programs under the terms of the AHPA. If the agency does not respond reasonably, one should ask the council and Interagency Archeological Services to allow one to review the determination. If one already knows that the determination is improper, and why, the basis for reaching this conclusion should be provided.

Escape through the AHPA

The agency may attempt to conduct salvage operations under terms of the Archeological and Historic Preservation Act without going through the advisory council's *Procedures* at all. This is contrary to OAHP's policy (36 CFR 66; Appendix A) and may earn the agency an adverse comment in Interagency Archeological Service's annual report to Congress, but it can permit the agency to escape review. By the time the advisory council catches up with the situation, archeologists are digging away and project planning is advancing. The council is loath to make an issue of such a situation, since things have advanced to the point where a memorandum of agreement would almost inevitably specify salvage anyway. Clearly, the solution here is to catch the agency before it begins salvage operations.

GETTING ARCHEOLOGISTS TO DESTROY THE
PROPERTIES

Even without an AHPA contract, archeologists can sometimes become the unwitting tools of agencies intent on avoiding review. If there are enough well-intentioned archeologists around who are ignorant of historic preservation policy, all the agency may have to do is release word of its impending project; college classes and amateur groups will mobilize to conduct salvage work. Particularly in urban areas where opportunities to dig and to train students in the field may be limited, archeologists may jump at such a chance. The archeologists will think they are responding properly to a crisis, and in some cases, of course, their work may be quite adequate. Their main effect, however, is usually destructive. The fact that they are digging at all—no matter how carefully—means that some information is lost. Because they usually lack substantial financing and regard the project as an "emergency" situation, their fieldwork is often sloppy and there is little guarantee that the results will be properly analyzed and reported. The lack of professional review means that it is quite possible for the work to be supervised by totally unqualified people. Even if the archeology is done very well, other aspects of the historic environment may be ignored; there is no reason to expect the archeologist to be automatically responsive to the needs of architectural history or to the cultural interests of local groups. The overall effect of all this is that the archeologist takes from the agency the responsibility for historic preservation; since the archeologist's financial, technical, and personnel resources are much more limited than those of the federal government, a poor and incomplete job usually results. If the archeologists are questioned, however, their professional reputations often appear to them to be threatened, and they become defensive. Meanwhile, the agency has gotten off the hook—either because the archeologists have destroyed the properties or because the situation has become too confused for the advisory council or OAHP to make an issue of it. Situations like this can only be avoided by developing among archeologists—and others who may be similarly used—a sensitivity to general preservation issues and an understanding of the responsibilities held by federal agencies. This is not to say that archeologists, or others, should never do free work; saving tax dollars is as desirable in archeology as in any other pursuit. One should simply be careful to know what one is doing, and to make sure that one's work contributes to preservation rather than destruction.

Summary

Determining whether and how an agency may be skirting its mitigation responsibilities may be relatively difficult. A preservation plan and clear evidence of compliance with the advisory council procedures should be included in the

EIS on a project. If an EIS is not prepared, or if surveys are done only after completion of the EIS for some reason, information on what is planned will be harder to come by. The safest strategy, generally, is to insist that the agency comply explicitly with its responsibilities under Section 800.4 of the *Procedures,* by consulting with the advisory council and the SHPO in developing plans for avoidance or mitigation of effects. If one is aware of other parties who should be directly or indirectly involved in approval of such plans—local groups, for instance—one should insist that they be involved and encourage them to demand such involvement themselves. Such demands should be repeated at regular intervals if they are not answered immediately, and the advisory council, SHPO, and OAHP should be informed and provided with copies of pertinent documents and correspondence. Addresses for the advisory council and OAHP are provided in Appendix D; names and addresses of current SHPOs can be obtained by writing either OAHP or the council.

TIMING AND NOMINATION FROM THE OUTSIDE

One can call for compliance with the advisory council's procedures, demand a survey, assert that a survey is inadequate, or press for proper avoidance or mitigation of effect at any point in the project planning process. Obviously, the extent to which one's efforts will be effective depends, in large measure, on the status of the project involved. Once a project is well underway, it is relatively difficult to get its sponsors to reconsider. Compliance with the advisory council's procedures is required regardless of whether an EIS is prepared on the project, so there is no reason to await the EIS to begin promoting compliance. As a rule, the earlier one can get into the agency's planning process, the better.

It is obviously best to provide the agency with some tangible—as well as simply procedural—reason for compliance. In other words, if one knows about some property or properties that may be affected by the project, one should tell the agency about the fact. If one has good reason to suspect that effects will occur, the basis for such suspicions should be provided to the agency. One should not get hooked into doing an agency's work for it, but it is poor form to demand that the agency collect data when one is unwilling to supply any. In some instances, it may be advisable to try and conduct at least a cursory inspection of the area and, if possible, to nominate properties to the National Register. Nomination by a private party is done through the SHPO (36 CFR 60; Appendix A), who can provide instructions. In urgent cases, copies of the nomination should go to OAHP and the advisory council with the request that they advise the agency of its responsibilities. Nomination, if based on good data, shows the review groups that there really is a problem, and enhances the likelihood that they will vigorously take issue with the errant agency. On the other hand, one should avoid preparing an incomplete nomination that is likely to be rejected by the SHPO; this can be twisted by the agency to indicate (to those who do not know better) that the project will *not* impact valuable properties.

Even if one fails to press the agency into compliance with all these notifications, requests, and demands, if one has worked carefully and maintained good documentation one will have clearly shown one's willingness to find administrative remedies to the problem, and one will have documented the agency's failure to respond. This documentation will be useful in court.

GOING TO COURT AND CONGRESS

The importance of litigation in the making of historic preservation law cannot be overestimated. Many of the uncertainties in the administration of the historic preservation system today result from the fact that relatively few cases have been brought to court for interpretation. Ultimately, too, the courts are a citizen's best hope for actually forcing an agency to comply with the law. At the same time, litigation is no small undertaking, and one should not go into it lightly. It is unwise to go to court without relatively assured access to several thousand dollars and an attorney who understands both environmental and historic preservation law. One cannot afford to lose; a positive judgment may help clarify an uncertain point in law and demolish an irrational and destructive agency policy, but a judgment that allows the agency policy to stand will obviously set a disastrous precedent, at least in the district where the case is heard. One's case should be chosen carefully, and carefully developed to demonstrate both that the agency has failed to comply with the law and that by so doing it has endangered or destroyed real historic properties on or eligible for inclusion in the National Register. Attorneys who understand historic preservation law are relatively hard to find, since rather few cases have been heard. A good environmental lawyer can usually grasp the basics of historic preservation law quickly, however, and provide good advice. A good starting place for the attorney (or the attorney's client) in becoming familiar with the law is *Historic Preservation Law: An annotated Bibliography,* by the National Trust for Historic Preservation (1976b).

If one chooses not to litigate, there remains one good—if rather post hoc—way to take a crack at the agency, if archeological values are involved. Under Section 5(c) of the Archeological and Historic Preservation Act, the secretary of the interior (that is, Interagency Archeological Services in OAHP) must report annually to Congress on the scope and effectiveness of the national program carried out under the act. Cases where agencies have shirked their responsibilities should always be reported, with all possible documentation, to OAHP for investigation and possible inclusion in the report to Congress.

10

THE FUTURE

The separation between rhetoric and reality remains considerable in historic preservation, but there is no doubt that the field and its needs are becoming more visible to all branches of the federal government. In August of 1976, President Gerald Ford signed Public Law 94-422, amending the NHPA to authorize, among other things, the $150 million Historic Preservation Fund. On October 22, in a televised debate, then-candidate for the presidency, Jimmy Carter, called for the increased protection of archeological sites. There is thus some reason to believe that the crisis decried by preservationists and archeologists since World War II is at last eliciting a response. Funding for historic preservation has increased dramatically at both the federal and state levels, and more and more preservationists are being employed in federal and state service. For many agencies, consideration of historic properties and their protection has become an expectable part of planning and management. There is still a long way to go, but the machinery of federally financed destruction no longer seems as unmanageable as it did a decade ago.

FEARS

Plenty of dangers still exist, however, and many of these are embedded in the developing historic preservation system itself.

The SHPO

Perhaps the most crucial link in the procedural chains of American historic preservation is the state historic preservation officer. The SHPO is the planner, the surveyor, the local authority, the consultant, the watchdog. The SHPO is also appointed by the governor, and hence is subject to great political pressure in many cases. This pressure is a fact of life for most SHPOs, and some do not bear up well under it. Collusion between SHPOs and agencies building things of economic importance to their states is not unknown (cf. *NYAC* v. *Train*), and no one has yet developed a generally effective method for avoiding it.

The Advisory Council

The 1976 amendments to the NHPA added substantially to the authority exercised by the Advisory Council on Historic Preservation, but there is as yet little guarantee that the council will exercise its power with much wisdom. A bias toward a narrow concern only for "landmark" properties can be noted in much of the council's rhetoric; council representatives have repeatedly called for a relaxation of concern for properties of less than "national significance" (McDermott 1976). The composition of the council and its staff are far from representative, as of early 1977, for instance, there were no archeologists on the council and only one archeologist on the 25-person staff. The council has been known to violate its own *Procedures*, in an apparent effort to make things easy for federal agencies by allowing them to avoid effective review. For example, the council's staff has been known to concur in determinations of no adverse effect, or otherwise offer no objection, on projects affecting properties that had not been evaluated for National Register eligibility by OAHP. In some instances not even the SHPO's comments had been received prior to the council action. The danger in such concurrences goes beyond their technical distortion of the council's *Procedures.* Considering that it is through the process of eligibility determination that properties are fully described and their significant attributes defined, it is difficult to see how one could decide, in the absence of a determination of eligibility, what actions might or might not adversely affect the value of a particular property. The dangers are especially great with respect to archeology; the council has occasionally concurred in determinations of no adverse effect on archeological sites that had not been determined eligible, basing its concurrence on the fact that the responsible agency planned a salvage operation, sometimes without even reviewing the salvage plans (King personal observation 1977).

The Office of Archeology and Historic Preservation

The OAHP continues to have difficulty in issuing procedures and guidelines, and sometimes seems to lose track of its large responsibilities in the bustle of day-to-day business. A simple procedure is sometimes substituted for creative thought; at times it seems, for instance, that a photograph of an endangered property is more important to a determination of eligibility than is a solid argument for or against a property's significance. The National Register itself, as a roster of significant properties, remains a relatively unhelpful planning tool. It does not effectively differentiate among kinds of historic value—the fact that something is on the Register does not tell one whether it is valuable for archeological research, its contribution to a community's ambiance, or the quality of its carved lintels. The National Register also provides no way of assessing negative data; if there are no National Register properties in an area, the Register gives one no clue as to whether this means a dearth of historic properties or a lack of surveys. As yet, OAHP has done little to increase the sophistication of its recordkeeping system. The position of OAHP in the National Park Service, meanwhile, does little to enhance its effectiveness. Many layers of review lie between the operational staff of OAHP and the agencies that need its advice and cooperation. The National Park Service, as a whole, has little reason to be supportive of OAHP; OAHP has little pertinence to park operations, and it has taken away, in part, the interagency salvage program that once belonged to the regional directors. The Office of Archeology and Historic Preservation competes with a welter of other, often contradictory National Park Service functions, for funding and for the attention of upper management. It is not often the winner, and the time spent in competition is time not spent on its basic coordinative functions.

Contractors and Others

The consultants, contractors, and agency employees who do preservation's legwork remain largely unregulated. Many archeological surveys done under terms of the historic preservation statutes are embarassingly bad examples of scientific research; little attention is given to maintaining high standards of scholarship or documentation. Much contract work is done by people primarily interested in financial gain or security of employment; as a result, both price-gouging and "whitewashing" of destructive projects occur. All this diminishes the credibility of historic preservation with the public and Congress, while it permits important historic properties to be lost.

LONG-RANGE DANGERS

A short distance beyond these current dangers, others are visible that may loom larger in the future. The lack of effective standards and procedures now may lead to overregulation in the future, and this regulation is likely to be undertaken by those people and agencies least well equipped to do it. Such regulation will be a comfort to the unimaginative, but will drive creative thinkers into other fields of endeavor.

For years, American universities have accepted large numbers of graduate students, in anthropology at least, with the expectation that at least some would be "washed out" en route to the PhD. Often, those who have been eliminated in accordance with this expectation have been given Master's degrees as consolation prizes, regardless of their scholarly competence. While many MA holders are excellent scholars (and, of course, many PhDs are not), it remains a fact that many people have been given MAs not because they have good minds and scholarly qualities but precisely because they have been found to lack them. Since "government work" is generally held in low esteem among at least anthropologists and historians, it is the terminal MA holders who quite often have been recommended by their university departments for jobs with the SHPO, positions as state archeologists, and employment by federal agencies. As a result, many of the people who now occupy key decision-making roles in the historic preservation system are those who simply are not very smart. In the positions they assume, they experience pressure with which they are often unequipped to deal. There is a strong motivation for employees of many agencies to be "part of the team" concerned with the efficient execution of the agency's major missions. In an agency like the Corps of Engineers this creates obvious conflicts for the preservationist. There should be no substantial conflict between preservation needs and the constructive activities of the Corps, given wise planning, but in the conflict situations that continue to occur the preservationist often comes under considerable pressure to stick with the agency's position regardless of its destructive results. In a planning organization like the Bureau of Land Management or an SHPO program, the situation can be more complex. In such an organization, the preservationist comes under pressure to bend regulations and compromise principles in favor of what are taken to be long range, pragmatic preservation goals. The preservationist is often naive about the motivations of his or her superiors, and often has insufficient professional breadth to either articulate preservation principles effectively or seek support outside the agency. Thus there often seems to be no option but to give in. Pressure is aggravated by the low educational level at which most agency preservationists are employed. An archeologist or historian with a BA or MA who loses a job with a federal agency is unlikely to find work in academia; such a person cannot afford to risk very seriously being fired. Within the agency, such people often have rather marginal potential for professional advancement. They are seldom encouraged to obtain further academic training, and their prospects for advancement within their agency structures are usually limited. If one is the only archeologist in a given region of the Forest Service, for example, one can advance only so far up the salary ladder before one has to change regions or stop being an archeologist in favor of being a forest supervisor or some other sort of general-purpose administrator.

Thus as things now stand, people who are often not very well equipped as scholars to begin with, and who have been selected out of academia for just this reason, are assuming high-pressure positions with little potential for satisfactory advancement. Here they exercise great power over preservation activities, while experiencing strong motivation to conform to agency goals and maintaining little contact with either the central historic preservation system or their professional peers outside government. The danger in this situation, above and beyond the creation of a very frustrated group of preservation professionals, is that the policies adopted by the agencies that employ them will become increasingly narrow, self-serving, and intellectually sterile. It is easy to envision a future of research-by-rote and preservation only of those properties that represent dominant Anglo-American conceptions of historicity, propriety, and aesthetics.

NEEDS

We believe that these dangers can be avoided, and we have written this book with the hope that—by helping to involve anthropologists in historic preservation in a sensitive way and by offering some proposals about how preservation problems can be dealt with—it may be helpful in avoiding them. We obviously believe that historic preservation should seek to maintain properties and data about properties that are important to each segment of the American people and to our understanding of humanity in general. We believe that this was the intent of Congress in passing the historic preservation statutes, and that this is the direction in which historic preservation has evolved. We have tried to show how anthropologists can work with the existing laws and policies to help realize this goal. Some structural changes would certainly be desirable, however, both in the way historic preservation is managed and the way anthropologists participate and prepare for participation.

ORGANIZATION

The present national organization of historic preservation is inefficient and prone to the generation of conflicts. It would at least be desirable to remove

OAHP from the National Park Service, recognizing that it plays a special role that cannot be effectively subsumed under the interests of a land-managing agency. It might well be advisable, as some advisory council representatives have urged, to combine OAHP and the advisory council. This proposition is dangerous in that it would destroy such balance as now exists between OAHP as a proponent of preservation and the advisory council as an adjudicator of the public interest, but it would have the advantage of reducing communication difficulties, centralizing agency contacts, providing the advisory council with professional breadth and depth, and giving OAHP access to more clear-cut coordinative authority over the national historic preservation system.

Besides the merging of the two primary preservation agencies, it might be possible—and would almost certainly be advantageous—to transfer all historic preservationists working in other agencies to the new consolidated body. Preservation professionals could then be loaned to agencies like the Corps of Engineers, the National Park Service, and the Bureau of Land Management for periods of time, but could be given opportunities for advancement in their fields within the preservation agency and could be discouraged from becoming too devoted to the borrowing agency's mission. It is tempting to imagine a still larger agency concerned with the maintenance of all sorts of cultural diversity— bringing programs like the recently established National Folklife Center in the Library of Congress together with the historic preservation programs to seek the maintenance of both the tangible and intangible expressions of America's cultures. Finally, such cultural preservation programs might be consolidated with the environmental protection activities now lodged in various agencies of the federal government to form a Department of the Environment, an agency without land management or construction responsibilities and solely responsible for providing other agencies with objective advice and review in order to protect both the social and natural environments.

With or without such radical changes in the core of the historic preservation system, states and federal agencies responsible for land management and construction projects need to adopt more systematic approaches to preservation planning. The idea that preservation is in conflict with modern land-use and development should decline in favor of a recognition that preservation is a rational part of general management planning. As responsible state and regional plans are developed, the advisory council and OAHP should be able to relax their present procedures, which center on project-by-project and property-by-property review, in favor of general, programmatic approval and monitoring.

A vital element in any modification of the historic preservation system should be the de-politicization of the state historic preservation officer. The power of the governor to appoint and control the SHPO should be circumscribed; the SHPO should be a knowledgeable professional and should be insulated as much as possible from political pressure.

Participation by Anthropologists

Anthropologists—both archeologists and sociocultural anthropologists—should take a more active part in the operation of the historic preservation system, and this requires a more sophisticated understanding of the system than most now possess. This is not just a matter of learning procedures, or learning to say "mitigation of effect" instead of "salvage." It is a matter of seeking to understand the procedures and how they are implemented, and considering how they relate to anthropological practice. Anthropologists working on contract survey projects should regard their work as legitimate research, not just as a way to support themselves or their graduate students. Planning a contract project, defining and implementing a field methodology, and evaluating properties should be recognized as exacting intellectual exercises, not mere bureaucratic requirements.

In conduct of statewide surveys and implementation of statewide plans, anthropologists should participate in establishing research goals, helping to specify the kinds of properties that should be identified and preserved or investigated to attain these goals, and developing methods to identify and treat such properties. They should help to identify sociocultural groups that may have interests in the preservation of particular kinds of properties, help contact such groups to bring them into the planning process, and help make sure that their interests are represented.

Anthropologists should serve as critics, advisors, and watchdogs over both statewide survey and planning and over the execution of particular projects. They should not be shy about criticizing their fellow professionals; the discipline is certainly mature enough to tolerate disharmony, and only the least sophisticated of public agencies expect full agreement among their professional advisors. Here again, preservation work should be thought of just as is any other form of research, in which argument and criticism do not necessarily impugn professional reputations but serve to improve research results. It is important to recognize, however, that the forum in which complaints about preservation activities can be most effectively aired is different from that in which other professional differences are fought out. A letter to the American Anthropological Association *Newsletter,* or a paper delivered at a meeting of a regional society, cannot substitute for a well-documented complaint to OAHP, the advisory council, the SHPO, or one's Congressperson.

Training

While work in preservation has much in common with research, it is certainly true that one needs to know specific things in order to participate in preservation, and that such participation requires some character traits that are not necessarily selected for by standard forms of anthropological training. Institutions that wish to train students for work in historic preservation, and students seeking such training, should consider what curriculum changes may be necessary to properly prepare for the work.

Preservation work involves a constant tension between scholarship and activism. Because the review procedures and the very nature of work in connection with destructive projects creates frequent adversary situations, one must in some ways be a better scholar in historic preservation than one would need to be in standard academic work. One's work is constantly open to challenge in much less polite ways than are normal in an academic context. At the same time, and for many of the same reasons, in most historic preservation activities it is not enough to be a scholar. One must know the law, politics, and the operations of agencies, and must be prepared to use that knowledge in a vigorous way.

Success in historic preservation is impossible to attain alone; one needs the support of associates, their intellectual stimulation, their special expertise. Moreover, one needs to be able to say, "The needs of archeological research (or architecture, or history, etc.) indicate that X, Y, and Z should be done," with a fair assurance that X, Y, and Z are really what is rationally needed. This demands a rather broad acquaintance with one's field and an ability to obtain help from one's colleagues quickly. One also needs to feel that one is not alone—that one has a constituency. If a fight with your boss over a principle may cost your job, you want to know—and be able to demonstrate—that there are taxpayers who are on your side. Conversely, one should feel sensitive enough to the needs of the preservation constituency to feel bad if one lets the boss get away with destroying historic properties in order to save one's job. A feeling of responsibility for one's discipline, and a willingness to work closely with other practicioners, are not necessarily engendered by the normal teaching of anthropology; the tradition of the "lone wolf" scholar still infuses the discipline. In the training of historic preservationists, a self-conscious effort should be made to promote responsibility and cooperation.

An historic preservationist's training in anthropology should be broad and comprehensive, both areally and, particularly, theoretically. A scholar trained solely in a cultural materialist tradition is likely to have difficulty dealing with a rock art site, and with the value of such a site to a local Indian community. Conversely, a specialist in psychological anthropology may have very little to say about flake scatters.

At least a passing acquaintance with each of the nonanthropological subdisciplines in historic preservation is desirable. The prehistoric archeologist should know a dog trot from a salt box, and should be able to say more about the War of 1812 than when it began.

The historic preservationist is well advised to get a background in law—not only the historic preservation and environmental statutes themselves but the law as a dynamic system of decision-making. Technical skills in using legal references and finding things in law libraries are also useful.

A working acquaintance with the sometimes rather nebulous field of regional and urban planning will be very useful, particularly to those who find themselves working in local or regional preservation programs, in state offices, or in land managing agencies. One should at least understand in general what planners do, and what sorts of information they seek in setting out to do it.

Specific training devises to develop skills in dealing with people, agencies, and adversary situations should be considered. Mock courts, mock public hearings, participation in the work of local professional and preservation organizations, internships with federal agencies, SHPOs, the National Trust, and other organizations, and first-hand participation in ongoing local preservation programs can all go far toward acquainting the preservation trainee with the conditions under which he or she will have to live, and toward providing a vital feeling of connectedness with preservation's participating disciplines.

CONCLUSION

We can conclude on a note that is encouraging to us if not to our publisher. Growth and change is continual in historic preservation, and at this writing, on balance, the direction of change seems consistent with the approaches we have advocated in this book. This of course means that much of what is in this book will rapidly go out of date. We hope, however, that it will continue to serve as a useful introduction to historic preservation, at least for those with anthropological biases, and that it will stimulate its readers to explore the field more deeply and participate in its continuing evolution.

Appendix **A**

STATUTES, PROCEDURES.
AND ASSOCIATED MEMORANDA

All draft regulations given in this appendix were undergoing continuing revision in 1977. The drafts given here provide a general picture of the direction in which rulemaking is proceeding, but do not necessarily reflect the final forms of the regulations. Consolidation and simplification of most drafts can be expected, as can a more clear-cut separation between actual rulemaking, which demands compliance, and guidance, which may be followed at the discretion of the affected agency. For the most current forms of rulemaking, the reader should contact the Office of Archeology and Historic Preservation or the Advisory Council on Historic Preservation.

ANTIQUITIES ACT OF 1906

An Act For the Preservation of American Antiquities, Approved June 8, 1906
(Public Law 59-209; 34 STAT. 225; 16 U.S.C. 431-433)
Be it enacted by the Senate and House of Representatives of the United
States of America in Congress assembled. That any person who shall appropriate, excavate, injure or destroy any historic or prehistoric ruin or
monument, or any object of antiquity, situated on lands owned or controlled
by the Government of the United States, without the permission of the
Secretary of the Department of the Government having jurisdiction over the
lands on which said antiquities are situated, shall upon conviction, be
fined in a sum of not more than five hundred dollars or be imprisoned for
a period of not more than ninety days, or shall suffer both fine and
imprisonment, in the discretion of the court.

Section 2

That the President of the United States is hereby authorized, in his
discretion, to declare by public proclamation historic landmarks, historic
and prehistoric structures, and other objects of historic or scientific
interest that are situated upon the lands owned or controlled by the
Government of the United States to be national monuments, and may reserve
as a part thereof parcels of land, the limits of which in all cases shall
be confined to the smallest area compatible with the proper care and
management of the objected to be protected: *Provided,* That when such
objects are situated upon a tract covered by a bona fide unperfected claim
or held in private ownership, the tract, or so much thereof as may be
necessary for the proper care and management of the object, may be relin-
quished to the Government, and the Secretary of the Interior is hereby
authorized to accept the relinquishment of such tracts in behalf of the
Government of the United States.

Section 3

That permits for the examination of ruins, the excavation of archaeological sites, and the gathering of objects of antiquity upon the lands
under their respective jurisdictions may be granted by the Secretaries of
the Interior, Agriculture, and War to institutions which they may deem
properly qualified to conduct such examinations, excavation, or gathering,
subject to such rules and regulations as they may prescribe: *Provided,*
That the examinations, excavations, and gatherings are undertaken for
the benefit of reputable museums, universities, colleges, or other recognized scientific or educational institutions, with a view to increasing
the knowledge of such objects, and that the gatherings shall be made for
permanent preservation in public museums.

Section 4

That the Secretaries of the Departments aforesaid shall make and
publish from time to time uniform rules and regulations for the purpose of
carrying out the provisions of this Act.

UNIFORM RULES AND REGULATIONS PRESCRIBED BY THE SECRETARIES OF THE INTERIOR,
AGRICULTURE, AND WAR TO CARRY OUT THE PROVISIONS OF THE "ACT FOR THE
PRESERVATION OF AMERICAN ANTIQUITIES,"

1. Jurisdiction over ruins, archaeological sites, historic, and prehistoric monuments and structures, objects of antiquity, historic landmarks, and other objects of historic or scientific interest, shall be
exercised under the act by the respective Departments as follows:
By the Secretary of Agriculture over lands within the exterior limits
of forest reserves, by the Secretary of War over lands within the exterior
limits of military reservations, by the Secretary of the Interior over all
other lands owned or controlled by the Government of the United States,
provided the Secretaries of War and Agriculture may by agreement cooperate
with the Secretary of the Interior in the supervision of such monuments
and objects covered by the act of June 8, 1906, as may be located on lands
near or adjacent to forest reserves and military reservations, respectively.
2. No permit for the removal of any ancient monument or structure
which can be permanently preserved under the control of the United States
in situ, and remain an object of interest, shall be granted.
3. Permits for the examination of ruins, the excavation of archaeological sites, and the gathering of objects of antiquity will be granted, by
the respective Secretaries having jurisdiction, to reputable museums,
universities, colleges, or other recognized scientific or educational
institutions, or to their duly authorized agents.
4. No exclusive permits shall be granted for a larger area than the
applicant can reasonably be expected to explore fully and systematically
within the time limit named in the permit.
5. Each application for a permit should be filed with the Secretary
having jurisdiction, and must be accompanied by a definite outline of the
proposed work, indicating the name of the institution making the request,
the date proposed for the beginning the field work, the length of time
proposed to be devoted to it, and the person who will have immediate
charge of the work. The application must also contain an exact statement
of the character of the work, whether examination, excavation, or gathering,
and the public museum in which the collections made under the permit are
to be permanently preserved. The application must be accompanied by a
sketch plan or description of the particular site or area to be examined,
excavated, or searched, so definite that it can be located on the map with
reasonable accuracy.
6. No permit will be granted for a period of more than three years,
but if the work has been diligently prosecuted under the permit, the
time may be extended for proper cause upon application.
7. Failure to begin work under a permit within six months after it is
granted, or failure to diligently prosecute such work after it has begun,
shall make the permit void without any order or proceeding by the
Secretary having jurisdiction.
8. Applications for permits shall be referred to the Smithsonian
Institution for recommendation.
9. Every permit shall be in writing and copies shall be transmitted to
the Smithsonian Institution and the field officer in charge of the land
involved. The permittee will be furnished with a copy of these rules and
regulations.
10. At the close of each season's field work the permittee shall
report in duplicate to the Smithsonian Institution, in such form as its
secretary may prescribe, and shall prepare in duplicate a catalogue of the
collections and the photographs made during the season, indicating therein
such material, if any, as may be available for exchange.

11. Institutions and persons receiving permits for excavation shall, after the completion of the work, restore the lands upon which they have worked to their customary condition, to the satisfaction of the field officer in charge.

12. All permits shall be terminable at the discretion of the Secretary having jurisdiction.

13. The field officer in charge of land owned or controlled by the Government of the United States shall, from time to time, inquire and report as to the existence, on or near such lands, of ruins and archaeological sites, historic or prehistoric ruins or monuments, objects of antiquity, historic landmarks, historic and prehistoric structures, and other objects of historic or scientific interest.

14. The field officer in charge may at all times examine the permit of any person or institution claiming privileges granted in accordance with the act and these rules and regulations, and may fully examine all work done under such permit.

15. All persons duly authorized by the Secretaries of Agriculture, War, and Interior may apprehend or cause to be arrested, as provided in the act of February 6, 1905 (33 Stat. 700), any person or persons who appropriate, excavate, injure, or destroy any historic or prehistoric ruin or monument, or any object of antiquity on lands under the supervision of the secretaries of Agriculture, War, and Interior, respectively.

16. Any object of antiquity taken, or collection made, on lands owned or controlled by the United States, without a permit, as prescribed by the act and these rules and regulations, or there taken or made, contrary to the terms of the permit, or contrary to the act and these rules and regulations, may be seized whenever found and at any time, by the proper field officer or by any person duly authorized by the Secretary having jurisdiction, and disposed of as the Secretary shall determine, by deposit in the proper national depository or otherwise.

17. Every collection made under the authority of the act and of these rules and regulations shall be preserved in the public museum designated in the permit and shall be accessible to the public. No such collection shall be removed from such public museum without the written authority of the Secretary of the Smithsonian Institution, and then only to another public museum, where it shall be accessible to the public; and when any public museum, which is a depository of any collection made under the provisions of the act and these rules and regulations, shall cease to exist, every such collection in such public museum shall thereupon revert to the national collections and be placed in the proper national depository.

Washington, D.C., December 28, 1906.

The foregoing rules and regulations are hereby approved in triplicate and under authority conferred by law on the Secretaries of the Interior, Agriculture, and War, are hereby made and established, to take effect immediately. *E.A. Hitchcock, Secretary of the Interior, James Wilson, Secretary of Agriculture, William H. Taft, Secretary of War.*

HISTORIC SITES ACT OF 1935

An Act To Provide for the Preservation of Historic American Sites,
Buildings, Objects, and Antiquities of National Significance, and for
Other Purposes, Approved August 21, 1935 (Public Law 74-292; 49 STAT. 666;
16 U.S.C. 461-467)
*Be it enacted by the Senate and House of Representatives of the United
States of America in Congress assembled*, That it is hereby declared that
it is a national policy to preserve for public use historic sites,
buildings and objects of national significance for the inspiration and
benefit of the people of the United States. (16 U.S.C. sec. 461.)

Section 2
The Secretary of the Interior (hereinafter referred to as the Secretary), through the National Park Service, for the purpose of effectuating
the policy expressed in section 1 hereof, shall have the following powers
and perform the following duties and functions:
(a) Secure, collate, and preserve drawings, plans, photographs, and
other data of historic and archaeologic sites, buildings and objects.
(b) Make a survey of historic and archaeologic sites, buildings,
and objects for the purpose of determining which possess exceptional
value as commemorating or illustrating the history of the United States.
(c) Make necessary investigations and researches in the United States
relating to particular sites, buildings, or objects to obtain true and
accurate historical and archaeological facts and information concerning
the same.
(d) For the purpose of this Act, acquire in the name of the United
States by gift, purchase, or otherwise any property, personal or real, or
any interest or estate therein, title to any real property to be satisfactory to the Secretary: *Provided*, That no such property which is owned
by any religious or educational institution, or which is owned or administered for the benefit of the public shall be so acquired without the
consent of the owner: *Provided further*, That no such property shall be
acquired or contract or agreement for the acquisiton thereof made which
will obligate the general fund of the Treasury for the payment of such
property, unless or until Congress has appropriated money which is available for that purpose.
(e) Contract and make cooperative agreements with States, municipal
subdivisions, corporations, associations, or individuals, with proper bond
where deemed advisable, to protect, preserve, maintain, or operate any
historic or archaeologic building, site, object, or property used in
connection therewith for public use, regardless as to whether the title
thereto is in the United States: *Provided*, That no contract or cooperative
agreement shall be made or entered into which will obligate the general
fund of the Treasury unless or until Congress has appropriated money for
such purpose.
(f) Restore, reconstruct, rehabilitate, preserve, and maintain historic or prehistoric sites, buildings, objects, and properties of national
historical or archaeological significance and where deemed desirable
establish and maintain museums in connection therewith.

(g) Erect and maintain tablets to mark or commemorate historic or prehistoric places and events of national historical or archaeological significance.

(h) Operate and manage historic and archaeologic sites, buildings, and properties acquired under the provisions of this Act together with lands and subordinate buildings for the benefit of the public, such authority to include the power to charge reasonable visitation fees and grant concessions, leases, or permits for the use of land, building space, roads, or trails when necessary or desirable either to accommodate the public or to facilitate administration: *Provided*, That such concessions, leases, or permits, shall be let at competitive bidding, to the person making the highest and best bid.

(i) When the Secretary determines that it would be administratively burdensome to restore, reconstruct, operate, or maintain any particular historic or archaeologic site, building, or property donated to the United States through the National Park Service, he may cause the same to be done by organizing a corporation for that purpose under the laws of the District of Columbia or any State.

(j) Develop an education program and service for the purpose of making available to the public facts and information pertaining to American historic and archaeologic sites, buildings, and properties of national significance. Reasonable charges may be made for the dissemination of any such facts or information.

(k) Perform any and all acts, and make such rules and regulations not inconsistent with this Act as may be necessary and proper to carry out the provisions thereof. Any person violating any of the rules and regulations authorized by this Act shall be punished by a fine of not more than $500 and be adjudged to pay all cost of the proceedings. (16 U.S.C. sec. 462.)

Section 3

A general advisory board to be known as the "Advisory Board on National Parks, Historic Sites, Buildings, and Monuments" is hereby established, to be composed of not to exceed eleven persons, citizens of the United States, to include representatives competent in the fields of history, archaeology, architecture, and human geography, who shall be appointed by the Secretary and serve at his pleasure. The members of such board shall receive no salary but may be paid expenses incidental to travel engaged in discharging their duties as members.

It shall be the duty of such board to advise on any matters relating to national parks and to the administration of this Act submitted to it for consideration by the Secretary. It may also recommend policies to the Secretary from time to time pertaining to national parks and to the restoration, reconstruction, conservation, and general administration of historic and archaeologic sites, buildings, and properties. (16 U.S.C. sec. 463.)

Section 4

The Secretary, in administering this Act, is authorized to cooperate with and may seek and accept the assistance of any Federal, State, or municipal department or agency, or any educational or scientific institution, or any patriotic association, or any individual.

(b) When deemed necessary, technical advisory committees may be established to act in an advisory capacity in connection with the restoration or reconstruction of any historic or prehistoric building or structure.

(c) Such professional and technical assistance may be employed without regard to the civil-service laws, and such service may be established as may be required to accomplish the purposes of this Act and for which money may be appropriated by Congress or made available by gifts for such purpose. (16 U.S.C. sec. 464.)

Section 5

Nothing in this Act shall be held to deprive any State, or political subdivision thereof, of its civil and criminal jurisdiction in and over lands acquired by the United States under this Act. (16 U.S.C. sec. 465.)

Section 6

There is authorized to be appropriated for carrying out the purposes of this Act such sums as the Congress may from time to time determine. (16 U.S.C. sec. 466.)

Section 7

The provisions of this Act shall control if any of them are in conflict with any other Act or Acts relating to the same subject matter. (16 U.S.C. sec. 467.)

NATIONAL HISTORIC PRESERVATION ACT OF 1966

An Act to Establish a Program for the Preservation of Additional Historic Properties throughout the Nation, and for Other Purposes, Approved October 15, 1966 (Public Law 89-665; 80 STAT. 915; 16 U.S.C. 470 *as amended* by Public Law 91-243, Public Law 93-54, Public Law 94-422, and Public Law 94-458)

Be it enacted by the Senate and House of Representatives of the United States of America in Congress assembled, That Congress finds and declares--

(a) That the spirit and direction of the National are founded upon and reflected in its historic past;

(b) That the historical and cultural foundations of the Nation should be preserved as a living part of our community life and development in order to give a sense of orientation to the American people;

(d) That, in the face of ever-increasing extensions of urban centers, highways, and residential, commercial, and industrial developments, the present governmental and nongovernmental historic preservation programs and activities are inadequate to insure future generations a genuine opportunity to appreciate and enjoy the rich heritage of our Nation; and

(d) That, although the major burdens of historic preservation have been borne and major efforts initiated by private agencies and individuals, and both should continue to play a vital role it is nevertheless necessary and appropriate for the Federal Government to accelerate its historic preservation programs and activities, to give maximum encouragement to agencies and individuals undertaking preservation by private means, and to assist State and local governments and the National Trust for Historic Preservation in the United States to expand and accelerate their historic preservation programs and activities.

TITLE I

Section 101

(a) The Secretary of the Interior is authorized--

(1) to expand and maintain a national register of districts, sites, buildings, structures, and objects significant in American history, architecture, archaeology, and culture, hereinafter referred to as the National Register, and to grant funds to States for the purpose of preparing comprehensive statewide historic surveys and plans, in accordance with criteria established by the Secretary, for the preservation, acquisition, and development of such properties;

(2) to establish a program of matching grants-in-aid to States for projects having as their purpose the preservation for public benefit of properties that are significant in American history, architecture, archaeology, and culture;

(3) to establish a program of matching grants-in-aid to the National Trusts for Historic Preservation in the United States, chartered by act of Congress approved October 26, 1949 (63 STAT. 927), as amended, for the purpose of carrying out the responsibilities of the National Trust; and

(4) to withhold from disclosure to the public information relating to the location of sites or objects listed on the National Register whenever

he determines that the disclosure of specific information would create a risk of destruction or harm to such sites or objects.

(b) As used in this Act--

(1) The term "State" includes, in addition to the several States of the Union, the District of Columbia, the Commonwealth of Puerto Rico, the Virgin Islands, Guam, American Samoa, and the Trust Territory of the Pacific Islands.

(2) The term "project" means programs of State and local governments and other public bodies and private organizations and individuals for the acquisition of title or interests in, and for the development of, any district, site, building, structure, or object that is significant in American history, architecture, archaeology, and culture, or property used in connection therewith, and for its development in order to assure the preservation for public benefit of any such historical properties.

(3) The term "historic preservation" includes the protection, rehabilitation, restoration, and reconstruction of districts, sites, buildings, structures, and objects significant in American history, architecture, archaeology, or culture.

(4) The term "Secretary" means the Secretary of the Interior.

Section 102

(a) No grant may be made under this Act--

(1) unless application therefor is submitted to the Secretary in accordance with regulations and procedures prescribed by him;

(2) unless the application is in accordance with the comprehensive statewide historic preservation plan which has been approved by the Secretary after considering its relationship to the comprehensive statewide outdoor recreation plan prepared pursuant to the Land and Water Conservation Fund Act of 1965 (78 STAT. 897);

(3) for more than 50 per centum of the total cost involved, as determined by the Secretary and his determination shall be final;

(4) unless the grantee has agreed to make such reports, in such form and containing such information as the Secretary may from time to time require;

(5) unless the grantee has agreed to assume, after completion of the project, the total cost of the continued maintenance, repair, and administration of the property in a manner satisfactory to the Secretary; and

(6) until the grantee has complied with such further terms and conditions as the Secretary may deem necessary or advisable.

(b) The Secretary may in his discretion waive the requirements of subsection (a), paragraphs (2) and (5) of this section for any grant under this Act to the National Trust for Historic Preservation in the United States, in which case a grant to the National Trust may include funds for the maintenance, repair, and administration of the property in a manner satisfactory to the Secretary.

(c) The Secretary may in his discretion waive the requirements of paragraph (3) of subsection (a), of this section for the purposes of making grants for the preparation of statewide historic preservation plans and surveys and project plans. Any grant made pursuant to this subsection may not exceed 70 per centum of the cost of a project, and the total of such grants made pursuant to this subsection in any one fiscal year may not exceed one-half of the funds appropriated for that fiscal year pursuant to section 108 of this Act.

(d) No State shall be permitted to utilize the value of real property obtained before the date of approval of this Act in meeting the remaining cost for which a grant is made under this Act.

Section 103

(a) The amounts appropriated and made available for grants to the States for comprehensive statewide historic surveys and plans under this Act shall be apportioned among the States by the Secretary on the basis of needs as determined by him;

(b) The amounts appropriated and made available for grants to the States for projects under this Act for each fiscal year shall be apportioned among the States by the Secretary in accordance with needs as disclosed in approved statewide historic preservation plans.

The Secretary shall notify each State of its apportionment, and the amounts thereof shall be available thereafter for payment to such State for projects in accordance with the provisions of this Act. Any amount of any apportionment that has not been paid or obligated by the Secretary during the fiscal year in which such notification is given, and for two fiscal years thereafter, shall be reapportioned by the Secretary in accordance with this subsection.

Section 104

(a) No grant may be made by the Secretary for or on account of any survey or project under this Act with respect to which financial assistance has been given or promised under any other Federal program or activity, and no financial assistance may be given under any other Federal program or activity for or on account of any survey project with respect to which assistance has been given or promised under this Act.

(b) In order to assure consistency in policies and actions under this Act with other related Federal programs and activities, and to assure coordination of the planning acquisition, and development assistance to States under this Act with other related Federal programs and activities, the President may issue such regulations with respect thereto as he deems desirable, and such assistance may be provided only in accordance with such regulations.

Section 105

The beneficiary of assistance under this Act shall keep such records as the Secretary shall prescribe, including records which fully disclose the disposition by the beneficiary of the proceeds of such assistance, the total cost of the project or undertaking in connection with which such assistance is given or used, and the amount and nature of that portion of the cost of the project or undertaking supplied by other sources, and such other records as will facilitate an effective audit.

Section 106

The head of any Federal agency having direct or indirect jurisdiction over a proposed Federal or federally assisted undertaking in any State and the head of any Federal department or independent agency having authority to license any undertaking shall, prior to the approval of the expenditure of any Federal funds on the undertaking or prior to the issuance of any license, as the case may be, take into account the effect of the undertaking on any district, site, building, structure, or object that is included in or eligible for inclusion in the National Register. The head of any such Federal agency shall afford the Advisory Council on Historic Preservation established under Title II of this Act a reasonable opportunity to comment with regard to such undertaking.

Section 107

Nothing in this Act shall be construed to be applicable to the White House and its grounds, the Supreme Court building and its grounds, or the United States Capitol and its related buildings and grounds.

Section 108

To carry out the provisions of this Act, there is hereby established the Historic Preservation Fund (hereafter referred to as the "fund") in the Treasury of the United States.

There shall be covered into such fund $24,400,000 for fiscal year 1977, $100,000,000 for fiscal year 1978, $100,000,000 for fiscal year 1979, $150,000,000 for fiscal year 1980, and $150,000,000 for fiscal year 1981, from revenues due and payable to the United States under the Outer Continental Shelf Lands Act (67 STAT. 462, 469) as amended (43 U.S.C. 338), and/or under the Act of June 4, 1920 (41 STAT. 813), as amended (30 U.S.C. 191), notwithstanding any provision of law that such proceeds shall be credited to miscellaneous receipts of the Treasury. Such moneys shall be used only to carry out the purposes of this Act and shall be available for expenditure only when appropriated by the Congress. Any moneys not appropriated shall remain available in the fund until appropriated for said purposes: *Provided*, That appropriations made pursuant to this paragraph may be made without fiscal year limitation.

Section 201

(a) There is established as an independent agency of the United States Government an Advisory Council on Historic Preservation (hereinafter referred to as the Council) which shall be composed of twenty-nine members as follows:
- (1) The Secretary of the Interior;
- (2) The Secretary of Housing and Urban Development;
- (3) The Secretary of Commerce;
- (4) The Administrator of the General Services Administration;
- (5) The Secretary of the Treasury;
- (6) The Attorney General;
- (7) The Secretary of Agriculture;
- (8) The Secretary of Transportation;
- (9) The Secretary of State;
- (10) The Secretary of Defense;
- (11) The Secretary of Health, Education, and Welfare;
- (12) The Chairman of the Council on Environmental Quality;
- (13) The Chairman of the Federal Council on the Arts and Humanities;
- (14) The Architect of the Capitol;
- (15) The Secretary of the Smithsonian Institution;
- (16) The Chairman of the National Trust for Historic Preservation;
- (17) The President of the National Conference of State Historic Preservation Officers; and
- (18) Twelve appointed by the President from outside the Federal Government. In making these appointments, the President shall give due consideration to the selection of officers of State and local governments and individuals who are significantly interested and experienced in the matters to be considered by the Council.

(b) Each member of the Council specified in paragraphs (1) through (17) of subsection (a) may designate another officer of his department, agency, or organization to serve on the Council in his stead.

(c) Each member of the Council appointed under paragraph (18) of subsection (a) shall serve for a term of five years from the expiration of his predecessor's term; except that the members first appointed under that paragraph shall serve for terms of from one to five years, as designated by the President at the time of appointment, in such manner as to insure that the terms of not less than one nor more than two of them will expire in any one year.

(d) A vacancy in the Council shall not affect its powers, but shall be filled in the same manner as the original appointment (and for the balance of the unexpired term).

(e) The Chairman and the Vice Chairman of the Council shall be designated by the President. During the absence or disability of the Chairman or when the office is vacant, the Vice Chairman shall act in the place of the Chairman.

(f) Fifteen members of the Council shall constitute a quorum.

Section 202

(a) The Council shall--

(1) advise the President and the Congress on matters relating to historic preservation; recommend measures to coordinate activities of Federal, State, and local agencies and private institutions and individuals relating to historic preservation; and advise on the dissemination of information pertaining to such activities;

(2) encourage, in cooperation with the National Trust for Historic Preservation and appropriate private agencies, public interest and participation in historic preservation;

(3) recommend the conduct of studies in such areas as the adequacy of legislative and administrative statutes and regulations pertaining to historic preservation activities of State and local governments and the effects of tax policies at all levels of government on historic preservation;

(4) advise as to guidelines for the assistance of State and local governments in drafting legislation relating to historic preservation; and

(5) encourage, in cooperation with appropriate public and private agencies and institutions, training and education in the field of historic preservation.

(b) The Council shall submit annually a comprehensive report of its activities and the results of its studies to the President and the Congress and shall from time to time submit such legislative enactments and other actions as, in the judgment of the Council, are necessary and appropriate to carry out its recommendations.

Section 203

The Council is authorized to secure directly from any department, bureau, agency, board, commission, office, independent establishment or instrumentality of the executive branch of the Federal Government information, suggestions, estimates, and statistics for the purpose of this title; and each such department, bureau, agency, board, commission, office, independent establishment or instrumentality is authorized to furnish such information, suggestions, estimates, and statistics to the extent permitted by law and within available funds.

Section 204

The members of the Council specified in paragraphs (1) through (17) of section 201(a) shall serve without additional compensation. The members of the Council appointed under paragraph (18) of section 201(a) shall receive $100 per diem when engaged in the performance of the duties of the Council. All members of the Council shall receive reimbursement for necessary traveling and subsistence expenses incurred by them in the performance of the duties of the Council.

Section 205

(a) There shall be an Executive Director of the Council who shall be
appointed in the competitive service by the Chairman with the concurrence
of the Council. The Executive Director shall report directly to the
Council and perform such functions and duties as the Council may prescribe.

(b) The Council shall have a General Counsel, who shall be appointed
by the Executive Director. The General Counsel shall report directly to
the Executive Director and serve as the Council's legal advisor. The
Executive Director shall appoint such other attorneys as may be necessary
to assist the General Counsel, represent the Council in courts of law
whenever appropriate, assist the Department of Justice in handling litigation concerning the Council in courts of law, and perform such other
legal duties and functions as the Executive Director and the Council may
direct.

(c) The Executive Director of the Council may appoint and fix the
compensation of such officers and employees in the competitive service as
are necessary to perform the functions of the Council at rates not to
exceed that now or hereafter prescribed for the highest step for grade 15
of the General Schedule under section 5332 of Title 5, United States Code:
Provided. however, That the Executive Director, with the concurrence of
the Chairman, may appoint and fix the compensation of not to exceed five
employees in the competitive service at rates not to exceed that now or
hereafter prescribed for the highest rate of grade 17 of the General
Schedule under section 5332 of Title 5, United States Code.

(d) The Executive Director shall have power to appoint and fix the
compensation of such additional personnel as may be necessary to carry
out its duties, without regard to the provisions of the civil service laws
and the Classification Act of 1949.

(e) The Executive Director of the Council is authorized to procure
expert and consultant services in accordance with the provisions of
section 3109 of Title 5, United States Code.

(f) Financial and administrative services (including those related
to budgeting, accounting, financial reporting, personnel and procurement)
shall be provided the Council by the Department of the Interior, for
which payments shall be made in advance, or by reimbursement, from funds
of the Council in such amounts as may be agreed upon by the Chairman of
the Council and the Secretary of the Interior: *Provided*, That the
regulations of the Department of the Interior for the collection of
indebtedness of personnel resulting from erroneous payments (5 U.S.C. 46e)
shall apply to the collection of erroneous payments made to or on behalf
of a Council employee, and regulations of said Secretary for the administrative control of funds (31 U.S.C. 665(g)) shall apply to appropriations
of the Council: *And provided further*, That the Council shall not be
required to prescribe such regulations.

(g) The members of the Council specified in paragraphs (1) through
(16) of section 201(a) shall provide the Council, with or without reimbursement as may be agreed upon by the Chairman and the members, with
such funds, personnel, facilities, and services under their jurisdiction
and control as may be needed by the Council to carry out its duties, to
the extent that such funds, personnel, facilities, and services are
requested by the Council and are otherwise available for that purpose.
To the extent of available appropriations, the Council may obtain, by
purchase, rental, donation, or otherwise, such additional property,
facilities, and services as may be needed to carry out its duties.

Section 206

(a) The participation of the United States as a member in the International Centre for the Study of the Preservation and Restoration of Cultural Property is hereby authorized.

(b)   The Council shall recommend to the Secretary of State, after consultation with the Smithsonian Institution and other public and private organizations concerned with the technical problems of preservation, the members of the official delegation which will participate in the activities of the Centre on behalf of the United States.   The Secretary of State shall appoint members of the official delegation from the persons recommended to him by the Council.

(c)   For the purposes of this section there are authorized to be appropriated not more than $175,000 per year for fiscal years 1977, 1978, and 1979:   *Provided*, That no appropriation is authorized and no payment shall be made to the Centre in excess of 25 per centum of the total annual assessment of such organization.

Section 207

So much of the personnel, property, records, and unexpended balances of appropriations, allocations, and other funds employed, held, used, programed, or available or to be made available by the Department of the Interior in connection with the functions of the Council, as the Director of the Office of Management and Budget shall determine, shall be transferred from the Department to the Council within 60 days of the effective date of this Act.

Section 208

Any employee in the competitive service of the United States transferred to the Council under the provisions of this section shall retain all the rights, benefits, and privileges pertaining thereto held prior to such transfer.

Section 209

The Council is exempt from the provisions of the Federal Advisory Committee Act (86 STAT. 770), and the provisions of the Administrative Procedure Act (80 STAT. 381) shall govern the operations of the Council.

Section 210

Whenever the Council transmits any legislative recommendations, or testimony, or comments on legislation to the President or the Office of Management and Budget, it shall concurrently transmit copies thereof to the House Committee on Interior and Insular Affairs and the Senate Committee on Interior and Insular Affairs.   No officer or agency of the United States shall have any authority to require the Council to submit its legislative recommendations, or testimony, or comments on legislation to any officer or agency of the United States for approval, comments, or review, prior to the submission of such recommendations, testimony, or comments to the Congress.   In instances in which the Council voluntarily seeks to obtain the comments or review of any officer or agency of the United States, the Council shall include a description of such actions in its legislative recommendations, testimony, or comments on legislation which it transmits to the Congress.

Section 211

The Council is authorized to promulgate such rules and regulations as it deems necessary to govern the implementation of section 106 of this Act.

Section 212

(a) The Council shall submit its budget annually as a related agency
of the Department of the Interior. To carry out the provisions of this
title, there are authorized to be appropriated not more than $1,500,000
in fiscal year 1977, $1,750,000 in fiscal year 1978, and $2,000,000 in
fiscal year 1979.

(b) Whenever the Council submits any budget estimate or request to
the President or the Office of Management and Budget, it shall concurrently
transmit copies of that estimate or request to the House and Senate
Appropriations Committees and the House Committee on Interior and Insular
Affairs and the Senate Committee on Interior and Insular Affairs.

TITLE 5 OF THE UNITED STATES CODE IS AMENDED

§5316. *Positions at level V*

Level V of the Executive Schedule applies to the following positions,
for which the annual rate of basic pay is $28,000:

(135) Executive Director, Advisory Council on Historic Preservation.

1969 Increases in Salaries

Salaries of positions at Level V increased from $28,000 to $36,000
per annum, commencing on the first day of the pay period which begins after
February 14, 1969, upon recommendation of the President of the United
States, see note set out under section 358 of Title 2, The Congress.

EXECUTIVE ORDER 11593

Executive Order 11593 expands upon the responsibilities of federal agencies with respect to the purposes of the National Historic Preservation Act. It also specifies a relationship between the act and the National Environmental Policy Act.

PROTECTION AND ENHANCEMENT OF THE CULTURAL ENVIRONMENT

By virtue of the authority vested in me as President of the United States and in furtherance of the purposes and policies of the National Environmental Policy Act of 1969 (83 Stat. 852, 42 U.S.C. 4321 et seq.), the National Historic Preservation Act of 1966 (80 Stat. 915, 16 U.S.C. 470 et seq.), the Historic Sites Act of 1935 (49 Stat. 666, 16 U.S.C. 461 et seq.), and the Antiquities Act of 1906 (34 Stat. 225, 16 U.S.C. 431 et seq.), it is ordered as follows:

Section 1. Policy

The Federal Government shall provide leadership in preserving, restoring, and maintaining the historic and cultural environment of the Nation. Agencies of the executive branch of the Government (hereinafter referred to as "Federal agencies") shall (1) administer the cultural properties under their control in a spirit of stewardship and trusteeship for future generations, (2) initiate measures necessary to direct their policies, plans and programs in such a way that federally owned sites, structures, and objects of historical, architectural or archaeological significance are preserved, restored and maintained for the inspiration and benefit of the people, and (3), in consultation with the Advisory Council on Historic Preservation (16 U.S.C. 470i), institute procedures to assure that Federal plans and programs contribute to the preservation and enhancement of non-federally owned sites, structures and objects of historical, architectural or archaeological significance.

Section 2. Responsibilities of Federal Agencies

Consonant with the provisions of the acts cited in the first paragraph of this order, the heads of Federal agencies shall:

(a) no later than July 1, 1973, with the advice of the Secretary of the Interior, and in cooperation with the liaison officer for historic preservation for the State or territory involved, locate, inventory, and nominate to the Secretary of the Interior all sites, buildings, districts, and objects under their jurisdiction or control that appear to qualify for listing on the National Register of Historic Places.

(b) exercise caution during the interim period until inventories and evaluations required by subsection (a) are completed to assure that any federally owned property that might qualify for nomination is not inadvertently transferred, sold, demolished or substantially altered. The agency head shall refer any questionable actions to the Secretary of the Interior for an opinion respecting the property's eligibility for inclusion on the National Register of Historic Places. The Secretary shall consult with the liaison officer for historic preservation for the State or territory involved in arriving at his opinion. Where, after a reasonable period in which to review and evaluate the property, the Secretary determines that

the property is likely to meet the criteria prescribed for listing on the
National Register of Historic Places, the Federal agency head shall reconsider the proposal in light of national environmental and preservation
policy. Where, after such reconsideration, the Federal agency head proposes to transfer, sell, demolish or substantially alter the property he
shall not act with respect to the property until the Advisory Council on
Historic Preservation shall have been provided an opportunity to comment
on the proposal.

(c) initiate measures to assure that where as a result of Federal
action or assistance a property listed on the National Register of Historic
Places is to be substantially altered or demolished, timely steps be taken
to make or have made records, including measured drawings, photographs
and maps, of the property, and that copy of such records then be deposited
in the Library of Congress as part of the Historic American Buildings
Survey or Historic American Engineering Record for future use and reference.
Agencies may call on the Department of the Interior for advice and technical assistance in the completion of the above records.

(d) initiate measures and procedures to provide for the maintenance,
through preservation, rehabilitation, or restoration, of federally owned
and registered sites at professional standards prescribed by the Secretary
of the Interior.

(e) submit procedures required pursuant to subsection (d) to the
Secretary of the Interior and to the Advisory Council on Historic Preservation no later than January 1, 1972, and annually thereafter, for review
and comment.

(f) cooperate with purchasers and transferees of a property listed on
the National Register of Historic Places in the development of viable plans
to use such property in a manner compatible with preservation objectives
and which does not result in an unreasonable economic burden to public or
private interests.

Section 3. Responsibilies of the Secretary of the Interior

The Secretary of the Interior shall:

(a) encourage State and local historic preservation officials to
evaluate and survey federally owned historic properties and, where appropriate, to nominate such properties for listing on the National Register
of Historic Places.

(b) develop criteria and procedures to be applied by Federal agencies
in the reviews and nominations required by section 2(a). Such criteria
and procedures shall be developed in consultation with the affected agencies.

(c) expedite action upon nominations to the National Register of
Historic Places concerning federally owned properties proposed for sale,
transfer, demolition or substantial alteration.

(d) encourage State and Territorial liaison officers for historic
preservation to furnish information upon request to Federal agencies regarding their properties which have been evaluated with respect to historic, architectural or archaeological significance and which as a result
of such evaluations have not been found suitable for listing on the
National Register of Historic Places.

(e) develop and make available to Federal agencies and State and local
governments information concerning professional methods and techniques for
preserving, improving, restoring and maintaining historic properties.

(f) advise Federal agencies in the evaluations, identification, preservation, improvement, restoration and maintenance of historic properties.

(g) review and evaluate the plans of transferees of surplus Federal
properties transferred for historic monument purposes to assure that the
historic character of such properties is preserved in rehabilitation, restoration, improvement, maintenance and repair of such properties.

(h)   review and comment upon Federal agency procedures submitted
pursuant to section 2(e) of this order.

Dated: May 13, 1971
RICHARD M. NIXON

36 CFR PART 60

*This regulation sets forth basic procedures of nomination to
the National Register of Historic Places (for expanded instructions see OAHP 1977) and for the operations of state historic
preservation officers. The associated memorandum, "Recommendations to Archaeologists," issued in 1976 by the National Register,
clarifies the methods to be used in describing and evaluating properties of archaeological value when nominating them to the National Register or when reporting them for a determination of
eligibility (see 36 CFR 63).*

NATIONAL REGISTER OF HISTORIC PLACES: NOMINATIONS BY STATES AND FEDERAL
AGENCIES

Section 60.1.   The National Historic Preservation Act of 1966

In the National Historic Preservation Act of 1966, 80 Stat. 915, 16
U.S.C. 740, the Congress found and declared:
(a) That the spirit and direction of the Nation are founded upon and
reflected in its historic past.
(b) That the historic and cultural foundations of the Nation should
be preserved as a living part of our community life and development in
order to give a sense of orientation to the American people.
(c) That, in the face of ever-increasing extensions of urban centers,
highways, and residential, commercial, and industrial developments, the
present governmental and nongovernmental historic preservation programs and
activities are inadequate to insure future generations a genuine opportunity to appreciate and enjoy the rich heritage of our nation; and
(d) That, although the major burdens of historic preservation have been
borne and major effects initiated by private agencies and individuals, and
both should continue to play a vital role, it is nevertheless necessary
and appropriate for the Federal Government to accelerate its historic
preservation programs and activities, to give maximum encouragement to
agencies and individuals undertaking preservation by private means, and
to assist State and local governments and the National Trust for Historic
Preservation in the United States to expand and accelerate their historic
preservation programs and activities.

Section 60.2.   Authorization and Expansion of the National Register

(a) The National Historic Preservation Act of 1966, 80 Stat. 915,
16 U.S.C. 470, authorizes the Secretary of the Interior to expand and
maintain a National Register of districts, sites, buildings, structures,
and objects significant in American history, architecture, archaeology,
and culture. Previously, the National Register included only nationally
significant properties that were historical or archaeological units of the
National Park System, or that had been declared eligible for designation
as national historic landmarks. Because they must meet exacting criteria
of national significance, such properties are few in number. The National
Historic Preservation Act of 1966 provides a means for States to nominate
properties of State and local significance, regardless of location within

the State, and whether publically or privately owned for placement in the National Register.

(b) The National Register is an authoritative guide to be used by Federal, State, and local governments, private groups, and citizens to identify the Nation's cultural resources and to indicate what properties should be considered for protection from destruction or impairment. It is also the legal instrument to insure that registered properties affected by undertakings that are executed, licensed, or financially assisted by the Federal Government will be the subject of review and comment in accordance with section 106 of the Act. Such review and comment is the function of the Advisory Council on Historic Preservation. The Advisory Council has adopted procedures concerning, inter alia, their commenting responsibility in 36 CFR Part 800.

(c) The National Register was designed to be and is administered as a planning tool without restraint upon private property interests. Federal agencies undertaking a project having an effect on a listed property must provide the Advisory Council on Historic Preservation a reasonable opportunity to comment pursuant to 36 CFR Part 800. Having complied with this procedural requirement the Federal agency may adopt any course of action it may feel appropriate. While the Advisory Council comments must be taken into account and integrated into the decisionmaking process, the program decision rests with the agency implementing the undertaking. No requirements of any kind are imposed upon private initiative.

(d) The National Register is enlarged by:

(1) Acts of Congress and Executive orders which create areas of the National Park System administered by the National Park Service, all or portions of which may be determined to be of historic significance consistent with the intent of Congress;

(2) Properties declared by the Secretary of the Interior as eligible for designation as national historic landmarks;

(3) Nominations prepared by the States and approved by the National Park Service; and,

(4) Nominations of Federal properties prepared by Federal agencies as directed by Executive Order 11593 and approved by the National Park Service.

Section 60.3. *Grants for Historic Preservation*

The National Historic Preservation Act also authorizes 50 percent matching grants-in-aid to the States and the National Trust for Historic Preservation. Grants to the States are authorized for comprehensive statewide historic site surveys and preservation plans and for preservation projects in accordance with approved statewide plans. With the exception of grants to the National Trust for Historic Preservation, all grants are made through the States. The State Historic Preservation Officer may then distribute the funds to other approved public and private recipients. Funds may be used for acquisition, protection, rehabilitation, restoration, and reconstruction of properties included in the National Register. For further information relating to the historic preservation grants-in-aid program, consult Chief, Division of Grants, National Park Service, U.S. Department of the Interior, Washington, D.C. 20240.

Section 60.4. *Federal Nominations Pursuant to Executive Order 11593, "Protection and Enhancement of the Cultural Environment," May 13, 1971 (36 FR 8921, see 16 U.S.C. 470).*

(a) The Executive order states that the Federal Government shall provide leadership in preserving, restoring, and maintaining the historic and cultural environment of the Nation. Federal agencies are directed to

administer cultural properties under their control in a spirit of stewardship and trusteeship for future generations and to initiate measures to
direct their activities in such a way that federally owned properties
of historical, architectural, or archaeological significance are preserved,
restored, and maintained for the inspiration and benefit of the people.

(b) Section 2(a) of Executive Order 11593 provides that Federal
agencies shall locate, inventory, and nominate to the Secretary of the
Interior all sites, buildings, districts, and objects under their jurisdiction or control that appear to qualify for listing on the National
Register of Historic Places.

(c) Additional responsibilities of Federal agencies are detailed in
Executive Order 11593, the National Historic Preservation Act of 1966,
the National Environmental Policy Act of 1969, the Archaeology and
Historic Preservation Act of 1974, procedures developed pursuant to these
authorities, and other related legislation. Detailed administrative
procedures for the further implementation of Executive Order 11593 are
being developed to set forth inter alia criteria and procedures to be
applied by Federal agencies in the review and nomination required by
section 2(a).

Section 60.5. Appointment and Responsibilities of the State Historic Preservation Officer

(a) Implementation of the National Historic Preservation Act of 1966
is accomplished primarily by the State Historic Preservation Officers
(formerly known as State Liaison Officers), who are responsible for
administering the National Register program within their jurisdictions.
These officers are appointed by the Governors of the 50 States, Guam,
American Samoa, the Commonwealth of Puerto Rico, the Virgin Islands, the
Trust Territory of the Pacific Islands, and the Mayor of the District of
Columbia.

(b) The State Historic Preservation Officer is responsible for the
development and implementation of a comprehensive State Historic preservation plan, based clearly on the State's history and established in conformance with local, State, and Federal legislation and mechanisms, and
approved by the Secretary of the Interior. The State Historic Preservation
Officer supervises a professional staff in conducting a statewide survey
of historic resources addressed to every aspect of the State's history.
From this continuing inventory of historic resources, an integral part of
the State historic preservation plan, the State Historic Preservation
Officer should nominate properties for inclusion in the National Register.
The nominated properties which are approved by the National Park Service
are entered in the National Register by the Director, Office of Archaeology
and Historic Preservation, National Park Service.

(c) The State Historic Preservation Officer has been requested to
assume certain responsibilities for compliance under section 106 of the
National Historic Preservation Act as outlined by the Advisory Council on
Historic Preservation in "Procedures for the Protection of Historic and
Cultural Properties" (36 CFR Part 800).

(d) The following officials have been designated by their Governors
to act as State Historic Preservation Officers responsible for State
activities under the National Historic Preservation Act:

State Historic Preservation Officers

Alabama
Chairman, Alabama Historical Commission, Alabama Department of Archives
and History, Archives and History Building, Montgomery, Alabama 36104.

Alaska
Director, Department of Natural Resources, Division of Parks, 323 East
Fourth Avenue, Anchorage, Alaska 99501.

Arizona
Director, State Parks Board, 1688 West Adams, Phoenix, Arizona 85007.

Arkansas
Director, Department of Natural and Cultural Heritage, the Old State House,
300 West Markham, Little Rock, Arkansas 72201.

California
Director, Department of Parks and Recreation, State Resources Agency,
P. O. Box 2390, Sacramento, California 95811.

Colorado
Chairman, State Historical Society, Colorado State Museum, 200 14th Avenue,
Denver, Colorado 80203.

Connecticut
Director, Connecticut Historical Commission, 59 South Prospect Street,
Hartford, Connecticut 06106.

Delaware
Director, Division of Historical and Cultural Affairs, Hall of Records,
Dover, Delaware 19901.

Florida
Director, Division of Archives, History and Records Management, Department
of State, 401 East Gaines Street, Tallahassee, Florida 32304.

Georgia
Chief, Historic Preservation Section, Department of Natural Resources, 270
Washington Street SW., Room 403-C, Atlanta, Georgia 30334.

Hawaii
State Historic Preservation Officer, P.O. Box 621, Honolulu, Hawaii 96808.

Idaho
Director, Idaho Historical Society, 610 North Julia Davis Drive, Boise,
Idaho 83706.

Illinois
Director, Department of Conservation, 602 State Office Building, 400 South
Spring Street, Springfield, Illinois 62706.

Indiana
Director, Department of Natural Resources, 608 State Office Building,
Indianapolis, Indiana 46204.

Iowa
Director, State Historical Department, Division of Historic Preservation,
B-13 MacLean Hall, Iowa City, Iowa 52242.

Kansas
Executive Director, Kansas State Historical Society, 120 West 10th Street,
Topeka, Kansas 66612.

Kentucky
Director, Kencuky Heritage Commission, 401 Wapping Street, Frankfort,
Kentucky 40601.

Louisiana
Director, Department of Art, Historical and Cultural Preservation, Old
State Capitol, Baton Rouge, Louisiana 70801.

Maine
Director, Maine Historical Preservation Commission, 31 Western Avenue,
Augusta, Maine 04330.

Maryland
Director, Maryland Historical Trust, The John Shaw House, 21 State Circle,
Annapolis, Maryland 24101.

Massachusetts
Executive Director, Massachusetts Historical Commission, 294 Washington
Street, Boston, Massachusetts 02108.

Michigan
Director, Michigan History Division, Department of State, Lansing,
Michigan 48918.

Minnesota
Director, Minnesota Historical Society, 690 Cedar Street, St. Paul,
Minnesota 55101.

Mississippi
Director, State of Mississippi Department of Archives and History, P.D.
Box 571, Jackson, Mississippi 39205.

Missouri
Director, Missouri Department of Natural Resources, P.O. Box 176, 1204
Jefferson Building, Jefferson City, Missouri 65101.

Montana
Administrator, Recreation and Parks Division, Department of Fish and
Game, Helena, Montana 59601.

Nebraska
Director, The Nebraska State Historical Society, 1500 R Street, Lincoln,
Nebraska 68508.

Nevada
Administrator, Division of State Parks, 201 South Fall Street, Carson
City, Nevada 89701.

New Hampshire
Commissioner, Department of Resources and Economic Development, P. O. Box
856, Concord, New Hampshire 03301.

New Jersey
Commissioner, Department of Environmental Protection, P. O. Box 1420,
Trenton, New Jersey 08625.

New Mexico
State Planning Officer, State Capitol, 403 Capitol Building, Santa Fe,
New Mexico 87501.

New York
Commissioner, Parks and Recreation, Room 303, South Swan Street Building,
Albany, New York 12223.

North Carolina
Director, Division of Archives and History, Department of Cultural
Resources, 109 East Jones Street, Raleigh, North Carolina 27611.

North Dakota
Superintendent, State Historical Society of North Dakota, Liberty Memorial
Building, Bismarck, North Dakota 58501.

Ohio
Director, The Ohio Historical Society, Interstate #71 at 17th Avenue,
Columbus, Ohio 43211.

Oklahoma
State Historic Preservation Officer, 1108 Colcord Building, Oklahoma City,
Oklahoma 73102.

Oregon
State Parks Superintendent, 300 State Highway Building, Salem, Oregon 97310.

Pennsylvania
Executive Director, Pennsylvania Historical and Museum Commission, Box 1026,
Harrisburg, Pennsylvania 17120.

Rhode Island
Director, Rhode Island Department of Community Affairs, 150 Washington
Street, Providence, Rhode Island 02903.

South Carolina
Director, State Archives Department, 1430 Senate Street, Columbia, South
Carolina 29211.

South Dakota
Director, Office of Cultural Preservation, Department of Education and
Cultural Affairs, State Capitol, Pierre, South Dakota 57501.

Tennessee
Executive Director, Tennessee Historical Commission, 170 2nd Avenue North,
Suite 100, Nashville, Tennessee 37219.

Texas
Executive Director, Texas State Historical Survey Committee, P.O. Box 12276,
Capitol Station, Austin, Texas 78711.

Utah
Director, Division of State History, 603 East South Temple, Salt Lake City,
Utah 84102.

Vermont
Director, Vermont Division of Historic Sites, Pavilion Building, Montpelier,
Vermont 05602.

Virginia
Executive Director, Virginia Historic Landmarks Commission, 221 Governor
Street, Richmond, Virginia 23219.

Washington
Director, Washington State Parks and Recreation Commission, P.O. Box 1128,
Olympia, Washington 98504.

West Virginia
State Historic Preservation Officer, P.O. Box 937, Morgantown, West
Virginia 26505.

Wisconsin
Director, State Historical Society of Wisconsin, 816 State Street,
Madison, Wisconsin 53706.

Wyoming
Director, Wyoming Recreation Commission, 604 East 25th Street, Box 309,
Cheyenne, Wyoming 82001.

District of Columbia
Director, Office of Housing and Community Development, 14th and E Street
NW., Washington, D.C. 20004.

American Samoa
Territorial Historic Preservation Officer, Department of Public Works,
Government of American Samoa, Pago Pago, American Samoa 96799.

Commonwealth of Puerto Rico
State Historic Preservation Officer, Institute of Puerto Rico Culture,
Apartado 4184, San Juan, Puerto Rico 00905.

Guam
Director, Department of Parks and Recreation, P.O. Box 682, Agana, Guam
96910.

Trust Territory
Chief, Land Resources Branch, Department of Resources and Development,
Trust Territory of the Pacific Islands, Saipan, Mariana Islands 96950.

Virgin Islands
Planning Director, Virgin Islands Planning Board, Charlotte Amalie,
St. Thomas, Virgin Islands 00801.

(e) When a new State Historic Preservation Officer is appointed by a
Governor, a letter must be sent to the Director of the National Park
Service providing notice of the appointment. Similar written notification
must also be sent in cases involving a successor to the State Historic
Preservation Officer when the original appointment was made to the *office*
rather than specifically to the *individual* (*by name*) holding the office.
The National Park Service also requires notification when the State
Historic Preservation Officer delegates authorities to other parties.
Changes of address, telephone number, or personnel should also be brought
promptly to the attention of the National Park Service.
(f) Questions concerning authorized signatures should be addressed to
the Director, Office of Archaeology and Historic Preservation, National
Park Service, U.S. Department of the Interior, Washington, D.C. 20240.

Section 60.6. Criteria for Evaluation

The criteria applied to evaluate properties for possible inclusion in
the National Register are listed below. These criteria are worded in a
manner to provide for the diversity of resources. The following criteria
shall be used in evaluating properties for nomination to the National
Register, by the National Park Service in reviewing nominations, and for
evaluating National Register eligibility of properties affected by Federal
agency undertakings.

National Register criteria for evaluation. The quality of significance
in American history, architecture, archaeology, and culture is present in
districts, sites, buildings, structures, and objects of State and local
importance that possess integrity of location, design, setting, materials,
workmanship, feeling, and association, and
(a) That are associated with events that have made a significant
contribution to the broad patterns of our history; or
(b) That are associated with the lives of persons significant in our
past; or
(c) That embody the distinctive characteristics of a type, period,
or method of construction, or that represent the work of a master, or that
possess high artistic values, or that represent a significant and distinguishable entity whose components may lack individual distinction; or
(d) That have yielded, or may be likely to yield, information important in prehistory or history.

Criteria considerations. Ordinarily cemeteries, birthplaces, or graves
of historical figures, properties owned by religious institutions or used

for religious purposes, structures that have been moved from their original locations, reconstructed historic buildings, properties primarily commemorative in nature, and properties that have achieved significance within the past 50 years shall not be considered eligible for the National Register. However, such properties will qualify if they are integral parts of districts that do meet the criteria or if they fall within the following categories:

(a) A religious property deriving primary significance from architectural or artistic distinction or historical importance.

(b) A building or structure removed from its original location but which is significant primarily for architectural value, or which is the surviving structure most importantly associated with a historic person or event.

(c) A birthplace or grave of a historical figure of outstanding importance if there is no appropriate site or building directly associated with his productive life.

(d) A cemetery which derives its primary significance from graves of persons of transcendent importance, from age, from distinctive design features, or from association with historic events.

(e) A reconstructed building when accurately executed in a suitable environment and presented in a dignified manner as part of a restoration master plan, and when no other building or structure with the same association has survived.

(f) A property primarily commemorative in intent if design, age, tradition, or symbolic value has invested it with its own historical significance.

(g) A property achieving significance within the past 50 years if it is of exceptional importance.

Section 60.7. *The State Historic Preservation Plan*

(a) Before properties are nominated for inclusion in the National Register, a continuing statewide survey of historic, architectural, archaeological, and cultural resources is undertaken. This survey may be conducted with matching funds from the grants-in-aid program of the National Park Service.

(b) The survey is the basis of a State historic preservation plan which is organized into three volumes. Volume I of this document provides a summary of the State's history and background of its preservation activities, a statement of its long-range goals, and its methods of operation. Volume II, an inventory of the State's cultural resources, identifies significant districts, sites, buildings, structures, and objects regardless of title, boundaries, or ownership, so that properties which meet the criteria for evaluation can be nominated to the National Register. Volume III is the annual work program, which must be submitted annually with an apportionment warrant stating and explaining the State's request for historic preservation grants-in-aid. This volume includes a review of the past year's work, updates of Volumes I and II, and plans for the next fiscal year.

(c) A State's eligibility to participate in the National Register program and the grants-in-aid program depends upon its submission of an acceptable State historic preservation plan to the National Park Service.

(d) More detailed information on the State historic preservation plan may be obtained by writing the Branch of Plans, National Register Division, National Park Service, U.S. Department of the Interior, Washington, D.C. 20240.

Section 60.8.   State Professional Staff

The State plan and all nominations submitted to the National Register by a State for consideration must first be prepared under the supervision of a full-time professional staff, responsible to the State Historic Preservation Officer.   The staff must possess professionally recognized qualifications by education and experience in the fields of history, archaeology, architecture (architectural history), and other appropriate disciplines, such as planning, as may be necessary.   The credentials for each proposed staff member must be presented to the National Park Service for approval as part of the State historic preservation plan, volume III, or whenever there is a change in the composition of the staff.

Section 60.9.   State Review Board

(a)   Volumes I and II of the State plan and all nominations submitted to the National Register by a State Historic Preservation Officer must first have been approved by a professional review board.   The State Historic Preservation Officer must identify the proposed members of the review board and present their credentials to the National Park Service for approval in volume III of the State historic preservation plan or whenever there is a change in the composition of the board.   The members of the review board may be proposed to the National Park Service either by the Governor or by the State Historic Preservation Officer.

(b)   A minimum membership of five is required, including an authority in each of the following fields: history, archaeology, architectural history, or architecture, and such other professional disciplines as may be appropriate (i.e. urban or regional planning).   Employees of the State agency having the responsibility for survey and planning under the provisions of the act may be members of this body but may not vote on documents which they have supervised or have prepared themselves.   Employees of the State agency may not fill one of the five professional positions except with special written permission of the National Park Service.

Section 60.10.   Nomination Forms

All nominations to the National Register are to be made on standard National Register forms (revised October 1974) as follows:

No.	Form title	User	Color
10-300	Inventory-nomination.	State	White
10-306	do	Federal	Blue
10-300a	Continuation sheet	State and Federal	White
10-301	Property map	do	Do
10-301a	Property photograph	do	Do

These forms are provided upon request to the State Historic Preservation Officers and to the participating Federal agencies by the National Park Service.   For archival reasons, no other forms, photocopied or otherwise, will be accepted.

Section 60.11.   Concurrent State and Federal Nominations

(a)   State Historic Preservation Officers and Federal Representatives are encouraged to cooperate in loacting, inventorying, evaluating, and nominating all properties possessing historical, architectural, archaeological, or cultural value.

(b)   When a portion of the area included in a Federal nomination is not located on land under the jurisdiction or control of the Federal agency, but is an integral part of the cultural resource, the completed nomination

form should be sent to the State Historic Preservation Officer for submission to the State review board, notification to property owners, and
the solicitation of written comments.

(c) If the review board approves the nomination, the form should be
signed by the State Historic Preservation Officer and returned to the
Federal agency initiating the nomination along with a letter confirming
that the nomination has been reviewed and approved by the State Historic
Preservation Officer and the review board, that the appropriate owner or
owners have been notified, and that all other State procedures have been
fulfilled. Comments received by a State concerning the significance of
the property should be included.

(d) Federally owned properties may be nominated by the State as well.
In such cases the State Historic Preservation Officer shall notify the
appropriate Federal representative in writing and, if possible, an agency
official within the State before the nomination is forwarded to the
National Park Service.

Section 60.12. Notification

(a) As indicated previously in §60.2 (c), the National Register was
designed and has been implemented as a planning tool. Federal agencies
that undertake a project having an effect on such a listed property must
provide the Advisory Council on Historic Preservation a reasonable opportunity to comment pursuant to 36 CFR Part 800. Having complied with this
requirement, the agency may adopt any course of action it may feel appropriate. While the Advisory Council comments must be taken into account
and integrated into the decisionmaking process, the program decision rests
with the agency implementing the undertaking. No requirements of any kind
are imposed upon private initiative.

(b) The State Historic Preservation Officer concept has been developed
within the various States at the urging of the Secretary of the Interior
both to expand the National Register and to implement the historic preservation grants-in-aid program created by the National Historic Preservation
Act of 1966, 16 U.S.C. 470 et seq. (1970 ed.). As such, this position has
come to serve as a vital link between a State's participation in these
programs and the National Park Service, and as a blending of State and
Federal programs. This is particularly true of the identification and
nomination of properties to the National Register by a State, which is
required as a portion of the comprehensive statewide historic and cultural
survey and a condition precedent to participation in the grants-in-aid
program.

(c) The identification and nomination of historic and cultural resources, as a function that has been assumed by the various States, is
essentially a State action. The nomination of a property is a proposal
to the National Park Service and does not constitute listing. However,
nominations received from the various States are, in the vast majority of
situations, accepted by the National Park Service. Listing in the National
Register is a Department of the Interior decision. As a part of the
nomination process, each State is required to notify property owners in
writing except as specified in subsection (d) below of the State's intent
to nominate a property and to allow a reasonable opportunity for the
presentation of written comments concerning the property's significance
prior to review board consideration. The required notice shall advise the
property owner that certain Federal tax consequences may result from
listing in the National Register and refer to section 2124 of the Tax
Reform Act of 1976. The States are also strongly encouraged to notify
appropriate State, county, or municipal authorities and to allow them a
reasonable opportunity to present written comments concerning the property's
significance prior to review board consideration.

(d)   In the event of a nomination of a historic district of multiple
ownerships where notice to individual property owners is not practicable,
each State is required to notify appropriate State, county, or municipal
authorities; to provide other means of general notice concerning the
State's intent to nominate the district; and to allow a reasonable opportunity for the presentation of written comments concerning the district's
significance prior to review board consideration.   Such notice must point
out that certain Federal tax consequences may result from listing of the
district in the National Register and must refer to section 2124 of the
Tax Reform Act of 1976 in this respect.

(e)   State Historic Preservation Officers are required to obtain and
submit to the National Park Service at the time of nomination the names and
addresses of the owners of record of all properties nominated to the
National Register by the State, including all owners of properties in historic districts.   When the State Historic Preservation Officer signs the
nomination and forwards it to the National Park Service, he is certifying
that the owners of record have been obtained from the most current list
available as of the date of the nomination.

(f)   State Historic Preservation Officers are required to inform
property owners or appropriate local authorities when properties are
added to the National Register.

(g)   In consultation with the State's Attorney General, each State
should adopt general notification procedures consistent with the considerations of this section and provide the National Park Service with a copy
of these procedures when completed, and thereafter include them in the
annual State historic preservation plan or whenever changes are made.

Section 60.13.   Notification of Owners of Record and Publication in the "Federal Register"

(a)   When a nomination from a State is received, the National Park
Service shall notify in writing each owner of record submitted by the
State that the property (or proposed historic district within which it is
located) has been nominated to the National Register and shall allow a
reasonable opportunity for the presentation of written comments concerning
the property's significance prior to listing the property in the National
Register.   Such notice shall advise property owners that certain Federal
tax consequences may result from listing of the property in the National
Register and refer to section 2124 of the Tax Reform Act of 1976 in this
respect.   The notice shall also advise the owner of the National Register
criteria of evaluation as set forth herein.

(b)   When a nomination is received, the National Park Service shall
publish notice in the "Federal Register" that the property is being
considered for listing and shall receive additional written comments
concerning the significance of the property under the National Register
criteria for evaluation to the extent practicable.

(c)   The National Park Service shall notify the State Historic Preservation Officer of the listing of the property and publish notice of listing
in the "Federal Register" on a regular basis and in a cumulative edition
which shall appear once a year, usually in February.

Section 60.14.   Other State and Local Programs

State and local authorities that utilize the National Register nominations as the base for more restrictive provisions, such as halt-in-demo-
lition provisions, must be aware that such uses of the information provided to the National Register are purely matters of State and local
initiative and subject to the scope of a State's police powers.   Such State

and local provisions must be clearly separated from the role of the
National Register as a planning tool and as the basis for participation
in the historic preservation grants-in-aid program.

Section 60.15. Processing of Nominations

Nominations of properties to the National Register follow the process
set forth below.

(a) *Nominations by the State Historic Preservation Officer*.

(1) Nomination forms (10-300) are prepared under the supervision of
the State Historic Preservation Officer.

(2) Notice is provided of the intent to nominate the property and
written comments are solicited. With regard to property under Federal
jurisdiction or control, completed nomination forms should be submitted
to the Federal representative for review and comment regarding the significance of the property. After receiving the comments of the Federal
representative, or if there has been no response within 45 days, the
State Historic Preservation Officer may approve the nomination and forward
it to the Keeper, National Register, National Park Service, Washington,
D.C. 20240. The comments of the Federal representative are appended to
the nomination; or, if there are no comments, an explanation is attached.

(3) Completed nomination forms or the documentation proposed for
submission on the nominations forms are submitted to the State review
board for approval prior to submission to the National Register.

(4) Nomination forms approved by the State review board are reviewed
by the State Historic Preservation Officer and, if approved, signed with
the affirmation that all appropriate procedures have been followed.

(5) The State Historic Preservation Officer submits the completed
nomination and comments received by a State concerning the significance
of the property to the Keeper, National Register, National Park Service,
Washington, D.C. 20240.

(6) Notice will be provided in the FEDERAL REGISTER that the nominated
property is being considered for listing in the National Register of Historic Places and comments will be received whenever possible concerning
the significance of the property. Copies of these written comments will
be supplied to the State Historic Preservation Officer.

(7) Nominations are reviewed by the Office of Archaeology and Historic
Preservation to determine technical and professional sufficiency and
conformance to the National Register criteria for evaluation and comments
are considered.

(8) Nominations found to be technically and professionally sufficient
and in conformance with the National Register criteria for evaluation will
be approved by the Director, Office of Archaeology and Historic Preservation,
and entered in the National Register. Nominations found technically or
professionally inadequate will be returned for correction and re-submission.
When a property does not appear to meet the National Register criteria for
evaluation, the nomination will be returned with an explanatory letter.

(b) *Nominations by a Federal agency*.

(1) Nomination forms (10-306) are prepared under the supervision of
the Federal Representative designated by the head of a Federal agency to
fulfill agency responsibilities under Executive Order 11593.

(2) Completed nominations are submitted to the appropriate State
Historic Preservation Officer for review and comment regarding the significance of the property and its eligibility for the National Register.

(3) After receiving the comments of the State Historic Preservation
Officer, or if there has been no response within 45 days, the Federal
Representative may approve the nomination and forward it to the Keeper,
National Register, National Park Service, Washington, D.C. 20240. The

comments of the State Historic Preservation Officer are appended to the
nomination, or, if there are no comments, an explanation is attached.
Concurrent nominations cannot be submitted, however, until the nomination
has been approved by the State in accord with §60.11, supra. Comments
received by the State concerning concurrent nominations must be submitted
with the nomination.

(4) Notice will be provided in the FEDERAL REGISTER that the nominated
property is being considered for listing in the National Register of
Historic Places and comments will be received whenever possible concerning
the significance of the property. Copies of these written comments will
be supplied to the Federal representative and to the State Historic Preservation Officer.

(5) Nominations are reviewed by the Office of Archaeology and Historic
Preservation to determine technical and professional sufficiency and conformance to the National Register criteria for evaluation and comments are
considered.

(6) Nominations found to be technically and professionally sufficient
and in conformance with the National Register criteria for evaluation will
be approved by the Director, Office of Archaeology and Historic Preservation,
and entered in the National Register. Nominations found technically or
professionally inadequate will be returned for correction and resubmission.
When a property does not appear to meet the National Register criteria for
evaluation, the nomination will be returned with an explanatory letter.

*Section 60.16. Changes and Revisions to Properties Listed in the National
Register*

(a) *Boundary changes.*

(1) A boundary alteration should be handled as a new property nomination supplanting the old nomination form. All forms, criteria, and
procedures used in nominating a property to the National Register must be
used at both the State and Federal levels. A professionally justified
recommendation by the State Historic Preservation Officer or Federal
Representative must be presented to the National Park Service. During
this process, the property is not taken off the National Register. If
the National Park Service finds the recommendation in accordance with the
National Register criteria for evaluation, the change will be accepted. If
the boundary change is not accepted, the old boundaries will remain.

(2) Two justifications exist for altering a boundary: Professional
error in the initial nomination or loss of historic integrity. In some
cases, accretion of additional significance may also be reason for altering property boundaries. No enlargement of a boundary should be recommended
unless the additional area possesses previously unrecognized significance in
American history, architecture, archaeology, or culture. No diminution of
a boundary should be recommended unless the properties being removed have
lost the characteristics that endowed them with such significance and
qualified them for the initial nomination. Any proposal to alter a boundary has to be documented in detail in order to avoid the necessity of
an onsite inspection by National Park Service personnel. Specifically,
the structures or other historic resources falling between the existing
boundary and the other proposed boundary should be photographed.

(3) Attention should be given to the "Criteria for Effect," promulgated by the Advisory Council on Historic Preservation in "Procedures for
the Protection of Historic and Cultural Properties" (36 CFR Part 800), for
use in the application of section 106 of the National Historic Preservation
Act. According to these criteria a project need not fall within the
boundaries of a National Register property for an effect to exist.

(b) Relocating properties listed in the National Register.

(1) Properties listed in the National Register should be moved only when there is no feasible alternative for preservation. When a property is moved, every effort should be made to reestablish its historic orientation, immediate setting, and general environment.

(2) If it is proposed that a structure listed in the National Register be moved and the State or Federal agency wishes the property to remain in the National Register during and after the move, the State or Federal agency must submit documentation prior to the move which should discuss:

(i) The reasons for the move;

(ii) The effect on the property's historical integrity; and

(iii) The new setting and general environment of the proposed site, including evidence that the proposed site does not possess historical significance that would be adversely affected by the intrusion of the structure.

In addition, photographs showing the proposed location must be sent along with the documentation. Any such proposal submitted by a State must be approved by the State review board and will continue to follow normal review procedures.

(3) If the National Park Service approves the proposal, the property will remain on the National Register during and after the move unless the integrity of the property is, in some unforeseen manner, destroyed, If the National Park Service does not approve the proposal, the property will be automatically deleted from the National Register when moved. If the State or Federal agency has proof that previously unrecognized significance exists, or has accrued, the State or Federal agency may resubmit a nomination for the property as outlined below.

(4) In the event that a structure is moved, deletion from the National Register will be automatic unless the above procedures are followed prior to the move. If the property has already been moved, it is the State or Federal agency's responsibility to notify the National Register. Assuming that the State or Federal agency wishes to have the structure reentered in the National Register, it must be nominated again on new forms which should discuss:

(i) The reasons for the move;

(ii) The effect on the property's historical integrity, and

(iii) The new setting and general environment, including evidence that the new site does not possess historical significance that would be adversely affected by the intrusion of the site.

In addition, new photographs showing the structure at its new location must be sent along with the revised nomination. Any such nomination submitted by a State must be approved by the State review board.

(5) Properties moved in a manner consistent with the comments of the Advisory Council on Historic Preservation, in accord with its procedures (36 CFR Part 800), are granted an exception to §60.16 (b). Moving of properties in accord with the Advisory Council's procedures should be dealt with individually in each memorandum of agreement.

Section 60.17. *Removing Properties from the National Register*

(a) Properties nominated by the States or Federal agencies will be removed from the National Register only when they have ceased to meet the criteria for the National Register: when the qualities which caused them originally to be nominated have been lost or destroyed; upon proof that an error in professional judgment has been made; or, for failure to follow the procedures set forth herein. Information concerning the loss of integrity, error in judgment, or procedural error should be submitted through the appropriate State Historic Preservation Officer or Federal representative to the Keeper, National Register, National Park Service, Washington, D.C. 20240.

Dated: January 5, 1976.
GARY EVERHARDT
Director, National Park Service

THE NATIONAL REGISTER AND ARCHAEOLOGY
SUGGESTIONS TO ARCHAEOLOGISTS NOMINATING PROPERTIES
TO THE NATIONAL REGISTER OF HISTORIC PLACES

The National Register includes properties of value to many and diverse segments of the public, and the value of such properties requires definition by many kinds of specialists--historians, historic and prehistoric archaeologists, and anthropologists, to name a few. Since the inception of the National Register program, the involvement of these professional disciplines has become increasingly sophisticated, as review boards, state staffs, and the National Register staff have become increasingly professional. At the same time, the increase in section 106 and section 2(b) actions before the Advisory Council on Historic Preservation and the courts, and the increasing impact of historic preservation statues on Federal undertakings require that entries in the National Register be highly defensible.

In view of these historical developments, it seems appropriate to review the kind and level of professionalism necessary in the preparation of nominations to the National Register. While similar clarifications may be expected with regard to many kinds of cultural resources, recent circumstances have called our attention to districts, sites, structures, buildings, and objects nominated for their archaeological value.

Nominating an archaeological property should be an exacting, intellectual activity, designed to provide not only documentation that the property exists, but also a reasonable argument for the property's research significance. Archaeological properties do not have to be large, impressive, or rich in artifacts or data to qualify for the National Register, nor do they have to be suitable for public interpretation. Any archaeological resource is potentially eligible if one can legitimately argue that it is likely to be associated with a cultural pattern, process, or activity important to the history or prehistory of its locality, the United States, or humanity as a whole, provided its study can contribute to an understanding of that pattern, process, or activity.

Archaeologists are encouraged to participate in the development of regional and state research designs, overviews, and plans that will facilitate the development of arguments for and against the eligibility of specific properties and districts. Some properties that have little significance as individual entities may be eligible as segments of archaeological districts. In some cases an archaeological property or district may also qualify because of an association with a particular event or person, or on the basis of its intrinsic historicity or utility as an interpretive location. Properties that have lost their integrity by being completely excavated or otherwise totally disturbed do not normally qualify, unless they are of outstanding historical significance for the data they have yielded.

Both historic and prehistoric properties may be considered archaeological if they are valuable for scientific study to elucidate patterns important in history or prehistory. Historic (and some prehistoric) properties may, of course, also be important for nonarchaeological reasons; for example, a historic archaeological property may include a building with important architectural characteristics. Archaeologists engaged in identifying cultural resources for nomination to the National Register should be sensitive to nonarchaeological values, and obtain professional assistance in describing and evaluating them.

DESCRIPTIONS OF ARCHAEOLOGICAL PROPERTIES

In the nomination of an archaeological property to the National
Register, two types of information should be included in the property
description.

A. *Contextual Data Should Place the Site in a Framework Understandable*
   to the General Public, and Should Include Information as to:

(1) the nature of the survey or other study that led to the identification of the property. How was the property searched for? What lands
were surveyed and what methods were used in finding it? Were other
cultural resources discovered that might also be eligible for the National
Register?

(2) the historic or prehistoric context of the property, historic
descriptions, assignment to a place in a local cultural-historical framework, and possible activities represented by the property's characteristics.
Assumptions about age, cultural affiliation, and function should be sub-
stantiated with supporting data.

B. *Descriptive Data Should Include:*

(1) boundaries and justification-location, boundaries, and size of
the property; reasons for the selection of boundaries; and location maps
and planimetric or sketch maps of the property.

(2) internal composition-for a district: descriptions of sites,
structures, buildings, and objects that make up the property; for a site:
structure, building or object, descriptions of important component parts,
features, strata, rooms, artifacts, attributes, etc. (may be summarized,
tabulated or mapped).

(3) environment-pertinent elements of the surrounding natural environment, biological and geological features, and micro-environments.

(4) intrusions-impinging development, agricultural practices, erosion,
vandalism, etc.

(5) archaeological activities-subsurface testing or other special
studies (may be summarized with maps and plans as appropriate).

(6) data limitations-any areas of uncertainty concerning the nature
of the property that should be considered.

STATEMENTS OF SIGNIFICANCE OF ARCHAEOLOGICAL PROPERTIES

A statement of significance should be more than a simple professional
opinion that the property is significant or that it meets one or more of
the National Register criteria. A well-reasoned argument for the property's usefulness to research is appropriate. If a State, regional, or
local plan or research design has been developed or is being developed
that sets forth standards for the preservation or other treatment of
archaeological resources, the significance of particular properties should
be discussed with reference to these standards. In any case, the following
three steps are not rigidly required for statements of significance, but
should serve as general guides.

A. Consider all known and/or expected data categories and cultural
features of the property in terms of the information they may yield. Does
the site contain many strata that might yield information on cultural-change?
Does it consist of a single stratum or surface assemblage that might provide data on activity patterns during a short time span? Does the building
contain papers, artifacts, or patterns of material that could yield information on social interaction, use of space, or economic activities? Does
the district represent a settlement pattern that could be studied to learn

about land use or social organization? Is the object a petroglyph rock
that might yield information on concepts of space and symbolism?
      B. Consider any research topics that might form a basis for study
of the property, including topics currently addressed in the area and
topics suggested by one's professional training as future possibilities.
      C. Discuss how study of the data categories and features represented
by the property may (or may not) contribute to study of the research
topics.
      The three examples appended are hypothetical statements of significance
illustrating some of the problems encountered with many such statements as
they are now received.

DETERMINATIONS OF ELIGIBILITY

      The comments above, while framed with reference to National Register
nominations, apply to requests for determinations of eligibility as well.
In the case of determinations, of course, presentation of descriptive
data and a statement of significance in strict nomination format is not
required; reports of archaeological surveys and evaluations are adequate,
provided that they include the necessary descriptive and evaluatory
material outlined above. Archaeologists preparing reports for use in
making determinations of eligibility should organize their reports in such
a way as to insure that the necessary data are presented in a clear and
understandable way. Descriptive and evaluative statements should be
clearly separated from recommendations or proposals for salvage excavation
or other forms of impact-mitigation; defining the nature and significance
of a property and reaching conclusions about how best to treat it in project planning are separate processes, and should not be confused.
      Determinations of ineligibility for the National Register should be docu-
mented in the same way as determinations of eligibility. The property should
be fully described, and a viable argument should be set forth to show that
the property lacks research value.

Example 1. Insufficient Statement of Significance

      *Lewis and Clark, in 1795, describe a "large Indian village" at this
location, consisting of 17 temple mounds and a chiefly residence.*

      Comment. The fact that the site has an association with an historic
event, or that it was described historically, does not by itself give it
research value.

      *The site today contains stratified deposits representing 4,000 years of
prehistory.*

      Comment. Stratigraphy and time-depth do not equal significance. Why
are these 4,000 years of prehistory important for research?

      *The large number of artifacts recovered from the test excavation, the
architectural remains represented by the temple mounds, and the deeply
stratified medden deposits indicate that this site can yield important
information about local prehistory.*

      Comment. Artifacts, architecture and middens do not equal significance.
Why are these artifacts of the site important for research?

*Example 2. Sufficient Statement of Significance Based on Known Research
Date*

      *As indicated in the description, the site contains nonrandom clusters
of flakes and stone tools typical of the Archaic period, suggesting work*

areas and (possibly) residential locations.

Comment. Pertinent data categories, described in the descriptive section of the nomination, are noted.

Local research has long focused on the reconstruction of culture history through the study of changes in artifact type. There is evidence of rapid change from an Archaic pattern of low-density land use by mobile hunter-gatherers to a prehistoric pattern of high-density sedentary residence in nucleated village clusters. The nature of this change is poorly understood, but Twiddletrowl (1975) has proposed that it reflects the rise of warrior-priests in response to hostile actions by neighboring groups, while Marshalltown (1976) has argued that it reflects the ability of large populations to support themselves in high-density communities following the domestication of the armadillo. These alternative propositions reflect contrasting general theoretical positions concerning the origins of the state.

Comment. Local research problems are synopsized, and related to problems of general theoretical interest.

Since this site appears to contain data categories reflective of different residential groups, it should be possible to use it in the reconstruction of Archaic period community organization. Resolution of the Twiddletrowl/Marshalltown controversy will require the comparative analysis of settlement organization through time, to identify the demographic and economic events with which organization changes are associated. It is in this comparative framework that the site attains its significance.

Comment. The ways in which the site could be studied to address research questions are synopsized.

Example 3. Sufficient Statement of Significance Based on Research Data

The State Historic Preservation Plan, in discussing the historic archaeology of this region, defines 14 types of sites representative of the Chinese-American community during the Whaling period, and recommends that at least 10% of all sites representing each type be preserved for purposes of future, as yet undefined research. This site, as noted in the description, is a Type 12 Chinese-American Whaling period site. Only two such sites have thus far been nominated to the National Register, and both are on the other side of the mountain, farther from the main population center during the Whaling period. The site thus represents a type which is not as yet adequately recognized or preserved, in a geographic and social environment different from those in which those sites now recognized as representative of the type exist.

Comment. Here, although no specific research value is assigned to the property, an argument is advanced for its potential research value, based on a systematic regional study that has defined types of sites that are likely to be of future reserach interest (in this case, the State Historic Preservation Plan).

36 CFR PART 60:   DRAFT AMENDMENTS

The following draft amendments to 36 CFR Part 60 were circula-
ted to State Historic Preservation Officers and others for comment
during the summer of 1976. As of early 1977 they were undergoing
revision preparatory to publication in the FEDERAL REGISTER. They
expand upon the responsibilities of the State Historic Preserva-
tion Officer in statewide survey and planning.

CRITERIA FOR COMPREHENSIVE STATEWIDE HISTORIC SURVEYS AND PLANS

On January 9, 1976, a notice of new rulemaking was published in the
"Federal Register" (41 FR 1590) to amend Chapter I of Title 36 of the
Code of Federal Regulations by adding a new Part 60 concerning the
National Register of Historic Places program administered by the National
Park Service, Department of the Interior. The purpose of the rulemaking
was to draw together procedures that had been developed to implement the
National Historic Preservation Act of 1966, 80 Stat. 915, 16 U.S.C. 470
et seq. (1970 ed.), and Executive Order 11593, Protection and Enhancement
of the Cultural Environment, 16 U.S.C. 470 (Supp. 1, 1971). Specifically,
the aforementioned rulemaking articulated certain actions taken by this
Department to meet its responsibilities to "expand and maintain a national
register of districts, sites, buildings, structures, and objects significant in American history, architecture, archaeology, and culture" as
prescribed by section 101(a)(1) of the 1966 Act.
In addition to authorizing the Secretary of the Interior to expand
and maintain the National Register, the 1966 Act authorized the Secretary
to grant funds to States for the purpose of preparing comprehensive
statewide historic surveys and plans, in accordance with criteria established by the Secretary, for the preservation, acquisition, and development
of districts, sites, buildings, structures, and objects significant in
American history, architecture, archaeology, and culture. The Act also
authorized the Secretary to establish a program of matching grants-in-aid
to States for projects having as their purpose the preservation for public
benefit of properties that are significant in American history, architecture,
archaeology, and culture, and a program of matching grants-in-aid to the
National Trust for Historic Preservation in the United States, for the
purpose of carrying out the responsibilities of the National Trust. The
Act stipulates that grants shall be made on the basis of approved statewide historic preservation plans.
The purpose of this proposed rulemaking is to set forth the criteria
established by the Secretary of the Interior for preparing comprehensive
statewide historic surveys and plans under the National Historic Preservation Act of 1966. Planning requirements for the National Trust and administration of the grants program, as it affects both the States and the
National Trust, will be the subject of subsequent rulemaking.
This proposed rulemaking adds to the existing Part 60 new sections
60.1a (Definitions), 60.6a (Comprehensive statewide survey process),
60.7a (Environmental review), and 60.8a (Professional qualifications) and
substitutes new language for existing sections 60.5 (Appointment and
responsibilities of the State Historic Preservation Officer), 60.7 (State

historic preservation plan), 60.8 (State professional staff), and 60.9
(State Review Board).

In preparing these regulations and reviewing the National Register and
grants program, the intent, requirements, and spirit of the National
Environmental Policy Act of 1969 (Public Law 91-190, 42 U.S.C. 4321-4347)
have been carefully considered. As established by the National Historic
Preservation Act of 1966 and expanded by Executive Order 11593, these
programs have as their purpose the identification, protection, and enhancement of the historic, architectural, archaeological, and cultural
resources of the manmade environment. It has been administratively
determined that, beyond the overall program purpose, which is intended
to enhance the environment, this proposed rulemaking will have no significant effect on the environment. These regulations serve to expand the
regulations previously published in the "Federal Register" and should
further insure the environmentally beneficial effects of the National
Register and grants programs. Further information, including a memorandum
of environmental assessment, is on file in the Office of Archaeology and
Historic Preservation, National Park Service, Department of the Interior,
Washington, D.C. 20240. It has been administratively determined that
this proposed rulemaking is not "major" within the intent of Executive
Order 11821 (39 FR 41501, November 27, 1974) and that an inflationary
impact certification is therefore not required.

It is the policy of the Department of the Interior, whenever practicable,
to afford the public an opportunity to participate in the rulemaking process.
Accordingly, interested persons may submit written comments, suggestions, or
objections regarding the proposed procedures to the Keeper of the National
Register, National Park Service, Department of the Interior, Washington,
D.C. 20240, on or before (*30 days from date of publication*).

Dated:_____
NATHANIEL P. REED
Assistant Secretary for Fish and Wildlife and Parks

60.1a DEFINITIONS

As used in these procedures:
(a) "State" means, in addition to the several States of the Union, the
District of Columbia, the Commonwealth of Puerto Rico, the Virgin Islands,
Guam, American Samoa, the Trust Territory of the Pacific Islands, and any
other jurisdictions that may be authorized by Congress to receive grants
under the National Historic Preservation Act of 1966.
(b) "National Register" means the national register of districts,
sites, buildings, structures, and objects significant in American history,
architecture, archaeology, and culture that the Secretary of the Interior
was authorized by section 101(a)(1) of the National Historic Preservation
Act of 1966 to expand and maintain.
(c) "National Register program" means the survey, planning, and registration program that has evolved under the Secretary of the Interior's
authority in section 101(a)(1) of the National Historic Preservation Act
of 1966, including, but not limited to, the responsibilities of the
State Historic Preservation Officers as outlined in section 60.5(b) of
these regulations.
(d) "Grants program" means the program of matching grants-in-aid to
States authorized by section 101(a)(2) of the National Historic Preservation Act of 1966.
(e) "Secretary" means the Secretary of the Interior or his designee
authorized to carry out his responsibilities.

(f) "Cultural resource" means any district, site, building, structure, or object significant in American history, architecture, archaeology, and culture at the national, State or local level.

60.5 DESIGNATION AND RESPONSIBILITIES OF THE STATE HISTORIC PRESERVATION OFFICER

(a) The State Historic Preservation Officer is the official within each State who has been designated by the Governor or chief executive of the State to administer the National Register and grants programs within the State.

(b) The responsibilities of the State Historic Preservation Officer shall include:

(1) Development of an administrative framework for the State historic preservation program, consisting of (a) the State historic preservation office, which shall be an official part of State government; (b) a full-time professional staff working under the direction of the State Historic Preservation Officer; and (c) a State Review Board duly appointed by the State Historic Preservation Officer.

(2) Direction of a comprehensive statewide survey of cultural resources.

(3) Registration, or official recognition, of cultural resources through (a) preparation and submission of nominations to the National Register and (b) participation in the Secretary's determinations that cultural resources meet the National Register criteria and are therefore eligible for listing in the National Register.

(4) Development of effective working relationships with (a) Federal agencies, (b) other State offices, and (c) local governmental units that participate in the identification, registration, protection, enhancement, and management of cultural resources and in project planning that may affect cultural resources; and integration of historic preservation planning with all levels of planning, in order to ensure that the need to preserve cultural resources is taken into consideration by all planning agencies.

(5) Development and operation of an environmental review procedure for undertakings that may affect cultural resources within the State.

(6) Participation in the review of Federal, federally assisted, and federally licensed undertakings that may affect cultural resources included in or eligible for inclusion in the National Register under section 106 of the National Historic Preservation Act and Executive Order 11593, in accordance with the Advisory Council on Historic Preservation's "Procedures for the Protection of Historic and Cultural Properties" (36 CFR Part 800).

(7) Assisting Federal agencies in fulfilling their historic preservation responsibilities under Federal laws and regulations.

(8) Liaison with organizations of professional archaeologists, historians, architects, architectural historians, planners, and others concerned or potentially concerned with historic preservation, and utilizing their expertise wherever possible.

(9) Development and operation of a public information program concerning the National Register and grants program.

(10) Administration of the grants program within the State.

(11) Preparation and maintenance of a comprehensive statewide historic preservation plan, subject to approval by the Secretary.

(c) A list of State Historic Preservation Officers shall be published in the "Federal Register" annually and shall be amended as changes occur.

(d) When a new State Historic Preservation Officer is designated by a Governor, a letter shall be sent to the Director of the National Park

Service providing notice of the designation. Similar written notification shall also be sent in cases involving a successor to the State Historic Preservation Officer when the original designation was made to the office rather than specifically to the individual (by name) holding the office. The National Park Service also requires notification when the State Historic Preservation Officer delegates authorities to other parties. Changes of address, telephone number, or personnel shall also be brought promptly to the attention of the National Park Service.

(e) Questions concerning authorized signatures shall be addressed to the Director, Office of Archaeology and Historic Preservation, National Park Service, Department of the Interior, Washington, D.C. 20240.

60.6a COMPREHENSIVE STATEWIDE SURVEY PROCESS

(a) A comprehensive statewide survey of cultural resources shall be conducted in each State under the direction of the State Historic Preservation Officer. The goal of the comprehensive survey shall be the identification of all districts, sites, buildings, structures, and objects within the State that are significant in American history, architecture, archaeology, and culture at the national, State, and local levels. The survey shall be conducted in as timely a manner as possible and shall include all cultural resources, regardless of title, boundaries, or ownership.

(b) In conducting the survey, the State Historic Preservation Officer shall develop a systematic method to ensure comprehensive statewide coverage including every aspect of the State's prehistory and history. Documentation concerning the survey methods employed shall be maintained in the State historic preservation office.

(c) Insofar as possible, the State Historic Preservation Officer shall coordinate all cultural resource survey efforts in the State, including surveys conducted by other State offices, local governmental units, universities, and other public and private institutions and organizations, and shall cooperate with surveys conducted by Federal agencies. Records of the methods as well as the results of such surveys shall be maintained in the State historic preservation office.

(d) All information in the State historic preservation office resulting from Federal, State, and local cultural resource surveys shall be known as the State Survey Data. The State Survey Data shall include, but not be limited to, the following:

(1) The State inventory of cultural resources, defined as those cultural resources that have been evaluated and have been found to be significant in American history, architecture, archaeology, and culture at the national, State, and local levels. These resources include (a) resources listed in the National Register, (b) resources nominated to the National Register or approved by the State Review Board for nomination, (c) resources determined eligible by the Secretary for listing in the National Register, and (d) resources that may potentially meet the National Register criteria, as determined by the State professional staff, the State Historic Preservation Officer, and/or the State Review Board. The last category will normally include cultural resources in State and local registers.

(2) Survey data that indicate after evaluation by the Secretary or by the State professional staff, the State Historic Preservation Officer, and/or the State Review Board that (a) specific cultural resources are ineligible for listing in the National Register or (b) specific geographical areas that have been fully surveyed do not contain significant cultural resources other than those already included in the State inventory.

(3) Predictive statements concerning the probable distribution of

cultural resources in different parts of the State, different environmental
zones, etc., based on systematic background research and sample fieldwork.

(4) Specification of those areas of the State for which inadequate
survey data are available and about which no reliable predictions can yet
be made.

(e) All State Survey Data shall be continually evaluated to identify
cultural resources for nomination to the National Register and to make
predictions about the distribution of cultural resources or resource types
that may meet the criteria for listing in the National Register.

(f) State Survey Data shall be maintained by the State Historic Preservation Officer in a central location and shall be kept up-to-date so
that the information is readily accessible to Federal, State, and local
planners during the decisionmaking process. The State Survey Data need
not be published but shall be physically organized and/or indexed in a
manner to provide for easy access.

(g) The culmination of the overall survey process is nomination of
resources significant in American history, architecture, archaeology,
and culture at the national, State, or local level to the National
Register. The State Historic Preservation Officer shall establish priorities and a rationale behind the priorities for submission of National
Register nominations to the National Park Service, procedures for review
of National Register nominations by the State Review Board, and a mechanism
for reporting to the National Park Service changes in State notification
procedures under section 60.12. Nominated cultural resources that are
approved by the National Park Service are entered in the National Register
by the Director, Office of Archaeology and Historic Preservation, National
Park Service.

60.7 STATE HISTORIC PRESERVATION PLAN

(a) A comprehensive statewide historic preservation plan shall be
prepared in each State under the direction of the State Historic Preservation Officer. The plan shall consist of a report or series of reports
on the State historic preservation plan. These reports, which shall be
submitted in such form and at such time as the Secretary shall determine,
shall describe, analyze, and make future projections about the program.
One required report shall be an annual Apportionment Warrant disclosing
the State's historic preservation project funding needs as a basis for
the Secretary's apportionment of grant appropriations. The State Review
Board shall review and approve all State historic preservation plan
reports, except the annual Apportionment Warrant, prior to submission.

(b) The State historic preservation plan shall include the following
information for each component of the State historic preservation program: an explanation of the philosophy or rationale behind the program
component, a report on current status, an evaluation of effectiveness,
and a projection of future plans. The program components to be reported
on in the State historic preservation plan shall include, but not be
limited to, the following:

(1) Organizational framework of the State historic preservation office,
including the composition and qualifications of the State professional
staff and the State Review Board and the position of the office in the
hierarchy of State government.

(2) Comprehensive statewide survey methods, timetable, and progress.

(3) National Register nominations and other registration activity,
including a report on notification procedures when changes are made.

(4) Environmental review procedures and activity.

(5) Compliance activity under section 106 of the National Historic

Preservation Act of 1966 and Executive Order 11593, and participation under
other Federal laws and regulations related to historic preservation.

(6) Progress in integrating historic preservation planning into
general planning processes at the Federal, State, and local levels.

(7) Public information activity.

(8) Grants program activity, including both survey and planning
operations and acquisition and development projects, and including the
annual Apportionment Warrant.

(c) A State's eligibility to participate in the National Register and
grants programs shall be contingent upon its submission of a State historic
preservation plan and upon approval of that plan by the Secretary. The
Secretary may waive any of the requirements of this or any other section
of this Part if in his opinion, expressed in writing to the State Historic
Preservation Officer, the State historic preservation program would benefit
from such waiver and the purposes, conditions, and requirements of the
National Historic Preservation Act of 1966 would not be compromised.

60.7a ENVIRONMENTAL REVIEW

The State Historic Preservation Officer is responsible for the review
of proposed Federal or federally funded, licensed, or approved undertakings that may potentially have an effect on cultural resources within
the State, in accordance with procedures of the National Historic Preservation Act of 1966, Executive Order 11593, the National Environmental
Policy Act of 1969, the Archaeological and Historic Preservation Act of
1974, and other environmentally related legislation and regulations.
Consequently, the State Historic Preservation Officer shall develop and
operate environmental review procedures for the State.

(a) The State Historic Preservation Officer shall review all notices
of Federal or federally funded, licensed, or approved undertakings having
a potential effect on cultural resources. These notices include, but are
not limited to, those received through the A-95 Clearinghouse process,
documents prepared in accordance with the National Environmental Policy
Act of 1969, and other notices or requests from Federal agencies or
their consultants.

(b) The State Historic Preservation Officer shall consult with Federal,
State, and local planning officials at the earliest planning stages of
proposed undertakings and shall make available to the appropriate officials the following data for the environmental impact areas of the undertakings:

(1) All information in the State Survey Data as outlined in section
60.6a(d). Agencies may be requested to avoid or limit publication of such
data if in the opinion of the State Historic Preservation Officer such
publication might result in damage to cultural resources.

(2) Recommendations that there is need for a survey of cultural resources unless the State Survey Data indicate that additional survey is
not required.

(3) Recommendations to Federal agencies and to communities conducting
surveys on methods for conducting comprehensive surveys and on sources of
professional expertise.

(4) Results from review of Federal and community surveys and opinions
on the eligibility of cultural resources for listing in the National
Register.

(c) Where the State Survey Data indicate that additional survey of
cultural resources is needed in the environmental impact area of an undertaking, the State Historic Preservation Officer may conduct such survey
under contract with Federal, State, or local officials or their consultants.

60.8   STATE PROFESSIONAL STAFF

   (a) The State staff shall include at a minimum at least one full-time
professional in each of the following disciplines: history, archaeology,
and architectural history or architecture. All of these professionals
shall meet the minimum qualifications set forth in section 60.8a. Two
or more part-time staff members may be substituted for one full-time
person in any of the required disciplines, as long as the equivalent of
one full-time professional is achieved in each discipline. The State
Historic Preservation Officer shall determine what other professional
disciplines and/or additional staffing are needed to carry out the
responsibilities of the National Register and grants programs.
   (b) After October 1, 1978, each State staff shall include at a minimum at least one full-time professional in each of the following disciplines: history, archaeology, architectural history, and historical
architecture.
   (c) The State Historic Preservation Officer shall submit the professional qualifications of the State staff to the Secretary for review and
approval. Such submission shall be made as part of the State historic
preservation plan and whenever changes occur.

60.8a PROFESSIONAL QUALIFICATIONS

   In the following definitions, a year of full-time professional experience need not consist of a continuous year of full-time work but may be
made up of discontinuous periods of full-time or part-time work adding
up to the equivalent of a year of full-time experience.
   (a) History. The minimum professional qualifications in history are
a graduate degree in history or closely related field; or a bachelor's
degree in history or closely related field plus one of the following:
(1) at least two years of full-time experience in research, writing,
teaching, interpretation, or other demonstrable professional activity
with an academic institution, historical organization or agency, museum,
or other professional institution; or (2) substantial contribution
through research and publication to the body of scholarly knowledge in
the field of history.
   (b) Archaeology. The minimum professional qualifications in archaeology
are a graduate degree in archaeology, anthropology, or closely related
field plus (1) at least one year of full-time professional experience or
equivalent specialized training in archaeological research, administration, or management; (2) at least four months of supervised field and
analytic experience in general North American archaeology; and (3) demonstrated ability to carry research to completion. In addition to these
minimum qualifications, a professional in prehistoric archaeology shall
have at least one year of full-time professional experience at a supervisory level in the study of archaeological resources of the prehistoric
period. A professional in historic archaeology shall have at least one
year of full-time professional experience at a supervisory level in the
study of archaeological resources of the historic period.
   (c) Architectural history. The minimum professional qualifications
in architectural history are a graduate degree in architectural history,
art history, historic preservation, or closely related field, with course
work in American architectural history; or a bachelor's degree in architectural history with concentration in American architecture; or a
bachelor's degree in architectural history, art history, historic preservation, or closely related field plus one of the following: (1) at
least two years of full-time experience in research, writing, or teaching
in American architectural history or restoration architecture with an

academic institution, historical organization or agency, museum, or other
professional institution; or (2) substantial contribution through research
and publication to the body of scholarly knowledge in the field of American architectural history.

(d) Architecture. The minimum professional qualifications in architecture are a professional degree in architecture plus at least two years
of full-time professional experience in architecture; or a State license
to practice architecture.

(e) Historical architecture. The minimum professional qualifications
in historical architecture are a professional degree in architecture or
State license to practice architecture, plus one of the following: (1) at
least one year of graduate study in architectural preservation, American
architectural history, preservation planning, or closely related field and
at least one year of full-time professional experience on preservation and
restoration projects; or (2) at least two years of full-time professional
experience on preservation and restoration projects. Experience on
preservation and restoration projects shall include detailed investigations
of historic structures, preparation of historic structures research
reports, and preparation of plans and specifications for preservation
projects.

60.9 STATE REVIEW BOARD

(a) Members of the State Review Board shall be designated by the
State Historic Preservation Officer.

(b) The State Review Board shall consist of at least five persons,
a majority of whom shall be recognized professionals. At a minimum,
the State Review Board shall include one professional in each of the
following disciplines: history, archaeology, and architectural history
or architecture. All of these professionals shall meet the minimum
standards of professional qualifications set forth in section 60.8a.
The State Historic Preservation Officer shall determine what other professional disciplines and/or additional members are needed. Nonprofession-
al citizen members may be appointed to the State Review Board, as long as
the majority of the membership consists of professionals.

(c) After January 1, 1978, each State Review Board shall include at a
minimum one professional in each of the following disciplines: history,
archaeology, architectural history, and architecture. After January 1,
1978, the professional in archaeology shall be qualified in both prehistoric and historic archaeology, or an additional professional shall be
appointed to the State Review Board so that expertise in both prehistoric
and historic archaeology will be represented.

(d) The State Historic Preservation Officer shall submit the professional qualifications of the members of the State Review Board to the
Secretary for review and approval. Such submission shall be made as part
of the State historic preservation plan and whenever changes occur.

(e) The State Review Board shall meet at least four times a year and
shall adopt bylaws governing its operations consistent with the provisions
of this section.

(f) The responsibilities of the State Review Board shall include, but
not be limited to, the following:

(1) Reviewing and approving each completed National Register nomination
form, or the documentation proposed for submission on the nomination form,
prior to submission to the National Register.

(2) Reviewing and approving each completed State historic preservation
plan report, except the annual Apportionment Warrant, prior to submission
to the Secretary.

(3)   Providing general oversight, guidance, and professional recommendations to the State Historic Preservation Officer in conducting the comprehensive statewide survey, preparing the State historic preservation
plan, and carrying out the other duties and responsibilities of the State
historic preservation office.

36 CFR PART 63:   DRAFT

*A draft of 36 CFR Part 63, "Procedures for Requesting Deter-
minations of Eligibility," was published for comment in the Federal
Register on April 27, 1976. After an extensive comment period, the
draft was extensively re-written and, in the form presented here,
was being readied for publication as final rulemaking as of early
1977.*

PROCEDURES FOR REQUESTING DETERMINATIONS OF ELIGIBILITY FOR INCLUSION IN
THE NATIONAL REGISTER

Section 63.1.   Purpose and Authorities

(a) These procedures, which have been developed to assist Federal
agencies in identifying and evaluating a property's eligibility for
inclusion in the National Register in a timely fashion as part of the
planning process, define how to request determinations of eligibility
under section 2(b) of Executive Order 11593 and the procedures of the
Advisory Council on Historic Preservation (36 CFR 800) for the implementation of sections 1(3) and 2(b) of Executive Order 11593 and the National
Historic Preservation Act of 1966. Federal agencies request determinations
of eligibility in considering historic resources on lands under their
jurisdiction or control or on lands to be affected by proposed projects.

Section 63.2.   Determination of Eligibility Process

The Department of the Interior will respond within 45 days of receipt
of an adequately documented request for a determination of eligibility
when it is submitted in accordance with the following procedures.
(a) The department recommends that agencies consult the State Historic
Preservation Officer as the first step in identifying historic resources,
for information concerning:
(1) resources listed in the National Register.
(2) resources in the process of nomination to the National Register or
approved by the State Review Board for nomination.
(3) resources determined eligible by the Secretary for listing in the
National Register.
(4) resources that may potentially meet the National Register criteria,
as determined by the State Historic Preservation Officer. This
will normally include historic resources in State and local
registers or inventories.
(5) survey data, if surveys have been conducted, that indicate, after
evaluation by the Secretary or by the State Historic Preservation
Officer that (a) specific properties are ineligible for listing in
the National Register or (b) specific geographical areas that have
been fully surveyed do not contain significant historic resources
other than those already included in the State inventory.
(6) predictive statements concerning the probable distribution of
historic resources in different parts of the State, different environmental zones, etc., based on systematic background research
and sample fieldwork, if such research has been conducted.
(7) advice concerning the need for the agency to conduct a historic

resource survey of the proposed project area. If such a survey is necessary, the State Historic Preservation Officer may be able to assist the agency in developing an appropriate method of survey, based on a careful analysis of the potential effects of the proposed action.

(b) In accord with an agency's planning responsibilities under the National Historic Preservation Act of 1966, Executive Order 11593, and the National Environmental Policy Act of 1969, the agency shall, in consultation with the State Historic Preservation Officer, apply the National Register criteria contained in 36 CFR Part 60.6 to all potentially eligible properties identified by the agency through consultation with the State Historic Preservation Officer, a Federal agency sponsored survey, or other means. If a property appears to meet the criteria, or if it is questionable whether the criteria are met, the agency should follow the determination of eligibility procedures as stated below. A question on whether a property meets the National Register criteria for evaluation may occur when there is a difference of opinion on eligibility either between the agency and the State Historic Preservation Officer or the agency and the State Historic Preservation Officer on the one hand and private groups or citizens on the other.

(c) The agency shall submit a letter of request for a determination of eligibility with a description, statement of significance, photographs, and a map, or a statement in accord with 63.3 below, if applicable, directly to the Chief, Office of Archaeology and Historic Preservation, National Park Service, Department of the Interior, Washington, D.C. 20240. If available, the opinion of the State Historic Preservation Officer on the eligibility of the property should also be forwarded with the request. Guidance concerning adequate documentation for specific types of resources is set forth in Appendix A.

(d) The Chief, Office of Archaeology and Historic Preservation, will review the documentation submitted by the agency and will respond to the agency's request within 45 days of receipt of an adequately documented request submitted in accord with these procedures. If the opinion of the State Historic Preservation Officer is not included in the documentation submitted by the agency, the Chief, Office of Archaeology and Historic Preservation, will write directly to the State Historic Preservation Officer for his opinion, supplying the State Historic Preservation Officer with a copy of the agency's request and documentation submitted on the property. If the Chief does not receive a response from the State Historic Preservation Officer within three weeks of the State Historic Preservation Officer's receipt of the letter, the Chief will proceed with the determination of eligibility and indicate to the agency that the State Historic Preservation Officer did not give an opinion. If the Chief, Office of Archaeology and Historic Preservation, determines that documentation submitted with the request is not sufficient to make a professional evaluation of the significance of the property, he will advise the agency in writing of the additional information needed. The Chief, Office of Archaeology and Historic Preservation, will respond to the agency's request within 45 days of receipt of adequate documentation on the property.

Section 63.3. Special Procedures to Be Applied When the Agency and the State Historic Preservation Officer Agree a Property is Eligible

If, during the consultation described in section 63.2(b), both the Federal agency and the State Historic Preservation Officer agree that a property meets the criteria for listing in the National Register, the Federal agency may forward (1) a letter stating that the agency and the State Historic Preservation Officer agree that the property is eligible for inclusion in the National Register, (2) a statement signed by the

State Historic Preservation Officer that in his opinion the property is eligible for the National Register (see Appendix B), to the Chief, Office of Archaeology and Historic Preservation. Both the letter from the agency and the statement of the State Historic Preservation Officer must contain a substantive discussion describing the property and its significance and a statement concerning why the property is eligible for listing in the National Register. The property shall be deemed eligible for inclusion in the National Register as a determination by the Secretary of the Interior for the purpose of obtaining the Advisory Council's comments. The Chief, Office of Archaeology and Historic Preservation, shall review the determination and send a written acknowledgement upon receipt of this positive determination letter and the State Historic Preservation Officer's opinion to both the agency and the State Historic Preservation Officer. If the Chief, OAHP, determines that the property has not been accurately identified and evaluated, he will advise the agency and the SHPO of his objection in writing and recommend that the agency follow the procedure set forth at section 63.2(c). Documentation concerning properties determined eligible for the National Register in accord with section 63.3 should be kept on file with the agency and the State Historic Preservation Officer.

Section 63.4.   Publication of Properties Determined Eligible in the Federal Register

The Chief, Office of Archaeology and Historic Preservation, will provide written notice to the Federal agency and the State Historic Preservation Officer of a determination on the eligibility of a property for inclusion in the National Register. Notice of determination that a property is eligible for inclusion in the National Register will also be published in the "Federal Register" on a regular basis and in a cumulative edition which will appear once a year, usually in February. Determinations made in accord with the special procedures in 63.3 will be specified with an asterisk.

Section 63.5.   Review and Nomination of Properties Determined Eligible

The Office of Archaeology and Historic Preservation will review the list of properties determined eligible annually to ascertain the physical condition and status of plans affecting these properties. The Office of Archaeology and Historic Preservation will obtain from the advisory Council on Historic Preservation information on decisions made concerning the property in accord with a memorandum of agreement under the Advisory Council's "Procedures for the Protection of Historic and Cultural Properties" (36 CFR 800).

If there is no memorandum of agreement or if no provision has been made in the memorandum of agreement for nomination of the property and if the property retains the characteristics which made it eligible for the National Register after decisions have been made in the Federal planning process, the Department of the Interior will take the following steps:

(a) For properties under the jurisdiction or control of a Federal agency the Department of the Interior will request the Federal agency to nominate the property to the National Register within six months of receipt of the Secretary's request in accord with the National Register procedures for Federal nominations codified in Part 60 of Chapter I of Title 36 of the Code of Federal Regulations (41 Federal Register 1590).

(b) If the property is not under Federal jurisdiction or control, the Department of the Interior will request that the State Historic Preservation Officer nominate the property to the National Register within six months of receipt of the Secretary's request in accord with the National

Register procedures for State nominations codified in Part 60 of Chapter I of Title 36 of the Code of Federal Regulations (41 Federal Register 1590).

Appendix A. Guidelines for Level of Documentation to Accompany Request for Determination of Eligibility for Inclusion in the National Register

This appendix gives guidance to Federal agencies in the preparation of the basic documentation (description, statement of significance, maps, and photographs) necessary to evaluate the eligibility for the National Register of districts, sites, buildings, structures, and objects. Where possible this documentation should be prepared by professionals in the fields of history, architectural history, architecture, and archaeology. Although in some cases a determination of eligibility can be made on less information, the Department of the Interior recommends these guidelines as a general standard for the amount and kinds of documentation necessary to evaluate properties against the National Register criteria. The categories of information here are those required for nomination of pro- perties to the National Register. Documentation submitted with determin- ation of eligibility requests may be recorded on National Register nomin- ation forms, although such forms are not required. If the information on the property has been compiled through a survey, the agency should submit the survey report as part of the documentation. Information included in the survey report or in other material need not be recorded in the format suggested in this appendix. As long as the basic categories of informa- tion are provided, the agency may use any format for submitting this docu- mentation, which it finds convenient. Each category should be provided:

 I. Request for determination
 II. Property name
 III. Location
 IV. Classification: district, site, building, structure, or object
 V. Ownership
 VI. Representation in Existing Surveys
 VII. Description
 VIII. Significance
 IX. Bibliography
 X. Geographical Data, Maps, and Acreage
 XI. Photographs
 XII. Individual(s) compiling documentation

Many of these categories require only a very brief statement. Special attention should be given to VII Description and VIII Significance. Much of the guidance under VII and VIII applies to a specific classification of resource. Not all this information is required for each classification (building, site, district, structure, object).

I. **Request for Determination of Eligibility**

The name and address of the agency and the agency official making the request should appear in the letter of request or as part of the documen- tation. Communities requesting determinations of eligibility in accord with the "Environmental Review Procedures for Community Development Block Grant Program" (24 CFR 58) should certify that the request is made as part of planning for a community development block grant project.

II. **Property Name**

A. Historic Name. This name is generally preferred for a property and ordinarily represents one or more of the following:
 1. original owner or builder,
 2. significant persons or events associated with the property,
 3. innovative or unusual characteristics of the property,
 4. accepted professional scientific, technical, or traditional names.

B. Common Name. This is the name by which the property is known
locally.

C. Archaeological Site Name. Archaeological sites are generally named
for the project, a nearby geographic feature, an aspect of cultural significance, the owner of the property, etc. For an archaeological site with
no name, use the numbering system in use in the State. The State site
number should also be appended to the designation of a named site for
cross-reference purposes.

III. Location

Include the number and the name of the street or road on which the
property is located. If the road has a number rather than a name, indicate whether it is a Federal, State, or county road. If a property does
not have a specific address, give the names of the nearest roads. For
rural properties and others without specific street addresses, precise
location may be specified by indicating the side of the road (North, South,
East, or West) and exact distance from nearest intersection (North, South,
East, or West). If a property is rural and in the vicinity of a town or
city, this should be indicated. In the case of a historic district or
similarly complicated property, inclusive street address numbers for all
the properties within the district should be given.

IV. Classification

A. Categories. Classify the property in the appropriate category if
possible. If it is unclear what category is appropriate, this should be
indicated. Agencies may, for example, request assistance in determining
whether properties should be considered individually or together as a
district.
1. A "district" is a geographically definable area, urban or rural,
   possessing a significant concentration, linkage or continuity of
   site, buildings, structures, or objects which are united by past
   events or aesthetically by plan or physical development. A district may also be comprised of individual elements which are
   separated geographically but are linked by associations or history.
2. A "site" is the location of a significant event, a prehistoric
   or historic occupation or activity, or a building or structure
   whether standing, ruined, or vanished, where the location itself
   maintains historical or archaeological value.
3. A "building" is a structure created to shelter any form of human
   activity such as a house, barn, church, hotel, or similar structure.
   "Buildings" may refer to a historically related complex, such as
   a courthouse and jail or a house and barn.
4. A "structure" is a work made up of interdependent and interrelated
   parts in a definite pattern or organization. Constructed by man,
   it is often an engineering project large in scale.
5. An "object" is a material thing of functional, aesthetic, cultural,
   historical, or scientific value that may be, by nature or design,
   movable yet related to a specific setting or environment.

B. Multiple Classification. Some properties may be most properly
classified within two or more of the categories given above.

V. Ownership

Give the name of the owner of the property. Indicate "multiple
ownership" for districts.

VI. Representation in Existing Surveys

Identify local, State, or Federal historic resource surveys that include or refer to the property in question. Include name of survey, date,

and person or organization that conducted the survey. Federal surveys other than the National Register include, but are not limited to, the Historic American Buildings Survey, the Historic American Engineering Record, and the National Survey of Historic Sites and Buildings (National Historic Landmarks Program).

VII. Description

Description of the physical appearance and condition of a property is important in making an accurate assessment of its significance. To be useful, the description of the property should use appropriate professional terminology and should be concise, factual, detailed, and well-organized.

A. *Buildings, structures, or objects should be described in detail.* Marcus Whiffen's "American Architecture Since 1780: A guide to the Styles" (The M.I.T. Press, Cambridge, 1969) provides a standard guide to American architectural styles and should be consulted when questions of terminology arise. If local terms or styles are used, they should be accompanied by a description or explanation. Unique details or unusual features should be pointed out and should be visible in the accompanying photographs. The description of a building should include the following kinds of information where applicable:
   1. Kind of structure (dwelling, church, commercial, etc.).
   2. Building placement (detached, row, etc.)
   3. General characteristics:
       a. overall shape or plan (rectangle, ell, etc.).
       b. Number of stories.
       c. Number of vertical divisions or bays.
       d. Construction materials (brick, frame, stone, etc.) and wall finish (type of bond, coursing, shingle, etc.).
       d. Roof shape (gable, hip, shed, etc.).
   4. Specific Features-location, number, and appearance of:
       a. porches (verandas, stoops, attached sheds, etc.)
       b. windows
       c. doors
       d. chimneys
       e. dormers
   5. Important decorative elements.
   6. Significant interior features.
   7. Number, type, and location of outbuildings, as well as dates, if known.
   8. Other manmade elements (roadways, contemporary structures, landscaping included within the area).
   9. Information on moved properties
       a. date of move;
       b. descriptions of original and present locations;
       c. explanation of the effect of the move on the historic integrity of the property.
   10. Known alterations or changes to the property over time and dates if available. A restoration is considered an alteration even if an attempt has been made to restore the property to its original form. In cases involving numerous alterations it would be helpful to include a floor plan with the submission.
   11. Guidance in compiling information on industrial or engineering structures may be obtained by consulting the Historic American Engineering Record, National Park Service, Department of the Interior, Washington, D.C. 20240.

B. *Archaeological site descriptions should include the following information:*
   1. Site type (e.g., midden, rockshelter, flake scatter, historic

factory, etc.).
2. A description of the site including its immediate environment,
   using standard archaeological terminology. If local terms are
   used, they should be defined. The following data should be included:
   a. Boundaries of the site and methods by which these boundaries
      have been defined.
   b. The immediately surrounding environment, both as it probably
      was when the site was in use and as it is today.
   c. Any disrupting influences (urban development, roads, agri-
      culture) at work on or immediately around the site.
   d. Descriptions (or summaries) of known data on internal charac-
      teristics: stratigraphy, artifact classes and their distri-
      bution, structural remains, etc.
   e. Extent and nature of any excavation, testing, surface collecting
      etc.
   f. Descriptions of any standing or ruined structures or buildings
      that might be of architectural or historic importance.
3. A list of pertinent previous investigations at the site, if any,
   indicating dates, institutions, or organizations responsible, and
   bibliographic references.
4. Quality and intensity of survey that resulted in recording the site;
   any limitations this may impose on the data available for purposes
   of evaluation.

   C. *Historic site descriptions should include discussion of the
present condition of the site and its environment.* The integrity of the
site--the degree to which the setting is a visual reminder of the events
and activities that took place there--is very important and should be
thoroughly discussed in the submission.

   D. *District*
1. Architectural and historic district descriptions should include the
   following kinds of information, as appropriate:
   a. General description of the natural and manmade elements of
      the district: structures, buildings, sites, objects, promi-
      nent geographical features, density of development.
   b. General description of types, styles, or periods of archi-
      tecture represented in the district: scale, proportions,
      materials, color, decoration, workmanship, design quality.
   c. General physical relationships of buildings to each other and
      to the environment: facade lines, street plans, squares, open
      spaces, structural density, plantings, important natural
      features; changes in the relationships over time. Some of
      this information may be provided on a sketch map.
   d. General description of the district during the period(s) when
      it achieved significance.
   e. Building types found in district: commercial, residential,
      etc.; present and original uses of buildings and land.
   f. General condition of buildings: restoration or rehabilitation
      activities, alterations.
   g. Approximate number of buildings in district or a good indi-
      cation of size of district.
   h. Intrusions: include ratio and size of intrusions compared to
      the number of buildings within the district.
   i. Qualities that made the district distinct from its surroundings.
   j. A list of significant pivotal buildings within the district,
      with short descriptions where appropriate.
   k. Precise verbal boundary description: streets, property lines,

inclusive street addresses, geographical features, etc., which separate the district from its surroundings.

    1.   If the district also has qualities of an archaeological nature, the information indicated under 4 below should be provided.

  2. Industrial district descriptions, in addition to the information listed should include:

    a.   General description of the industrial activities and processes taking place within the district, important natural and geographical features, power sources;

    b.   General description of original machinery still in use; and/or

    c.   General description of linear systems within district (canals, railroads, roads) and their terminal points with approximate length and width of area to be encompassed in district.

  3. Rural district descriptions, in addition to the information listed above, should include:

    a.   General description of geography and topographical features (valleys, vistas, etc.) that convey a sense of cohesiveness; and/or

    b.   General description of the outbuildings and other examples of vernacular rural architecture within district boundaries.

  4. Archeological district descriptions should include:

    a.   General description of the natural and manmade elements of the district: structures, buildings, sites, objects, prominent geographical features, density of development.

    b.   A statement of the date, level, and kind of archaeological survey that has been done in the district.

    c.   A list of archaeological properties within the district, including their locations. Data on individual sites, as required by section VII. B, should be appended.

    d.   A statement of the cultural, historic or other relationships among the sites within the district that make the district a cohesive unit for investigation.

    e.   A summary of the nature and level of damage the sites within the district have received or are receiving.

    f.   A statement of the extent to which the intersite relationships that give the district its cohesion remain intact.

VIII. Significance

    A. *Summary statement of significance.* A statement of significance identifies qualities of the property that may make it eligible for listing in the National Register. A concise opening paragraph summarizing the possible importance of the property being considered should be followed by a more detailed account of the events, personalities, prehistoric or historic occupations, or activities associated with the property. This concise history of the property should be directed to a whole property, rather than some functional segment. Thus, it is inappropriate to discuss a mound and not an associated village, burial area, etc., or to submit a house and not the associated outbuildings, etc. A statement of significance should attempt to relate the property to a broad historical, architectural, archaeological, or cultural context: local, regional, State or national. For example, if a community has a number of neighborhoods with the same or similar qualities as the one being evaluated, this information should be included in the documentation. Any quoted material which appears in this section or the description should be footnoted. Quotations taken out of context must faithfully represent the meaning of the original source. Supplemental information, such as newspaper articles, letters from professional historians, architects, architectural historians, or archaeologists, etc. may also be submitted as appropriate. The state-

ment of significance for properties that are less than 50 years old;
moved; reconstructed; cemeteries and grave sites; birthplaces, primarily
commemorative in nature; or owned or used by religious institutions
should address the specific exceptions set forth in the National Register
criteria.

  B. *Period(s) and Area(s) of significance.* Identify the area(s) and
period(s) with which the property's significance is associated. This may
mean date of construction, major alterations, or association with an individual, event, or culture, etc. For some archaeological properties,
assignment to a very general time period or periods may be sufficient.

  The following areas of significance are listed on National Register
forms. Agencies may find it helpful to consider these areas in identifying and evaluating properties:

Archaeology--Prehistoric: the scientific study of life and culture of
    indigenous peoples before the advent of written records.

Archaeology--Historic: the scientific study of life and culture in the
    New World after the advent of written records.
Agriculture: farming, livestock raising, and horticulture.
Architecture: the style and construction of buildings and structures.
Art: concerning creative works and their principles; fine arts and
    crafts. Do not include architecture, sculpture, music, or litera-
    ture here; specific categories are established for these areas.
Commerce: production and exchange of goods and the social contracts
    thereby encouraged.
Communications: art or science of transmitting information.
Community Planning: the design of communities from predetermined
    principles.
Conservation: official maintenance or supervision of natural or man-
    made resources.
Economics: the science that deals with the production, distribution,
    and consumption of wealth.
Education: formal schooling or the methods and theories of teaching
    or learning.
Engineering: the applied science concerned with utilizing products
    and sources of power for supplying human needs in the form of
    structures, machines, etc.
Exploration/Settlement: the investigation of regions previously un-
    known; the establishment of a new colony or community.
Industry: enterprises producing goods and services.
Invention: something originated by experiment or ingenuity. (Proper-
    ties connected with the inventors themselves would be classified
    here.)
Landscape Architecture: the art or practice of planning or changing
    land and water elements for the enhancement of the physical environ-
    ment.
Literature: the production of writings.

Military: concerning the armed forces and individual soldiers.
Music: the art of combining vocal or instrumental sounds or tones.
Philosophy: system of principles for the conduct of life; the theory
    or analysis of the principles underlying thought or knowledge and
    the nature of the universe.
Politics/Government: an established system of political administration
    by which a nation, State, district, etc., is governed and the pro-
    cesses which determine how it is to be conducted.
Religion: systems and expressions of belief in a suprahuman power
    that have made a contribution to the patterns of culture.

Science: a systematic study of nature.

Sculpture: the art of forming material into three-dimensional representation.

Social/Humanitarian: concerning human beings living together in a group or the promotion of the welfare of humanity.

Theater: the dramatic arts and the places where they are enacted.

Transportation: concerning the work or business or means of conveying passengers or materials.

C. *Additional facts.* Additional facts to be included on specific categories of properties, as appropriate:

1. Buildings, structures, or objects
   a. The architect or builder, if known,
   b. Historically significant events and/or patterns of activity,
   c. Data concerning individuals significantly associated with the property, and
   d. Consideration of any possible archaeological significance present.

2. Sites
   a. A statement of the kinds of information known or thought likely to be present in the property; types of data that might be recovered if the property were thoroughly investigated by archaeologists, art historians, architectural historians, or other appropriate scholars. Some categories of information will be directly observable; others can be inferred based on knowledge of similar properties that have been extensively investigated. Reasons for believing that given categories of information are present and have been preserved in the property should be given.
   b. A statement of the relationships between the information believed to be present in the property and topics that might be studied there; i.e., what kinds of research could be done using the information known or thought to be present in the property.

3. Architectural and historic districts
   a. Concise statement of why the district may be significant.
   b. Origins and historical development of the district; inclusive dates, architects, builders, designers, planners; relationships of district to historic development of the area.
   c. General analysis of architectural styles or periods. If possible, relate the architecture in the district to the architectural resources of the area.
   d. Significant people or events associated with the district as a whole or with individual elements within the district.
   e. Preservation and/or restoration activities in the district (if considered to contribute to the significance for which the district is submitted).
   f. Effect of intrusions on the integrity of the district.
   g. Explanation of how district boundaries were chosen. Considerations may include the presence of a natural barrier or edge, such as a highway or new development, change in character of the area, or decline in concentration of significant properties to the point where the integrity of the district has been lost. (You may wish to refer to qualities discussed under VII. D. 1. k.). If the area on which the determination request is made appears to be only part of a larger district, this should be noted with an explanation (for example, the project may affect only part of the district). If possible the relation-

ship of this part of the district to the whole should be discussed.
   h. Consideration of any possible archaeological significance
      present in the district.
4. Archaeological districts
   a. A summary statement concerning the significance of individual
      properties within the district. (Data on individual proper-
      ties meeting the standards set forth in VIII. C. 2).
   b. A concise statement of the characteristics that give the dis-
      trict cohesion as a unit for study; what categories of data
      might be derived from study of the district that would not
      be derived from the study of individual properties within it?
   c. A concise statement explaining the scientific and/or inter-
      pretive yield or potential of the district in terms of the
      cultural and natural contexts or interrelationships described
      in VII. D. 4. d.
   d. Consideration of any possible architectural or historic signi-
      ficance present in the district, above and beyond its value
      for information purposes.
   e. An explanation of how district boundaries were chosen should
      be included. Considerations may include presence of a natural
      geographic barrier, such as a river or drainage divide; a pro-
      ject boundary if this delineates a group of resources which
      conform to the definition of a district given above; manmade
      features such as a highway or other structure; or decline in
      settlement density.

   D. *Federal agencies.* Federal agencies should attempt to answer the
following questions when seeking to determine whether a property meets
National Register criteria.
1. Building, structure, object
   a. If a building or structure is submitted for its architectural
      qualities, does it retain enough of its significant design,
      aspect, or feeling to be recognizable? If not, could the im-
      portant elements of design or appearance be restored? (This
      does not mean that buildings which have additions or altera-
      tions are not eligible, as they may reflect later significant
      styles and design).
   b. If a building or structure is submitted for historical asso-
      ciations, does the existing building have an identifiable
      relationship to the history described? Does it retain suffi-
      cient integrity to convey the feeling of the historical period
      when it achieved significance.
   c. If a building or structure is significant because of its asso-
      ciation with an individual, how long did that individual live
      there, or how long was he associated with the building, and
      during what period of his life? Are there other properties in
      the vicinity which also have strong associations with the indi-
      vidual? If so, the significance of the property in question
      should be compared to the significance of these other properties.
   d. If a building, structure, or object is submitted for its archae-
      ological associations, does it contain attributes that are
      amenable to study in order to extract useful information about
      history or prehistory? For example, has it been rebuilt or
      added to in ways that reveal changing concepts of style or
      beauty? Does it contain tools, equipment, furniture, trash or
      other materials whose distributions could be studied to learn
      about the social organization of its occupants, their rela-
      tions with other people and groups, their daily lives, etc.?

e. Does the building, structure, or object have an unusually important association with its location?

f. If the building or structure is no longer at its original location, are the reasons for the move fully explained? How does the new location affect the historical and architectural integrity of the building or structure?

g. What was the building or structure used for during the period it achieved historical significance?

2. Site

a. How does the site relate to the significant event, occupation, or activity that took place there?

b. How have alterations (destruction of original buildings, change in land use, changes in foliage or topography) affected the integrity of the site? (The site of a treaty signing which took place in a deep woods is probably not eligible if the area is now a suburban development.

c. If the site has been submitted for its archaeological significance, has the site contributed or does it have a potential for contributing useful information regarding human ecology, culture history, or culture process? What is the potential information yield of the site, and how does this information potential relate to theories, problems, and research questions that could be or have been addressed in the region or elsewhere? Evidence supporting these evaluations of significance should be provided, including references to specific scholarly investigations.

d. Does an excavated site retain interpretive value or did the information yielded make a fundamental contribution to knowledge of American cultures, such that the act of investigation constituted a historic event? Sites already completely excavated are eligible only if the answers to these questions are positive.

3. District (in addition to the questions on individual buildings, structures, and objects)

a. How does the district convey a sense of historic and architectural cohesiveness? (through design, setting, materials, workmanship, association, etc.) Is this sense expressed in the statement of significance?

b. How do architectural styles or elements within the district contribute to the feeling of time and place?

c. How have significant individuals or events contributed to the development of the district?

d. How has the district affected the historical development of the overall community, region, or State?

e. What effect do intrusions have on the integrity of the district?

f. How were district boundaries chosen? (Considerations may include boundaries at specific times in history; the presence of a visual barrier or edge, such as a river, highway or new development; change in character of the area; or decline in concentration of significant properties to the point where the integrity of the district has been lost.)

g. Are the qualities that distinguish the district from its surroundings identified and described?

h. If the district has been submitted for its research value, do the sites or individual resources have cohesion as a unit for study or do they have an identifiable geographical relationship?

    i. How does the district compare to other similar areas in the
        State, region, or locality?
  4. Industrial districts (in addition to the questions above)
    a. How do the industrial functions or processes relate to the
        broader industrial or technological developments of the county,
        region, State, or the Nation?
    b. How important are the entrepreneurs, engineers, designers, and
        planners who contributed to the development of the district?
  5. Rural (in addition to the questions above)
    a. How are the elements of the rural district linked historically,
        architecturally, by function, or by common ethnic or social
        background.

IX. Bibliography
    The bibliography should contain a list of sources from which informa-
tion on the property was compiled. General reference works on architecture,
archaeology, etc., should not be included unless they provide specific information which is of assistance in evaluating the property. Use standard
bibliographical style, listing author, full title, date and location of
publication, and publisher. For an article, list the magazine or journal
from which it was taken, volume number and date. For unpublished manu-
scripts, indicate where copies are available. Interviews should also be
listed here with the date of interview.

X. Geographical Data, Maps, and Acreage
    A map clearly locating the property within a city or broader context
must accompany each request. A 7.5 or 15 minute series United States
Geological Survey map, State highway map, or other suitable map will be
acceptable. Latitude and longitude coordinates or UTM (Universal Transverse Mercator) reference points are useful in identifying the geographical
location of properties. Photocopies of maps are acceptable provided they
are clear and properly referenced. If the property is a district, a
detailed sketch map should be included. The sketch map need not be pre-
cise in scale, but it should indicate:
  A. All buildings, structures, or sites in the district.
  B. Extent of district boundaries, carefully drawn.
  C. Street and place names, including inclusive street numbers.
  D. Highway numbers.
  E. Architectural styles or periods, if appropriate.
  F. Pivotal structures and important spaces (parks, squares, etc.).
  G. Present type of district (mixed, residential, commercial, public,
      etc.).
  H. Intrusions or other elements not contributing to the significance
      of the district.
  I. North arrow (magnetic or true), if not printed on map.
  J. Scale (on sketch map, or on printed maps when not indicated,
      scale may be approximate).
  K. Land use in rural district--woods, fields, swamps, etc.
  L. Significant aspects of the natural environment, if appropriate.
Sketch maps should also be provided for large archaeological sites, indicating significant cultural features and intrusions. Maps of archaeological
districts should clearly indicate the areas within the district boundaries
which have actually been surveyed. If portions of the districts have been
inspected using different techniques or at different levels of intensity,
this should be indicated on maps. The acreage of the property in question
should also be given.

XI. Photographs
    Along with written documentation and maps, photographs form the basis
of the Secretary of the Interior's determination of a property's eligibility

for inclusion in the National Register. For this reason, photographs submitted should give an honest visual representation of the property and should illustrate those qualities discussed in the description and statement of significance. Photographs should be contemporary with the request for a determination of eligibility and should be identified in detail, giving the name and location of the property, view or detail shown, and direction of photo. Historical photographs may also be useful but are not required. Black and white glossy photographs are preferred since these are required for National Register nominations, but other photo formats are also acceptable. Xeroxed copies of photographs rarely provide sufficient detail to accurately portray a property and should therefore be avoided. The number of photographs required for a determination varies according to the complexity of the property:

A. *Individual buildings, structures, or objects.* Include only as many photographs as are necessary to depict the property clearly. One of the photographs should show the environment or context in which the property is located. Additions, alterations, intrusions, and dependencies should appear in the photographs. If the significance for which the property is submitted includes interiors or particular details, representative views should be included.

B. *Archaeological Sites.* Photographs should document the condition of the property and, if relevant to the evaluation of significance, show artifacts that have been recovered and features present in the site. Drawings may be substituted for photographs of artifacts or other features where relevant and if it is not possible to take photographs. Site submissions must include at least one photograph, however, showing the physical environment and configuration of the site.

C. *Districts.* Districts should be represented visually in selected street, landscape, or aerial views. Include as many photographs as necessary to visually relate the essence of and the variety included in the district. Views of individual structures may not be necessary as streetscapes often reveal the architectural qualities of a district better than photographs of individual buildings. Pivotal structures, however, and elements which help define the quality of the district should be clearly shown. Streetscape views should include as many building types, styles, and uses as necessary to relate the variety of the district. Photographs of important topographical or spatial elements should be included, as well as representative types of intrusions in their settings. It is useful to indicate on the sketch map the location and direction of view of photographs. Views of archaeological districts should show significant natural and/or cultural aspects of the environment and typical sites, structures, buildings, and objects.

XII. Individual(s) Compiling Documentation

Names and qualifications of persons directly involved in compiling information on the property should be submitted as this information may be of assistance in the evaluation process. Addresses and phone numbers are also useful so that these individuals may be consulted if questions arise concerning the documentation.

APPENDIX B--SAMPLE FORM LETTER FOR

*Statement of the opinion of the State Historic Preservation Offi-
cer concerning the eligibility of a property for inclusion in the
National Register.*

I understand that the _____ is requesting the
                                (agency)
opinion of the State Historic Preservation Officer concerning the eligibility of _____ for inclusion in the National
                (property(ies))
Register and that my opinion may be submitted to the Secretary of the
Interior with a formal request for a determination of eligibility on this
property. This statement confirms that I have been consulted as part of
the determination of eligibility procedures.

__(1) In my opinion, the property is eligible for inclusion in the
       National Register. Below is a justification for this opinion.

__(2) In my opinion, the property is not eligible for inclusion in the
       National Register.

__(3) I have no opinion and prefer to defer to the opinion of the Secre-
       tary of the Interior.

Justification and comments:

Signed: _____
              State Historic Preservation Officer

36 CFR PART 64:   DRAFT

*This draft of 36 CFR Part 64, which sets forth procedures for
conducting surveys and other identificatory activities under
Section 2(a), Executive Order 11593, was circulated to all State
Historic Preservation Officers and others in early 1977, preparatory to publication for comment in the Federal Register.*

CRITERIA AND PROCEDURES FOR THE IDENTIFICATION OF HISTORIC PROPERTIES:
PROPOSED GUIDELINES

The Department of the Interior is considering rulemaking with respect
to its responsibilities under sections 3(b) and 3(f) of Executive Order
11593. Section 3(b) provides that the Secretary of the Interior shall
develop criteria and procedures to be used by Federal agencies in the
activities required by section 2(a) of that order. Section 2(a) provides
that Federal agencies shall locate, inventory, and nominate to the Secretary of the Interior all sites, buildings, districts, and objects under
their jurisdiction or control that appear to qualify for listing on the
National Register of Historic Places. Section 3(f) is a general requirement that the Secretary of the Interior advise Federal agencies in the
evaluation, identification, and preservation of historic properties.
Section 3(b) further provides that the criteria and procedures prepared under its authority be developed in consultation with the affected
agencies. This proposed rulemaking is designed to provide an opportunity
for such consultation. Further, it is the policy of the Department of
the Interior, whenever practicable, to afford the public an opportunity
to participate in the rulemaking process. Accordingly, interested persons
may submit written comments, suggestions, or objections regarding this
proposed rulemaking to the Acting Chief, Office of Archaeology and Historic
Preservation, National Park Service, U.S. Department of the Interior,
Washington, D.C. 20240, on or before _____.
These criteria procedures are also consistent with, and implement, this
Department's responsibility to expand and maintain a National Register of
Historic Places, established by section 101(a)(1), National Historic
Preservation Act of 1966. They have been in development for some time and
have been reviewed and commented on informally by other Federal agencies
throughout the development process. The formalization now proposed will
satisfy an obvious need for a clear and readily available statement of
the criteria and procedures to be used by Federal agencies in complying
with Executive Order 11593 and in assisting this Department in expanding
and maintaining the National Register.
It is important to understand the relationship between the identification requirements set forth below and (1) the identification provisions of
the Advisory Council on Historic Preservation (ACHP) procedures (36 CFR
Part 800) and (2) the responsibilities imposed by the National Environmental
Policy Act (NEPA). The ACHP procedures (36 CFR Part 800) pertain to the
authorities of section 106 of the National Historic Preservation Act and
to sections 1(3) and 2(b) of Executive Order 11593. Section 106 of the
National Historic Preservation Act, as amended by Public Law 94-422, requires that Federal agencies afford the ACHP the opportunity to comment
prior to approving the expenditure of Federal funds or issuing a license

for any undertaking that may have an effect on any National Register property or property qualifying for inclusion in the National Register.
Section 1(3) of Executive Order 11593 instructs Federal agencies to establish procedures regarding the preservation and enhancement of nonfederally
owned historic properties. Section 2(b) of Executive Order 11593 requires
that until the identification of historic properties required by section
2(a) has been completed by each Federal agency, each agency must exercise
caution to insure that Federally owned properties that might be eligible
for nomination to the National Register are not inadvertently lost or
damaged.

The procedures proposed herein, to be used by agencies in meeting the
responsibilities imposed by section 2(a) of Executive Order 11593, are

Recognizing that these three authorities are interconnected, the ACHP
procedures (36 CFR Part 800) set forth steps to be taken by Federal agencies
to identify properties on or eligible for the National Register, to determine the effects and adverse effects of proposed undertakings on such properties, and to consult with ACHP and pertinent State Historic Preservation
Officer (SHPO) to develop methods to avoid or mitigate adverse effects.

The procedures proposed herein, to be used by agencies in meeting the
responsibilities imposed by section 2(a) of Executive Order 11593, are
also appropriate for identifying historic properties on or eligible for
the National Register of Historic Places, on nonfederal as well as Federal
lands, pursuant to section 106 of the National Historic Preservation Act.
Their use will enable an agency to initiate compliance with the Procedures
of the ACHP by identifying "properties within the area of the (agency's)
undertaking's potential environmental impact that are included in or eligible for inclusion in the National Register (36 CFR 800.4(a)).

NEPA confers upon Federal agencies a broad and affirmative responsibility
to fully consider the maintenance of the natural and human environment in
their processes of planning and management. Among the environmental elements to be considered in compliance with NEPA are historic and cultural
elements (cf. NEPA section 101(b)(4)). These constitute an extremely
broad category commonly called "cultural resources," which the Department
interprets as including all phenomena that may be of cultural value to the
nation, a state, a locality, a community or an aggregate of people. The
category "cultural resources" includes but is not limited to historic properties as defined below. Other examples of cultural resources are social
institutions, traditions, and folkways that do not find expression in historic properties, and properties that have lost their physical integrity
or whose historicity cannot be demonstrated but which are nevertheless
regarded by local people as having historic or cultural value. In most
cases, the identification of historic properties is one part of an agency's
identification of cultural resources in compliance with NEPA. Identification of historic properties and compliance with section 106 of the
National Historic Preservation Act and Executive Order 11593 are necessary
regardless of whether NEPA requires preparation of an Environmental Impact
Statement (EIS) on a given Federal agency undertaking. Conversely, the
fact that an EIS must be prepared does not automatically mean that each
and every historic property subject to possible effect must be identified.
All Federal agencies have a positive mandate to protect historic properties together with other cultural and natural resources, but their consideration of such properties should be consistent with the nature of the
undertaking being planned. An EIS prepared for a type of undertaking that
could not damage historic properties need not treat historic preservation
interests. An EIS prepared on a program of general Federal activities
(e.g. a program of national energy development) need treat historic properties in only a general way, identifying possible kinds of conflicts
between the activity and historic preservation concerns and specifying ways
of resolving these conflicts if specific program elements are implemented

in specific areas. It is the view of this Department, however, that at
some time prior to the implementation of any Federal undertaking that
might damage historic properties.

Assistant Secretary, Fish and Wildlife Services

Section 64.1. Objective

This part establishes procedures for the identification of historic
properties and provides criteria for studies to locate, inventory, and
evaluate districts, sites, buildings, structures, and objects significant
in American history, architecture, archaeology, and culture. Procedures
and criteria for nomination of such properties to the National Register of
Historic Places are found in 36 CFR Part 60; procedures for requesting
determination of their eligibility for inclusion in the National Register
were published for comment as draft in the "Federal Register" April 27,
1976, 36 CFR Part 6.
Each agency must evaluate its particular program responsibilities and
define suitable methods for meeting the statutory and Executive order
directives discussed at section 64.2; these procedures are designed for
use in developing such methods. These procedures shall be used by all
agencies in fulfilling their responsibilities under sections 2(a) and 2(b)
of Executive Order 11593. It is the opinion of the Department of the
Interior that these procedures should also be used for identifying historic
properties subject to possible effect by Federal, federally assisted and
federally permitted undertakings in compliance with section 102(a)(c) of
the National Environmental Policy Act, Section 106 of the National Historic Preservation Act as amended, section 1(3) of Executive Order 11593,
and requirements of 36 CFR Part 800.4(a).

Section 64.2. Statutory and Executive Directives

(A) Executive Order 11593, section 2(a), provides that Federal agencies
shall locate, inventory, and nominate to the Secretary of the Interior all
sites, buildings, districts, and objects under their jurisdiction or control
that appear to qualify for listing on the National Register of Historic
Places.
(B) Executive Order 11593, section 3(b) provides that the Secretary of
the Interior shall develop criteria and procedures to be applied by Federal
agencies in the reviews and nominations required by section 2(a).
(C) Executive Order 11593, section 3(f) provides that the Secretary
of the Interior shall advise Federal agencies in the evaluation, identification, preservation, improvement, restoration, and maintenance of historic
properties.
(D) The National Historic Preservation Act of 1966, 16 USC section
470 et seq. (1970 ed.), section 101(a)(1), authorizes the Secretary of
the Interior to expand and maintain a National Register of Historic
Places.
1. The National Register is a listing of the Nation's historic
    properties deemed to be potentially worthy of preservation. It
    is designed to serve as a planning tool eventually containing
    pertinent data on all historic properties worthy of consideration
    during the planning of projects and land uses.
2. The National Register concept was developed under section 2 of the
    Historic Sites Act of 1935, 16 USC section 467 et. seq. (1970 ed.)
3. Section 4 of the Historic Sites Act authorized the Secretary to
    cooperate with and to seek the assistance of any Federal agency in
    administering this Act.

Section 64.3. Definitions

(A) Advisory Council means the Advisory Council on Historic Preservation, established under Title II of the National Historic Preservation Act of 1966 (16 USC 470i).

(B) Agency Official means the head of the Federal agency having responsibility for compliance with these procedures or the subordinate employee of the Federal agency to whom such authority has been delegated.

(C) Area subject to environmental impact is that land area, or areas, where land may be disturbed, or buildings or structures altered, or the environment of historic properties changed, in such a way as to affect their historical value.

(D) Consultation means a process of notice and communication among various groups or interests but does not necessarily include concurrence or approval. The consultation concept encourages a free play of thoughts and an exchange of information. Agency officials cannot be expected to delay decisionmaking if responses are not received within a reasonable period although every effort should be made to provide ample time for comment.

(E) Determination of Eligibility means finding by the Secretary of the Interior or his designee that a district, site, building, structure or object meets the National Register criteria. Procedures for determining the eligibility of properties for listing in the National Register are set forth at Part 63 of this title.

(F) Executive Order means Executive Order 11593, May 13, 1971, "Protection and Enhancement of the Cultural Environment" 36 CFR 8921, 16 USC 470.

(G) History comprises the events, patterns, and processes of the human past, including those that have affected literate societies and those that have affected pro-literate or nonliterate groups, whose history is sometimes referred to as prehistory.

(H) Historic properties are districts, sites, buildings, structures, and objects that may meet the National Register criteria set forth at 36 CFR 60.6, by virtue of their possession of one or more kinds of historical value.

(I) Historical Values are those attributes of an historic property that make it eligible for inclusion in the National Register. Historical values include but are not limited to those values resulting from property's association with historical events, persons, patterns, or processes, a property's representativeness of styles, trends, traditions, or characteristics of formal or vernacular architecture, a property's association with the work of particular artists or craftspeople in the past, a property's importance in the aesthetic, social, or cultural fabric of a community, neighborhood, social group, or area, and a property's known or potential capacity to provide information important to the reconstruction, analysis, and understanding of history. Historical values are measured against the criteria set forth at 36 CFR 60.6 in order to determine whether a given property is eligible for the National Register.

(J) Inventory means adequately documented survey records of all historic properties, resulting from a location and identification study.

(K) Location and Identification Study means a study carried out in accordance with the criteria set forth in Appendix A, to locate and identify historic properties.

(L) *National Register* means the National Register of Historic Places.

(M) *Professional quality* defines work executed according to the standards set forth in these procedures, by or under the supervision of professionals as defined in these procedures.

(N) *Qualified person* means the State Historic Preservation Officer, State Archaeologist, State Historian, any duly appointed county, city, or local historian, architect, or archaeologist, any recognized professional historian, architectural historian, historical architect, art historian, archaeologist, or anthropologist, or any group or society including such persons among its members.

(O) *Questionable action* under section 2(b) or Executive Order 11593 means any action pertaining to the eligibility of a property for the National Register about which a question is raised by a qualified person.

(P) *Secretary* means the Secretary of the Interior, or his designee authorized to carry out the responsibilities of the Secretary of the Interior under these procedures.

(Q) *State Historic Preservation Officer* means the official within each State, or his designated representative, authorized by the State, at the request of the Secretary of the Interior to act as liaison for purposes of implementing the National Historic Preservation Act.

Section 64.4. *Procedures for Identification and Evaluation of Historic Properties*

(A) For all lands under the jurisdiction or control of a Federal agency, including any lands subject to affect as a result of a Federal, federally assisted, or federally permitted undertaking, the agency official shall:

1. Consult with the State Historic Preservation Officer and, if necessary, other qualified persons to ascertain:
    a. whether the lands in question have been the subject of a complete professional quality location and identification study as defined in Appendix A;
    b. if such a study has been completed, whether there is evidence of the existence of historic properties on the lands;
    c. if such a study has not been completed, whether there is any reason to believe that such a study is not necessary in order to identify historic properties;
    d. if such a study has not been completed, and there is no reason to believe that it is not necessary, what methods should be used to conduct a study consistent with the statewide historic preservation plan undertaken by the state pursuant to section 102(a)(2), National Historic Preservation Act, and Appendix A; and
    e. any other useful data about the area in question, including but not limited to lists of known or suspected historic properties, areas of predicted historic property concentration or absence, types of historic property that may occur in the area, and recommended sources of further data or professional expertise.

2. Conduct such location and identification studies as are necessary, consistent with the standards set forth in Appendix A. Such studies may be phased in such a way as to spread their cost over a number of years, insofar as such phasing is consistent with agency planning and with section 106 of the National Historic Preservation Act, section 2(b) of the Executive Order, and the Procedures of the Advisory Council on Historic Places (36 CFR Part 800).

(B)   Should a question or controversy occur between the agency official
and the State Historic Preservation Officer or other qualified person regarding the need for a location and identification study, or regarding the
elements to be included in such a study, the agency official, the State
Historic Preservation Officer, or any member of the public may request the
recommendation and advice of the Secretary by consulting the Acting Chief,
Office of Archaeology and History Preservation, National Park Service.

(C) Having compiled descriptive data and professional opinions as to
the significance of historic properties in accordance with Appendix A:

1. The agency official in consultation with the State Historic
Preservation Officer as well as other qualified persons as appropriate should evaluate all properties identified in the inventory
in accordance with the National Register criteria set forth at
36 CFR Part 60.6.

2. Where a property appears to meet the criteria for inclusion in the
National Register or where a question exists between the agency
official and any other qualified person regarding the eligibility
of a property for inclusion, the agency official shall request an
opinion from the Secretary respecting the property's eligibility
for the National Register or prepare a nomination as specified
below.

3. The agency official should provide the Secretary with adequate
documentation in accordance with the criteria set forth in Appendix
A to the procedures published in the "Federal Register" for comment
on April 27, 1976, as 36 CFR Part 63 and in Appendix A: IV to this
part.

4. A determination by the Secretary that a property does not meet the
criteria for inclusion in the National Register shall not bar
subsequent nomination of the property by the State Historic Preservation Officer or a Federal agency upon receipt of new information or upon consideration, through the normal nomination process, nor its approval for listing by the Secretary.

5. Where properties will remain under the jurisdiction or control of
a Federal agency, nomination is required by section 2(a) of the
Executive Order, but may be undertaken subsequent to a determination of eligibility or noneligibility. Properties in the areas
subject to environmental impact by Federal undertakings may be
nominated after determination of their eligibility and after decisions have been made concerning disposition of the properties
in accordance with 36 CFR Part 800. Nominations should be prepared
in accordance with detailed instructions given in 36 CFR Part 60.

6. When an integral portion of a property described in a Federal
nomination is not located on land under the jurisdiction or control
of the Federal agency, the completed nomination should be sent to
the appropriate State Historic Preservation Officer for submission
the State Review Board as a concurrent nomination in accordance
with the detailed instructions as given in 36 CFR Part 60.

(D) *Properties not under Federal jurisdiction or control.* The agency
official is requested to advise the appropriate State Historic Preservation
Officer of all historic properties located by the agency but not under
Federal jurisdiction or control that appear to qualify for inclusion in
the National Register or that have been determined eligible for inclusion
in the National Register. The agency official shall make available to the
State Historic Preservation Officer for inclusion in the State Plan for
Historic Preservation such information as has been compiled on properties
including relevant plans, drawings, photographs, and maps and the results
of any request for the determination of eligibility on such property.

Section 64.5.   Protection of Properties

All properties entered in or determined eligible for inclusion in the National Register in accordance with this Section are subject to the consultation and review process set forth at 36 CFR 800.

Section 64.6.   Responsibilities of the Secretary

(A) Professional guidance and assistance. Pursuant to his responsibilities under section 101(a) of the National Historic Preservation Act, and sections 3(b) and 3(f) of the Executive Order, the Secretary will periodically issue guidelines for the location, identification, and evaluation of historic properties, and will provide professional advice upon request.

(B) Comments on adequacy of identification and preservation. The Secretary or his designee shall exercise, in part, his continuing responsibilities under sections 3(b) and 3(f) of the Executive Order by commenting upon the adequacy of survey work and/or other identification and preservation activities undertaken by Federal agencies pursuant to section 106 of the National Historic Preservation Act, sections 1(3), 2(a), and 2(b) of the Executive Order, the procedures set forth at 36 CFR Part 800 and sections 102(2)(C) of the National Environmental Policy Act whenever such comment appears to be appropriate within the spirit of the laws and Executive order.

(C) Determination of the eligibility of properties for the National Register. The Secretary of his designee shall make determinations regarding the eligibility for inclusion in the National Register of properties under the jurisdiction or control of Federal agencies in accordance with the procedures set forth at 36 CFR Part 800.4(a)(2), pursuant to sections 2(b) and 3(f) of Executive Order 11593, and pursuant to sections 101(A)(1) and 106 of the National Preservation Act of 1966.

Appendix A.   Location and Identification Standards

The following standards are set forth to guide Federal agencies in the identification of historic properties for the purpose of their evaluation, nomination to, or determination of eligibility for the National Register, and consideration in project planning.

(A) General Conduct of Location and Identification Studies

Although the exact activities necessary for the identification of historic properties will vary depending on the nature of the agency's undertakings, the following steps will generally be appropriate.

(B) Background Research and Evaluation of Existing Data

1. Since few areas of the Nation have yet been adequately surveyed for historic properties, current lists for such properties seldom provide adequate information for full identification. Documentary research is the starting place for any identification study, however. Systematic study and evaluation of documentary data will usually permit predictions to be made about the kinds of historic properties that may be encountered in the area, and about their possible distributions. Such study may also make it possible to develop a broad evaluatory framework within which the significance of particular properties can be judged. Finally, background research may pinpoint some particular properties that are already adequately documented, or properties that are known but need further study to obtain full documentation. In undertaking background research, answers to the following questions should be sought:

(a) Are there known historic properties in the area?

(b) Is knowledge about the presence or absence of historic properties

based on a survey or surveys carried out according to the standards set forth in this chapter?
(c)   If not, to what extent are survey data lacking?
(d)   If the area has not been systematically surveyed, what predictions
      can be made about the location or kinds of historic properties to
      be expected based on data from nearby surveyed areas, from the
      known history of the area, from the constraints known to be im-
      posed by the natural environment, etc.?
(e)   Given the known history and prehistory of the region, the social
      and cultural concerns of its people, and pertinent state, local,
      and regional plans, what kinds of historic properties might be
      important to the satisfaction of these priorities?
2.   The agency undertaking a location and identification study, should
be vigorous in searching out useful sources of data, and should encourage
innovative approaches in their use to predict the locations of properties
and to develop evaluatory frameworks. It must be recognized, however, that
some institutions and organizations that maintain lists, files, or other
bodies of unpublished data are legitimately concerned about the integrity
of these documents and/or about the cost involved in permitting their use;
these concerns should be ascertained and, if legitimate, honored. At
least the following sources of background data should be consulted:
(a)   The State Historic Preservation Officer should be consulted with
      reference to the State Historic Preservation Plan maintained by
      his office, to obtain such data as:
      (1)   information on properties listed in or nominated to the
            National Register, properties on other lists, inventories,
            or registers known to the State Historic Preservation Offi-
            cer, and properties on which the State has evaluated and un-
            evaluated survey data;
      (2)   information on predictive data regarding potential properties
            in the area;
      (3)   recommendations as to the need for surveys in the area;
      (4)   recommendations concerning methods that should be used in
            conducting such surveys and possible sources of professional
            expertise;
      (5)   results of any previous surveys in the area, and the State
            Historic Preservation Officer's comments thereon; and
      (6)   recommendations concerning pertinent State or local laws and
            policies concerning historic properties.
(b)   Basic published and unpublished sources on local history, pre-
      history, anthropology, ethnohistory, and ecology should be studied
      to obtain an overview of the region's potential historic property
      distributions and research or preservation values.
(c)   The National Register and other lists or files of data on historic
      properties should be consulted. The National Register is published
      in its entirety in the "Federal Register," usually in February of
      each year; additions are published regularly in the "Federal
      Register." The most recent full publication and subsequent addi-
      tions should be consulted to determine whether any properties
      exist in an area to be affected by a Federal undertaking. The
      National Register listings are also accompanied by a list of pro-
      perties in both Federal and nonfederal ownership which have been
      determined to be eligible for inclusion as well as a list of
      pending nominations. The catalogs of the Historic American Build-
      ings Survey and the Historic American Engineering Record main-
      tained by the National Park Service, and any similar surveys and
      published reports should be utilized. State, university, or pro-
      fessional society historians, architects, architectural historians,

and archaeologists, and local organizations may also have
registers, inventories, catalogs, or other lists of sites or
areas with known or presumed historic values.

(d) Persons with first-hand knowledge of historic properties and/or
their historic values should be interviewed where feasible and
appropriate. Such interviews, and a proper respect for the
opinions expressed by those interviewed, are of particular importance where properties of cultural importance to local communities or social groups may be involved. Oral data should be elicited and recorded using existing professional methods such as those
prescribed by the Oral History Association, Box 13734, N.T. Station,
Denton, Texas 76203.

3. Background research should be undertaken by or under the supervision
of professional historians, architectural historians, historical
architects, and/or archaeologists. It will often be necessary to
draw upon the services of specialists such as ethnohistorians,
anthropologists, sociologists, and cultural geographers to make
full use of documentary data.

(C) Field Inspection
If review and evaluation of existing information fails to produce complete data based upon prior professional examination of the area subject
to environmental impact, then the background research should be supplemented by direct examination of the area of concern.

1. *Staff and Planning.* Field inspection usually can be performed
only by professional historians, archaeologists, architectural historians,
and historical architects. It will sometimes be necessary or useful to
call upon additional specialists to deal with particular characteristics
of the area. For example, if industrial properties are present, the
services of an industrial historian or an industrial archaeologist may be
appropriate, and if the continuing ways of life of local social or ethnic
groups are important to an understanding of the area's historic properties,
social and cultural anthropologists and folklorists may be necessary
additions to the staff. The exact nature of the appropriate staff will
depend on the kinds of resources that can be reasonably expected to occur.
For example, it is obviously unreasonable to employ an architectural historian or historical architect if the area of concern contains no standing
or ruined buildings or structures.

The nature of the area will also affect the kinds of methods that must
be employed to identify and record historic properties. Urban areas and
rural areas require different approaches. Terrain, vegetation, land
ownership and other factors will also affect the time required to conduct
an inspection and the kinds of techniques that will be required to complete
it. For example, if few indications of archaeological sites are likely to
appear on the surface of the ground because of vegetation, alluviation, or
other factors, it will probably be necessary for archaeologists to undertake subsurface testing both to locate sites and to obtain sufficient information for evaluation purposes.

Agencies planning field inspection should take factors such as the
above into account in preparing work plans, and should consult with the
Secretary, the State Historic Preservation Office, and/or other qualified
persons or groups to determine exactly what special approaches may be
necessary.

Adequate records must be kept of all field inspections to clearly
indicate what lands were inspected, the degree of intensity with which
they were inspected, the kinds of historic properties sought, all historic
properties recorded, and any factors that may have affected the quality of
the observations.

    2. Levels of field inspections. The intensity of field inspection
in advance of an undertaking should be commensurate with the projected
impact of the undertaking.

    An undertaking whose effects will be indirect and diffuse--for
instance an undertaking that will permit generalized population growth
in a large area--will generally require a systematic sample reconnaissance,
or some other less intensive field inspection than will an undertaking
having definable direct impacts.

    The level of project planning will also affect the nature of field
inspection undertaken; at an early level of planning, when many options
are open for location of project-facilities, low-intensity reconnaissance
may be appropriate to provide planning guidance; when alternative project
locations have been reduced, a much more intensive survey will usually be
necessary.

    Although many different types of field inspections may be appropriate
in different situations, such inspections generally fall into two types:
reconnaissance surveys and intensive survey.

D. Reconnaissance Survey

    Full identification of historic properties for purposes of determina-
tion of eligibility and detailed planning normally requires that an intensive survey be conducted as discussed at section 1.2(b) of this
appendix. Some agencies, however, may find it helpful to their planning
activities to conduct reconnaissance surveys in order to obtain preliminary
or predictive data on the distribution and nature of historic properties.
Reconnaissance survey is designed to provide a general impression of an
area's historic properties and their values, and involves small-scale field
work relative to the overall size of the area being studied. Although
reconnaissance survey will seldom if ever provide sufficient data to insure identification of all historic properties in an area, it should make
it possible to identify obvious or well-known properties, to check the
existence and condition of properties tentatively identified or predicted
from background research, to identify areas where certain kinds of properties are obviously lacking, and to indicate where certain kinds of
properties are likely to occur, thus making possible a more informed and
efficient intensive survey at a later stage in planning.

    In areas of potential direct impact from Federal undertakings, re-
connaissance survey should be used only as a preliminary to an intensive
survey, unless the reconnaissance reveals that it is impossible or extremely unlikely for historic properties to occur in the area. In areas
of potential indirect impact, reconnaissance may provide sufficient data
to permit an agency to evaluate its possible impacts and to develop plans
to assist local agencies in avoiding or mitigating such impacts. In cases
where a Federal agency intends to license or permit a State, local, or
private undertaking, particularly if the undertaking involves large land
areas, a reconnaissance may provide the agency with sufficient information
to permit the development of protective stipulations in the permit or license. An agency that participates in many small-scale undertakings in a
large region may find it useful to undertake a reconnaissance of the
region in order to develop a basis for making decisions about the need for
intensive surveys on individual projects, or to obtain guidance in the
kinds of survey activities that may be needed. Although a reconnaissance
survey will not ordinarily provide sufficient data to insure identification
of all historic properties under the jurisdiction or control of, or subject
to impact by a federal agency, it may be a very useful tool for effective
agency planning. A reconnaissance survey is preceded by adequate background research as discussed above. In the field an effort is made to
gain a sufficient impression of the area under consideration, and its
cultural resources, at least to permit predictions to be made about the

distribution of historic properties within the area and the potential significance of such properties. For small areas, a superficial visit to the
area by professionals in pertinent disciplines (architectural historians,
historians, archaeologists, and others whose expertise is appropriate to
the study of the area) may be sufficient for reconnaissance purposes. Such
a reconnaissance should provide an informed general opinion about the kinds
of properties that might be encountered and the appropriate methods to be
used in completing an intensive survey if such a survey is necessary. For
larger areas, a more systematic approach to reconnaissance survey is
usually necessary. For archaeological resources this usually involves the
detailed inspection of selected lands representing a statistically valid
sample of the entire area, from which projections can be made to the entire
area. Comprehensive drive-through or walking inspections of architecturally
significant resources, or at least spot-checks of various neighborhoods
within the area, are appropriate for the characterization of architectural
resources in such a reconnaissance. Coordination in the field with local
parties interested in or knowledgeable about the area's history and historic properties is appropriate during a reconnaissance as during an intensive survey.

E. Intensive Survey
     An intensive survey is a systematic, detailed, field inspection done
by or under the supervision of professional architectural historians,
historians, archaeologists, and/or other appropriate specialists. This
type of study is usually required to determine the significance of properties and their eligibility for listing in the National Register. It
is preceded by adequate background research as discussed above. All
districts, sites, buildings, structures, and objects of possible historical
or architectural value are examined by or under the supervision of a
professional historian, architectural historian, or historical architect.
Persons knowledgeable in the history, prehistory, and folkways of the area
are interviewed by or under the supervision of a professional historian,
ethnohistorian, cultural anthropologist, or folklorist. The surface of
the land and all districts, sites, buildings, structures, and objects of
possible archaeological value are inspected by or under the supervision
of a professional archaeologist. Historic archaeologists are employed
where historic sites are likely, prehistoric archaeologists are used if
prehistoric sites are probable. Systematic subsurface testing is conducted
if necessary to locate or obtain full descriptive and evaluative data.
Documentary data necessary to the evaluation of specific properties are
compiled and analyzed. A systematic effort is made to identify all properties within the area of concern that might qualify for the National
Register, and to record sufficient information to permit their evaluation.
All historic properties should be evaluated against the criteria established at 36 CFR 60.6, and supporting documentation should be developed
with reference to the standards published in the "Federal Register" for
comment on April 27, 1976, as 36 CFR 63, Appendix A. Since the precise kinds
of field activities necessary to fully identify historic properties vary
among the different regions of the United States, it is vital that agencies
preparing to undertake intensive surveys consult with the State Historic
Preservation Officer and other sources of professional guidance in developing plans for such surveys.

F. Special Archaeological Methods for Application to General Land-Use
Programs
     Agencies having responsibilities for the general management of land, or
for assisting or regulating land-use planning, will ordinarily not find it
possible to immediately conduct intensive archaeological surveys of all
lands under their jurisdiction or control, and often even a comprehensive

reconnaissance of such lands within a short period of time will be unfeasible
Such agencies should undertake a systematic, phased program of predictive
studies that will eventually result in full identification of all historic
properties and that will in the meantime provide planning data that will be
of assistance in complying with Section 2(b) of the Executive Order.

Studies of the kind set forth below are widely used by archaeologists
for research purposes; their utility in predicting the distribution and
nature of non-archaeological properties is less certain. Agencies are
encouraged to experiment with the application of such studies to the
whole range of historic properties, in order to determine their feasibility.

Regional predictive archaeological studies will ordinarily include the
following sequential steps:

1. Research Design: In consultation with the relevant State Historic
Preservation Officer (SHPO) and with archaeologists, anthropologists,
historians, and others having competence and interests in the archaeology
of the region, a research design and plan (or plans) are developed to
guide the study.

2. Initial Predictions: Using pertinent ethnographic, historical, and
environmental data as well as available archaeological documentation,
initial predictions are derived about the probable distributions of both
historic and prehistoric archaeological properties. These predictions,
being untested through fieldwork, will seldom be trustworthy as bases for
planning.

3. Significance-Measures: In consultation with appropriate scholars
and the SHPO, research questions and problems are formulated to serve as
guides in judging the significance of archaeological properties. These
must be consistent with, and reflect scholarly consideration of, the
National Register Criteria set forth in the approved State Historic Preservation Plan pertinent to the region.

4. Sampling Design: Plans for fieldwork are developed to test and
refine the initial predictions. These plans must reflect high professional standards. Sampling in Archaeology, J.S. Mueller, editor, University of Arizona Press, 1975, and Archaeological Sampling Procedures for
Large Land Parcels: A Statistically Based Approach, L. D. Smith and
D. F. Green, U.S. Department of Agriculture, Forest Service, Albuquerque,
1977 are recommended as methodological guides.

5. Sample fieldwork: A valid sample of the entire area is subjected
to intensive survey. Based on the results of this fieldwork, the initial
predictions are tested and refined. Specific properties recorded are
nominated for inclusion in the National Register.

6. Refined predictions and evaluation: Based on the sample fieldwork,
new and refined predictions can be made about the distribution and nature
of archaeological properties. Preliminary evaluations of the types of
properties now known to occur in the area can be made, with reference to
the National Register criteria and the significance measures developed
under paragraph 3 above. Depending on the size and reliability of the
sample inspected, these refined predictions may be of considerable value
in general planning and in decisionmaking about the need for particular
kinds of surveys or other preservation activities in advance of particular
land-use projects.

7. Further fieldwork: Another sample of the area is now selected for
survey to test the refined predictions. This should result in further
refinement of the predictions.

8. *Consultation:* The SHPO and appropriate scholars are consulted regularly in order to update research plans, methods, predictions, and research problems, as well as to incorporate data from pertinent studies conducted by others.

9. *Further studies:* The general predictive data from the study is used to guide project-specific surveys. The study continues until all land areas have been physically inspected in accordance with the research plans, and all archaeological properties identified and nominated for inclusion in the National Register, except cases where fully reliable predictive data now show that specific lands lack reasonable potential for containing archaeological properties.

G. Special Considerations with Respect to Submerged Lands

For submerged lands documentary research by qualified researchers may serve to indicate the need for, and recommended location of, physical and/or electronic surveys for submerged archaeological sites and sunken vessels. Because of the specialized nature and problems attending underwater survey activities, agency officials may wish to determine specific survey procedures in consultation with the Director, Office of Archaeology and Historic Preservation, National Park Service, Washington, D.C. 20240.

H. Documenting Locating and Identification Studies

The nature and level of specificity required in documenting a location and identification study will vary somewhat with the scope and kind of undertaking (if any) for which the study is conducted, the kinds of information already on hand about the area being studied, and other factors. In general, however, it is necessary to document the methods used in conducting the study, the assumptions that guided the application of the methods, the results of applying the methods, and any deficiencies in these results that may have arisen from the application or misapplication of the methods. Typically, the report of a location and identification study should contain the following types of information.

1. *Description of the study area.* Boundaries of the area should be indicated and the rationale used in defining the boundaries should be presented. Topographic and environmental characteristics that might affect the distribution, significance, or preservation of historic properties should be described.

2. *Background research and preparation.* Documentary data and, where relevant, data from oral sources pertinent to the study should be discussed and evaluated. Sources utilized should be identified, and methods of analysis presented and discussed. Background data should be analyzed in such a way to form a basis for planning any necessary field investigations, and for evaluating the significance of properties that may be discovered. Accordingly, the researcher should indicate a familiarity not only with local history and prehistory, but also with the professional literature in history, architecture, anthropology, archaeology, or other disciplines that may provide bases for evaluating historic properties.

3. *Research Design.* The report should also set forth the research design or plan of study that guided the work, discussing what sorts of historic properties were expected in the area, what historic values they might represent, and what strategies were to be employed in seeking the resources. Often it will be possible to make predictions about what kinds of properties can be expected in the field and how they ought to appear. The researcher should also set forth any biases or sources of error that can be identified as having potentially influenced the results of the study. For example, researchers trained specifically in prehistoric archaeology may be unable to accurately observe historic properties; if

this bias is not corrected by adding an historian, historic archaeologist, or architectural historian to the study team, it should be explicitly acknowledged in the report as a possible source of error.

4. *Field Inspection.* The composition of the field study team should be presented. An attempt should be made to insure that all pertinent professional disciplines are presented in this team. Names and qualifications of team members and consultants should be presented and their duties discussed. It is the researcher's obligation to employ persons and methods that will insure the accurate recognition of all classes of historic properties. Methods used in seeking, observing, and recording historic properties should be clearly set forth. The extent to which the study area was fully covered by inspectors on foot should be presented, textually and/ or using maps and charts. Any portions of the area not inspected, or inspected at a lower level of intensity, should be indicated and discussed. On-the-ground observational procedures should be presented.

    a.   In reporting the inspection of lands thought to contain non-structural properties, or structures in ruins, the following should normally be discussed:

        (1) how surveyors were distributed over the study area, how far apart they were placed and in what directions they walked;

        (2) what signs of historic and/or prehistoric activity surveyors were instructed to seek;

        (3) what special techniques, if any, were used to seek special kinds of properties thought to occur in the area (e.g., rock art, standing structures), and/or to cope with special environmental difficulties (e.g., pavement, heavy brush, overburden);

        (4) if subsurface testing was done, under what conditions it was done, what techniques were used, and where it was done; and

        (5) if less than the entire area was inspected, a sampling design should be presented and justified.

    b.   In reporting the inspection of lands containing buildings, and/or structures, the following should normally be discussed:

        (1) how surveyors covered the area--by foot, auto, etc.;

        (2) whether surveyors proceeded individually or as teams;

        (3) intensity of inspection of properties; did the inspection address only facades? exteriors? interiors?

        (4) how much of the area was covered at a time; did the inspection cover the entire area, proceed in stages, or cover only a portion? The rationale for the coverage strategy should be presented; and

        (5) what kinds of properties were surveyors instructed to seek (e.g., industrial as well as domestic buildings; vernacular architecture as well as "high style" buildings; buildings representing different "themes")?

    c.   The above categories are not presented as a "check list," but as examples of the kinds of questions that should be answerable using the report of a field inspection. To the extent possible, archaeological and architectural/historical inspections should be coordinated, since many properties discovered may be of both archaeological and historic architectural importance.

    d.   All procedures used should be justified in terms of their applicability to the area, its potential properties, its environment, and the plan of study.

5. *Results.*

    a.   If an intensive survey has been done, all historic properties should be clearly and completely described. To the extent

  possible, documentation of properties should refer to Appendix A
to the "Procedures for Requesting Determination of Eligibility,"
36 CFR Part 63, published for comment in the "Federal Register,"
April 27, 1976. Documentation can be provided on standard forms
or as text, but should be complete and internally consistent.

 b. If a reconnaissance survey has been done, the predicted distributions
of historic properties should be presented and justified on the basis of background research and field inspection. Specific historic
properties actually recorded during the field inspection should be
described, insofar as possible, as set forth at Section III(5)(a)
above.

 c. Negative data, as well as positive data should be presented and discussed, i.e., if historic properties were not found, this fact
should be noted and, if possible, accounted for.

6. Evaluation.

 a. Evaluations of historic properties should be made in sufficient
detail to provide an understanding of the historical values that
they represent, so that this understanding can serve as a basis
for managing the properties of planning impact-mitigation programs
if necessary. Properties valuable for their data content should be
evaluated in such a way as to facilitate the development of research designs for data recovery programs if such programs become
necessary. Properties of importance to a community, neighborhood,
social or ethnic group should be discussed with reference to the
values and concerns of those to whom the properties may be important.

 b. If an intensive survey has been done, all historic properties should
be evaluated against the criteria of eligibility for the National
Register of Historic Places set forth at 36 CFR 60.6.

 c. If a reconnaissance survey has been done, to the extent possible,
the predicted significance of each kind of historic property likely
to occur within the study area should be presented and justified
in relation to its general cultural setting, with reference to the
criteria set forth at 36 CFR 60.6.

 7. Recommendations. In most cases it is expected that the report
will provide recommendations concerning any need that may exist for further
study, evaluation or, where applicable, impact mitigation.

 8. Accompanying photographs, graphics, and tabular material. A location and identification study report should contain sufficient photographs,
maps, charts, tables, and appendix material to insure its accurate use for
study and planning purposes.

Appendix B. *Professional Qualifications*

 1. It is essential that any location and identification study be
staffed by qualified persons. While students, interns, trainees, and
volunteers are commonly and effectively used as team members on such
studies, it is vital that they be properly supervised by persons with
appropriate training and experience.

 2. A wide variety of specialists may be appropriate for work in particular kinds of location and identification studies. Geologists, geographers, ethnographers, ethnohistorians, folklorists, art historians,
and marine survey archaeologists are among the specialists quite commonly
employed in such studies. In general, however, the core disciplines represented in location and identification studies are history, architectural
history, architecture, historical architecture, and archaeology, and it is
for these disciplines that the Secretary has developed qualification stan-

dards. Standards for other professional disciplines may be issued from
time to time as the need arises.

3. In the following definitions, a month of professional experience
need not consist of a continuous month of full-time work but may be made
up of discontinuous periods of full-time or part-time work adding up to
the equivalent of a month of full-time experience.

a. *History.* The minimum professional qualifications in history are a
graduate degree in American history or closely related field; or a bachelor's degree in history or closely related field plus one of the following:
(a) at least two years of full-time experience in research, writing,
teaching, interpretation, or other demonstrable professional activity with
an academic institution, historical organization or agency, museum, or
other professional institution; or (b) substantial contribution through
research and publication to the body of scholarly knowledge in the field
of history.

b. *Archaeology.* The minimum professional qualifications in archaeology are (a) a graduate degree in archaeology, anthropology, or a closely
related field, or equivalent training accepted for accreditation purposes
by the Society of Professional Archaeologists, (b) demonstrated ability
to carry research to completion, usually evidenced by timely completion
of theses, research reports, or similar documents, and (c) at least 16
months of professional experience and/or specialized training in archaeological field, laboratory, or library research, administration, or management, including at least 4 months experience and/or specialized training
in the kind of activity the individual proposes to practice. For example,
persons supervising field archaeology should have at least 1 year or its
equivalent in field experience and/or specialized field training, including at least six months in a supervisory role. Persons engaged to
do archival or documentary research should have had at least 1 year of
experience and/or specialized training in such work. Archaeologists engaged in regional or agency planning or compliance with historic preservation procedures should have at least 1 year of experience in work directly pertinent to planning, compliance actions, etc., and/or specialized
historic preservation or cultural resource management training. A practitioner of prehistoric archaeology should have had at least 1 year of
experience or special training in research concerning archaeological resources of the prehistoric period. A practitioner of historic archaeology
should have had at least 1 year of experience in research concerning archaeological resources of the historic period.

c. *Architectural History.* The minimum professional qualifications in
architectural history are a graduate degree in architectural history,
historic preservation, or closely related field, with course work in
American architectural history; or a bachelor's degree in architectural
history, with a concentration in American architecture; or a bachelor's
degree in architectural history, art history, historic preservation, or
closely related field plus one of the following:

(1) at least two years of full-time experience in research, writing,
or teaching in American history or restoration architecture with
an academic institution, historical organization or agency, museum, or other professional institution; or

(2) substantial contribution through research and publication to the
body of scholarly knowledge in the field of American architectural history.

d. *Architecture.* The minimum professional qualifications in architecture are a professional degree in architecture plus at least 2 years
of full-time professional experience in architecture; or a State license

to practice architecture, plus one of the following:
  (1)   at least 1 year of graduate study in architectural preservation,
        American architectural history, preservation planning, or closely
        related field and at least 1 year of full-time professional ex-
        perience on preservation and restoration projects; or
  (2)   at least 2 years of full-time professional experience on preser-
        vation and restoration projects. Experience on preservation and
        restoration projects shall include detailed investigations of
        historic structures, preparation of historic structures research
        reports, and preparation of plans and specifications for preser-
        vation projects.

Other Specialists
      A wide variety of specialists may be appropriate for work in parti-
cular kinds of location and identification studies. Geologists, geographers, ethnographers, ethnohistorians, folklorists, art historians,
and marine survey archaeologists are among the specialists commonly employed
in such studies. The professional staff of the Office of Archaeology and
Historic Preservation is available to assist agencies in locating such
specialists when needed, and in identifying the need for them.

Use of less qualified personnel
      Nothing in this appendix should be taken to imply that *all* personnel
employed in a location and identification study need meet the criteria
given in Section 1. Personnel supervising such studies should meet the
criteria, but employment of less qualified persons, including volunteers,
in supervised positions is appropriate.

36 CFR PART 800

*The Procedures of the Advisory Council on Historic Preservation
set forth the basic steps for compliance with both section 106
of the National Historic Preservation Act and sections 2(b)
and 1(3) of the Executive Order. The associated memorandum
concerning determinations of "adverse effect" and "no adverse
effect" with regard to archaeological resources is an elaboration on portions of the Procedures with respect to archaeological considerations.*

PROCEDURES FOR THE PROTECTION OF HISTORIC AND CULTURAL PROPERTIES

Pursuant to the National Historic Preservation Act of 1966 (80 Stat.
915, 16 U.S.C. 470) and Executive Order 11593, May 13, 1971, "Protection
and Enhancement of the Cultural Environment" (36 FR 8921, 16 U.S.C. 470),
the Advisory Council on Historic Preservation has established Procedures
for Compliance, set forth in the FEDERAL REGISTER of February 28, 1973
(38 FR 5388), to implement the purposes of those authorities. Proposed revisions to those procedures were published in the FEDERAL REGISTER of
November 5, 1973 (38 FR 30464) and 30 days were allowed for public comment.
Federal agencies were also solicited to consult with the Advisory Council
with regard to the development of procedures for the protection of non-
federally owned historic and cultural properties as required by section
1(3) of Executive Order 11593.

In response to comments received by the Advisory Council and in consultation with Federal agencies, the proposed procedures have been revised to
incorporate suggestions from Federal and State agencies and private citizens. It is the purpose of this notice, through publication of revised
"Procedures for the Protection of Historic and Cultural Properties," to
apprise the public as well as government agencies, associations, and all
other organizations and individuals interested in historic preservation,
that the following procedures are hereby adopted as set forth below. The
procedures will appear in the Code of Federal Regulations in Title 36,
Chapter 8 at Part 800. The procedures are being codified because they
affect State and local governmental agencies, private organizations, and
individuals, in addition to Federal agencies, to which they are specifically directed, and because of the resultant need to make them widely
and readily available.

Federal agencies are advised that the procedures set forth certain
steps for agencies to follow to fulfill their obligations pursuant to
section 1(3) of Executive Order 11593 and to use as a guide in the development of their required internal procedures in consultation with the
Council. The Advisory Council reiterates its solicitation of Federal
agencies to consult with the Council on the development of those procedures. Inquiries regarding such consultation, as well as inquiries regarding the substance of and compliance with the procedures in general,
should be directed to the Executive Secretary, Advisory Council on Historic Preservation, Suite 430, 1522 K Street NW., Washington, D.C. 20005.

Effective date: January 25, 1974.
ROBERT R. GARVEY, Jr.
Executive Director, Advisory Council on Historic Preservation

Section 800.1. Purpose and Authorities

(a) The National Historic Preservation Act of 1966 created the Advisory Council on Historic Preservation, an independent agency of the Executive branch of the Federal Government, to advise the President and Congress on matters involving historic preservation. Its members are the Secretary of the Interior, the Secretary of Housing and Urban Development, the Secretary of the Treasury, the Secretary of Commerce, the Attorney General, the Secretary of Transportation, the Secretary of Agriculture, the Administrator of the General Services Administration, the Secretary of the Smithsonian Institution, the Chairman of the National Trust for Historic Preservation, and 10 citizen members appointed by the President on the basis of their outstanding service in the field of historic preservation.

(b) The Council reviews Federal, federally assisted, and federally licensed undertakings affecting cultural properties as defined herein in accordance with the following authorities:

(1) *Section 106 of the National Historic Preservation Act.* Section 106 requires that Federal, federally assisted, and federally licensed undertakings affecting properties included in the National Register of Historic Places be submitted to the Council for review and comment prior to the approval of any such undertaking by the Federal agency.

(2) *Section 1(3) of Executive Order 11593, May 13, 1971, "Protection and Enhancement of the Cultural Environment."* Section 1(3) requires that Federal agencies, in consultation with the Council, establish procedures regarding the preservation and enhancement of non-federally owned historic and cultural properties in the execution of their plans and programs. After soliciting consultation with the Federal agencies, the Advisory Council has adopted procedures, set forth in §§800.3 through 800.10, to achieve this objective and Federal agencies should fulfill their responsibilities under section 1(3) by following these procedures. The Council further recommends that Federal agencies use these procedures as a guide in the development, in consultation with the Council, of their required internal procedures.

(3) *Section 2(b) of Executive Order 11593, May 13, 1971, "Protection and Enhancement of the Cultural Environment."* Federal agencies are required, by section 2(a) of the Executive Order, to locate, inventory, and nominate properties under their jurisdiction or control to the National Register. Until such processes are complete, Federal agencies must submit proposals for the transfer, sale, demolition, or substantial alteration of federally owned properties eligible for inclusion in the National Register to the Council for review and comment. Federal agencies must continue to comply with section 2(b) review requirements, even after the initial inventory is complete, when they obtain jurisdiction or control over additional properties that are eligible for inclusion in the National Register or when properties under their jurisdiction or control are found to be eligible for inclusion in the National Register subsequent to the initial inventory.

Section 800.2. Coordination with Agency Requirements under the National Environmental Policy Act

Section 101(b)(4) of the National Environment Policy Act (NEPA) declares that one objective of the national environmental policy is to "preserve important historic, cultural, and natural aspects of our national heritage and maintain, wherever possible, an environment which supports diversity and variety of individual choice." In order to meet this objective, the Advisory Council instructs Federal agencies to coordinate NEPA compliance with the separate responsibilities of the National Historic Preservation Act and Executive Order 11593 to ensure that historic and

cultural resources are given proper consideration to the preparation of
environmental impact statements. Agency obligations pursuant to the
National Historic Preservation Act and Executive Order 11593 are independent from NEPA and must be complied with even when an environmental impact
statement is not required. However, where both NEPA and the National
Historic Preservation Act or Executive Order 11593 are applicable, the
Council on Environmental Quality, in its *Guidelines for the Preparations
of Environmental Impact Statements* (40 CFR Part 1500), directs that compliance with section 102(2)(C) of NEPA should, to the extent possible,
be combined with other statutory obligations--such as the National Historic
Preservation Act and Executive Order 11593--to yield a single document
which meets all applicable requirements. To achieve this objective, Federal
agencies should undertake, to the fullest extent possible, compliance with
the procedures set forth below whenever properties included in or eligible
for inclusion in the National Register are involved in a project to ensure
that obligations under the National Historic Preservation Act and Executive
Order 11593 are fulfilled during the preparation of a draft environmetal
impact statement required under section 102(2)(C) of NEPA. The Advisory
Council recommends that compliance with these procedures be undertaken
at the earliest stages of the environmental impact statement process to
expedite review of the statement. Statements on projects affecting properties included in or eligible for inclusion in the National Register
should be sent directly to the Advisory Council for review. All statements involving historic, architectural, archaeological, or cultural
resources, whether or not included in or eligible for inclusion in the
National Register, should be submitted to the Department of Interior for
review.

Section 800.3. Definitions

As used in these procedures:
(a) "National Historic Preservation Act" means Public Law 89-665,
approved October 15, 1966, an "Act to establish a program for the preservation of additional historic properties throughout the Nation and
for other purposes," 80 Stat. 915, 16 U.S.C. 470, as amended, 84 Stat.
204 (1970) and 87 Stat. 139 (1973) hereinafter referred to as "the Act."
(b) "Executive Order" means Executive Order 11593, May 13, 1971,
"Protection and Enhancement of the Cultural Environment," 36 FR 8921,
16 U.S.C. 470.
(c) "Undertaking" means any Federal action, activity, or program, or
the approval, sanction, assistance, or support of any other action,
activity or program, including but not limited to:
(1) Recommendations or favorable reports relating to legislation, including requests for appropriations. The requirement for following these
procedures applies to both: Agency recommendations on their own proposals
for legislation and agency reports on legislation initiated elsewhere.
In the latter case only the agency which has primary responsibility for
the subject matter involved will comply with these procedures.
(2) New and continuing projects and program activities: directly
undertaken by Federal agencies; or supported in whole or in part through
Federal contracts, grants, subsidies, loans, or other forms of funding
assistance; or involving a Federal lease, permit, license, certificate, or
other entitlement for use.
(3) The making, modification, or establishment of regulations, rules,
procedures, and policy.
(d) "National Reigster" means the National Register of Historic Places,
which is a register of districts, sites, buildings, structures, and objects,
significant in American history, architecture, archaeology, and culture,
maintained by the Secretary of the Interior under authority of section 2(b)

of the Historic Sites Act of 1935 (49 Stat. 666, 16 U.S.C. 461) and
section 101(a)(1) of the National Historic Preservation Act. The National
Register is published in its entirely in the FEDERAL REGISTER each year
in February. Addenda are published on the first Tuesday of each month.

(e) "National Register property" means a district, site, building,
structure, or object included in the National Register.

(f) "Property eligible for inclusion in the National Register" means
any district, site, building, structure, or object which the Secretary
of the Interior determines is likely to meet the National Register Criteria.
As these determinations are made, a listing is published in the FEDERAL
REGISTER on the first Tuesday of each month, as a supplement to the
National Register.

(g) "Decision" means the exercise of agency authority at any stage of
an undertaking where alterations might be made in the undertaking to
modify its impact upon historic and cultural properties.

(h) "Agency Official" means the head of the Federal agency having
responsibility for the undertaking or a subordinate employee of the Federal agency to whom such authority has been delegated.

(i) "Chairman" means the Chairman of the Advisory Council on Historic
Preservation, or such member designated to act in his stead.

(j) "Executive Director" means the Executive Director of the Advisory
Council on Historic Preservation established by Section 205 of the Act,
or his designated representative.

(k) "State Historic Preservation Officer" means the official within
each State, authorized by the State at the request of the Secretary of the
Interior, to act as liaison for purposes of implementing the Act, or his
designated representative.

(1) "Secretary" means the Secretary of the Interior, or his designee
authorized to carry out the responsibilities of the Secretary of the Interior under Executive Order 11593.

Section 800.4. Agency Procedures

At the earliest stage of planning or consideration of a proposed undertaking, including comprehensive or area-wide planning in which provision
may be made for an undertaking or an undertaking may be proposed, the Agency
Official shall take the following steps to comply with the requirements of
section 106 of the National Historic Preservation Act and sections 1(3)
and 2(b) of Executive Order 11593.

(a) *Identification of resources.* As early as possible and in all cases
prior to agency decision concerning an undertaking, the Agency Official
shall identify properties located within the area of the undertaking's
potential environmental impact that are included in or eligible for inclusion in the National Register.

(1) To identify properties included in the National Register, the
Agency Official shall consult the National Register, including monthly
supplements.

(2) To identify properties eligible for inclusion in the National
Register, the Agency Official shall, in consultation with the appropriate
State Historic Preservation Officer, apply the National Register Criteria,
set forth in Section 800.10, to all properties possessing historical,
architectural, archaeological, or cultural value located within the area
of the undertaking's potential environmental impact. If the Agency
Official determines that a property appears to meet the Criteria, or if it
is questionable whether the Criteria are met, the Agency Official shall
request, in writing, an opinion from the Secretary of the Interior respecting the property's eligibility for inclusion in the National Register.
The Secretary of the Interior's opinion respecting the eligibility of a

property for inclusion in the National Register shall be conclusive for
the purposes of these procedures.

(b) *Determination of effect.* For each property included in or eligible
for inclusion in the National Register that is located within the area of
the undertaking's potential environmental impact, the Agency Official, in
consultation with the State Historic Preservation Officer, shall apply the
Criteria of Effect, set forth in Section 800.8, to determine whether the
undertaking has an effect upon the property. Upon applying the Criteria
and finding no effect, the undertaking may proceed. The Agency Official
shall keep adequate documentation of a determination of no effect.

(c) *Effect established.* Upon finding that the undertaking will have
any effect upon a property included in or eligible for inclusion in the
National Register, the Agency Official, in consultation with the State
Historic Preservation Officer, shall apply the Criteria of Adverse Effect,
set forth in § 800.9, to determine whether the effect of the undertaking
is adverse.

(d) *Finding of no adverse effect.* Upon finding the effect not to be
adverse, the Agency Official shall forward adequate documentation of the
determination, including evidence of the views of the State Historic
Preservation Officer, to the Executive Director for review. Unless the
Executive Director notes an objection to the determination within 45 days
after receipt of adequate documentation, the Agency Official may proceed
with the undertaking.

(e) *Finding of adverse effect.* Upon finding the effect to be adverse
or upon notification that the Executive Director does not accept a
determination of no adverse effect, the Agency Official shall: (1) Request,
in writing, the comments of the Advisory Council; (2) notify the State
Historic Preservation Officer of this request; (3) prepare a preliminary
case report; and (4) proceed with the consultation process set forth in
Section 800.5.

(f) *Preliminary case report.* Upon requesting the comments of the
Advisory Council, the Agency Official shall provide the Executive Director
and the State Historic Preservation Officer with a preliminary case report,
containing all relevant information concerning the undertaking. The
Agency Official shall obtain such information and material from any applicant, grantee, or other beneficiary involved in the undertaking as may
be required for the proper evaluation of the undertaking, its effects, and
alternative courses of action.

Section 800.5. *Consultation Process*

(a) *Response to request for comments.* Upon receipt of a request for
Advisory Council comments pursuant to Section 800.4(e), the Executive
Director shall acknowledge the request and shall initiate the consultation
process.

(b) *On-site inspection.* At the request of the Agency Official, the
State Historic Preservation Officer, or the Executive Director, the Agency
Official shall conduct an on-site inspection with the Executive Director,
the State Historic Preservation Officer and such other representatives of
national, State, or local units of government and public and private organizations that the consulting parties deem appropriate.

(c) *Public information meeting.* At the request of the Agency Official, the State Historic Preservation Officer, or the Executive Director,
the Executive Director shall conduct a meeting open to the public, where
representatives of national, State, or local units of government, representatives of public or private organizations, and interested citizens can
receive information and express their views on the undertaking, its effects
on historic and cultural properties, and alternate courses of action. The

Agency Official shall provide adequate facilities for the meeting and shall afford appropriate notice to the public in advance of the meeting.

(d) *Consideration of alternatives.* Upon review of the pending case and subsequent to any on-site inspection and any public information meeting, the Executive Director shall consult with the Agency Official and State Historic Preservation Officer to determine whether there is a feasible and prudent alternative to avoid or satisfactorily mitigate any adverse effect.

(e) *Avoidance of adverse effect.* If the Agency Official, the State Historic Preservation Officer, and the Executive Director select and unanimously agree upon a feasible and prudent alternative to avoid the adverse effect of the undertaking, they shall execute a Memorandum of Agreement acknowledging avoidance of adverse effect. This document shall be forwarded to the Chairman for review pursuant to Section 800.6(a).

(f) *Mitigation of adverse effect.* If the consulting parties are unable to unanimously agree upon a feasible and prudent alternative to avoid any adverse effect, the Executive Director shall consult with the Agency Official and the State Historic Preservation Officer to determine whether there is a feasible and prudent alternative to satisfactorily mitigate the adverse effect of the undertaking. Upon finding and unanimously agreeing to such an alternative, they shall execute a Memorandum of Agreement acknowledging satisfactory mitigation of adverse effect. This document shall be forwarded to the Chairman for review pursuant to Section 800.6(a).

(g) *Memorandum of Agreement.* It shall be the responsibility of the Executive Director to prepare each Memorandum of Agreement required under these procedures. In preparation of such a document the Executive Director may request the Agency Official to prepare a proposal for inclusion in the Memorandum, detailing actions to be taken to avoid or mitigate the adverse effect.

(h) *Failure to avoid or mitigate adverse effect.* Upon the failure of consulting parties to find and unanimously agree upon a feasible and prudent alternative to avoid or satisfactorily mitigate the adverse effect, the Executive Director shall request the Chairman to schedule the undertaking for consideration at the next Council meeting and notify the Agency Official of the request. Upon notification of the request, the Agency Official shall delay further processing of the undertaking until the Council has transmitted its comments or the Chairman has given notice that the undertaking will not be considered at a Council meeting.

Section 800.6. Council Procedures

(a) *Review of Memorandum of Agreement.* Upon receipt of a Memorandum of Agreement acknowledging avoidance of adverse effect or satisfactory mitigation of adverse effect, the Chairman shall institute a 30-day review period. Unless the Chairman shall notify the Agency Official that the matter has been placed on the agenda for consideration at a Council meeting, the memorandum shall become final: (1) Upon the expiration of the 30-day review period with no action taken; or (2) when signed by the Chairman. Memoranda duly executed in accordance with these procedures shall constitute the comments of the Advisory Council. Notice of executed Memoranda of Agreement shall be published in the FEDERAL REGISTER monthly.

(b) *Response to request for consideration at Council meeting.* Upon receipt of a request from the Executive Director for consideration of the proposed undertaking at a Council meeting, the Chairman shall determine whether or not the undertaking will be considered and notify the Agency Official of his decision. To assist the Chairman in this determination, the Agency Official and the State Historic Preservation Officer shall pro-

vide such reports and information as may be required. If the Chairman decides against consideration at a Council meeting, he will submit a
written summary of the undertaking and his decision to each member of the
Council. If any member of the Council notes an objection to the decision
within 15 days of the Chairman's decision, the undertaking will be
scheduled for consideration at a Council meeting. If the Council members
have no objection, the Chairman shall notify the Agency Official at the
end of the 15-day period that the undertaking may proceed.

(c) *Decision to consider the undertaking.* Upon determination that
the Council will consider an undertaking, the Chairman shall: (1) Schedule
the matter for consideration at a regular meeting no less than 60 days
from the date the request was received, or in exceptional cases, schedule
the matter for consideration in an unassembled or special meeting; (2)
notify the Agency Official and the State Historic Preservation Officer of
the date on which comments will be considered; and (3) authorize the
Executive Director to prepare a case report.

(d) *Content of the case report.* For purposes of arriving at comments,
the Advisory Council prescribes that certain reports be made available to
it and accepts reports and statements from other interested parties.
Specific informational requirements are enumerated below. Generally, the
requirements represent an explication of elaboration of principles contained in the Criteria of Effect and in the Criteria of Adverse Effect.
The Council notes, however, that the Act recognizes historical and cultural
resources should be preserved "as a living part of our community life and
development." Consequently, in arriving at final comments, the Council
considers those elements in an undertaking that have relevance beyond historical and cultural concerns. To assist it in weighing the public interest, the Council welcomes information not only bearing upon physical,
sensory, or esthetic effects but also information concerning economic,
social, and other benefits or detriments that will result from the undertaking.

(e) *Elements of the case report.* The report on which the Council re-
lies for comment shall consist of:

(1) A report from the Executive Director to include a verification of
the legal and historical status of the property; an assessment of the historical, architectural, archaeological, or cultural significance of the
property; a statement indicating the special value of features to be most
affected by the undertaking; an evaluation of the total effect of the
undertaking upon the property; a critical review of any known feasible
and prudent alternatives and recommendations to remove or mitigate the
adverse effect;

(2) A report from the Agency Official requesting comment to include
a general discussion and chronology of the proposed undertaking; when
appropriate, an account of the steps taken to comply with section 102(2)(A)
of the National Environmental Policy Act of 1969 (83 Stat. 852, 42 U.S.C.
4321); an evaluation of the effect of the undertaking upon the property,
with particular reference to the impact on the historic, architectural,
archaeological and cultural values; steps taken or proposed by the agency
to take into account, avoid, or mitigate adverse effects of the undertaking; a thorough discussion of alternate courses of action; and, if
applicable and available, a copy of the draft environmental statement
prepared in compliance with section 102(2)(C) of the National Environmental
Policy Act of 1969;

(3) A report from any other Federal agency having under consideration
an undertaking that will concurrently or ultimately affect the property,
including a general description and chronology of that undertaking and discussion of the relation between that undertaking and the undertaking being
considered by the Council;

(4) A report from the State Historic Preservation Officer to include an assessment of the significance of the property; an identification of features of special value; an evaluation of the effect of the undertaking upon the property and its specific components; an evaluation of known alternate courses of action; a discussion of present or proposed participation of State and local agencies or organizations in preserving or assisting in preserving the property; an indication of the support or opposition of units of government and public and private agencies and organizations within the State; and the recommendations of his office;

(5) A report by any applicant or potential recipient when the Council considers comments upon an application for a contract, grant, subsidy, loan, or other form of funding assistance, or an application for a Federal lease, permit, license, certificate, or other entitlement for use. Arrangements for the submission and presentation of reports by applicants or potential recipients shall be made through the Agency Official having jurisdiction in the matter; and

(6) Other pertinent reports, statements, correspondence, transcripts, minutes, and documents received by the Council from any and all parties, public or private. Reports submitted pursuant to this section should be received by the Council at least two weeks prior to a Council meeting.

(f) *Coordination of case reports and statements.* In considerations involving more than one Federal department, either directly or indirectly, the Agency Official requesting comment shall act as a coordinator in arranging for a full assessment and discussion of all interdepartmental facets of the problem and prepare a record of such coordination to be made available to the Council. At the request of the Council, the State Historic Preservation Officer shall notify appropriate governmental units and public and private organizations within the State of the pending consideration of the undertaking by the Council, and coordinate the presentation of written statements to the Council.

(g) *Council meetings.* The Council does not hold formal hearings to consider comments under these procedures. Two weeks notice shall be given, by publication in the FEDERAL REGISTER, of all meetings involving Council review of Federal undertakings in accordance with these procedures. Reports and statements will be presented to the Council in open session in accordance with a prearranged agenda. Regular meetings of the Council generally occur on the first Wednesday and Thursday of February, May, August and November.

(h) *Oral statements to the Council.* A schedule shall provide for oral statements from the Executive Director; the referring Agency Official presently or potentially involved; the applicant or potential recipient, when appropriate; the State Historic Preservation Officer; and representatives of national, State, or local units of government and public and private organizations. Parties wishing to make oral remarks shall submit written statements of position in advance to the Executive Director.

(i) *Comments by the Council.* The comments of the Council, issued after consideration of an undertaking at a Council meeting, shall take the form of a three-part statement, including an introduction, findings, and a conclusion. The statement shall include notice to the Agency Official of the report required under section 800.6(j) of these procedures. Comments shall be made to the head of the Federal Agency requesting comment or having responsibility for the undertaking. Immediately thereafter, the comments of the Council will be forwarded to the President and the Congress as a special report under authority of section 202(b) of the Act and published as soon as possible in the FEDERAL REGISTER. Comment shall be available to the public upon receipt of the comments by the head of the Federal agency.

(j) *Report of agency action in response to Council comments.* When a
final decision on the undertaking is reached by the Federal Agency, the
Agency Official shall submit a written report to the Council containing
a description of actions taken by the Federal Agency subsequent to the
Council's comments; a description of actions taken by other parties pursuant to the actions of the Federal Agency; and the ultimate effect of
such actions on the property involved. The Council may request supplementary reports of the nature of the undertaking requires them.

(k) *Records of the Council.* The records of the Council shall consist
of a record of the proceedings at each meeting, the case report prepared
by the Executive Director, and all other reports, statements, transcripts,
correspondence, and documents received.

(l) *Continuing review jurisdiction.* When the Council has commented
upon an undertaking pursuant to Section 800.6 such as a comprehensive or
area-wide plan that by its nature requires subsequent action by the Federal
Agency, the Council will consider its comments or approval to extend only
to the undertaking as reviewed. The Agency Official shall ensure that
subsequent action related to the undertaking is submitted to the Council
for review in accordance with §800.4(e) of these procedures when that
action is found to have an adverse effect on a property included in or
eligible for inclusion in the National Register.

Section 800.7. Other Powers of the Council

(a) *Comment or report upon non-Federal undertaking.* The Council will
exercise the broader advisory powers, vested by section 202(a)(1) of the
Act, to recommend measures concerning a non-Federal undertaking that will
adversely affect a property included in or eligible for inclusion in the
National Register: (1) upon request from the President of the United
States, the President of the U.S. Senate, or the Speaker of the House of
Representatives, or (2) when agreed upon by a majority vote of the members
of the Council.

(b) *Comment or report upon Federal undertaking in special circumstances.*
The Council will exercise its authority to comment to Federal agencies in
certain special situations even though written notice that an undertaking
will have an effect has not been received. For example, the Council may
choose to comment in situations where an objection is made to a Federal
agency finding of "no effect."

Section 800.8. Criteria of Effect

A Federal, federally assisted, or federally licensed undertaking shall
be considered to have an effect on a National Register property or property eligible for inclusion in the National Register (districts, sites,
buildings, structures, and objects, including their settings) when any
condition of the undertaking causes or may cause any change, beneficial or
adverse, in the quality of the historical, architectural, archaeological,
or cultural character that qualifies the property under the National
Register Criteria.

Section 800.9. Criteria of Adverse Effect

Generally, adverse effects occur under conditions which include but
are not limited to:

(a) Destruction or alteration of all or part of a property;

(b) Isolation from or alteration of its surrounding environment;

(c) Introduction of visual, audible, or atmospheric elements that are
out of character with the property or alter its setting;

(d) Transfer or sale of a federally owned property without adequate
conditions or restrictions regarding preservation, maintenance, or use; and

(e) Neglect of a property resulting in its deterioration or destruction.

Section 800.10. National Register Criteria

(a) "National Register Criteria" means the following criteria established by the Secretary of the Interior for use in evaluating and determining the eligibility of properties for listing in the National Register: The quality of significance in American history, architecture, archaeology, and culture is present in districts, sites, buildings, structures,
and objects of State and local importance that possess integrity of location, design, setting, materials, workmanship, feeling and association and:
(1) That are associated with events that have made a significant
contribution to the broad patterns of our history; or
(2) That are associated with the lives of persons significant in our
past; or
(3) That embody the distinctive characteristics of a type, period, or
method of construction, or that represent the work of a master, or that
possess high artistic values, or that represent a significant and distinguishable entity whose components may lack individual distinction; or
(4) That have yielded, or may be likely to yield, information important in prehistory or history.
(b) *Criteria considerations.* Ordinarily cemeteries, birthplaces, or
graves of historical figures, properties owned by religious institutions
or used for religious purposes, structures that have been moved from their
original locations, reconstructed historic buildings, properties primarily
commemorative in nature, and properties that have achieved significance
within the past 50 years shall not be considered eligible for the National
Register. However, such properties will qualify if they are integral
parts of districts that do meet the criteria or if they fall within the
following categories:
(1) A religious property deriving primary significance from architectural or artistic distinction or historical importance;
(2) A building or structure removed from its original location but
which is the surviving structure most importantly associated with a
historic person or event;
(3) A birthplace or grave of a historical figure of outstanding
importance if there is no appropriate site or building directly associated
with his productive life;
(4) A cemetery which derives its primary significance from graves
of persons of transcendent importance, from age, from distinctive design
features, or from association with historic events;
(5) A reconstructed building when accurately executed in a suitable
environment and presented in a dignified manner as part of a restoration
master plan, and when no other building or structure with the same
association has survived;
(6) A property primarily commemorative in intent if design, age,
tradition, or symbolic value has invested it with its own historical
significance; or
(7) A property achieving significance within the past 50 years if it
is of exceptional importance.

FR Doc.74-1936 Filed 1-24-74; 8:45 am

GUIDELINES FOR MAKING "ADVERSE EFFECT" AND "NO ADVERSE EFFECT" DETERMIN-
ATIONS FOR ARCHAEOLOGICAL RESOURCES IN ACCORDANCE WITH 36 CFR PART 800

Archaeological properties included in or eligible for inclusion in the
National Register of Historic Places are generally nominated under National
Register Criterion "d" (36 CFR Part 60.6) which states that a property may
qualify if it has "yielded, or may be likely to yield, information important in prehistory or history." While disturbance of archaeological properties should be avoided, under certain circumstances, properties primarily significant for the data they contain can be said to realize their sig-
nifiance when this data is retrieved in an appropriate manner.

In such cases where a Federal undertaking (36 CFR Part 800.3(c)) can
result in the recovery of data from an archaeological property on or
eligible for inclusion in the National Register of Historic Places, the
Agency Official should take the following steps to decide whether a
"no adverse effect" determination can be made:

*The Agency Official shall, in consultation with the State Historic
Preservation Officer (SHPO), apply the criteria set forth in Part
I below. If these criteria are not met, the Agency Official shall
comply with the procedures set forth at 36 CFR Part 800.4(e) et
seq. If the criteria are met, the Agency Official may issue a
determination of no adverse effect for any data recovery program
conducted in accordance with the requirements set forth in Part
II below. Documentation that the criteria and requirements set
forth in Parts I and II below have been met, along with the
comments of the SHPO, shall be forwarded to the Council for review in accordance with 36 CFR Part 800.4(d).*

PART I: CRITERIA

1. The property is not a National Historic Landmark, a National Historic Site in non-federal ownership, or a property of national
   historical significance so designated within the National Park
   System.
2. The SHPO has determined that in-place preservation of the property
   is not necessary to fulfill purposes set forth in the State Historic Preservation Plan.
3. The SHPO and the Agency Official agree that:
   a. The property (including properties that are subsidiary ele-
      ments in a larger property defined in Criterion 1) has minimal
      value as an exhibit in place for public understanding and en-
      joyment;
   b. Above and beyond its scientific value, the property is not
      known to have historic or cultural significance to a community,
      ethnic, or social group that would be impaired by the retrieval
      of data;
   c. Currently available technology is such that the significant
      information contained in the property can be retrieved.
4. Funds and time have been committed to adequately retrieve the data.

PART II: DATA RECOVERY REQUIREMENTS

1. The data recovery will be conducted under the supervision of an archaeologist who meets the "Proposed Department of the Interior Qualifications for the Supervisory Archaeologist (Field Work Projects)." (See Attachment #1.)
2. The data recovery will be conducted in accordance with "Professional Standards for Data Recovery Programs." (See Attachment #2.)
3. A specified date has been set for completion and submission of the final report to the Agency official.
4. Plans have been made for disposition of the material recovered after they have been analyzed for the final report. (See Attachment #3.)
5. Regarding the status of the affected property, documentation of the condition and significance of the property after data recovery will be provided the Agency Official and SHPO for forwarding to the National Register of Historic Places for action to include nominations, boundary changes or removal of National Register or eligibility status, in accordance with National Register procedures (36 CFR Part 60.16 and 60.17).

ATTACHMENT #1.   PROPOSED DEPARTMENT OF THE INTERIOR QUALIFICATIONS FOR THE SUPERVISORY ARCHAEOLOGIST (FIELD WORK PROJECTS)

The minimum professional qualifications for the Supervisory Archaeologist are a graduate degree in archaeology, anthropology, or a closely related field, or equivalent training accepted for accreditation purposes by the Society of Professional Archaeologists, plus:
   (1)   at least sixteen months of professional experience or specialized training in archaeology field, laboratory, or library research, including
     (a)   at least four months of experience in general North American archaeology, and
     (b)   at least six months of field experience in a supervisory role;
   (2)   a demonstrated ability to carry research to completion, usually evidence by timely completion of theses, research reports, or similar documents.
For work involving prehistoric archaeology, the Supervisory Archaeologist should have had at least one year of experience in research concerning archaeological resources of the prehistoric period.
For work involving historic archaeology, the Supervisory Archaeologist should have had at least one year of experience in research concerning archaeological resources of the historic period.

ATTACHMENT #2.   PROFESSIONAL STANDARDS FOR DATA RECOVERY PROGRAMS

1. The data recovery program should be conducted in accordance with a professionally adequate recovery plan (research design):
   a.   The plan shall be prepared or approved by the Supervisory Archaeologist and shall reflect a familiarity with previous relevant research;
   b.   The plan shall include a definite set of research objectives, taking into account previous relevant research, to be answered in analysis of the data to be recovered;
   c.   The plan shall provide for recovery of a usable sample of data on all significant research topics that can reasonably be addressed using the property or a justification for collecting data on a smaller range of topics at the expense of others;

    d. The plan shall specify and justify the methods and techniques to be used for recovery of the data contained in the property. (Methods destructive of data or injurious to the natural features of the property should not be employed if non-destructive methods are feasible.)

2. The data recovery program should provide for adequate personnel, facilities, and equipment to fully implement the recovery plan.

3. The data recovery program should insure that full, accurate and intelligible records will be made and maintained of all field observations and operations, including but not limited to excavation and recording techniques, stratigraphic and/or associational relationships where appropriate, and significant environmental relationships.

4. Particularly when a data recovery program is conducted upon a potentially complex historic or prehistoric property (e.g., an historic town site; a prehistoric site that may contain many occupation layers, cemeteries, or architectural remains), situations may arise or data be encountered that were not anticipated in designing the program. Adequate provision should be made for modification of the data recovery plan to cope with unforeseen discoveries or other unexpected circumstances.

5. The data recovery program should include provisions for dissemination of the results of the program. Generally, the final report should be made available to the SHPO, the State archivist, the State archaeologist, the Departmental Consulting Archaeologist of the Department of the Interior, and the Chairman, Department of Anthropology, Smithsonian Institution.

ATTACHMENT #3. TREATMENT OF RECOVERED MATERIALS

The recommended professional treatment of recovered materials is curation and storage of the artifacts at an institution that can properly insure their preservation and that will make them available for research and public view. If such materials are not in Federal ownership, the consent of the owner must be obtained, in accordance with applicable law, concerning the disposition of the materials after completion of the report.

ARCHAEOLOGICAL AND HISTORIC PRESERVATION ACT

An Act to amend the Act of June 27, 1960 (74 Stat. 220), relating to the preservation of historical and archaeological data (Public Law 93-291, 93rd Congress, S. 514, May 24, 1974).

Be it enacted by the Senate and House of Representatives of the United States of America in Congress assembled, That the Act entitled "An Act for the preservation of historical and archaeological data (including relics and specimens) which might otherwise be lost as the result of the construction of a dam, approved June 27, 1960 (74 Stat. 220; 16 U.S.C. 469), is amended as follows: "That it is the purpose of this Act to further the policy set forth in the Act entitled 'An Act to provide for the preservation of historic American sites, buildings, objects, and antiquities of national significance, and for other purposes,' approved August 21, 1935 (16 U.S.C. 461-467), by specifically providing for the preservation of historical, and archaeological data (including relics and specimens) which might otherwise be irreparably lost or destroyed as the result of (1) flooding, the building of access roads, the erection of workmen's communities, the relocation of railroads and highways, and other alterations of the terrain caused by the construction of a dam by any agency or (2) any alteration of the terrain caused as a result of any Federal construction project or federally licensed activity or program.

Section 2

Before any agency of the United States shall undertake the construction of a dam, or issue a license to any private individual or corporation for the construction of a dam it shall give written notice to the Secretary of the Interior (hereafter referred to as the "Secretary") setting forth the site of the proposed dam and the approximate area to be flooded and otherwise changed if such construction is undertaken: Provided, That with respect to any floodwater retarding dam which provides less than five thousand acre-feet of detention capacity and with respect to any other type of dam which creates a reservoir of less than forty surface acres the provisions of this section shall apply only when the constructing agency, in its preliminary surveys, finds, or is presented with evidence that historical, or archaeological materials exist or may be present in the proposed reservoir area.

Section 3

(a) Whenever any Federal agency finds, or is notified, in writing, by an appropriate historical or archaeological authority, that its activities in connection with any Federal construction project or federally licensed project, activity, or program may cause irreparable loss or destruction of significant scientific, prehistorical, historical, or archaeological data, such agency shall notify the Secretary, in writing, and shall provide the Secretary with appropriate information concerning the project, program, or activity. Such agency may request the Secretary to undertake the recovery, protection, and preservation of such data (including preliminary survey, or other investigation as needed, and analysis and publication of the reports resulting from such investigation), or it may, with funds appropriated for such project, program, or activity, undertake such activities. Copies of reports of any investigations made pursuant to this section shall be sub-

mitted to the Secretary, who shall make them available to the public for
inspection and review.

(b) Whenever any Federal agency provides financial assistance by
loan, grant, or otherwise to any private person, association, or public
entity, the Secretary, if he determines that significant scientific,
prehistorical, historical, or archaeological data might be irrevocably
lost or destroyed, may with funds appropriated expressly for this purpose
conduct, with the consent of all persons, associations or public entities
having a legal interest in the property involved, a survey of the affected
site and undertake the recovery, protection, and the preservation of such
data (including analysis and publication). The Secretary shall, unless
otherwise mutually agreed to in writing, compensate any person, association,
or public entity damaged as a result of delays in construction or as a
result of the temporary loss of the use of private or any non-federally
owned lands.

Section 4

(a) The Secretary, upon notification, in writing, by any Federal or
State agency or appropriate historical or archaeological authority that
scientific, prehistorical, historical, or archaeological data is being or
may be irrevocably lost or destroyed by any Federal or federally assisted
or licensed project, activity, or program, shall, if he determines that
such data is significant and is being or may be irrevocably lost or
destroyed and after reasonable notice to the agency responsible for funding or licensing such project, activity, or program, conduct or cause to
be conducted a survey and other investigation of the areas which are or may
be affected and recover and preserve such data (including analysis and
publication) which, in his opinion, are not being, but should be, recovered and preserved in the public interest.

(b) No survey or recovery work shall be required pursuant to this
section which, in the determination of the head of the responsible agency,
would impede Federal or federally assisted or licensed projects or activities undertaken in connection with any emergency, including projects or
activities undertaken in anticipation of, or as a result of, a natural
disaster.

(c) The Secretary shall initiate the survey or recovery effort within sixty days after notification to him pursuant to subsection (a) of
this section or within such time as may be agreed upon with the head of
the agency responsible for funding or licensing the project, activity, or
program in all other cases.

(d) The Secretary shall, unless otherwise mutually agreed to in
writing, compensate any person, association, or public entity damaged as
a result of delays in construction or as a result of the temporary loss
of the use of private or non-federally owned lands.

Section 5

(a) The Secretary shall keep the agency responsible for funding or
licensing the project notified at all times of the progress of any survey
made under this Act, or of any work undertaken as a result of such survey,
in order that there will be as little disruption or delay as possible in
the carrying out of the functions of such agency and the survey and recovery programs shall terminate at a time mutually agreed upon by the
Secretary and the head of such agency unless extended by mutual agreement.

(b) The Secretary shall consult with any interested Federal and State
agencies, educational and scientific organizations, and private institutions and qualified individuals, with a view to determining the ownership
of and the most appropriate repository for any relics and specimens re-

covered as a result of any work performed as provided for in this section.

(c) The Secretary shall coordinate all Federal Survey and recovery activities authorized under this Act and shall submit an annual report at the end of each fiscal year to the Interior and Insular Affairs Committees of the United States Congress indicating the scope and effectiveness of the program, the specific projects surveyed and the results produced, and the costs incurred by the Federal Government as a result thereof.

Section 6

In the administration of this Act, the Secretary may--

(1) enter into contracts or make cooperative agreements with any Federal or State agency, any educational or scientific organization, or any institution, corporation, association, or qualified individual; and

(2) obtain the services of experts and consultants or organizations thereof in accordance with section 3109 of title 5, United States Code; and

(3) accept and utilize funds made available for salvage archaeological purposes by any private person or corporation or transferred to him by any Federal agency.

Section 7

(a) To carry out the purposes of this Act, any Federal agency responsible for a construction project may assist the Secretary and/or it may transfer to him such funds as may be agreed upon, but not more than 1 per centum of the total amount authorized to be appropriated for such project, except that the 1 per centum limitation of this section shall not apply in the event that the project involves $50,000 or less: *Provided*, That the costs of such survey, recovery, analysis, and publication shall be considered nonreimbursable project costs.

(b) For the purposes of subsection 3(b), there are authorized to be appropriated such sums as may be necessary, but not more than $500,000 in fiscal year 1974; $1,000,000 in fiscal year 1975; $1,500,000 in fiscal year 1976; $1,500,000 in fiscal year 1977; and $1,500,000 in fiscal year 1978.

(c) For the purposes of subsection 4(a) there are authorized to be appropriated not more than $2,000,000 in fiscal year 1974; $2,000,000 in fiscal year 1975; $3,000,000 in fiscal year 1976; $3,000,000 in fiscal year 1977; and $3,000,000 in fiscal year 1978.

36 CFR PART 66:   DRAFT

These regulations concern the basic professional standards
to be employed in complying with the terms of the Archaeological
and Historic Preservation Act. They were printed for comment in
the Federal Register on January 28, 1977.

RECOVERY OF SCIENTIFIC, PREHISTORIC, HISTORIC, AND ARCHAEOLOGICAL DATA:
METHODS, STANDARDS, AND REPORTING REQUIREMENTS: PROPOSED GUIDELINES

On August 13, 1975, The Department of the Interior distributed a
"Statement of Program Approach" with respect to its responsibilities under
Public Law 93-291, the Archaeological and Historic Preservation Act of
May 24, 1974 (88 Stat. 174. 16 U.S.C. Section 469a-1 *et seq*; hereinafter,
"the Act"). Comments have been received from many Federal agencies, State
Historic Preservation Officers, and members of the public. The Department
expects to publish proposed rulemaking with respect to this aspect of the
Act, for comment, in the near future.

Many of the comments received indicate a need for the Department to
provide substantive guidance to agencies that undertake to recover scientific, prehistoric, historic, and archaeological data; such guidance is
also contemplated by the Act. It is the purpose of this notice of proposed
rulemaking to provide this information as a part of the Department's proposed overall rulemaking with respect to the Act. This guidance will facilitate the Department's coordination of activities authorized under the
Act, and its reporting to Congress on the scope and effectiveness of the
program, as required by section 5(c) of the Act. It will also help guarantee the uniform high quality of reports submitted to the Department
pursuant to the requirements of section 3(a) of the Act.

The Act provides Federal agencies with a method of mitigating impacts
of their undertakings upon those historic properties that contain scientific, prehistoric, historic, or archaeological data. This method, data
recovery, is not the only method that may be properly applied in order to
mitigate project impacts identified through the process prescribed by the
National Environmental Policy Act of 1969 (Public Law 91-190, hereinafter, "NEPA"). Actions that preserve historic properties in place are
usually preferable to the preservation of data alone through data recovery
activities, both because such actions usually extend the useful lives of
the properties and their data and because they often are less costly.

The activities authorized by the Act must also be understood as applicable
only to the mitigation of project impacts on the data or research value of
historic properties, not on those historic cultural attributes that are
not data related. For example, the Act does not pertain to actions that
may be appropriate under NEPA or the National Historic Preservation Act
of 1966 (Public Law 89-665; hereinafter, "NHPA") to preserve the historical
or cultural meaning or integrity of a property to a neighborhood, community,
or group.

In order to ascertain when application of the Act to impact mitigation
activities may be appropriate, and to apply its provisions wisely, it is
necessary that the planning steps required by NEPA, NHPA, and Executive
Order 11593 be taken before the Act is invoked; the Act is not a substitute
for these planning authorities. It is also obvious that before data can

be recovered under the terms of the Act, the districts, sites, buildings, structures, and objects that contain or represent such data must be carefully located and identified. Accordingly, Appendix B is provided, setting forth the Department's general guidelines for the location and identification of historic properties.

It is the policy of the Department of the Interior, whenever practicable, to afford the public an opportunity to participate in the rulemaking process. Accordingly, interested persons may submit written comments, suggestions, or objections regarding these proposed guidelines to the Chief, Office of Archaeology and Historic Preservation, National Park Service, U.S. Department of the Interior, Washington, D.C. 20240 on or before _____.

Under the terms of the Act, these guidelines are a Department of the Interior responsibility. The budget implications the Act for other Federal agencies have been presented to the Office of Management and Budget for coordination therewith. It is hereby certified that the economic and inflationary impacts of these proposed guidelines have been carefully evaluated in accordance with Executive Order 11821. The impact will be minor and preparation of an infation impact statement is not required. This rulemaking is developed under the authority, *inter alia*, of section 5(c) of the Archaeological and Historic Preservation Act of 1974, 16 U.S.C. §469a-3 *et seq* (1970 ed.). In consideration of the foregoing, it is proposed to amend Chapter 1 of Title 36, Code of Federal Regulations, to add a new Part 66 as follows:

Section 66.1. Definitions

1. *Area subject to environmental impact* is that land area, or areas, where land may be disturbed, or buildings or structures altered, or the environment of historic properties changed, in such a way as to affect their historical value.

2. *Historic properties* are sites, districts, structures, buildings, and objects that may meet the National Register criteria set forth at 36 CFR 60.6, by virtue of their possession of one or more kinds of historical value. One kind of historical value is data or research value, the known or potential capacity of a property to provide information important to the reconstruction, analysis, and understanding of history.

3. *History* comprises the events, patterns, and processes of the human past, including those that have affected literate societies and those that have affected pre-literate or nonliterate groups, whose history is sometimes referred to as prehistory.

4. *Significant...data*, as used by the Act, are data that can be used to answer research questions, including questions of present importance to scholars and questions that may be posed in the future.

5. *Archaeological data* are data embodied in material remains (artifacts, structures, refuse, etc.) produced purposely or accidentally by human beings, and in the spatial relationships among such remains.

6. *Historical data* are data useful in the study and understanding of human life during the period since the advent of written records in the area of concern. The date of inception of the historic period varies from area to area within the United States.

7. *Prehistoric data* are data useful to the study and understanding of human life during the prehistoric period, i.e., at all time periods prior to substantial contact between the native people of the United States and literate societies. The end point of the prehistoric period varies from area to area within the United States.

8. *Scientific data*, as used by the Act, are data provided by sciences other than archaeology, history, and architecture, that are relevant to an understanding of human life during either historic or prehistoric periods. Ethnographic, biological, geological, paleontological, ecological, and geophysical data, among others, are often important to the understanding of the human past.

9. *Location and identification study* is the study necessary to determine the locations of, and to evaluate, historic properties. At a minimum it requires background research; if existing data are inadequate to permit the location and evaluation of historic properties, it requires field inspection as well (See Appendix B).

10. *Data recovery* is the systematic removal of the scientific, prehistoric, historic, and/or archaeological data that provide an historic property with its research or data value. Data recovery may include preliminary survey of the historic property or properties to be affected for purposes of research planning, the development of specific plans for research activities, excavation, relocation, preparation of notes and records, and other forms of physical removal of data and the material that contains data protection of such data and material, analysis of such data and material, preparation of reports on such data and material, and dissemination of reports and other products of the research. Examples of data recovery include archaeological research producing monographs, descriptive, and theoretical articles, study collections of artifacts and other materials; architectural or engineering studies resulting in measured drawings, photogrammetry, or photography; historic or anthropological studies of recent or living human populations relevant to the understanding of historic properties, and relocation of properties whose data value can best be preserved by so doing.

11. *Material* means actual objects removed from an historic property as a part of a data recovery program, including but not limited to artifacts, byproducts of human activity such as flakes of stone, fragments of bone, and organic waste of various kinds, architectural elements, soil samples, pollen samples, skeletal material, and works of art.

12. *Principal Investigator* means the contractor or other person directly responsible for a location and identification, or data recovery project.

13. *Research design* is a plan, usually generated by the principal investigator, outlining the proposed approach to a location, identification, or data recovery project. Minimally, the design should spell out relevant research problems, research methods, and some predicted results of the study. Research designs are often modified as the course of research yields new findings.

14. *Research methods* are procedures and techniques used to record, recover, and/or analyze a body of data such that conclusions may be drawn concerning research problems.

15. *Research problems* are questions in anthropology, sociology, geography, history, architectural history, art history, and other disciplines of the sciences and humanities that can potentially be answered by studying historic properties. Scientific, prehistoric, historic and archaeological data are valuable insofar as they are potentially applicable to the investigation of research problems. Research problems are typically posed as questions about human behavior, thought, or history. Potential answers to such questions, and the ways in which such possible answers may be reflected in the data content of specific historic properties are often spelled out in research designs as hypotheses and test implications.

Section 66.2. Data Recovery Operations

1. Data recovery program operations carried out under the authority
of the Act should meet at least the following minimum standards:
   a. all operations should be conducted under the supervision of qualified professionals in the disciplines appropriate to the data
   that are to be recovered. Qualifications commonly required for
   professionals are set forth in Appendix C;
   b. the program should be conducted in accordance with a professionally
   adequate research design. This design should reflect:
      (1) An understanding by the principal investigator of the data
          or research value of the property. This value will normally
          have been defined as a result of a location and identification
          study as discussed in Appendix B.
      (2) An acquaintance on the part of the principal investigator with
          previous relevant research, including research in the vicin-
          ity of the proposed undertaking and research on topics ger-
          mane to the data recovery program regardless of where such
          research has been carried out.
      (3) The development of a definite set of research problems, taking
          into account the defined research value of the property, other
          relevant research and general theory in the social and natur-
          al sciences and the humanities that may be pertinent to the
          data to be recovered.
      (4) A responsiveness to the need to recover from the property to
          be investigated, a usable sample of data on all research
          problems that reflect the property's research value, or a
          clear and defensible rationale for collecting data on a
          smaller range of problems at the expense of others.
      (5) Competence on the part of the principal investigator and his
          or her staff in the methods and techniques necessary to re-
          cover the data contained in the property, and an intention to
          utilize these methods and techniques in the research;
   c. the program should provide for adequate personnel, facilities, and
   equipment to fully implement the research design;
   d. the program should provide for adequate consultation with scholars
   whose research interests would enable them to contribute to the
   research;
   e. the program should employ methods that insure full, clear, and
   accurate descriptions of all field operations and observations,
   including excavation and recording techniques, stratigraphic and/
   or associational relationships where appropriate, significant
   environmental relationships, etc. Where architectural characteristics are recorded, such recording should be consistent with the
   standards published by the Historic American Building Survey
   (HABS) in "Recording Historic Buildings," by H. J. McKee (National
   Park Service, 1970). Updated guidelines for recording architectural, engineering, and archaeological data may be obtained from
   the Director, Office of Archaeology and Historic Preservation,
   National Park Service;
   f. if portions or elements of the property under investigation can
   be preserved, the program should employ methods that make econo-
   mical use of these portions or elements. Destructive methods
   should not be applied to such portions or elements if nondestructive methods are feasible;
   g. the program should result in a report or reports detailing the
   reasons for the program, the research design, the methods employed
   in both fieldwork and analysis, the data recovered, and the knowledge or insights gained as a result of the data recovery, with

reference to the research design and the research value of the property. The report or reports should meet contemporary professional standards, and should be prepared in accordance with the format guidelines set forth in Appendix A;

h. the program should provide for adequate perpetuation of the data recovered, as discussed at Section 66.3. Care should be taken during curation and handling of specimens and records to insure that data are not lost or decimated. Provision must be made for disseminating the report of the program. Appropriate methods for dissemination of results include but are not limited to publication in scholarly journals, monographs, and books, presentation on microfilm or microfiche through the National Technical Information Service or other outlets, and distribution in manuscript form to State Historic Preservation Officers and other appropriate archives and research libraries. Reports submitted to the Department of the Interior pursuant to section 3(a) of the Act will be disseminated as set forth in section 66.4, but nonredundant independent distribution is encouraged. At a minimum, a copy of each report should be provided to the State Historic Preservation Officer; and

i. particularly when a data recovery program is conducted upon a potentially complex historic property (e.g., a recent town site; a prehistoric site that may contain many occupation layers, cemeteries, or architectural remains), situations may arise or data be encountered that were not anticipated in designing the program. Adequate provision should be made for modification of the program plan to cope with unforeseen discoveries or other unexpected circumstances.

2. These guidelines should be regarded as flexible, inasmuch as (a) some specialized types of data recovery (e.g., the relocation of a structure or object) may not require all the operations discussed above, and (b) innovative approaches to data recovery should be encouraged, as long as these have as their purpose the basic purpose set forth in section 1 of the Act.

Section 66.3. *Protection of Data and Materials*

1. Data recovery programs result in the acquisition of notes, photographs, drawings, plans, computer output, and other data. They also often result in the acquisition of architectural elements, artifacts, soil, bone, modified stones, pollen, charcoal, and other physical materials subject to analysis, interpretation, and in some instances display. Analytic techniques that can be applied to such data and material change and improve through time, and interpretive questions that may be asked using such data and material also change and develop. For these reasons, and to maintain data and material for public enjoyment through museum display, it is important that the data and material resulting from data recovery programs be maintained and cared for in the public trust.

a. Data and materials recovered from lands under the jurisdiction or control of a Federal agency are the property of the United States Government. They shall be maintained by the Government or on behalf of the Government by qualified institutions through mutual agreement. A qualified institution is one equipped with proper space, facilities, and personnel for the curation, storage, and maintenance of the recovered data and materials. The exact nature of the requisite space, facilities, and personnel will vary depending on the kinds of data and materials recovered, but in general it is necessary for a qualified institution to maintain a laboratory where specimens can be cleaned, labeled, and preserved

or restored if necessary; a secure and fireproof storage facility
organized to insure orderly maintenance of materials; a secure
and fireproof archive for the storage of photographs, notes, etc.,
and a staff capable of caring for the recovered data and material.
b. Data recovered from lands not under the control or jurisdiction of
a Federal agency, as a condition of a Federal license, permit, or
other entitlement, are recovered on behalf of the people of the
United States and thus are the property of the United States Government. They should be maintained as provided under section
66.3(1)(a) above. The nonfederal provider of funds should be
provided with copies of such data upon request. Material recovered under such circumstances should be maintained in the manner
prescribed under section 66.3(1)(a) insofar as is possible.
2. Data and material resulting from a data recovery program should
be maintained by a qualified institution or institutions as close as
possible to their place of origin, and made available for future research.
3. Data on architectural and/or engineering characteristics, recorded
in accordance with the standards discussed at section 66.2.1(e) above,
should be filed with the Library of Congress.

Section 66.4. Provision of Reports to the Department

1. Pursuant to the terms of section 3(a) of the Act, any Federal
agency that undertakes a program of data recovery as authorized by the Act
shall provide the Department of the Interior with copies of the resulting
reports. The Department shall make these reports available to the public.
2. In order to facilitate public access to these reports, the Department, represented by the Office of Archaeology and Historic Preservation, National Park Service, has entered into an agreement with the National
Technical Information Service, which agreement provides for the storage on
microfiche, and reproduction upon demand, of all final reports on data
recovery programs either undertaken by the Department or provided to the
Department under the authority of the Act.
3. Two (2) copies of each final report shall be filed with the
Director, Office of Archaeology and Historic Preservation, National Park
Service, Washington, D.C. 20240. All final reports shall be prepared in
accordance with the format standards set forth in Appendix A.
4. In order to facilitate the Department's fulfillment of its responsibilities under Section 5(c) of the Act, to report to Congress concerning the scope and effectiveness of the National Survey and Data Recovery effort, each agency engaging in such activities shall also file
with the Director, Office of Archaeology and Historic Preservation:
a. two (2) copies of each final report on any location and identification study, regardless of whether the study resulted in the
actual identification of historic properties;
b. one (1) copy of each scope-of-work or other description of a
proposed location and identification or data recovery program;
c. one (1) copy of each contract let for any location and identification or data recovery program;
d. together with each final report of a location and identification
or data recovery program, a statement of the costs incurred by
the Federal Government in the conduct of the program; and
e. together with each final report of a location and identification
or data recovery program, the comments of at least one (1) professional in the field of study represented by the report, and
of the State Historic Preservation Officer(s) in whose State(s)
the program took place, on the scope and effectiveness of the
program reported.

Appendix A.   Format Standards for Final Reports of Data Recovery Programs

The following format standards are required for reports provided to the Department of the Interior under terms of section 3(a) of the Act. They are recommended for other reports provided to the Department pursuant to section 66.4.4(a) as well.

1. Text and line drawings should be clean, clear, and easily reproducible.
2. Photographs should be original black and white positive prints, or high-quality reproductions.
3. Typescript should be single spaced.
4. All pages should be numbered in sequence.
5. Form NTIS-35, available from the National Technical Information Service, U.S. Department of Commerce, Springfield, Virginia, 22161 should be enclosed with each report, partially completed in accordance with the example shown in Figure 1.

Appendix B.   Guidelines for the Location and Identification of Historic Properties Containing Scientific, Prehistoric, Historical or Archaeological Data

In order to notify the Secretary of the potential loss or destruction of significant scientific, prehistoric, historical, or archaeological data pursuant to sections 2, 3, and 4 of the Act, in a manner that will permit the Secretary to act effectively in response to this notification, it is necessary that the agency provide appropriate documentation concerning the nature and significance of all historic properties, subject to impact, that may contain such data. It is recommended that such documentation be generated by agencies in the course of their planning activities carried out under the authorities of the National Environmental Policy Act of 1969 (Public Law 91-190)(NEPA), the National Historic Preservation Act of 1966 (Public Law 89-665 as amended)(NHPA), Executive Order 11593, and related authorities.

It is important that agencies understand the relationship among NEPA, such general historic preservation authorities as the NHPA, and the Archaeological and Historic Preservation Act. NEPA mandates the evaluation of project impacts on the entire environment, including all kinds of cultural resources. One kind of cultural resource is the historic property which is the concern of the NHPA and Executive Order 11593. Section 106 of the NHPA sets forth specific actions to be taken when this kind of cultural resource is subject to effect. Some historic properties contain scientific, prehistoric, historical, and archaeological data; the Archaeological and Historic Preservation Act of 1974 provides mechanisms for the recovery of such data if and when the planning processes provided for by NEPA, NHPA, and related authorities have resulted in the conclusion that data recovery constitutes the most prudent and feasible method of impact-mitigation.

Identification of cultural resources is an obvious prerequisite to the evaluation of impact on such resources, and to the planning of methods for the mitigation of such impacts. Identification of cultural resources in general through the NEPA process involves a broad, general, interdisciplinary study of all those social and cultural aspects of the environment, both tangible and intangible, that may be affected by the undertaking. Identification of historic properties requires the location of those tangible places and things that may contain or represent historic values, and sufficient study of these properties to determine what their values are and whether these values are of sufficient importance to make the properties eligible for the National Register of Historic Places. In the process of such study, it should become apparent which properties contain significant

BIBLIOGRAPHIC DATA SHEET	1. Report No.	2.	3. Recipient's Accession No.
4. Title and Subtitle			5. Report Date
			6.
7. Author(s)			8. Performing Organization Rept. No.
9. Performing Organization Name and Address			10. Project/Task/Work Unit No.
			11. Contract/Grant No.
12. Sponsoring Organization Name and Address			13. Type of Report & Period Covered
			14.
15. Supplementary Notes			
16. Abstracts			

17. Key Words and Document Analysis. 17a. Descriptors

17b. Identifiers/Open-Ended Terms

17c. COSATI Field/Group

18. Availability Statement	19. Security Class (This Report) UNCLASSIFIED	21. No. of Pages
	20. Security Class (This Page) UNCLASSIFIED	22. Price

INSTRUCTIONS FOR COMPLETING FORM NTIS-35   (Bibliographic Data Sheet based on COSATI Guidelines to Format Standards for Scientific and Technical Reports Prepared by or for the Federal Government, PB-180 600).

1. **Report Number.** Each individually bound report shall carry a unique alphanumeric designation selected by the performing organization or provided by the sponsoring organization. Use uppercase letters and Arabic numerals only. Examples FASEB-NS-73-87 and FAA-RD-73-09.

2. Leave blank.

3. **Recipient's Accession Number.** Reserved for use by each report recipient.

4. **Title and Subtitle.** Title should indicate clearly and briefly the subject coverage of the report, subordinate subtitle to the main title. When a report is prepared in more than one volume, repeat the primary title, add volume number and include subtitle for the specific volume.

5. **Report Date.** Each report shall carry a date indicating at least month and year. Indicate the basis on which it was selected (e.g., date of issue, date of approval, date of preparation, date published).

6. **Performing Organization Code.** Leave blank.

7. **Author(s).** Give name(s) in conventional order (e.g., John R. Doe, or J.Robert Doe). List author's affiliation if it differs from the performing organization.

8. **Performing Organization Report Number.** Insert if performing organization wishes to assign this number.

9. **Performing Organization Name and Mailing Address.** Give name, street, city, state, and zip code. List no more than two levels of an organizational hierarchy. Display the name of the organization exactly as it should appear in Government indexes such as Government Reports Index (GRI).

10. **Project/Task/Work Unit Number.** Use the project, task and work unit numbers under which the report was prepared.

11. **Contract/Grant Number.** Insert contract or grant number under which report was prepared.

12. **Sponsoring Agency Name and Mailing Address.** Include zip code. Cite main sponsors.

13. **Type of Report and Period Covered.** State interim, final, etc., and, if applicable, inclusive dates.

14. **Sponsoring Agency Code.** Leave blank.

15. **Supplementary Notes.** Enter information not included elsewhere but useful, such as: Prepared in cooperation with . . . Translation of . . . Presented at conference of . . . To be published in . . . Supersedes . . .   Supplements . . . Cite availability of related parts, volumes, phases, etc. with report number.

16. **Abstract.** Include a brief (200 words or less) factual summary of the most significant information contained in the report. If the report contains a significant bibliography or literature survey, mention it here.

17. **Key Words and Document Analysis. (a). Descriptors.** Select from the Thesaurus of Engineering and Scientific Terms the proper authorized terms that identify the major concept of the research and are sufficiently specific and precise to be used as index entries for cataloging.
(b). **Identifiers and Open-Ended Terms.** Use identifiers for project names, code names, equipment designators, etc. Use open-ended terms written in descriptor form for those subjects for which no descriptor exists.
(c). **COSATI Field/Group.** Field and Group assignments are to be taken from the 1964 COSATI Subject Category List. Since the majority of documents are multidisciplinary in nature, the primary Field/Group assignment(s) will be the specific discipline, area of human endeavor, or type of physical object. The application(s) will be cross-referenced with secondary Field/Group assignments that will follow the primary posting(s).

18. **Distribution Statement.** Denote public releasability, for example "Release unlimited", or limitation for reasons other than security. Cite any availability to the public, other than NTIS, with address, order number and price, if known.

19 & 20. **Security Classification.** Do not submit classified reports to the National Technical Information Service.

21. **Number of Pages.** Insert the total number of pages, including introductory pages, but excluding distribution list, if any.

22. **NTIS Price.** Leave blank.

scientific, prehistoric, historic, or archaeological data. Once the undertaking's impact on such properties has been evaluated, it will then be possible to ascertain whether data recovery constitutes an appropriate mitigation action, and it is at this point that the Archaeological and Historic Preservation Act can be effectively utilized.

The guidelines presented in this appendix are the same as those required to identify properties eligible for the National Register of Historic Places pursuant to Section 106 of NHPA as amended and to sections 2(a), 2(b), and (where applicable) 1(3) of Executive Order 11593. Although prepared for publication under these authorities, they are presented here for the convenience of Federal agencies and other users.

AUTHOR'S NOTE: The remainder of the material in Appendix B to this regulation, and all of Appendix C to this regulation, concerning professional qualifications, are duplicated in material appended to 36 CFR 64, printed on pages 000-000.

Appendix D. *Recommendations for the Procurement of Location, Identification, and Data Recovery Programs*

The following recommendations are provided under the Department of the Interior's responsibilities under section 5(c) of the Act, to coordinate all Federal survey and data recovery activities authorized by the Act. They are based on the Department's 30 years of experience in the procurement of archaeological, architectural, and historical services in the location, identification, and study of historic properties.

1. The nature of required identification and data recovery programs varies with the kinds of historic properties expected or data to be recovered. The kinds of data to be recovered depend on both the information content of the properties to be investigated and the research questions that can be asked about the properties. Designing responsible identification and data recovery programs is a complex, professional activity, as is judging the quality of proposals from potential contractors and evaluating the final products of work performed. To the extent possible, the Department will assist Federal agencies in designing high-quality scopes-of-work and in evaluating offerers. Those agencies intending to undertake substantial independent data recovery activities, however, should review their staffs and procedures to insure that (1) adequate expertise in archaeology, history, and/or other appropriate disciplines is represented to provide professional oversight of contract operations, and (2) adequate provision is made for receiving and utilizing input from agencies, institutions, organizations, and qualified individuals who can advise the agency in professional matters relating to archaeological and historic data recovery.

2. Because the requirements of any given data recovery program will depend both on the data content of the property and the research questions relevant to its investigation, it is extremely difficult to define standard specifications for required contractual services and end products. As a result, negotiated competitive procurement is recommended for most kinds of data recovery activities. Sole source contracting has been found by the Office of Archaeology and Historic Preservation to often result in low quality work by restricting intellectual competition among offerers, and has been difficult to justify within Federal procurement regulations. On the other hand, formal advertising with price as the sole criterion for selection of a contractor has proven to be unsatisfactory as a method of insuring high-quality work because of the lack of a clearly specifiable end product. As a rule, negotiated competitive pro-

curement has been found to be the most effective approach to obtaining high-
quality services for location and identification of historic properties
as well. Agencies that anticipate the need for very small-scale location
and identification projects may find it useful to group these together and
solicit proposals for an annual package of jobs. The following procedural
steps are recommended in general for the procurement of location, identification, and data recovery programs:

    a.   Preparation of a Request for Proposals. The request for proposals
should include a scope-of-work usually including the following
elements:

        (1) a description of the undertaking requiring the identification
or data recovery activity, including a statement of the present status of planning, status of compliance with historic
preservation authorities, and a projected timetable for
future actions;

        (2) the location of the undertaking including information on the
size of the area to be affected, the terrain, access, land
ownership, or other factors that might affect the logistics
of identification or data recovery;

        (3) for identification projects, the kinds of descriptive and
evaluatory output required by statute and procedures; and

        (4) for data recovery projects, the property or properties to be
investigated, and the data or research values the property
or properties are (is) known or thought to represent.

    b.   The request for proposals should be circulated to all qualified
and potentially interested contractors, including both local and
non-local universities, colleges, museums, private firms, and
individuals, and should be advertised in "Commerce Business Daily."
Advertising in journals, newsletters, and other media likely to
be seen by potential offerers, and distribution through the State
Historic Preservation Officer, are desirable. The Department
will assist agencies in compiling lists of potential offerers
upon request.

    c.   Offerers should provide proposals for undertaking the requested
work, setting forth their staff qualifications, facilities, research designs, and project plans.

    d.   Proposals should be evaluated for responsiveness and professional
quality, and ranked accordingly, prior to a consideration of bids.
The Department will provide qualified assistance in evaluating
proposals upon request, to the extent permitted by staff limitations.

GARY EVERHARDT
Director, National Park Service

Appendix **B**

A COMPLETED NATIONAL REGISTER NOMINATION

Form No. 10-300   (Rev. 10-74)

UNITED STATES DEPARTMENT OF THE INTERIOR
NATIONAL PARK SERVICE

NATIONAL REGISTER OF HISTORIC PLACES
INVENTORY -- NOMINATION FORM

SEE INSTRUCTIONS IN *HOW TO COMPLETE NATIONAL REGISTER FORMS*
TYPE ALL ENTRIES -- COMPLETE APPLICABLE SECTIONS

1 NAME

HISTORIC   Po-wint   (Name refers to Unicorn Rock only: property includes environs)

AND/OR COMMON
Unicorn Rock; Daugherty Ridge Site; 53-Lng-523

2 LOCATION

STREET & NUMBER   On Daugherty Ridge, between north and central branches, Dry Hole
Canyon   __NOT FOR PUBLICATION

CITY, TOWN   CONGRESSIONAL DISTRICT
N/A   __ VICINITY OF   town of Dry Hole

STATE   Langleland   CODE   COUNTY Very   CODE

3 CLASSIFICATION

CATEGORY	OWNERSHIP	STATUS	PRESENT USE	
__DISTRICT	X PUBLIC	__OCCUPIED	__AGRICULTURE	__MUSEUM
__BUILDING(S)	__PRIVATE	X UNOCCUPIED	__COMMERCIAL	__PARK
__STRUCTURE	__BOTH	__WORK IN PROGRESS	X EDUCATIONAL	__PRIVATE RESIDE
X SITE	PUBLIC ACQUISITION	ACCESSIBLE	__ENTERTAINMENT	X RELIGIOUS
__OBJECT	__IN PROCESS	__YES: RESTRICTED	__GOVERNMENT	__SCIENTIFIC
	__BEING CONSIDERED	X YES: UNRESTRICTED	__INDUSTRIAL	__TRANSPORTATI
		__NO	__MILITARY	__OTHER:

4 OWNER OF PROPERTY

NAME   Langleland Water Conservation Commission

STREET & NUMBER
1066 West Narwhal Highway

CITY, TOWN   STATE
Langles   __ VICINITY OF   Langleland

5 LOCATION OF LEGAL DESCRIPTION

COURTHOUSE,
REGISTRY OF DEEDS, ETC.   Very County Courthouse, Office of the Tax Assessor

STREET & NUMBER
890 Main Street

CITY, TOWN   STATE
Plain   Langleland

6 REPRESENTATION IN EXISTING SURVEYS

TITLE   Cupalava University Archeological Survey Records

DATE
1972   __FEDERAL __STATE __COUNTY X LOCAL

DEPOSITORY FOR
SURVEY RECORDS   Archeological Survey, Dept. of Anthropology, Cupalava University

CITY, TOWN   STATE
Cupalava   Langleland

DESCRIPTION

CONDITION		CHECK ONE	CHECK ONE
__EXCELLENT	__DETERIORATED	__UNALTERED	X __ORIGINAL SITE
X GOOD	__RUINS	X ALTERED	__MOVED DATE 10/1/79
__FAIR	__UNEXPOSED		

DESCRIBE THE PRESENT AND ORIGINAL (IF KNOWN) PHYSICAL APPEARANCE

The Unicorn Rock Site, 53-Lng-523 on Daugherty Ridge, is the only historic property discovered during an intensive survey of optional location 5 for Dry Hole Reservoir (Grifford & Binin 1972). Daugherty Ridge separates the north and central branches of Dry Hole Canyon. It is clearly visible from a distance because of Unicorn Rock, a 200' pinnacle of basalt. Around the base of Unicorn Rock is a band of petroglyphs (see photos and sketches attached), consisting of interlocking squares, concentric circles, and cupules. Extending for about 50 meters E-W along the ridge is a scatter of basalt flakes and cores; this scatter is some 30 meters across on a N-S axis, but boundaries are somewhat obscured by down-slope erosion (see sketch-map; map of property boundaries). Five 1x2 meter test units (see sketch-map) showed no evidence of depth to the lithic deposit.

According to the traditions of the Lang-Les Indian people, Unicorn Rock (Po-wint) is the connection between this world and that occupied during earlier times by Coyote and other first people. Coyote, after committing an indiscretion with Hummingbird, daughter of the Creator, escaped the Creator's wrath by sliding down Po-wint with his paramour in his cheek-pouch. From their union came the Lang-Les people.

Prior to 1950, the east end of the site was occupied by Sliding Lava, the first major work of the distinguished local architect Dry Hole Daugherty (1873-1922?). Fortunately documented by the Historic American Buildings Survey in 1939, Sliding Lava was destroyed by Typhoon Carol, which ravaged the area in 1949. Its remains were cleared by the Water Conservation Commission in 1950, and no trace remains.

8 SIGNIFICANCE

PERIOD		AREAS OF SIGNIFICANCE -- CHECK AND JUSTIFY BELOW		
X PREHISTORIC	X ARCHEOLOGY-PREHISTORIC	__COMMUNITY PLANNING	__LANDSCAPE ARCHITECTURE	X RELIGION
X 1400-1499	X ARCHEOLOGY-HISTORIC	__CONSERVATION	__LAW	__SCIENCE
X 1500-1599	__AGRICULTURE	X ECONOMICS ?	__LITERATURE	__SCULPTURE
X 1600-1699	__ARCHITECTURE	X EDUCATION	__MILITARY	__SOCIAL/HUMANITARIAN
X 1700-1799	__ART	__ENGINEERING	__MUSIC	__THEATER
X 1800-1899	X COMMERCE ?	__EXPLORATION/SETTLEMENT	__PHILOSOPHY	__TRANSPORTATION
X 1900- Present	__COMMUNICATIONS	__INDUSTRY	__POLITICS/GOVERNMENT	__OTHER (SPECIFY)
		__INVENTION		

SPECIFIC DATES   N/A   BUILDER/ARCHITECT

STATEMENT OF SIGNIFICANCE

To the Lang-Les people, Po-wint has considerable importance because of its association with the origin of the world and its people in their present forms. The petroglyphs around the base of Po-wint may reflect activities based upon this association. In recent years, with the development of the Lang-Les Revitalization Council (Veloria 1974), Po-wint has been used as the site for periodic group meditation sessions and instruction of young people in the group's history and traditions.

The Unicorn Rock Site as a whole is of archeological importance both because of its association with Po-wint and hence with one people's view of the world and its origin, and because of its basalt. Daugherty Ridge is one of the best basalt sources in the Langles area; its basalt is chemically distinctive and is unusually fine-grained, easily flaked. Daugherty Ridge basalt is widespread in prehistoric sites throughout the Langles area and as far away as the Shriek Site on the north slope of the Screaming Plateau. An equally good source of basalt -- visually distinguishable from Daugherty Ridge basalt -- exists on Cupalava Island. However, there is no evidence that this source was ever used by prehistoric people. Cauldron (1973) has suggested that the Langles area was characterized in prehistory by what she calls the Greater Langles Co-Prosperity Sphere, dominated by the village of Selgnel near Dry Hole. The Selgnelites, according to Cauldron's proposition, controlled Daugherty Ridge and quarried its basalt both for use within the Co-Prosperity Sphere and for trade with outside groups. The importance of Daugherty Ridge basalt to the functioning of the Co-Prosperity Sphere served as a disincentive to use of the Cupalava source (Cauldron 1973:213).

If Cauldron is correct, one would expect considerable consistency in the technology of quarrying used at Daugherty Ridge, because only the people of Selgnel would have been quarrying. If Daugherty Ridge were not quarried exclusively by Selgnelites, greater variability would be expected in quarrying technology, since at different sites in the Langles area Daugherty Ridge basalt has been found to have been used for a wide variety of tools. For example, it was used solely for burins at Thunter Cave (Junnings 1962); knives and drills at the Very Plain Flake Site (Grubtree 1976); and hoes at the Coaster Site on the Very Plains (Slivver 1970). Consistency would of course not prove Cauldron's proposition, but it would lend support to it.

***** See Continuation Sheet *****

▌MAJOR BIBLIOGRAPHICAL REFERENCES

Cauldron, J.A.: "The Greater Langles Co-Prosperity Sphere". CUPALAVA REVIEW 33:4:200-250, 1973, Cupalava.

Grifford, J.R. & L.R. Benin: "Archeological Reconnaissance: Optional Location 5; Proposed Dry Hole Reservoir". Report to the U.S. Army Corps of Engineers, Langles District, 1972.

Grubtree, R.A.: "Flake-tool Technology at the Very Plain Flake Site". CUPALAVA REVIEW 36:2:22-35, 1976, Cupalava.

▌GEOGRAPHICAL DATA

ACREAGE OF NOMINATED PROPERTY _____ 50 acres _____

UTM REFERENCES

A |9,5| |4,7,2,7,8,0| |6,3,5,6,7,6,0|
ZONE EASTING NORTHING

B |9,5| |4,7,2,7,8,0| |6,3,5,6,7,4,0|
ZONE EASTING NORTHING

C |9,5| |4,7,2,6,7,0| |6,3,5,6,7,4,0|

D |9,5| |4,7,2,6,7,0| |6,3,5,6,7,6,0|

VERBAL BOUNDARY DESCRIPTION

A rectangular area of 50 acres running E-W along Daugherty Ridge encompasses all concentrations of basalt debitage and the environs of Po-wint.

LIST ALL STATES AND COUNTIES FOR PROPERTIES OVERLAPPING STATE OR COUNTY BOUNDARIES

STATE	CODE	COUNTY	CODE
STATE	CODE	COUNTY	CODE

▌FORM PREPARED BY

NAME / TITLE   Marvin Midden, Staff Archeologist

ORGANIZATION   Langleland State Historic Preservation Office   DATE 10/30/79

STREET & NUMBER 1776 West Dairy Street   TELEPHONE

CITY OR TOWN   Langles   STATE Langleland

▌STATE HISTORIC PRESERVATION OFFICER CERTIFICATION

THE EVALUATED SIGNIFICANCE OF THIS PROPERTY WITHIN THE STATE IS:

NATIONAL ___   STATE ___   LOCAL ___

As the designated State Historic Preservation Officer for the National Historic Preservation Act of 1966 (Public Law 89-665), I hereby nominate this property for inclusion in the National Register and certify that it has been evaluated according to the criteria and procedures set forth by the National Park Service.

STATE HISTORIC PRESERVATION OFFICER SIGNATURE

TITLE   DATE

FOR NPS USE ONLY
I HEREBY CERTIFY THAT THIS PROPERTY IS INCLUDED IN THE NATIONAL REGISTER

.   DATE

DIRECTOR, OFFICE OF ARCHEOLOGY AND HISTORIC PRESERVATION
ATTEST: DATE

KEEPER OF THE NATIONAL REGISTER

Form No 10-300a
(Rev 10-74)

UNITED STATES DEPARTMENT OF THE INTERIOR
NATIONAL PARK SERVICE

NATIONAL REGISTER OF HISTORIC PLACES
INVENTORY -- NOMINATION FORM

FOR NPS USE ONLY
RECEIVED
DATE ENTERED

CONTINUATION SHEET   ITEM NUMBER   8   PAGE   2

    Although 53-Lng-523 contains a vast amount of basalt debitage, this debris
has never been thoroughly described or analyzed. Such study should provide a
partial test for the Cauldron hypothesis, and thus provide information important
to an understanding of at least local prehistory. Potentially, this information
may be valuable to the comparative study of regional trade relationships and
perhaps to the study of economic systems in general.

    Although Sliding Lava, Dry Hole Daugherty's creation on the site, certainly
possessed considerable architectural value, its total destruction in 1949-50
eliminated this area of significance. No other buildings or structures exist on
the site.

                          Item Number 9   Page 2

Junnings, J.J.: THUNTER CAVE. Cupalava University Press, 1962, Cupalava and
          East Langles.

Slivver, S.A.: "Preliminary Report on the Coaster Site". ARCHEOLOGY TOMORROW:
          2:3:15-23, 1970, Taos.

Appendix C

A MEMORANDUM OF AGREEMENT

MEMORANDUM OF AGREEMENT

WHEREAS, the U.S. Army, Corps of Engineers, proposes to construct a dam and reservoir at Optional Location 7 in Dry Hole Canyon, Very County, Langleland; and,

WHEREAS, the U.S. Army, Corps of Engineers, has determined that this undertaking as proposed will have an adverse effect on certain properties qualifying for inclusion in the National Register of Historic Places, and pursuant to the procedures of the Advisory Council on Historic Preservation has requested the Comments of the Advisory Council on Historic Preservation; and,

WHEREAS, pursuant to the procedures of the Advisory Council on Historic Preservation (36 CFR Part 800), representatives of the Advisory Council on Historic Preservation, the U.S. Army, Corps of Engineers, and the Langleland State Historic Preservation Officer have consulted and reviewed the undertaking to consider feasible and prudent alternatives to satisfactorily mitigate the adverse effect; now,

THEREFORE:

It is mutually agreed that the implementation of the undertaking, in accordance with the following:

1. Salvage excavation of the 15 prehistoric archeological sites identified as 53-Lng-500 through 514 will be conducted by Interagency Archeological Services, Office of Archeology and Historic Preservation, National Park Service, utilizing funds transferred to Interagency Archeological Services by the U.S. Army, Corps of Engineers, in accordance with the research design provided to the U.S. Army, Corps of Engineers on June 23, 1978 by the Archeological Survey, Cupalava University under contract, with the following additions:

      a. All research will be subject to the overall control and supervision of Interagency Archeological Services;

      b. The program shall be reviewed after 1 year by the Advisory Council on Historic Preservation, the Langleland State Historic Preservation Officer, and representatives of the Langleland Archeological Council; alterations may be negotiated at that time;

      c. The U.S. Army, Corps of Engineers shall provide financial support for, and cooperate with, monitoring of the archeological program by representatives of the Lang-Les Revitalization Council; and

      d. A full report, or reports, will be prepared at the conclusion of the work, in accordance with Interagency Archeological Services standards, and will be submitted to the Langleland State Historic Preservation Officer, the Advisory Council on Historic Preservation, the U.S. Army, Corps of Engineers, and Interagency Archeological Services.

MEMORANDUM OF AGREEMENT
DRY HOLE RESERVOIR - 2

2. Chicken Run, last work of the architect Dry Hole Daugherty, will be relocated to the Dry Hole Reservoir Visitors' Center by the U.S. Army, Corps of Engineers, under the supervision of the Langleland State Historic Preservation Officer. The original site of Chicken Run will be excavated in accordance with the research plan adopted in conference on April 18, 1979 by the parties to this Memorandum.

3. Archeological site 53-Lng-523, the site of Unicorn Rock or Po-wint, will under no circumstances be intruded upon. Should the need arise to conduct any work within one-quarter (¼) mile of this site, the Corps will first consult with the Lang-Les Revitalization Council, the Langleland State Historic Preservation Officer, and the Advisory Council on Historic Preservation. The Corps will provide financial support for, and cooperate with, guards to be employed by the Lang-Les Revitalization Council to stand watch over the site throughout the construction period to discourage vandalism.

will satisfactorily mitigate any adverse effect on the properties, qualifying for inclusion in the National Register of Historic Places, that lie within the area of direct environmental impact of the proposed undertaking.

_____ (date) _____
Executive Director
Advisory Council on Historic Preservation

_____ (date) _____
U.S. Army, Corps of Engineers

_____ (date) _____
Langleland State Historic Preservation Officer

_____ (date) _____
Chairman,
Advisory Council on Historic Preservation

Appendix D

LETTERS TO AGENCIES TO NOTIFY OF COMPLIANCE PROBLEMS AND TO SOLICIT INFORMATION; PERTINENT ADDRESSES

NOTE: With the exception of Mr. Robert Garvey, all names given in this appendix are fictitious. The italic column provides comments on the texts of the letters.

NOTE: Photos and maps are not included.

Mr. H.I. Weyman
Supervisor, Environmental Branch
Federal Highway Administration,
  District 99
22 West 98th Street
Langles, Langleland

Dear Mr. Weyman:

I understand that the Federal Highway
Administration is planning to assist the
Langleland Department of Transportation in
construction of Section 1040.3.8 of Inter-   *Precisely identifies undertaking*
state Highway 5055 from the vicinity of the
town of Dry Hole to West Langles, Langleland.
I further understand that plans for this
undertaking include construction of an
access ramp at Dry Hole.

Several citizens of Dry Hole have
expressed concern to me about the effect
this project will have on their community.   *Identifies general nature of*
They believe that improved access to Dry   *the problem*
Hole from West Langles will result in a
population influx and new construction that
will alter the historic character of their
community and its social institutions.

My own brief visits to Dry Hole have
convinced me that the town is eligible for in-   *Refers specifically to the*
clusion in the National Register of Historic   *National Register, thus*
Places. The town contains many well-preserved   *alerting agency and reviewers*
late 19th century structures, and many more in   *to consider NHPA and Executive*
ruins. Its residents maintain patterns of   *Order responsibilities. Since*
social interaction and a sense of community   *property has not been placed on*
that depend substantially on the town's   *Register or determined eligible,*
historic traditions. They take pride in main-   *provides brief justification for*
taining both the traditions and the town it-   *belief that property is eligible*
self.

I understand that the I-5055 project is in   *Urges reasonable consideration,*
the very early stages of planning. I urge you   *not that project simply be*
to insure that a full study is made of this pro- *halted.*
ject's potential effects on Dry Hole, and of the
historical value of this town, in consultation
with the Langleland State Historic Preservation   *Refers specifically to Advisory*
Officer, the National Park Service, and the   *Council's procedures. This gives*
Advisory Council on Historic Preservation as   *the agency direction and also*
required by the latter's "procedures" (36 CFR   *indicates that the writer knows*
Part 800).   *what he or she is talking about*

If I can be of assistance to you with
respect to this matter, please do not hesitate
to contact me.

Sincerely yours,

Ethyl Nographer
Dept. of Anthropology
Cupalava University

Mr. Robert Garvey
Executive Director
Advisory Council on Historic Preservation
1522 K St. NW, Suite 1030
Washington D.C. 20005

Dear Mr. Garvey:

I wish to draw your attention to the potential destruction of a significant historic property by a federally permitted project.

Indicates that this is a problem letter

Dry Hole National Forest, a unit of the U.S. Department of Agriculture, Forest Service, plans to issue a special use permit to the Greater Langles Pulp Cooperative to construct a haul road across National Forest land. Construction of this road will make it possible for the Cooperative to harvest timber on land it controls within the National Forest; logging of the Cooperative's land is thus a contingent effect of the issuance of the permit by the Forest Service.

Identifies agency involved

Identifies type of involvement

Identifies nature of effect

The area to be logged has not been subjected to a survey to identify historic properties. The National Forest has conducted a survey of the haul road, and re-routed the right-of-way to avoid a prehistoric site. In her report of the survey, consulting archeologist J.A. Cauldron of Cupalava University strongly urged that the private inholding to be logged be subjected to a survey, because of rumors that historic buildings and sites existed there. Cauldron's report, dated June 28, 1978 and titled "An Archeological Survey of Road 48 NS 84, Dry Hole National Forest" is on file with the office of the Langleland State Historic Preservation Officer.

Indicates what has and has not been done about the area's historic properties

Identifies authoritative documentation and where to find it

My own research concerns patterns of social change among late 19th-century immigrants to the Langles area. Among the major immigrant groups were Lithuanians and Tibetans who became loggers on Dry Hole Mountain to provide fuel and shoring timbers to the lead mines on the Screaming Plateau, about 20 miles to the northwest. Ethnographic and ethnohistorical data indicate that between 1879 and 1892 a community of these immigrant loggers and their families existed within what is now the Pulp Co-operative's inholding. Remnants of this community, including buildings and extensive refuse dumps, have been reported in the area by hunters and fishermen. If these reports are true, the archeological site or sites represented could contain vital information on the nature of Lithuanian-Tibetan interaction, and thus be eligible for inclusion in the National Register of Historic Places. Logging the area will undoubtedly damage or destroy any archeological sites that exist there.

Describes what may be affected, its possible significance, how the writer knows about it

I have provided this information to the
Pulp Cooperative and urged that a survey be
done and the sites protected; the Cooperative
has refused (See copies of correspondence
enclosed). I have provided the same information to the Forest Service and urged that
your comments be requested pursuant to your
procedures. I have also suggested that the
special use permit might be conditioned upon
the conduct of a survey and preservation
program by the Cooperative. The Forest Service has maintained that it lacks authority
to do this, and has not to my knowledge initiated consultation with you. The Forest
may issue its permit within the next 30
days.

*Describes and documents
actions already taken by the
writer to solve the problem*

*Indicates time-frame within
which Council action should
occur*

I hope it will be possible for you to
advise the Forest Service of its responsibilities in this matter. Forest Supervisor
Woodsie Woodchuck is familiar with this project and can be reached at (999)296-3880.
Marvin Midden, Archeologist on the Langleland
State Historic Preservation Officer's staff,
is also familiar with the project. I would
appreciate being kept advised of your actions,
and those of the Forest Service, with respect
to this matter.

*Facilitates contact for
further information,
consultation*

Sincerely yours,

H.S. Torian
Department of Anthropology
  and Social Work
Narwhal Community College

cc: Office of Archeology & Historic
      Preservation, NPS
    Langleland SHPO

Mr. B.L. Durt
Assistant to the Administrator
   for Environmental Development
Soil Conservation Service, Department of Agriculture
Washington, D.C. 20250

    A FREEDOM OF INFORMATION ACT REQUEST

Dear Mr. Durt:

    I believe that significant historic
properties lying on the Very Plains, within
the Very Plains Soil Conservation District
of Langleland, are endangered by the actions
of the Soil Conservation Service in connection with the West Dry Hole Land Leveling Project, a Soil Conserservation Service
assisted activity. Therefore, pursuant to
the Freedom of Information Act, I request
documentation concerning the Soil Conservation Service's plans and programs for
historic preservation in connection with
this project, including identification of
and copies of:

    (1) all memoranda, position papers,
and policy statements of the Soil Conservation Service and/or the Very Plains
Soil Conservation District concerning
the archeological and historic preservation concomittants of this undertaking;

    (2) any and all archeological and/or
historical survey reports concerning this
undertaking, whether prepared by the Soil
Conservation Service, Very Plains Soil
Conservation District, or their consultants,
or submitted to the SCS or VPSCD by others;

    (3) any and all correspondence between
SCS and VPSCD, and/or between SCS or VPSCD
and any other party, including but not
limited to the Advisory Council on Historic
Preservation and the Office of Archeology
and Historic Preservation, National Park
Service, with respect to this project; and

*Red flag: assures prompt
           attention*

*Brief statement of concern
to establish that inquiry
is legitimate; specification
of object of concern*

Clear reference to Act.

*Specification of information
requested. Be as specific
as possible*

B.L. Durt - 2

(4) any and all minutes, transcripts, or other records of meetings in which SCS personnel have participated, in which archeological and/or historic preservation considerations with respect to this project have been discussed.

I do not desire Environmental Impact Statements or other documents that were circulated to state and local agencies for review.

Exclusion of unwanted, readily available material

Should the Soil Conservation Service propose to exclude from release to me any documents or portions of documents, I desire to have all such documents identified, and I request release of all portions of such documents containing factual matter not excluded from release.

Statement of alternative; keeps agency from withholding whole documents because of a single paragraph that can be legitimately withheld.

I am willing to pay a reasonable photocopy fee, not to exceed $35.00, for this material.

Avoids delay. Any amount can be specified. Many agencies will not bill unless large amounts of reproduction are involved

Sincerely yours,

Melvin Birdman
Hopeless Research Center

cc: Hon. J.C. Fogbottom, M.C.
    Office of Archeology &
    Historic Preservation, NPS
    Advisory Council on
    Historic Preservation

Information copies

PERTINENT ADDRESSES

Office of Archeology and Historic Preservation
National Park Service
Department of the Interior
Washington, D.C. 20240

Advisory Council on Historic Preservation
1522 K Street NW, Suite 1030
Washington, D.C. 20005

or

Post Office Box 25085
Denver, Colorado 80225

National Trust for Historic Preservation
740-748 Jackson Place, NW
Washington, D.C. 20006

BIBLIOGRAPHY

BOOKS, PERIODICALS, AND OTHER LITERATURE

Advisory Council on Historic Preservation
  1976   *Procedures for making determinations of "adverse effect" and "no adverse effect" for archeological resources in accordance with 36 CFR Part 800.* Memorandum; see Appendix A.
Airlie Airs
  1974   Airlie Airs: Compendium of limericks and poetry composed and distributed at the Seminars on the Future Direction of Archeology, Airlie, Virginia.
Anonymous
  1974   Untitled apocryphal poem circulated at the second Seminar on the Future Direction of Archeology, Airlie, Virginia.
Apple, R.A., and J.L. Rogers
  1976   Historical integrity and local significance in the Pacific Island Context. *Guam Reporter* 1:33–36.
Aten, L.E.
  1975   Archeological Planning. Paper presented at the Annual Meeting of the Conference of State Historic Preservation Officers, Washington D.C.

Bandelier, A.F.
  1881   Report on the ruins of the Pueblo of Pecos. *Papers of the Archeological Institute of America* 4:1–591.
Barnes, E.
  1967   Remarks: Annual Meeting of the Southwestern Anthropological Association, San Diego.
Berry, B.J.L., and D.F. Marble (Editors)
  1968   *Spatial Analysis: A Reader in Statistical Geography.* Prentice-Hall, Englewood Cliffs.
Binford, L.R.
  1962   Archeology as anthropology. *American Antiquity* 28:217–25.
Binford, L.R. *et al.*
  1970   Archeology at Hatchery West. *Memoir 24, Society for American Archeology.*
Chapman, C.
  1973   Archeology in the 1970s: Mitigating the Impact. *The Missouri Archeologist* 35:1–71.
Collier, J. Jr.
  1967   Visual Anthropology: Photography as a research method. Holt, Rinehart & Winston, New York.
Committee on Interior and Insular Affairs, U.S. House of Representatives
  1973   *Hearings before the Subcommittee on National Parks and Recreation, 93rd Congress, 1st Session, on H.R. 296 and Related Bills.* Serial Number 93-27, U.S. Government Printing Office, Washington, D.C.
Corps of Engineers, U.S. Army
  1975   *Identification and Administration of Cultural Resources.* Draft Regulation Number 1105-2-460, Office of the Chief of Engineers, Washington, D.C.
Deetz, J.F., and E.S. Dethlefsen
  1967   Death's head, cherub, urn & willow. *Natural History* 76:29–37.
Dincauze, D. and J. Meyer
  1976   Prehistoric resources in East Central New England: A preliminary predictive study. *Cultural Resource Management Studies.* Interagency Archeological Services, Office of Archeology and Historic Preservation, National Park Service, Washington D.C.
Forest Service, U.S. Department of Agriculture
  1976   *Training Guide: The archeological reconnaissance report.* R5-2700-37, California Region, San Francisco.
Gagliano, S. *et al.*
  1976   *Cultural resources evaluation of the northern Gulf of Mexico continental shelf.* Coastal Environments, Inc., Report to Interagency Archeological Services, Office of Archeology and Historic Preservation, National Park Service, Washington D.C.
Geertz, C.
  1973   *The interpretation of cultures.* Basic Books, New York.
Glassow, M.A., and L.W. Spanne, with J. Quilter
  1976   *Evaluation of archeological sites on Vandenberg Air Force Base, Santa Barbara, California.* Report to Interagency Archeological Services, San Francisco.
Grady, M., and W.D. Lipe
  1976   The Role of Preservation in Conservation Archeology. Paper presented at the Annual Meeting of the Society for American Archeology, St. Louis.
Gummerman, G.J. (Editor)
  1971   The distribution of prehistoric population aggregates: Proceedings of the South-

western Anthropological Research Group. *Prescott College Anthropological Reports 1.*

Haggett, P.
1965   *Locational Analysis in Human Geography.* Edward Arnold, London.

Harris, M.
1968   *The rise of anthropological theory.* Crowell, New York.

Hickman, P.P.
1977   Problems of significance: Two case studies of historic sites. In *Conservation archeology,* edited by M. Schiffer and G. Gummerman. Academic, New York.

Historic Preservation Team, Western Region, National Park Service
1975   *Keys Desert Queen Ranch, Joshua Tree National Monument.* National Park Service, Western Regional Office, San Francisco.

Hosmer, C.R., Jr.
1965   *Presence of the past.* Putnam, New York.

HUD (Housing and Urban Development, Department of)
1977   *Guidelines for Archeological Resources Assessment,* Washington D.C. (In preparation)

Interagency Archeological Services
1976a   *A status report to the archeological community.* Office of Archeology and Historic Preservation, National Park Service, Washington D.C.
1976b   *Staff Analysis: Review of conflicts in highway planning and cultural resource preservation as exemplified by conditions in the state of New York.* Office of Archeology and Historic Preservation, Washington D.C.

Interior, Department of
1976   *America 200: The legacy of our lands.* Conservation Yearbook Number 11, Washington D.C.

Jelks, E. *et al.*
1976   *Directory of professional archeologists.* Society of Professional Archeologists, Washington D.C.

Johnson, W., and G. Berg
1976   *Archeological impact evaluation: Stage one archeological survey: Canandaigua Lake County Sewer District Project No. C-36-841.* Report to Hershey, Malone & Associates, Consulting Engineers, & New York State Div. of Historic Preservation, Albany.

King, C.D.
1973   Documentation of tribelet boundaries, locations, and sizes. Appendix I to *The Southern Santa Clara Valley: A General plan for archeology.* By T.F. King and P.P. Hickman. A.E. Treganza Anthropology Museum, San Francisco State University, San Francisco.

King, T.F.
1971   A conflict of values in American archeology. *American Antiquity* 36:255–262, Washington D.C.
1975   *Cultural resource law and the contract archeologist: Methods of evaluation and reporting.* New York Archeological Council, Buffalo.
1976   The Citizen activist and cultural resources: A guide to strategies. In *In defense of rivers: A citizens' workbook.* Delaware Valley Conservation Association, Stroudsburg.
1977a   *Preservation law and the contract archeologist: Methods of evaluation and reporting.* New York Archeological Council, New York.
1977b   *The archeological survey: Methods and uses.* Interagency Archeological Services,

Office of Archeology and Historic Preservation, National Park Service, Washington D.C. (In preparation.)

1977 Personal observations, copies of outgoing Advisory Council on Historic Preservation correspondence.

King, T.F., and G. Berg

1975 *Archeological element: Environmental impact report, San Felipe water distribution system.* Environmental Science Associates, Foster City, California.

King, T.F., and P.P. Hickman

1973 *The Southern Santa Clara Valley: A General plan for archeology.* A.E. Treganza Anthropology Museum, San Francisco State University, San Francisco.

Klinger, T.

1975 State support for archeological research programs in the early 1970s. *American Antiquity* 40:94–97.

Lagacé, R.O.

1974 *Nature and use of the human relations area files: A research and teaching guide.* Human Relations Area Files, Inc., New Haven.

Laird, C.

1975 *Encounter with an angry god: Recollections of my life with John Peabody Harrington.* Malki Museum Press, Banning.

Lee, R.

1970 *The Antiquities Act of 1906.* Office of History and Historic Architecture, Eastern Service Center, National Park Service, Washington D.C.

Leoni, M.

1977 The New Mormon temple in Washington D.C. In *Historical archeology and the importance of material things,* edited by Leland Ferguson. Society for Historical Archeology Special Publication No. 2, Charleston.

Levine, F., and C.M. Mobley

1976 *Archeological resources at Los Esteros Lake, New Mexico.* Institute for the Study of Earth and Man, Department of Anthropology, Southern Methodist University, Dallas.

Lipe, W.D.

1974 A conservation model for American archeology. *The KIVA* 39:213–245, Tucson.

Lipe, W.D., and A.J. Lindsay

1974 *Proceedings of the 1974 Cultural Resource Management Conference, Denver, Colorado.* Technical Series No. 14, Museum of Northern Arizona, Flagstaff.

Longacre, W.A., and J.E. Ayres

1968 Archeological lessons from an Apache wickiup In *New perspectives in archeology,* edited by S.R. Binford and L.R. Binford. Aldine, Chicago.

Lovis, W.A.

1976 Quarter sections and forests: An example of probability sampling in the northeastern woodlands. *American Antiquity* 41:364–371, Washington D.C.

Lyons, R.R. (editor)

1977 *Remote sensing experiments in cultural resource studies: Nondestructive methods of archeological exploration, survey, and analysis.* National Park Service, Albuquerque.

McDermott, J.D.

1976 Comments at meeting of the Committee for the Recovery of Archeological Remains, Washington D.C.

McGimsey, C.R. III

1972 *Public archeology.* Seminar Press, New York.

1975   *The National Register and archeological resources: One view from the states.* Arkansas Archeological Survey, Fayetteville.

McGimsey, C.R., III, and H. Davis (editors)

1977   *The management of archeological resources: The Airlie House Report.* Society for American Archeology, Washington D.C.

McKee, H.J.

1970   *Recording historic buildings.* Historic American Buildings Survey, Office of Archeology and Historic Preservation, National Park Service, Washington D.C.

McMillan, B., *et al.*

1977   Cultural resource management. In *The management of archeological resources: The Airlie House Report,* edited by C.R. McGimsey III and H. Davis. Society for American Archeology, Washington D.C.

Moratto, M.J. *et al.*

1977   A consideration of law in archeology. In *The management of archeological resources: The Airlie House Report,* edited by C.R. McGimsey, III and H. Davis. Society for American Archeology, Washington D.C.

Mueller, J.W.

1974   The uses of sampling in archeological survey. *Memoir 28, Society for American Archeology,* Washington D.C.

1975   *Sampling in archeology.* University of Arizona Press, Tucson.

Mulloy, E.D.

1976   *The history of the National Trust for Historic Preservation, 1963–1973.* Preservation Press, Washington D.C.

National Park Service

1973   *Preparation of Environmental Statements: Guidelines for discussion of cultural (historical, archeological, architectural) resources.* Department of the Interior, Washington D.C.

National Trust for Historic Preservation

1976a   *A guide to federal programs: Programs and activities related to historic preservation.* National Trust for Historic Preservation, Washington D.C.

1976b   *Historic preservation law: An annotated bibliography.* National Trust for Historic Preservation, Washington D.C.

Noel-Hume, I.

1969   *Historical archeology.* Alfred A. Knopf, New York.

OAHP (Office of Archeology and Historic Preservation, NPS)

1977a   *Guidelines for local surveys: A basis for preservation planning.* Office of Archeology and Historic Preservation, National Park Service, Washington D.C.

1977b   *How to complete National Register forms,* 3rd Edition. Office of Archeology and Historic Preservation, National Park Service, Washington D.C.

OAHP/Advisory Council

1977   *A compendium of federal agency policies regarding historic preservation* (provisional title). Office of Archeology and Historic Preservation, National Park Service, and Advisory Council on Historic Preservation, Washington D.C. (In preparation.)

Putnam, F.W. (editor)

1879   Reports upon archeological and ethnological collections from the vicinity of Santa Barbara, California and from ruined Pueblos of Arizona and New Mexico, and certain interior tribes. In *Report upon U.S. geological surveys west of the one hundredth meridian, in charge of first lieutenant George M. Wheeler.* U.S. Government Printing Office, Washington D.C.

Rains, A., *et al.*
1965   *With heritage so rich: A report of a special committee on historic preservation under the auspices of the United States Conference of Mayors with a grant from the Ford Foundation.* Random House, New York.

Rathje, W.
1977   In praise of archeology: The projéct du garbáge. In *Historical archeology and the importance of material things,* edited by Leland Ferguson. Society for Historical Archeology Special Publication No. 2, Charleston.

Ritter, E. *et al.*
1976   Archeology: In *Final environmental analysis record, proposed geothermal leasing, Randsburg, Spangler Hills, and South Searles Lake.* Bureau of Land Management, Riverside District, Riverside, California.

Schiffer, M.B.
1973   The relationship between access volume and content diversity of storage facilities. *American Antiquity* 38:114–116.

Schiffer, M.B., and J.H. House
1975   *The Cache River Archeological Project: An experiment in contract archeology.* Research Series No. 18, Arkansas Archeological Survey, Fayetteville.

Schneider, W. *et al.*
1976   Personal communications to T.F. King regarding anthropological studies under Section 14(h), Alaska Native Claims Settlement Act; Washington D.C. and Anchorage.

Scovill, D.H.
1974   History of archeological conservation and the Moss–Bennett Bill. In *Proceedings of the 1974 Cultural Resource Management Conference, Denver, Colorado,* edited by W.D. Lipe and A.J. Lindsay, Jr. Technical Series No. 14, Museum of Northern Arizona, Flagstaff.
1976   Regional centers: Opportunities for federal–institutional partnership in cultural resource management. Paper presented at the Annual Meeting of the Society for American Archeology, St. Louis.

Scovill, D.H., G. Gordon, and K. Anderson
1972   *Guidelines for the preparation of statements on environmental impacts on archeological resources.* Arizona Archeological Center, National Park Service, Tucson.

Smith, L.D.
1977   *Archeological sampling procedures for large land parcels: A statistically based approach.* U.S. Forest Service, Albuquerque.

Society for California Archeology
1974   Recommended Procedures for Archeological Impact Evaluation. Appendix I to *The California Directory of archeological consultants,* Society for California Archeology, Fullerton.

Squire, E.G.
1849   Aboriginal monuments of New York. In *Smithsonian contributions to knowledge,* Vol. 2. Smithsonian Institution, Washington D.C.

Squire, E.G., and E. H. Davis
1848   Ancient monuments of the Mississippi Valley. In *Smithsonian Contributions to knowledge,* Vol. 1. Smithsonian Institution, Washington D.C.

Thomas, C.
1885   Who were the moundbuilders? *American Antiquarian and Oriental Journal* 2:65–74.

Vansina, J.
1961   Oral Tradition: A study in historical methodology. H.M. Wright, translator. Aldine, Chicago.
Vlachos, E. et al.
1975   Social impact assessment: An overview. U.S. Army Engineers Institute for Water Resources, Ft. Belvoir, Virginia.
Weide, M.S.
1974   Archeological element of the California desert study. Bureau of Land Management, Riverside District, Riverside.
Wilder, M.P., and E. F. Slafter
1882   Petition to the U.S. Senate. Congressional Record, 47th Congress, 1st Session, p. 3777, Washington D.C.
Wilke, P. (editor)
1975   The Cahuilla Indians of the Colorado Desert: Ethnohistory and prehistory. Ballena, Ramona.
Willey, G.R., and J.A. Sabloff
1974   A history of American Archeology. Freeman, San Francisco.

COURT CASES CITED

NYAC (New York Archeological Council) v. Russell Train et al.; 75 CV 488, USDC NDNY, 1975
Save the Courthouse Association v. Lynn; 8 ERC 1209 USDC SDNY, 1975
Stop H-3 Association et al. v. Coleman et al; 6 ELR 20424, CA 9 1976
Warm Springs Task Force et al. v. Gribble et al.; 378 F Sup. 240, 1974

FEDERAL STATUTES AND PROCEDURES CITED

Alaska Native Claims Settlement Act: Public Law 93-203
Antiquities Act: Public Law 59-209
Archeological and Historic Preservation Act: Public Law 93-291
Coastal Zone Management Act: Public Law 92-583
Department of Transportation Act: Public Law 89-670
Executive Order 11593: Protection and Enhancement of the Cultural Environment
Historic Sites Act: Public Law 74-292
Housing and Community Development Act: Public Law 93-383
National Environmental Policy Act: Public Law 91-190
National Housing Act: Public Law 83-560
National Historic Preservation Act: Public Law 89-665 (as amended, especially by Public Law 94-422).
Reservoir Salvage Act: Public Law 86-523
Tax Reform Act of 1976: Public Law 94-455
Water Pollution Control Act Amendments of 1972: Public Law 92-500
Wilderness Act of 1964: Public Law 88-557
7 CFR VI 656: Department of Agriculture, Soil Conservation Service: Procedures for the Protection of Archeological and Historical Properties Encountered in SCS-Assisted Programs.
36 CFR 60: National Register of Historic Places (See Appendix A)

36 CFR 60 (Draft Amendements): *Criteria for Statewide Comprehensive Surveys and Plans* (See Appendix A)

36 CFR 63 (Draft): *Procedures for Requesting Determinations of Eligibility* (See Appendix A)

36 CFR 64 (Draft): *Criteria and Procedures for the Identification of Historic Properties* (See Appendix A)

36 CFR 65 (Draft): *Recovery of Scientific, Prehistoric, Historic, and Archeological Data: Procedures for Coordination and Notification.* Office of Archeology and Historic Preservation, National Park Service, Washington D.C.

36 CFR 66 (Draft): *Recovery of Scientific, Prehistoric, Historic, and Archeological Data: Methods, Standards, and Reporting Requirements* (See Appendix A)

36 CFR 800: Procedures for the Protection of Historic and Cultural Properties (See Appendix A)

40 CFR V 1500: Guidelines for the Preparation of Environmental Impact Statements.

INDEX

A

Adverse effect (impact on historic
  properties)
  contingent, 58, 61, 78, 125, 136, 137
  criteria of, 91, 118–119
    Dry Hole Reservoir, application of at,
      128
    neglect defined as an, 143
    Very Plain Flake Site, special
      application at, 131–132
  direct, 57, 59–60, 78, 118, 121–125,
    135, 139–140
  discussion, 89
  identification of, 118
  infrastructural, 58–59, 62, 106, 118, 125,
    136
  managerial, 58, 60–61, 125
  permitted, 57–58, 60, 106

Advisory Council on Historic Preservation
  and archeological sites, "No Adverse
    Effect" guidelines, 131–132
  and archeologists, lack of in, 188
  CEQ and, 35
  comments, 90–93
  dangerous characteristics of, 188–189
  Department of Transportation Act,
    Section 4(f), 132–133
  divisions of, 74
  established, 31
  Executive Director of, 74
  IAS and, 70, 73–76
  legal council in, 74
  members of, 74
  memoranda of agreement and, 88–92, 119
  NHPA and, 36, 42, 47, 77–78
  NPS funding of, 32–33

329

STUDIES IN ARCHEOLOGY

Consulting Editor: Stuart Struever

Department of Anthropology
Northwestern University
Evanston, Illinois

James N. Hill and Joel Gunn (Eds.). **The Individual in Prehistory: Studies of Variability in Style in Prehistoric Technologies**

Michael B. Schiffer and George J. Gumerman (Eds.). **Conservation Archaeology: A Guide for Cultural Resource Management Studies**

Thomas F. King, Patricia Parker Hickman, and Gary Berg. **Anthropology in Historic Preservation: Caring for Culture's Clutter**

in preparation

Richard E. Blanton (Ed.). **Monte Alban: Settlement Patterns at the Ancient Zapotec Capital**

R. E. Taylor and Clement W. Meighan. **Chronologies in New World Archaeology**

Bruce D. Smith. **Prehistoric Patterns of Human Behavior: A Case Study in the Mississippi Valley**

Barbara L. Stark and Barbara Voorhies (Eds.). **Prehistoric Coastal Adaptations: The Economy and Ecology of Maritime Middle America**